The New Russian Nationalism

THE NEW RUSSIAN NATIONALISM

Imperialism, Ethnicity and Authoritarianism

2000–15

Edited by Pål Kolstø and Helge Blakkisrud

EDINBURGH
University Press

Edinburgh University Press is one of the leading university presses in the UK. We publish academic books and journals in our selected subject areas across the humanities and social sciences, combining cutting-edge scholarship with high editorial and production values to produce academic works of lasting importance. For more information visit our website: www.edinburghuniversitypress.com

© editorial matter and organisation Pål Kolstø and Helge Blakkisrud, 2016
© the chapters, their several authors, 2016

Edinburgh University Press Ltd
The Tun – Holyrood Road,
12(2f) Jackson's Entry
Edinburgh EH8 8PJ

Typeset in 11/13 Sabon by
Servis Filmsetting Ltd, Stockport, Cheshire

A CIP record for this book is available from the British Library
ISBN 978 1 4744 1042 7 (hardback)
ISBN 978 1 4744 1043 4 (webready PDF)
ISBN 978 1 4744 1044 1 (epub)

The right of Pål Kolstø and Helge Blakkisrud to be identified as the editor of this work has been asserted in accordance with the Copyright, Designs and Patents Act 1988, and the Copyright and Related Rights Regulations 2003 (SI No. 2498).

Contents

List of Figures	vii
List of Tables	x
Acknowledgements	xi
Notes on Contributors	xii

	Introduction: Russian nationalism is back – but precisely what does that mean? Pål Kolstø	1
1.	The ethnification of Russian nationalism Pål Kolstø	18
2.	The imperial syndrome and its influence on Russian nationalism Emil Pain	46
3.	Radical nationalists from the start of Medvedev's presidency to the war in Donbas: True till death? Alexander Verkhovsky	75
4.	Russian ethnic nationalism and religion today Anastasia Mitrofanova	104
5.	Everyday nationalism in Russia in European context: Moscow residents' perceptions of ethnic minority migrants and migration Natalya Kosmarskaya and Igor Savin	132

6. Backing the USSR 2.0: Russia's ethnic minorities and expansionist ethnic Russian nationalism 160
   Mikhail A. Alexseev

7. Rallying 'round the leader more than the flag: Changes in Russian nationalist public opinion 2013–14 192
   Mikhail A. Alexseev and Henry E. Hale

8. How nationalism and machine politics mix in Russia 221
   Henry E. Hale

9. Blurring the boundary between civic and ethnic: The Kremlin's new approach to national identity under Putin's third term 249
   Helge Blakkisrud

10. Russia as an anti-liberal European civilisation 275
    Marlene Laruelle

11. Ethnicity and nationhood on Russian state-aligned television: Contextualising geopolitical crisis 298
    Stephen Hutchings and Vera Tolz

12. The place of economics in Russian national identity debates 336
    Peter Rutland

Bibliography 362
Index 407

Figures

Figure 1.1:	A typology of Russian nationalisms	23
Figure 6.1:	Search frequency on Google for the term 'Crimean Tatars' in the Russian language in Tatarstan and the cities of Moscow and St Petersburg (January 2013–June 2014)	164
Figure 6.2:	Preferences for Russian territorial identity, ingroup pride, political preferences and economic valuations among ethnic Russian and non-Russian respondents in the 2013 NEORUSS surveys	175
Figure 6.3:	Russia territorial identity preferences in the 2013 NEORUSS surveys among ethnic Russian and non-Russian respondents	177
Figure 6.4:	Dominant preferences for Russia's state identity across ethnic groups in the 2013 NEORUSS survey	185
Figure 6.5:	Prospective group status in four Russia state identity scenarios	186
Figure 7.1:	Agreement that the current Ukrainian leadership is ...	196
Figure 7.2:	'If presidential elections were held today, for whom would you vote?'	199
Figure 7.3:	'Do you believe the ethnic diversity of the population strengthens or weakens	

	Russia?' – based on nationwide survey samples from 2005, 2013, and 2014	205
Figure 7.4:	Share of respondents who strongly opposed their family members marrying migrants belonging to ethnic groups other than their own	208
Figure 7.5:	Factors singled out by the respondents as most uniting/dividing the peoples of Russia and Ukraine	211
Figure 7.6:	Preferences for the territorial boundaries of the Russian Federation	214
Figure 8.1:	Per cent responses to 'What should be the borders of Russia?'	242
Figure 11.1:	Frequency and intensity of ethnicity-related news as a percentage of the overall news content	306
Figure 11.2:	Frequency of ethnicity-related news inside and outside the Russian Federation, *Vremia* and *Vesti*	307
Figure 11.3:	Intensity of ethnicity-related news inside and outside the Russian Federation, *Vremia* and *Vesti*	308
Figure 11.4:	Salience of ethnicity-related news, *Vremia* and *Vesti*	309
Figure 11.5:	Intensity of each category as a percentage of all ethnicity-related news, *Vremia*	311
Figure 11.6:	Intensity of each category as a percentage of all ethnicity-related news, *Vesti*	311
Figure 11.7:	Frequency of Russian Orthodox Church-coded stories over the total recording period, *Vremia* and *Vesti*	314
Figure 11.8:	Intensity of Russian Orthodox Church-coded stories over the total recording period, *Vremia* and *Vesti*	315
Figure 11.9:	Frequency of migration-coded stories inside and outside the Russian Federation over the total recording period, *Vremia*	321

FIGURES

Figure 11.10: Frequency of migration-coded stories inside and outside the Russian Federation over the total recording period, *Vesti*   322

Tables

Table 6.1:	Comparison of means test between ethnic Russian and non-Russian respondents in 2013 NEORUSS surveys on select outcome variables	173
Table 6.2:	Responsiveness to Putin's message that ethnic diversity strengthens Russia in a split-sample experiment, 2013 NEORUSS surveys in the Russian Federation and the cities of Moscow, Vladivostok and Krasnodar	181
Table 7.1:	'What is Novorossiia?'	198

Acknowledgements

This book has been made possible through a research project on 'Nation-building, nationalism and the new "other" in today's Russia' (NEORUSS)[1] funded by the Research Council of Norway, under the NORRUSS programme, project number 220599. Additional funding has been provided by the Freedom of Expression Foundation (Fritt Ord). The project involves researchers at the Department of Literature, Area Studies and European Languages at the University of Oslo, Norway and the Research Group on Russia, Eurasia and the Arctic at the Norwegian Institute of International Affairs, Oslo, Norway in addition to ten researchers from five different countries (France, Germany, Russia, United Kingdom and the United States).

---

[1] <www.hf.uio.no/ilos/english/research/projects/neoruss> (last accessed 9 March 2015).

Contributors

Mikhail A. Alexseev is Professor of Political Science at the San Diego State University, USA, where he has taught since 2000. His publications focus on threat assessment in interstate and internal wars, ethnic relations, immigration attitudes and nationalism, with a regional focus on Eurasia. He is the author of *Immigration Phobia and the Security Dilemma: Russia, Europe, and the United States* (Cambridge University Press, 2006), 'Societal Security, the Security Dilemma, and Extreme Anti-Migrant Hostility in Russia' (*Journal of Peace Research*, 2011) and 'The Asymmetry of Nationalist Exclusion and Inclusion' (*Social Science Quarterly*, 2015). In addition, he has published scholarly articles in *Political Science Quarterly, Political Behavior, Political Communication, Post-Soviet Studies, Eurasia Border Review, Europe–Asia Studies, Nationalities Papers, Post-Soviet Geography and Economics* and other peer-reviewed outlets. Alexseev has directed multi-year research projects on migration, ethnic demographics, xenophobia and ethnic relations funded by the National Science Foundation, the John D. and Catherine T. MacArthur Foundation and the National Council for Eurasian and East European Research (Title VIII). Since 1999 he is a member of the Program on New Approaches to Research on Security in Eurasia (PONARS Eurasia), currently based at the George Washington University, USA.

Helge Blakkisrud is Senior Researcher and Head of the Research Group on Russia, Eurasia and the Arctic, Norwegian Institute of

International Affairs, Oslo, Norway. He is also Editor in Chief of the Scandinavian language peer-reviewed area studies journal *Nordisk Østforum*. In 2009–10 he was a Fulbright Visiting Scholar, Institute of Slavic, East European, and Eurasian Studies, University of California, Berkeley, USA. His research interests include the development of centre–region relations in the Russian Federation, in particular the reform of intra-executive relations. He has also published on state- and nation-building in unrecognised states in Eurasia. His books include *Centre–Periphery Relations in Russia* (Ashgate, 2001, co-edited with Geir Hønneland), *Nation-building and Common Values in Russia* (Rowman & Littlefield, 2004, co-edited with Pål Kolstø), *Tackling Space: Federal Politics and the Russian North* (University Press of America, 2005, co-edited with Geir Hønneland), *The Governors' Last Stand: Federal Bargaining in Russia's Transition to Appointed Regional Heads* (Unipub, 2015). He has published peer-reviewed articles in *Post-Soviet Affairs, Europe–Asia Studies, Geopolitics, East European Politics, Ethnic and Racial Studies, Nationalities Papers* and *Communist and Post-Communist Studies*.

Henry E. Hale is Professor of Political Science and International Affairs at the George Washington University, USA and most recently the author of *Patronal Politics: Eurasian Regime Dynamics in Comparative Perspective* (Cambridge University Press, 2015). His previous work has won two awards from the American Political Science Association (APSA), for his book *Why Not Parties in Russia* (Cambridge University Press, 2006) and his article 'Divided We Stand' (*World Politics*, 2005). He is also the author of *The Foundations of Ethnic Politics* (Cambridge University Press, 2008) and a wide range of journal articles. During 2009–12, he served as Director of the Institute for European, Russian, and Eurasian Studies (IERES) at George Washington University's Elliott School of International Affairs, and he is currently editorial board chair of *Demokratizatsiya: The Journal of Post-Soviet Democratization*. His ongoing research focuses on issues related to nationalism, ethnic politics, political regimes and elections, with a focus on Russia and other post-Soviet countries.

Stephen Hutchings is Professor of Russian Studies at the University of Manchester, UK and Fellow of the Academy of Social Sciences. He has published six monographs and five edited volumes on various aspects of Russian literary, film and media studies, including *Russian Modernism: The Transfiguration of the Everyday* (Cambridge University Press, 1997), *Russian Literary Culture in the Camera Age: The Word as Image* (Routledge, 2004), *Television and Culture in Putin's Russia: Remote Control* (Routledge, 2009, co-authored with Natalia Rulyova) and *Nation, Ethnicity and Race on Russian Television: Mediating Post-Soviet Difference* (Routledge 2015, co-authored with Vera Tolz). He has held five large research grants with the UK's Arts and Humanities Research Council since 2000. Hutchings was President of the British Association for Slavonic and East European Studies 2010–13 and is currently Associate Editor of the *Russian Journal of Communication*.

Pål Kolstø is Professor of Russian Studies at the University of Oslo, Norway since 1990. His main research areas are nationalism, nation-building, ethnic conflicts and nationality policy in Russia, the former Soviet Union and the Western Balkans. Kolstø's main publications include: *Russians in the Former Soviet Republics* (Hurst & Co, 1995), *Nation-building and Ethnic Integration in Post-Soviet Societies: An Investigation of Latvia and Kazakstan* (Westview Press, 1999, editor), *Political Construction Sites: Nation-building in Russia and the Post-Soviet States* (Westview Press, 2000), *National Integration and Violent Conflict in Post-Soviet Societies: The Cases of Estonia and Moldova* (Rowman & Littlefield, 2002, editor), *Nation-building and Common Values in Russia* (Rowman & Littlefield, 2004, co-edited with Helge Blakkisrud), *Myths and Boundaries in South-Eastern Europe* (Hurst & Co, 2005, editor), *Media Discourse and the Yugoslav Conflicts: Representations of Self and Other* (Ashgate, 2009, editor), and *Strategies of Symbolic Nation-building in South Eastern Europe* (Ashgate, 2014, editor). He has published roughly forty articles in English-language refereed journals in addition to numerous publications in other languages. He is a recipient of six large research grants to study nation-building and ethnic relations in the post-Soviet world and the former Eastern Europe.

Natalya Kosmarskaya is Senior Researcher at the Centre for Central Eurasian Studies, Institute of Oriental Studies, Russian Academy of Sciences (Moscow, Russia). She is also a Deputy Editor in Chief of the Russian language academic journal *Diaspory*. Her areas of research are ethnic and diaspora studies, migration studies, urban sociology and Central Asian studies. Within these broad disciplines, she has prioritized post-Soviet migration to Russia, the position of the Russian-speakers in the newly independent states, trajectories of ethnic/social identity change in the post-Soviet (urban) context, adaptation of immigrant/minority communities and their relationships with the receiving population in different ethno-cultural milieus and formation and (de)construction of ethno-cultural stereotypes. Kosmarskaya has published extensively on the above-mentioned topics in Russian and English (more than seventy publications, including two books). She has contributed to a number of collected volumes and to academic journals both in Russia and in the West, such as *Acta Eurasica, Ethnographic Review, Nationalism and Ethnic Politics, Nationalities Papers, Europe–Asia Studies, Journal of Multicultural and Multilingual Development* and *Russian Journal of Communication*. Her last book is '*Children of the Empire' in Post-Soviet Central Asia: Mental Shifts and Practices of Adaptation (Russians in Kyrgyzstan, 1992–2002)* (Natalis, 2006, in Russian).

Marlene Laruelle is Research Professor of International Affairs and Associate Director of the Institute for European, Russian, and Eurasian Studies (IERES) at the Elliott School of International Affairs, George Washington University, USA. She explores contemporary political, social and cultural changes in Russia and Central Asia through the prism of ideologies and nationalism. She has authored *Russian Eurasianism: An Ideology of Empire* (Johns Hopkins University Press, 2008), *In the Name of the Nation: Nationalism and Politics in Contemporary Russia* (Palgrave, 2009) and *Russia's Strategies in the Arctic and the Future of* *the Far North* (M.E. Sharpe, 2013). She is currently working on Russian and Western European intellectual connections and has recently edited *Eurasianism and the European Far Right: Reshaping the Russia–Europe Relations* (Lexington, 2015).

Anastasia Mitrofanova is Chair of Political Science, Church–State Relations and the Sociology of Religion at the Russian Orthodox University of St John the Divine, Moscow, and Professor at the Financial University under the Government of the Russian Federation. Mitrofanova's research interests include religious politicisation, religio-political movements, Orthodox Christianity and politics, fundamentalism and nationalism in post-Soviet states. She has published the books *Politizatsiia 'pravoslavnogo mira'* (Nauka, 2004) and *The Politicization of Russian Orthodoxy: Actors and Ideas* (ibidem-Verlag, 2005). Her most recent publications include 'The Russian Orthodox Church' (co-authored with Zoe Knox) in *Eastern Christianity and Politics in the Twenty-First Century* (Routledge, 2014, edited by Lucian N. Leustean) and 'Orthodox Fundamentalism: Intersection of Modernity, Postmodernity and Tradition' in *Orthodox Paradoxes: Heterogeneities and Complexities in Contemporary Russian Orthodoxy* (Brill, 2014, edited by Katya Tolstaya).

Emil Pain is Director General of the Centre for Ethno-Political and Regional Studies, Moscow, and Professor of Political Science, National Research University–Higher School of Economics. He has published thirteen books and more than 300 articles, focusing on nationality politics, ethnic conflict and terrorism in Russia, Caucasus and Central Asia. From 1996 to 1999 he served as President Boris Eltsin's adviser on nationality issues. In 2000–1 he was a Galina Starovoitova Fellow on Conflict Resolution at the Kennan Institute (Washington, DC, USA). His main publications include *Between Empire and Nation: The Modernization Project and its Traditionalist Alternative in the National Policy of Russia* (Novoe izdatel'stvo, 2004, in Russian), *The Ethnopolitical Pendulum: Dynamics and Mechanisms of Ethnopolitical Processes in Post-Soviet Russia* (Institut sotsiologii RAN, 2004, in Russian), *Tolerance against Xenophobia: Foreign and Russian Experiences*

(Academia, 2005, in Russian, co-edited with Vladimir Mukomel), 'Socio-Cultural Factors and Russian Modernization' in *Waiting for Reform under Putin and Medvedev* (Palgrave Macmillan, 2012, edited by Lena Jonson and Stephen White), and 'The Ethno-political Pendulum: The Dynamics of the Relationship Between Ethnic Minorities and Majorities in Post-Soviet Russia' in *Managing Ethnic Diversity in Russia* (Routledge, 2013, edited by Oleh Protsyk and Benedikt Harzl).

Peter Rutland is a Professor of Government at Wesleyan University in Middletown, Connecticut, USA, where he has taught since 1989. He previously taught at the University of Texas, Austin, USA and the University of London, UK. He has been a Fulbright Fellow at the European University at Saint Petersburg, Russia and Sophia University in Tokyo, Japan. From 1995 to 1997 he was Assistant Director of the Open Media Research Institute in Prague. He is Associate Editor of *Russian Review* and Editor in Chief of *Nationalities Papers*, the journal of the Association for the Study of Nationalities. He blogs about nationalism at http://nationalismwatch.wordpress.com. He is the author of *The Myth of the Plan* (HarperCollins Publishers, 1985) and *The Politics of Industrial Stagnation in the Soviet Union* (Cambridge University Press, 1992) and editor of *Business and State in Contemporary Russia* (Westview Press, 2001). His current research topics include the state of research and development (R&D) in Russia and the role of identity politics in the failure of democracy in Russia.

Igor Savin is a Researcher at the Centre for Central Eurasian Studies, Institute of Oriental Studies, Russian Academy of Sciences (Moscow, Russia). His main research areas include ethnic identity in Central Asia, ethno-political conflicts in Central Asia, micro-level interaction between different ethno-cultural communities in Southern Kazakhstan and Southern Kyrgyzstan and labour migration from Central Asia to Russia and Kazakhstan, hereunder the integration of migrants into receiving societies. Savin is the author of more than fifty publications in Russian and in English on the above-mentioned topics. His main publications include the book chapters 'Titular Population Has the Edge in Kazakhstan' in *Local Governance and Minority Empowerment in the CIS* (Open Society Institute, 2003, edited by Valery Tishkov and Elena Filippova) and 'Successful Integration but Inadequate Protection: The Meskhetian Turks in Kazakhstan' in *The Meskhetian Turks at a Crossroads: Integration, Repatriation or Resettlement* (LIT Verlag, 2007, edited by Tom Trier and Andrei Khanzhin), as well as contributions to academic journals both in Russia and in the West. He is also co-editor and co-author of *North Caucasus: Views from Within* (Saferworld, 2012) and co-author of 'Kyrgyzstan: Tragedy in the South' (*Ethnopolitics Papers*, 2012, co-authored with Anna Matveeva and Bahrom Faizullaev).

Vera Tolz is Sir William Mather Professor of Russian Studies at the University of Manchester. She has published widely on various aspects of Russian nationalism, identity politics and the relationship between intellectuals and the state in the imperial and Soviet periods. Her books include *Russian Academicians and the Revolution* (Macmillan, 1997), *European Democratization since 1800* (Palgrave Macmillan, 2000, co-edited with John Garrard and Ralph White), *Gender and Nation in Contemporary Europe* (Manchester University Press, 2005, co-edited with Stephenie Booth), *Russia: Inventing the Nation* (Arnold, 2001), *'Russia's Own Orient': The Politics of Identity and Oriental Studies in the Late Imperial and Early Soviet Periods* (Oxford University Press, 2011) and *Nation, Ethnicity and Race on Russian Television: Mediating Post-Soviet Difference* (Routledge 2015, co-authored with Stephen Hutchings).

Alexander Verkhovsky is Director of the SOVA Center for Information and Analysis. His areas of research include nationalism, religion and politics and anti-extremism policies in Russia. He has published the books *Political Orthodoxy: Russian Orthodox Nationalists and Fundamentalists, 1995–2001* (SOVA Center for Information and Analysis, 2003, in Russian), *State Policy Towards National-Radical Organizations, 1991–2002* (SOVA Center for Information and Analysis, 2013, in Russian) and *Criminal Law in OSCE Countries against Hate Crimes, Incitement of Hatred and Hate Speech* (SOVA Center for Information and

Analysis, 2014, in Russian). Other recent publications include 'Counteracting "Religious Extremism": The Russian State in Search of Responses to the Challenges of Desecularisation' (*Gosudarstvo, religiia, tserkov'*, 2013, in Russian), 'The Russian Orthodox Church as a Church of the Majority' (*Pro et Contra*, 2013, in Russian), 'Language of Authorities and Radical Nationalists' in *Doublespeak: The Rhetoric of the Far Right since 1945* (ibidem-Verlag, 2014, edited by Matthew Feldman and Paul Jackson), 'Dynamics of Violence in Russian Nationalism' in *Russia is not Ukraine: Contemporary Accents of Nationalism* (SOVA Center for Information and Analysis, 2014, in Russian, edited by Alexander Verkhovsky), 'Federal Ethnopolitics and the Resurgence of Russian Nationalism' (*Pro et Contra*, 2014, in Russian) and 'Party-building on the Far Right Wing of the Political Spectrum' (*Polis*, 2014, in Russian, co-authored with Elena Strukova).

Introduction: Russian nationalism is back – but precisely what does that mean?

Pål Kolstø

Nationalism is featuring increasingly in Russian society and in public discourse. Previously dominated by 'imperial' tendencies – pride in a large, strong and multi-ethnic state able to project its influence abroad – Russian nationalism is now focusing more and more on ethnic issues. This new ethnonationalism comes in various guises – as racism and xenophobia, but also as a new intellectual movement of 'national democracy' that deliberately seeks to emulate conservative West European nationalism.

Western media often fail to grasp the important differences between the various strands of Russian nationalism. Traditionally, Russian nationalists have focused on the perceived need to maintain a large and strong state, and have been far less concerned with ethnic interests and racial purity. These nationalists are usually referred to as 'statists' (*gosudarstvenniki*) or with the more derogatory term 'imperialists' (*impertsy*). Opposed to them are ethnonationalists who fight for the interests not so much of the Russian state but of the *Russian people*, ethnically defined. These two groups distrust, even hate, each other in their pursuit of opposing political goals.

Achieving ethnic and cultural homogeneity will be impossible as long as Russia remains a huge multi-cultural state with a hegemonic position in the post-Soviet space. A consequence of Vladimir Putin's drive to maintain a high degree of influence in the Central Asian and Caucasian post-Soviet states has been his willingness to keep Russian borders open to labour migration from these regions. To be sure, also in the Soviet period there was significant movement of people between the various parts of the USSR, but the setting has now changed radically. Gone is the overarching common Soviet culture; knowledge of the Russian language among the non-Russians in the other post-Soviet states is dwindling; and the immigrants who now arrive in Moscow and other large Russian cities often have little or no education and establish themselves as a poorly integrated Lumpenproletariat. They can travel to Russia without a visa, but working there requires an official permit, which is generally not forthcoming – and so, the vast majority of them work illegally. This labour migration increased after the turn of the millennium: unemployment was rife in the Central Asian and Caucasian states, while the oil-driven Russian economy needed more work hands.

Widespread and growing migrantophobia in the Russian population soon became the main motor behind the nationalist mobilisation. It is no coincidence that the largest Russian nationalist organisation for a long time was the Movement against Illegal Immigration. In mid-December 2010 Moscow became the scene of the biggest riots in recent years, when thousands gathered at Manezhnaia Square to protest against the death of a Russian football supporter killed during a brawl with youth from North Caucasus. Rioters shouted nationalistic and anti-Caucasian slogans; when the mob became rowdy, more than a thousand were arrested (*Russia Today* 2010). The event marked a sea change in the approach of the Russian regime to the nationalists. Until then, the state authorities had largely condoned radical Russian nationalism, for instance allowing the 'Russian March' that gathers thousands of nationalists – including skinheads and neo-Nazis – in the streets of Moscow on 4 November, the official 'National Unity Day'. This leniency towards nationalists contrasted sharply with the regime's harsh reactions against the rallies of the pro-Western, liberal opposition, whose meetings were regularly broken up and the participants rounded up by the riot police. The Putin regime had apparently calculated that they could harness nationalist sentiments in the population and exploit them for their own purposes, as with the establishment of the pro-Putin youth movement Nashi, which sought to tap into the same nationalist sentiments. However, in about 2009/10, Kremlin strategists seem to have had second thoughts about the wisdom of this strategy.

The disenchantment was mutual: Russia's nationalists felt that Putin has betrayed them by welcoming immigrant labourers and sending billions of dollars to the majority Muslim North Caucasus (Grove 2011). When the hard-line nationalists were driven out of the Kremlin embrace, some ended up in the anti-Putin opposition. This became clear when huge anti-Putin rallies erupted in Moscow and other Russian cities after the fraudulent parliamentary elections of December 2011, one year almost to the day after the Manezhnaia riots. In these demonstrations pro-Western democrats marched together with vociferous nationalists, waving an incongruous medley of rightist, centrist and leftist banners. The new star of the anti-Putin opposition at the time, blogger Aleksei Navalnyi, was seen as a nationalist with liberal values (Laruelle 2014b; Kolstø 2014). Renowned for characterising the dominant, pro-Putin party United Russia as 'the party of scoundrels and thieves', he also endorsed more ominous slogans such as 'Stop feeding the Caucasus', and participated in the Russian Marches. Although controversial in some camps, Navalnyi epitomised the increased acceptance of nationalism in many parts of Russian society.

The backdrop to this rise of Russian nationalism was a state that was far *more* Russian in demographic terms than before 1991. When the Soviet Union broke up, the share of ethnic Russians rose from just above 50 per cent in the USSR, to 81 per cent in the Russian Federation. Observers commented that, for the first time in its history, Russia now had the chance to develop into a 'nation-state' based on a high degree of common values and common identity (Tishkov 1997: 246–71). The terms *'rossiiskii'* and *'rossiiane'* – non-ethnic words for 'Russian' and 'Russians' – were introduced to encapsulate this new non-ethnic national idea. Some twenty years later, however, the attempt to establish a *rossiiskii* nation seems for all practical purposes to have been discarded. The very concept of *'rossiiane'* is associated with the Eltsin era, and has been ditched along with shock therapy, oligarch economy and other elements of the failed transition to

Western-style pluralism and liberalism. Although the 'national question' still simmers beneath the surface in federal politics, the Putin regime has effectively centralised the Federation and emasculated the power of the once-mighty non-Russian elites in the republics.

While Russia became ethnically more homogeneous after 1991, it also experienced a serious demographic crisis. Due to high mortality and low reproduction rates, in addition to substantial out-migration (primarily to the West), the population has been contracting. This has led to a growing demand for guest workers and labour immigration, primarily unskilled or low-skilled workers from the former Soviet republics. In 2011 it was estimated that Russia was housing some four to six million labour migrants – but such figures are highly unreliable, as since as many as two out of three may be illegals not shown in official statistics (Visloguzov 2011). Moreover, the ethno-cultural distance between the new migrants and local populations was increasing: whereas at the turn of the millennium foreign labour migrants were mostly Ukrainians, South Caucasians, Moldovans and Chinese, they were increasingly being replaced by Tajiks, Kyrgyz and Uzbeks. The ethnic element in federal politics had largely been taken off the agenda – but migration, another ethnicity-related issue, loomed increasingly large in public discourse.

In addition to an influx of people from the 'near abroad', all major Russian cities also have a population stemming from the 'inner abroad'– the string of non-Russian republics north of the Caucasian Range. High fertility rates and low standards of living have induced many people from these tracts to migrate to other parts of Russia. Russian nationalist discourse often does not distinguish between labour (im)migrants from the near and the inner abroad, but lumps them together as one group of 'aliens' who allegedly threaten to dilute the (ethnic) Russian character of their neighbourhoods. This is paradoxical, since most Russian cities, including Moscow, are remarkably homogeneous in ethnic terms, indeed more so than most West European metropolises. The 2010 census gave the share of ethnic Russians in Moscow as 91.6 per cent (not including illegal residents), making Russia one of the very few countries in Europe where the capital is more ethnically homogeneous than the rest of the country.

In any case, ethnic composition as such does not influence the nationality debate directly: what matters is how it is perceived by the population. Research has shown that public assumptions often diverge significantly from demographic data. When Russians are asked to gauge the share of specific non-Russian ethnic groups in the population in their oblast or city, they almost invariably offer exaggerated figures (Alexseev 2010: 171–3). To Russian 'statists' and 'imperialists', it mattered not so much that the ethnic composition of Russia's population was heterogeneous as long as the state was large and strong. Historically, if non-Russians were willing to learn Russian and adapt to Russian customs, they were welcome to assimilate into the Russian nation – and historically, millions of non-Russians have done so (Kappeler 1993). Only the Jews were not allowed to assimilate (Kolstø 2009). If in the past the Jews were singled out as the main 'Other', xenophobes today – in Russia and elsewhere – more often vent their hatred against the other 'inner enemy': Muslim immigrants.

Regime responses

Writing in 2007, Lilia Shevtsova claimed that Russian officialdom not only condoned xenophobic attitudes and expressions, but actively *encouraged* and tried to exploit them for their own purposes:

> Xenophobia has always been endemic in Russia, but it was never allowed public expression. It hid behind imperial ideology. Now ethnic nationalism is often fanned by factions within the ruling elite. In its search for external and internal enemies, the elite focuses on [inter alia] immigrants. (Shevtsova 2007: 283)

If this was correct, the authorities seem, like the sorcerer's apprentice, to have created a monster they could not control. In about 2010/11, xenophobic nationalism was turning into a weapon that could be wielded against them.

As a part of his 2012 election campaign, Putin in January 2012 published an article in *Nezavisimaia gazeta* under the heading 'Russia: the national question' (Putin 2012b). Here he came across as a nationalist, but of a different kind from those found among the anti-system radicals. Putin denounced nationalism as such – but by presenting his own alternative version of it (Rutland 2012a). His national model differed significantly from the nonethnic *rossiiskii* model promoted by the Eltsin Administration in the 1990s, by clearly focusing on the historical role – indeed, 'the mission' – of the ethnically Russian people. At the same time, Putin's model retained the state-centred orientation that had characterised Russian nationalism before 'the ethnic turn' of recent years.

Then, in the spring of 2014 the scene changed again. In a reaction to the Euromaidan revolution in Kyiv, the Kremlin adopted much more of the rhetoric of the Russian nationalists, in effect stealing their thunder. The annexation of the Crimea was sold to the Russian people in starkly nationalist language. Putin's popularity, which had been flagging since the beginning of the financial crisis, now soared back to old heights, reaching 85–87 per cent.[1] Interestingly, with regard to the two dominant brands of nationalism in Russia – imperial nationalism and ethnonationalism – the annexation of Crimea allowed Putin to ride two horses: since the population of the peninsula is primarily ethnic Russians it was possible to present this act both as an ingathering of Russian lands in a strong Russian state *and* as a defence of ethnic Russians abroad.

The present book traces the vicissitudes of Russian nationalism over the last decade and a half. A grant from the Research Council of Norway allowed us to put together a team of twelve highly competent researchers from six countries, who started working in January 2013.[2] Underlying the analysis is a survey carried out in May 2013 by a major Moscow polling institute, Romir, which covered a representative sample of 1,000 respondents nationwide, plus an additional 1,800 respondents in three cities – Moscow, St Petersburg and Krasnodar – 600 respondents in each city. This survey provides a wealth of data on Russian attitudes towards ethno-centrism, xenophobia, patriotism, regime loyalty and other nationalism issues. However, it cannot, of course, tell us anything about reactions to the 2014 events in Ukraine. An additional grant,[3] however, made possible a follow-up survey, conducted in November that year, to shed light on how Russian attitudes have changed under the impact of the dramatic events that had unfolded since our first survey. The new survey repeated most of the questions from the May 2013 survey verbatim, to enable us to assess how the recent events may have prompted a re-orientation on nationalism issues among the Russian population. We also included some new questions that focused specifically on the Crimean annexation and the war in Eastern Ukraine.

Scope and structure of the book

The book is divided into two main parts: first, society-level Russian nationalism, and, second, nationalism at the level of the state. In Chapter 1 Pål Kolstø (University of Oslo, Norway) pursues three aims: he provides a literature synopsis on the study of Russian nationalism in Western scholarship; offers a brief historical overview over the development of Russian nationalism; and outlines in broad terms the trajectory of Russian nationalism from statist to ethno-centrist positions.

The turn towards ethnification in Russian national identity gained momentum with the collapse of the USSR. The state most Russians now live in – the Russian Federation – is far less multi-cultural than the states they and their forebears had lived in and identified with earlier – under the Tsarist Empire and the Soviet Union. Today's ethnification can also be seen as resulting from a 'contagion' from the ethnic/nationalist mobilisation of non-Russians under perestroika. Even so, in the first decade after state dissolution, nationalist sentiment in Russia continued to be dominated more by empire-nostalgia than by ethnonationalism. The new turn towards ethnonationalism came only after the turn of the millennium, spurred by two issues in particular: concern for Russian co-ethnics abroad, 'stranded' in the other former Soviet republics when the USSR collapsed; and, somewhat later, the influx of non-Russian migrants from the Caucasus and Central Asia into Russian cities. Kolstø concludes that the ethnification of Russian nationalism seems to stem from below, driven by opposition activists rather than by the regime, but that it also to some extent reverberates in official Russian rhetoric.

In Chapter 2 Emil Pain (National Research University – Higher School of Economics, Moscow, Russia) discusses the persistence of the imperial legacy in the political life in Russia and its influence on Russian nationalism. The enduring combination of nationalism and imperial consciousness in Russia has led to the creation of 'imperial nationalism'. While this term may seem unfamiliar and even unwarranted from a theoretical point of view, such a phenomenon does exist in Russia and has come to the fore several times, most recently after the 2014 annexation of Crimea.

Pain engages in two theoretical discussions: first, concerning the nature of empire, he proposes a unified theoretical concept of 'imperial syndrome' that encompasses several analytical perspectives: its political organisation (the imperial 'order'), its political 'body' (territorial arrangement) and, finally, the type of mass consciousness characteristic of an empire. Second, he discusses the causes behind the endurance of authoritarian and imperial features in Russian politics, first and foremost the mutual relationship between cultural traditions, on the one hand, and the intentional manipulations that lead to this persistence, on the other.

As Pain points out, when the idea of the *nation* first appeared in Russia under the influence of the French Revolution, it was understood by the Russian elite in the same way as in the 1789 Declaration of the Rights of Man and of the Citizen. Against this background he sets out to explain how it later turned into a very specific idea of imperial nationalism. Pain also analyses the appearance of a new, anti-imperial Russian nationalism after the turn of the last century, and examines its weaknesses after the annexation of Crimea in 2014.

In Chapter 3 Alexander Verkhovsky (SOVA Center for Information and Analysis, Moscow, Russia) examines the dynamics of the radical wing in Russian nationalism, from the beginning of Dmitrii Medvedev's presidency in 2008 to the war in the Donbas region in 2014. Based on extensive research carried out by the SOVA Center for Information and Analysis, Verkhovsky's analysis focuses on nationalists who oppose the authorities – typically, those who participate in the 4 November 'Russian March' – but not on the 'national democrats'. In the evolution of an aggressive ultra-nationalism promoting a 'White Power'-influenced model of an ethnically pure Russia in place of the lost empire, 2008 stands as the year in which racist violence peaked. Verkhovsky then considers the radical nationalists' fluctuating levels of engagement in political activities and in violence, and the dynamics of their relationship with the authorities. He identifies the 2010 Manezhnaia riots as the point at which the federal authorities were forced to elaborate statist nationalism as an alternative to ethnic nationalism. A surprise lapse in this policy came with the anti-migrant campaign of 2013, which significantly inflamed ethnic tensions and generated radical nationalist activity in the form of raids on 'illegal migrants'.

Notwithstanding this surge in activity, and despite reasonably effective leadership and a range of strategies for generating support (from raids and anti-paedophile campaigns to Kondopoga-type riots), Verkhovsky holds that the movement has been unable to broaden its support base. He ends by briefly summarising ultra-nationalist responses to the situation in Ukraine, and provisionally concludes that once the Euromaidan anti-authority protest in Kyiv escalated into armed conflict between 'Russians' and 'Ukrainians', the Russian nationalist movement became divided over whether to support the separatists or oppose them.

In Chapter 4 Anastasia Mitrofanova (Russian Orthodox University, Moscow, Russia) examines the religious attitudes of Russian ethnonationalist circles, whose ideology and political practice centre on the promotion of political self-determination for ethnic Russians, as well as the in/compatibility of the teachings of the Russian Orthodox Church with nationalism. She shows that the 'Russian world' concept as advocated by the Church is far from promoting ethnic Russian nationalism. Further, the concept is broader than 'imperial' nationalism and is currently used to support the universal soteriological ambitions of the Church.

Immediately after the dissolution of the USSR, nearly all nationalists – except a small neopagan anti-Christian minority – identified themselves with Orthodoxy. However, since ethnic nationalism apparently contradicts the teaching and the policy of the Church, this Orthodox nationalism as promulgated in the early 1990s has now become obsolete. Orthodox nationalists have invented two strategies to allow them to reconcile Christianity with ethnic supremacism: they either join various non-canonical Orthodox jurisdictions, or form non-territorial faith communities around like-minded priests within the mainstream Church.

The neopagans have long been a closed sub-culture in Russia, and support for them now seems to have reached its limits. Instead, it is secularism that has become the most widespread position for contemporary Russian ethnonationalists. Unlike the neopagans, the secularists have nearly unlimited opportunities for recruiting new members; and unlike Orthodox nationalists, they experience none of the ideological challenges or practical difficulties of having to satisfy the regulations of the Church. Secular nationalism has become the most promising stratum within Russian nationalism, where new leaders, new organisations and new ideas are emerging.

In Chapter 5 Natalya Kosmarskaya and Igor Savin (both at Institute of Oriental Studies of the Russian Academy of Sciences, Moscow, Russia) analyse perceptions of immigrants among Muscovites. Throughout the post-Soviet period, the Russian capital has been a magnet for labour migrants from the poverty- and/or war-stricken Caucasus, as well as from parts of Central Asia. In their analysis, Kosmarskaya and Savin draw parallels between the scale and manifestations of anti-migrant sentiments in various countries of Western Europe and among residents of Moscow. The authors examine how the main factors that provoke anti-migrant attitudes in Europe as well as the main concepts used in explaining these attitudes may operate also under the social conditions of the largest city in Russia.

Two features of the Muscovites' perceptions of labour migrants deserve special attention. First, respondents contextualise the 'migration issue' primarily within a wider social setting in Moscow: in their narratives, they associate migrants much more with disturbances of social/political life in Russia/Moscow in general than with any alleged 'ethno-cultural otherness'. Second, their opinions are marked by a 'demonstrative xenophobia'. Many of those who were interviewed through the large-N survey selected questionnaire options that reflected perceptions of migrants as a source of threat to Russian culture, economy and the like. By contrast, those who expressed their opinions through in-depth interviews made it clear that the actual migrants whom Muscovites meet in everyday life in various parts of the city are not perceived through any 'threat' lens.

In Chapter 6 Mikhail A. Alexseev (San Diego State University, California, USA) focuses on the repercussions of Putin's turn to ethnic Russian great-power nationalism at the time of the Crimean annexation in 2014 among Russia's ethnic minorities, and he asks whether the minorities will support majority ethnic nationalist expansionism. On the one hand, mass opinion surveys in Russia showed overwhelming support for the Crimean annexation across predominantly Russian and ethnic non-Russian regions. On the other hand, interpreting the survey data is difficult, given the government's control of the media.

Alexseev's main finding is that ethnic identity is contingent on state identity and prospective valuations of relative group position. Russians and non-Russians were almost equally likely to be proud of their ethnicity and Russian citizenship, to vote for Putin, to believe that Russia's economy was growing and to support Russian territorial expansion. However, when the non-Russian subsample was further divided into Slavic and non-Slavic respondents, systematic differences emerged as to views on Russia's state borders. Each group of respondents systematically supported the option under which its own size relative to that of others would increase the most. Thus, support for Russia without the ethnically non-Russian North Caucasus region was strongest among ethnic Russians. Support for a Slavic Union was strongest among non-Russian Slavs. And support for Russia expanding to the size of the former USSR was strongest among non-Slavic respondents.

As noted, the annexation of Crimea in March 2014 took place while all contributors to this volume were engaged in writing up their chapters. This momentous event moved questions of nationalism and national identity to the top of the political agenda in Russia. In order to gauge the changes that were taking place in Russian popular opinion, we carried out a follow-up survey in November 2014 to our original May 2013 survey. The two polls were analysed and compared by Mikhail A. Alexseev and Henry E. Hale (George Washington University, Washington DC, USA) who present their findings in Chapter 7. They find that attitudes regarding such typically 'nationalist' issues as ethnic pride and ethno-centrism had changed very little – possibly because Russians had scored high on these issues already prior to the Crimean annexation. What really changed was support for the regime in general and for President Putin in particular. To a greater extent than before, respondents now expressed the view that Putin was the right man to tackle all kinds of nationalist challenges to the state and in society. Thus, rather than the typical 'rally-around-the-flag' effect, Alexseev and Hale find what they call a 'rally-around-the-leader' effect.

The chapters in Section II in the book analyse state-level Russian nationalism under Putin. In Chapter 8 Henry E. Hale presents two competing pictures of Russian politics: Some Western researchers depict it as a realm of cynicism, where everything is for sale, leaders rudely dismiss public opinion and politicians mainly pursue their own power and enrichment through a mix of repression and corruption. Others claim that Russia's leadership is resolutely principled, driven at least in part by the nationalist goal of restoring Russian pride. In Hale's interpretation these two perspectives are not necessarily mutually exclusive: they can be explained if we employ the logic of 'patronal presidentialism'.

'Patronal presidentialism' refers to a constitutionally strong presidency that exists in a social context where political collective action unfolds primarily through extensive networks of personal acquaintances, networks that tend to give presidents 'informal' power far beyond the authority formally stipulated in the country's constitution. Even when such presidents use manipulation, coercion and fraud to win elections, they run significant risks of losing power if they lose popular support. For that reason, Russia's presidents have been highly sensitive to public opinion.

Nationalism comes into play here. The relationship between nationalism and political support in Russia is not straightforward – in fact, Putin did not rely heavily on Russian nationalism for political support during his first two presidential terms or his time as prime minister. However, a domestic political crisis that came to a head in late 2011, when tens of thousands of demonstrators poured into the streets, changed the Kremlin's calculus, forcing it to seek out new bases of public support. This eventually led to a far more prominent role for Russian nationalism in connection with Putin's leadership, and helped to bring about the crisis involving Crimea and Ukraine.

In Chapter 9 Helge Blakkisrud (Norwegian Institute of International Affairs (NUPI), Oslo, Norway) shows how the boundary between civic and ethnic has been blurred in Russian nationality policy under Putin's third term. Traditionally, the Russian – and later Soviet – state relied on an imperial approach to the 'national question': on loyalty to the state and the dynasty/Communist Party, rather than to an ethnically defined community. The breakup of the Soviet Union did not immediately change this. After 1991, the multi-ethnic 'Soviet people' was replaced by an equally multi-faceted *rossiiskii* civic identity intended to encompass everyone residing within the borders of the new state.

As the Soviet overlay began to wear off, however, a re-appraisal gradually took place. From around the beginning of Putin's third term, against a backdrop of internal and external challenges, with the mass protests in Moscow and St Petersburg after the 2011 State Duma elections and the evolving crisis in Ukraine, the Kremlin has undertaken a re-calibrating of its understanding of the national 'self'. There has been a growing tendency to redefine the citizenry in ethnonational terms. Traditional ethnopolitical correctness has been challenged: the space allocated to the ethnic Russian population within the state project has been expanded. The ethnic Russian (*russkii*) people together with Russian culture and language have increasingly taken centre stage, with ethnic Russians portrayed as the 'state-forming nation' (*gosudarstvo-obrazuiushchii narod*).

During the first two years of Putin's third term the civic identity in official rhetoric has become more explicitly Russian, with the Kremlin holding up Russian language, culture and traditional values as the core of this identity. At the same time, Blakkisrud also points out that the Kremlin has distanced itself from more extreme expressions of Russian ethnonationalism.

In Chapter 10 Marlene Laruelle (George Washington University, Washington DC, USA) explores a major ambiguity in Russia's state discourse about national identity since Putin's return to power: that of being increasingly anti-Western while at the same time insisting on Russia's European identity. The Kremlin developed an elaborate narrative dissociating the West's liberal values from 'Europe' as a philosophical and historical principle, and presenting Russia as the representative of authentic European values, the embodiment of those 'real' values that have been lost in the West. With the Kremlin's morality-turn and launching of Russia as the 'Christian saviour', Moscow was able to develop close connections with conservative groupings in the West, ranging from the Vatican and some US evangelical movements to family-oriented groups like the highly conservative World Congress of Families, with increasing support among European far-right and classic-right political parties.

This narrative reinforces the traditional idea of seeing Europe – in the sense of a civilisation – as Russia's main 'Other'. Laruelle goes on to show how this narrative accords with identity changes experienced by Russian public opinion since the turn of the millennium, especially the rise of xenophobia against migrants and the identification of Russians with Europe. These two trends are echoed even by some of the most radical opponents of Putin's regime, the 'national-liberal' movement, which holds that Russia should follow a European path of development. Seeing nationalism as a European legacy, this movement proclaims the Europeanisation of Russia as its goal.

In Chapter 11 Stephen Hutchings and Vera Tolz (both at the University of Manchester, UK) explore how Russian state-aligned television presents ethnicity and nationhood in its news broadcasts, considering the effectiveness of the medium as a tool for forging a sense of belonging among the citizens of the largest post-Soviet state. Their material covers the period from 2010 to 2014, with the authors' reading of it framed by the Ukraine crisis and by the role of Russian federal television in fanning the flames that continue to engulf the actors at its heart.

Neither the conflict with the West that Russia's actions in Ukraine precipitated, nor the rationale for those actions promoted

INTRODUCTION: RUSSIAN NATIONALISM IS BACK

in news broadcasts on state-aligned channels, can be understood without reference to tensions within the Putin regime's nation-building project – tensions that were long evident in television news broadcasts. On the one hand, television news reports present ethnic and cultural diversity as one of Russia's uniquely positive qualities. On the other hand, with multi-ethnicity and migration proving to be a powder keg within the population at large, and with xenophobia growing, state broadcasters find themselves caught between attempting to preserve ethnic cohesion by under-reporting inflammatory topics, and giving in to popular sentiments by echoing the prejudicial fears to which those topics gave rise. During Putin's third presidential term, representations of Russia as a multi-ethnic state have been increasingly marginalised by the broadcasters' promotion of specifically Russian ethno-cultural aspects of identity. Further, ethno-cultural Russian nationalism provided the dominant frame for television coverage of the annexation of the Crimea in March 2014; the ethnic-diversity frame was also utilised, but only occasionally.

In the twelfth and final chapter, Peter Rutland (Wesleyan University, Connecticut, USA) examines an issue often overlooked in discussions of Russian nationalism: the place of economics in Russian national identity debates. On the one side are modernisers who believe that embracing Western market institutions is the only way to restore Russia's prosperity and hence its standing in the world. On the other side are nationalists who hold that economic integration will erode the political institutions and cultural norms that are central to Russian identity. They argue that erecting barriers to Western economic influence and creating an alternate trading bloc are necessary to prevent the exploitation of the Russian economy and even the possible destruction of the Russian state.

There seems to be no middle position, no third way between the modernisers and the nationalists: a distinctive Russian economic model that could combine elements of trade openness with measures to ensure the country's long-term development. Putin was building such a model of state corporatism plus international integration in the period 2000–8; but the model revealed its limitations in the stagnation following the 2008 financial crash. He tried to develop an alternative in the form of the Eurasian

Economic Union: a regional trading bloc that would be under Russian control and partially insulated from the global economic institutions dominated by the USA and its allies. However, the change of government in Kyiv signalled that Ukraine was pulling away from economic integration with Russia. The subsequent military confrontation seems to have pushed Russia in the direction of autarky – or perhaps into the arms of China, which would pose new and different risks to national identity.

The dramatic news emanating from Crimea and Eastern Ukraine in 2014 has had a profound influence on popular attitudes among Russians. However, at the time of writing (spring 2015) the civil war in Ukraine is still going on, and as yet we can only speculate about the long-term effects of these momentous events. We can document that they have indeed led to a profound shift in Russian popular discourse and official rhetoric in the direction of a greater focus on various nationalism issues, but we cannot know whether this will lead to a more permanent reconfiguration of the debate. Will the new constellations between 'imperial' nationalism and 'ethnic' nationalism endure or will the 'correlation of forces' between these two currents fall back to the patterns that had crystallised at the beginning of Putin's third term? It is also too early to determine whether the regime will continue to take the driver's seat in the promotion of national sentiment in Russia, or whether oppositional nationalists will be able to set the agenda.

The trajectory of Russian nationalism has been affected not only by the country's relations to the outside world: the changing economic plight of the country is another exogenous factor that has turned the study of this phenomenon into a rapidly moving target. The recent downturn in the Russian economy had been prepared by the failure of Dmitrii Medvedev's modernisation programme, accelerated by falling oil prices. But it was only after the Western economic sanctions against Putin's Ukrainian ventures and Russia's counter-sanctions that Russia experienced a dramatic depreciation of the rouble and negative economic growth. According to media reports, this has already led to a reversal of migration flows into the country: many of the 'guest workers' who until recently arrived in droves from Central Asia are already returning home. When construction companies and other employers are laying people off, the immigrants – who often have no official work permit – will inevitably be the first ones to go. However, these rumours (and for the time being it amounts to no more than that) cannot yet be substantiated by firm statistics, so we cannot know the scope or the permanence of this new trend. It seems clear that to the extent that xenophobia has been fuelled by the sight of an increasing number of alien-looking faces in the streets of major Russian cities, the sudden disappearance of this poorly integrated demographic element is bound to affect the character of Russian nationalism. But how fast and in what direction – that is something we cannot tell.

The re-emergence of nationalism as a strong societal force and public topic in Russia is not unique. In many other European countries, it is precisely the influx of illegal immigrants from other parts of the world that has nourished nationalist sentiments, putting the liberal state under considerable strain. The difference is that Russia today cannot be described as a 'liberal' state in the first place. Under conditions of increasing authoritarianism and controlled civil society, it becomes tempting for both regime and opposition in Russia to play the ethnic card so as to tap into xenophobic sentiments in the population. The sudden politicisation of nationalist issues in Kremlin rhetoric after the Euromaidan revolution in order to justify the annexation of Crimea and Russia's covert military engagement in the Donbas is one recent and ominous example of what this can lead to.

Notes

1. According to the Levada polling institute, <www.levada.ru/eng> (last accessed 9 March 2015).
2. See 'Nation-building and nationalism in today's Russia (NEORUSS)', <www.hf.uio.no/ilos/english/research/projects/neoruss> (last accessed 9 March 2015). The project was funded over the Research Council of Norway's Russia and the High North/Arctic (NORRUSS) programme, project number 220599.
3. From the Freedom of Expression Foundation (Fritt Ord), Oslo.

1

The ethnification of Russian nationalism

Pål Kolstø

On 18 March 2014 Putin held a landmark speech to the Russian Federal Assembly, justifying the annexation of the Crimean peninsula that took place on the same day. Some of the arguments were vintage Putin rhetoric – the need to build and defend a strong Russian state, a lament over double Western standards in international relations and so on. What was new, however, were his references to the Russian people as an ethnic entity. Putin claimed that, with the dissolution of the Soviet Union 'the Russian people have become one of the largest divided nations in the world, if not the largest' (Putin 2014a). By 'the Russian people' he was clearly referring not to 'the (multi-ethnic) people of Russia', but to 'ethnic Russians' – wherever they may live, also abroad. The expression he used was *russkii narod*, a concept that in the modern Russian political lexicon had until then been used in the ethnic sense only, not in referring to the political nation. For the latter entity, the Eltsin Administration had introduced the term *rossiiskii narod*. It is true that in the Tsarist era the terms *rossiiskii* and *russkii* had often been used interchangeably (Tishkov 2013), and Putin was arguably trying to resurrect the pre-revolutionary terminology. In an article from January 2012 (Putin 2012b) he referred also to 'Russian Armenians', 'Russian Tatars' and 'Russian Germans' – using the term *russkii* rather than *rossiiskii*. In the context this seems to mean 'Armenians, Tatars and Germans who live in Russia and undergo some kind of acculturation into Russian culture'. However, his claim that 'the Russian people has become one of the largest divided nations in the world' clearly presupposes an ethnic understanding of 'the people'. As long as 'the Russian people' is understood as 'the total population of Russia', it can by definition not be divided among various states.

Ever since taking office, Putin has regularly been characterised in Western media as a 'nationalist'. His original brand of nationalism was clearly of the statist kind, *derzhavnost*, with a strong emphasis on the *state*, the *derzhava*. In his article 'Russia on the eve of the millennium', published on 30 December 1999, the day before he was appointed acting president, Putin stressed the centrality of a strong state for Russian identity and discussed the cultural foundations of Russian statehood (Putin 1999; see also Kolstø and Blakkisrud 2004). Remarkably, *not once* did he use the adjective *russkii* at this point. In a lengthy section, Putin discussed what he regarded as 'traditional Russian values' – but he consistently referred to them as *rossiiskie* values, even if these values were generally the same ones as those that numerous authors before him had singled out as typical of ethnic Russians and not necessarily of other peoples of Russia. At this stage Putin not only toed the terminological line of his benefactor President Eltsin but underplayed the ethnic component in the nation concept even more than his predecessor had done. Later, the term *russkii* gradually crept into his speeches.

The substitution of one word for 'Russian' with another in Russian political discourse, I hold, was not just a matter of phrasing: it reveals a fundamental shift in nationalism and national identity that has taken place in Russia in recent decades, from statist to ethnonationalist positions. This change is evident at various levels, societal and political. Before it found its way into Putin's speeches, it could be detected in oppositional public discourse.

Nikolai Mitrokhin (2003: 47) traces organised Russian ethnonationalism back to the 1950s and 1960s. In the pre-perestroika period the vast majority of Russian nationalists, also of the ethnonationalists, had the Soviet Union as their country of reference and could not contemplate any truncation of its territory. Most Soviet citizens took great pride in the fact that their state was one of the world's two superpowers and, indeed, the largest country on the planet. Among the first to claim that Russians should be ready to let go of the Asian parts of the state was Aleksandr Solzhenitsyn. But for a long time his remained an isolated voice in the wilderness. The leading contemporary Russian nationalist Konstantin Krylov (*Nazdem.info* 2010) maintains that Russian (ethno)nationalism is a 'new phenomenon', dating roughly from the first decade of the new millennium – an assessment echoed by Emil Pain, a keen observer of the Russian nationalist scene (Pain 2014: 48; Pain, this volume).

Whence, then, the new ethnic turn in Russian self-understanding? A simple answer would be that it is linked to the collapse of the USSR – but that is far from the whole story. Under Eltsin both the regime and its critics espoused various brands of state-focused nationalism: the hardliners (the 'red–brown' opposition) were Soviet nostalgics who longed for the defunct superpower, while the Eltsinites sought to inculcate in the population loyalty to the truncated Russian state, the Russian Federation. At that time, actual ethnonationalists were few and far between; they were to come later.

A typology of Russian nationalisms

Numerous books and articles have been written about Russian nationalism – under the tsars (Riasanovsky 1959; Seton-Watson 1986; Simon 1991; Tuminez 2000; Tolz 2001), in the Soviet Union (Yanov 1978; Dunlop 1983; Dunlop 1985; Carter 1990; Brudny 2000; Mitrokhin 2003), under perestroika (Szporluk 1989; Dunlop 1993), and in the post-communist period (Tuminez 2000; Tolz 2001; Laruelle 2008; Laruelle 2009a). These analyses have argued that nationalism has influenced the worldview of Russian thinkers and politicians and shaped events in Russia. For instance, Nikolai Mitrokhin (2003: 41) has claimed that Russian nationalism was 'a rather widespread phenomenon' in the USSR, while John Dunlop (1985: 92) expressed the view that Russian nationalism was well positioned to replace communism as state ideology. In contrast, in 1990 Alexander Motyl (1990: 161–73) claimed that Russian nationalism was a marginal phenomenon in

Russian society, indeed, a 'myth'; and David Rowley (2000) ten years later followed up by asserting the *absence* of nationalism in Russian history.

In fact, however, the apparent discrepancy among those who assert and those who deny the significance of Russian nationalism stems from the differing definitions employed. Rowley and Motyl claimed that most of what had passed for Russian nationalism on closer scrutiny proved to be *imperialism*, and, argued Motyl (1990: 162), 'nationalism and imperialism are polar types'. Scholars who adhere to this view equate nationalism with *ethnonationalism*. While that is an extremely important variety of this -ism, it is not the only possible one. The pioneers of nationalism studies such as Karl Deutsch (1966) and Ernest Gellner (1983) regarded as nationalism all strategies aimed at homogenising a country's population so as to create a common identity, attached to the state. The 'ties that bind' do not necessarily have to be ethnicity or a myth of common descent.

It is only if we equate nationalism with ethnonationalism that political, state-based nationalism in multi-ethnic states becomes a contradiction in terms. Perhaps one reason why Rowley and Motyl did so with regard to Russia is that, almost without exception, the nationalisms of the other, small- and medium-sized nations in the Russian Empire and the Soviet Union have belonged to the ethnonationalist variety (see, for example, Simon 1991; Carrère d'Encausse 1993). This is not surprising. As long as there was no Belarusian, Uzbek or Chechen state, nationalism among Belarusians, Uzbeks, Chechens and so on focused on the ethnic group rather than on the state. Indeed, in a typology attributed to Hans Kohn (1971),[1] nationalism among state-less, state-seeking groups has been characterised as 'Eastern' in contradistinction to 'Western', state-focused nationalism. While this distinction may help to explain the trajectory of nationalism among stateless nations in the eastern part of Europe, it is unsuited for analysing nationalist thinking in East European nations that identify with one of Europe's old states, such as the Poles, the Hungarians and the Russians.

Marlene Laruelle (2010a: 3) argues that since ethno-centrism and nationalism are not synonymous terms, 'there can be no question here of excluding from "nationalism" so-called imperialist or statist currents'. Similarly, Vera Tolz (2001: 18) has held that the term 'nationalism', 'as it is used in Western scholarly literature, is applicable to the Russian case'. Also Emil Pain and Sergei Prostakov (2014) think that in a Russian context the expression 'imperial nationalism' is not necessarily an oxymoron. I will follow these researchers and include in my definition of nationalism both state-centred and ethnocentric nationalisms.

According to Laruelle (2014a: 59), it does not make sense to try to distinguish between imperialist and ethnonationalist currents in Russian nationalism, since 'the main ideologues and politicians can use at the same time both imperialist and ethnonationalist arguments'. In my view, however, it is important to keep these tendencies analytically separate. Even if almost all 'real existing nationalisms' in Russia historically or today are of a mixed kind, clear differences become evident, with significant political consequences, when we ask which of these two concerns is the driving motor behind each of them: the interests of the state, or the interests of the Russian ethnic group. The most important distinction, I argue, runs between those that focus on ethnicity versus those that focus on the state. But since the borders of the Russian state have changed, we must also hold apart those nationalists who identify with the current Russian Federation, and those who orient themselves towards one of its much larger predecessors, whether the Tsarist Empire or the USSR. For these purposes I will use the two-axis model proposed by Sven Gunnar Simonsen in 1996 (see Figure 1.1).[2] The two axes should not be understood as dichotomies but rather as continua, and the four boxes as ideal types in a Weberian sense.

Until about 1988–9, most Russians, including virtually all nationalists, took it for granted that 'the state' in question was the USSR. It was only when this state was reeling under the increasing onslaught of non-Russian nationalism that the term became ambiguous. In a seminal article in 1989, Roman Szporluk (1989: 16) referred to those who wanted to preserve the USSR as 'empire-savers' while those few who were willing to contemplate a breakup of the unitary state and see the Russian Soviet Federative Socialist Republic (RSFSR) as a Russian nation-state –

Territorial orientation	Primarily statist A	Primarily ethnic B
I 'Empire' oriented	1 empire-saving nationalism	2 supremacist nationalism
II 'Core' oriented	3 Russian Federation nationalism	4 ethnic core nationalism

Figure 1.1 A typology of Russian nationalisms

or as a territorial area that could be developed into such an entity – he called 'nation-builders'.

Today, a quarter-century after Szporluk wrote his article, the USSR has ended up in the dustbin of history and a new generation of Russians have grown up who have never known any other 'homeland' than the Russian Federation. This is not to say that the 'empire-savers' have evaporated. They are still around, now in the guise of various kinds of 'empire-nostalgics' or 'Eurasianists'. Some celebrate the fact that the Soviet Union was a multinational state (quadrant 1), while others combine a desire for a large and strong state with Russian supremacism (quadrant 2).

On both axes intermediate positions can be found. With regard to territory, it is not uncommon to hear among contemporary Russian ethnonationalists that, while the Soviet Union is irredeemably lost and should not be resurrected, the two Slavic republics of Ukraine and Belarus, plus perhaps the Russian-populated part of Kazakhstan, ought to be incorporated into a Russian nation-state. The main motivation here is ethnic commonality among the Eastern Slavs rather than any harking for a big and strong state. As Oxana Shevel has pointed out (2011: 187–9), some Russian ethnonationalists include also the Ukrainians and the Belarusians among those whom they regard as 'Russians' alongside the Great Russians, or 'Russians proper'.

In this chapter I trace the historical trajectory of Russian nationalism, arguing that a clearly discernible movement has taken place from positions A to B on the *x*-axis in my typology and from positions I to II on the *y*-axis. This development did not gain speed until after the breakup of the Soviet Union and can be linked to two issues that resulted from this dissolution: the 'new diaspora' in the 1990s, and flow of unskilled labour from former Soviet Republics into Russia after the year 2000.

Russian nationalism before the nation-state

Tsarist Russia was an empire in name and self-understanding as well as in actual fact. Regime legitimation – often called 'official nationality' (Riasanovsky 1959) – was of a dynastic, statist kind, emphasising loyalty to the Tsar. Also virtually all nationalist currents among the intelligentsia were located on the 'empire-oriented' axis in my matrix.

Geoffrey Hosking (1998: 19) holds that the huge efforts expended on building the vast Russian Empire impeded attempts to create a Russian nation. Likewise, Astrid Tuminez (2000: 25) argues that since 'the state developed as a multiethnic, authoritarian empire, the idea of nation both in ethnic and civic terms never gained widespread influence'. Only towards the end of the nineteenth century did the Russian state introduce a policy of Russification toward some of its non-Russian subjects, but the effects were limited. 'Russia remained a state where the sense of nation (both ethnic and civic) was weak, and nationalism that effectively bound state and society did not exist' (Tuminez 2000: 39).

After the first Russian revolution in 1905 came the emergence of a Russian nationalism with a strong emphasis on blood, descent and ethnicity. The extremist pro-tsarist groups (often referred to as 'the Black Hundreds') 'defined membership in the nation chiefly in ethnic terms – only ethnic Russians were bona fide members of the nation' (Tuminez 2000: 126; see also Laqueur 1993). At the same time such moderate great power nationalists as Petr Struve and Petr Stolypin tried to combine a civic and ethnic strategy of nationalism (Struve 1997; Hosking 1998: 32; Tuminez 2000: 128) – but this could not save the empire.

The Bolshevik regime that took over in 1917 professed an anti-nationalist ideology: internationalist communism. Writing in 1986, Hugh Seton-Watson (1986: 28) held that 'the Soviet leadership, from 1917 to the present day, has not been inspired by Russian nationalism'. Frederick Barghoorn (1980: 57–8), however, insisted that for Stalin a 'new Soviet Russian ethnocentrism' was central to his 'socialist patriotism' while Brezhnev was 'a Russifier and exponent of neo-Stalinist Russian ethnocentrism' (see also Barghoorn 1956). The truth should be sought somewhere in-between Seton-Watson and Barghoorn's one-sided claims. The least we can say is that Stalin deliberately appealed to Russian national sentiments during and after the Second World War to bolster support for the regime (Brandenberger 2002). Brezhnev for his part accorded some leeway to Russophile ideas, within the party apparatus as well as among the cultural intelligentsia (Yanov 1978; Brudny 2000; Mitrokhin 2003). Scholars have identified various strands and currents within the spectrum of state-tolerated Russian nationalisms at the time. Some nationalisms veered towards aggressive statism, replete with vehement anti-Westernism and rather transparent anti-Semitism, while others, like the 'village prose writers', were far more concerned with the preservation of Russian cultural values. One thing they had in common: they took the continued existence of a Soviet unitary state for granted.

The same was true of Russian nationalism as it developed in émigré circles in the interwar period. The two parallel movements of National Bolshevism and Eurasianism were often at loggerheads, but on many crucial issues they advocated similar brands of nationalism. Both were strongly committed to the preservation of the unitary Russian state within the old borders. The main difference between them was that while the National Bolshevists trusted the Bolshevik regime to do this (Agurskii 2003), the Eurasianists developed their own ideology for a post-Bolshevik, unified Russia. This ideology was to build on values common to all residents of this state – but also on Russian Orthodoxy as the sole state religion. While Eurasianists paid considerable attention to cultural matters, the concerns of the state were nevertheless paramount for them.

Laruelle (2008: 29) sees their movement as 'an extreme form of statism'.

John Dunlop (1983, 1985) identified the vast majority of Russian nationalists in the post-war dissident movement as culturalists (or *vozrozhdentsy* in his terminology) rather than 'National Bolsheviks'. They were deeply preoccupied with preserving Russian cultural traditions and monuments, concerned about the decay of the Russian countryside and at least some of them professed the Orthodox faith. Other scholars have found a much larger element of statism and aggressive Messianism, even proto-fascism and fascism, among anti-regime Russian nationalists (Yanov 1978; Laqueur 1993; Duncan 2000: 82–96; Shenfield 2001: 40–4). Neither the dissident statists nor the *vozrozhdentsy* questioned the territorial integrity of the Soviet state – with a few notable exceptions. Best-known here is Solzhenitsyn, with his appeal to the Soviet leaders to let go of Central Asia and concentrate the resources of the state on developing the Russian North (Solzhenitsyn 1980). It is true that Solzhenitsyn under no circumstances envisioned relinquishing the demographically Slavic parts of the Soviet state such as Ukraine, Belarus and northern Kazakhstan. However, by combining an ethnic reasoning with a readiness to forego state grandeur he anticipated the later development of Russian ethnic core nationalism (quadrant 4 in my matrix). Also a few other dissident nationalists in the 1970s and 1980s can be seen as ethnonationalists, including Vladimir Balakhonov (Szporluk 1989: 25–6) and Sergei Soldatov (Dunlop 1983: 250).

Nationalism after the dissolution of the unitary Soviet state

The collapse of the USSR was a major watershed in Russian history in the twentieth century, and inevitably affected the trajectory of nationalist thinking as well (Dunlop 1993). According to Georgiy Mirsky, this almost immediately led to two separate, major reorientations in Russian perceptions: towards an ethnic Russian nationalism, on the one hand, and towards a non-ethnic loyalty towards the Russian Federation, on the other:

It would not be an exaggeration to say that it was at that juncture that Russians, for the first time in decades, became really conscious of their national identity. Now, it suddenly appeared that they belonged not to a great multinational empire transcending ethnicity but to a smaller Russian state. *The fact of being an ethnic Russian, formerly just taken for granted, became salient overnight . . . And it was at this juncture that ethnic Russian nationalism came to the fore.* Russians began to feel that they were left all alone, that they were not *Rossiyanie*, but *Russkie*, a purely ethnic community . . . Ethnicity became a sanctuary for people lacking other outlets for self-fulfilment. This is the first, and major, cause of the rise of Russian nationalism. (Mirsky 1997: 165–6, emphasis in the original)

According to Mirsky, the fourth quadrant in my matrix, hitherto inhabited by a few quirks only, suddenly became the abode of millions of Russians. At first, however, ethnic solidarity was eclipsed by another stronger sentiment, Mirsky asserts: the feeling that all these nations, regardless of their ethnic background, belonged to Russia. This was the basis for the new nation-building project launched by the Eltsin Administration in the 1990s (Mirsky 1997: 165–7). The third quadrant, characterised by non-ethnic, Russian Federation-focused nationalism, for a while attracted many Russians.

In Mirsky's view, post-Soviet Russian nationalism has moved through three stages in a remarkably short time – from a subdued feeling of Russianness overshadowed by an overall Soviet loyalty, via a *rossiiane* period, marked by non-ethnic loyalty to the Russian Federation, to a 'genuine Russian ethnic nationalism with chauvinistic overtones' (Mirsky 1997: 167). While Mirsky's observations are important and basically astute, I think he errs on two accounts. First, the two varieties of Russian Federation-focused nationalism should not be seen as *stages* in which one supplants the other, but as coexisting phenomena. The ethnic orientation has indeed grown stronger over time at the expense of the state-centred variety, but this development, I hold, came *after* Mirsky published his book in 1997. Second, Mirsky downplays the enduring strength of the Soviet-focused varieties of Russian nationalism (the 'empire-oriented' axis in my matrix). Indeed, it can be argued that the empire-focused nationalisms initially gained strength, becoming *more* articulate and better organised, in the perestroika period – as 'empire-saving' – and in its immediate aftermath – as 'empire-nostalgia'. Below I will present the four major trends in post-Soviet Russian nationalism in the categories defined above.

USSR-focused statism

The unprecedented upsurge of ethnic nationalism among non-Russians during perestroika did not initially trigger a similar movement among ethnic Russians. Instead, as the nationalist effervescence led to demands for secession in the Union republics, ethnic Russians responded by creating organisations aimed at preserving the unitary state. Notably, in many republics these organisations were called *'intermovements'*, short for 'international movements', a name chosen in deliberate contrast to the nationalist movements among the non-Russians (Kolstø 1995). In the Congress of People's Deputies – the new superparliament established by Mikhail Gorbachev in 1989 – the 'Soiuz' (= Union) group of deputies fought tooth and claw to keep the Soviet Union together (Dunlop 1993: 147–51).

In his heated disputes in the 1980s with Alexander Yanov about the character of Russian nationalism, John Dunlop had claimed that the 'culturalists' were the stronger force and would carry the day. Yanov for his part predicted that the anti-regime culturalists (or nationalism 'A' in his terminology) would eventually be won over by hard-core anti-Western isolationism ('nationalism B'), finally merging into military imperialism ('nationalism C') (Yanov 1978: 19). Perestroika and its immediate aftermath seemed to prove Yanov right. In the late 1980s and early 1990s several Russian nationalists whom Dunlop had identified as leading *vozrozhdentsy* (Dunlop 1985: 88) such as Vladimir Osipov and Igor Shafarevich, made common cause with the 'empire-savers'. In 1992, both of these former dissident anti-communists were among the signatories when the leading red–brown organisation, the National Salvation Front, was established. Their names appeared alongside those of hard-line imperial nationalists like Aleksandr Prokhanov, Albert Makashov and Sergei Baburin, all of whom have been characterised by Stephen Shenfield (2001) as 'fascists'. The same appeal was signed also by 'red' statist nationalists like Communist Party leaders Gennadii Ziuganov and Aman Tuleev (*Den'* 1992).

The major aim of the 'red–brown' coalition – first against Mikhail Gorbachev, later against Boris Eltsin – was in fact not to preserve the communist ideology or the planned economy but to hold the Soviet Union together as state. In a public appeal, the organisers of the National Salvation Front used highly emotive language:

> Dear *rossiiane*! Citizens of the USSR! Fellow citizens! An enormous, unprecedented misfortune has befallen us: the motherland, our country, a great state, which has been given us by history, by nature, and by our glorious forefathers, is perishing, is being broken apart, is being buried in darkness and non-existence. ('Slovo k narodu' 1992)

The National Salvation Front pledged to 'work consistently for the restoration of the state unity of our country'.

The 'red-browns' failed in their bid for power in October 1993, when the besieged Russian parliament that they controlled was shelled into surrender by Eltsin-loyal troops. After this defeat, the 'red' and the 'brown' statists drifted apart and important differences in their thinking came to the fore. Even so, both factions continued to adhere to a basically ethnicity-neutral variety of statism. Ziuganov promoted cultural Russian nationalism but generally eschewed an emphasis on ethnicity in his argumentation (Simonsen 1996: 103), while Vladimir Zhirinovskii and his Liberal-democratic Party are somewhat more difficult to pin down. According to Laruelle, Zhirinovskii cannot reasonably be classified as either an 'imperialist' or an 'ethnonationalist'. On the one hand he has campaigned for a self-sufficient regime in which ethnic Russians would enjoy legal primacy, but at the same time 'he refuses . . . to provide a racial definition of Russianness, emphasizing instead a linguistic and cultural sense of belonging to a Russian world' (Laruelle 2009a: 100).

A more ethnocentric orientation could be expected from the Congress of Russian Communities (KRO), which was explicitly devoted to the support of Russians in the 'near abroad'. The adjective 'Russian' in the name of the movement was indeed *russkii*, not *rossiiskii* – but, according to Alan Ingram (1999: 688), KRO 'rejects an ethnic nationalism based on blood ties and descent, but neither is its nation fully civic, embracing all regardless of culture and identity. While descent ties are important in defining an ethnos, it is not these ties that constitute the nation; this arises out of state formation and a high culture' (see also Tuminez 2000: 191).

In the mid-1990s, neo-Eurasianism became one of the strongest currents of Russian nationalism, if not *the* strongest. Like their interwar namesakes, most latter-day Eurasianists adhered to a non-ethnic definition of the nation. Aleksandr Panarin, for instance, warned that 'the logic of ethnic sovereignty takes us back to pre-medieval times and jeopardises Eurasian unity' (Laruelle 2008: 96), while Aleksandr Dugin denounced ethnonationalism and called for 'a rational, dispassionate nationalism' instead (Laruelle 2008: 128). Dugin proclaimed the coming of 'a new Eurasian stage in Russian history in which the traditional expansion of the historical mission of the state will reach its final limits'; in this state 'the preservation of each and every people and ethnos will be regarded as a highest historical value' (Dugin 1999: 32, 134–5).

Russian supremacist nationalism

While most empire-oriented Russian nationalists steer clear of ethnocratic thinking, certain groups nevertheless adhere to what I have here called supremacism. These are groupings in line with the tradition of the pre-revolutionary Black Hundred movements. First and foremost this was the case with the Pamiat movement, which gained notoriety under perestroika for its combination of monarchism, stringent Orthodoxy and fascist-inspired symbols and ideology elements (Laqueur 1993). The same tendency is found in several smaller groups that at various points splintered off from Pamiat but kept its Russian supremacist orientation, such as the Russian National Union (RNS) and the National-Republican Party of Russia (NRPR) (Shenfield 2001: 225–44). RNS soon developed in the direction of pure neo-Nazism. NRPR leader Nikolai Lysenko initially declared that his party would lean heavily on the ideas of Solzhenitsyn; evidently, it was Solzhenitsyn's emphasis on Russian ethnic concerns that appealed to him. However, Solzhenitsyn's rejection of imperial aspirations was not to Lysenko's liking; in the end, NRPR ideology became a combination of Russian ethnic nationalism and great power imperialism (Shenfield 2001: 233).

Both of the above-mentioned parties had hundreds of members, but they were overshadowed by a third supremacist movement, Russian National Unity (RNE), which for a time became the largest Russian nationalist organisation. At its apogee this militant and militarised movement allegedly had tens of thousands of members and 350 regional chapters (Laruelle 2009a: 56). RNE leader Aleksandr Barkashov took a definite stance against state patriotism in favour of ethnic Russian nationalism. Nationalism, he proclaimed, is to love one's nation and to recognise it as the highest value. Everything else, including the state and its political and economic system, must be subordinated to the goal of achieving the highest possible creative manifestations of the nation (Barkashov 1993: 2). The RNE featured several Nazi-inspired symbols, including a variety of the swastika, and must be characterised as a fascist movement ('O simvole . . .' 1993). The state, it held, ought to become 'an ethnic entity at the service of a titular Russian people' (Laruelle 2009a: 55). However, the RNE basically fell apart in the early 2000s; while there are still organised fascist groups in Russia, only some of them continue in the imperial tradition of the RNE.

Russian Federation-centred civic nationalism

During the power struggle between Mikhail Gorbachev and his nemesis Boris Eltsin in the late perestroika period, the Eltsinites secured control first over the RSFSR legislature in June 1990 and over the newly established RSFSR presidency in June 1991. As a result, Eltsin and his supporters began to identify with and promote the interests of the Russian republic above those of the Union centre (Dunlop 1993). From this starting point, the transformation of the RSFSR into a democratic nation-state based on civic nationalism, the Russian Federation, commenced (Breslauer and Dale 1997: 315–17; Kolstø 2000: 194–202).

In the 1990s it was widely predicted that the phenomenon of the 'new' Russian diaspora in the 'near abroad' would become a major impetus behind a revitalisation of Russian ethnic identity. Accounts of discrimination of their fellow Russians in the other Soviet successor state would lead to an outburst of ethnic solidarity (Melvin 1995: 127; Zevelev 2001: 5). However, while the diaspora issue figured prominently in Russian media for a while, no large-scale mobilisation around this issue took place, neither in Russia nor among the diaspora communities themselves (Kolstø 2011). There were various reasons for this, but probably most important was the attitude of the Russian government at the time. Little support for the diaspora was forthcoming, rhetorically or financially; and, crucially, the official policy was coached in deliberately non-ethnic terms (Zevelev 2001). The diaspora – Russians as well as others with roots in the RSFSR – were referred to as *sootechestvenniki*, 'compatriots' or 'fellow countrymen'. Ostensibly a purely political, 'civic', term, it is probably more correctly regarded as multi-ethnic but cultural. It defined as 'compatriots abroad' not only all persons holding Russian passports, but also all direct descendants of Russian citizens living abroad who identify with Russian culture (Federal'nyi zakon 1999).

The theoretical underpinnings of the Russian Federation-centred nation-building project are practically the work of one man, Valerii Tishkov, director of the Institute of Ethnography and Anthropology at the Russian Academy of Sciences. In contrast to most of his Russian colleagues, Tishkov is a convinced constructivist who believes that nations are the product of nationalists, not the other way around. He liked to quote the nineteenth-century Italian nationalist Massimo D'Azeglio who wrote, 'We have created Italy – now we have to create Italians' (Shakina 1992). Tishkov saw no reason why Russia could not develop into a modern nation-state with the same kind of identity and the same attributes as other European states. The structural as well as the cultural preconditions are in place: 'Russia is more culturally homogenous than many other large and even small countries considered to be nation-states' (Tishkov 1995: 49). Tishkov acknowledges that Russia indeed is a multi-ethnic federation but the ties that bind the various groups together are strong. The all-encompassing knowledge of the Russian language throughout the country's population provides the means for pervasive social communication and facilitates the development of a strong common, supra-ethnic national identity as *rossiiane*. Tishkov strongly urges the depoliticisation of ethnicity in Russia, but he does not challenge the existing system of ethno-territorial autonomy. As Oxana Shevel (2011: 183) has remarked, it may therefore be difficult to see exactly how his *rossiiskii* nation concept differs from the more traditional concept of the multinational *rossiiskii* people.

Tishkov noted with satisfaction that some of his notions found their way into official Russian statements and documents in the Eltsin era – in particular in the president's address to the Federal Assembly in February 1994, when Eltsin defined the nation as 'co-citizenship' (*sograzhdanstvo*) (El'tsin 1994; Tishkov 1995: 48). Tishkov eventually became disappointed with Eltsin's inability to follow through with these ideas, but he regained hope when Vladimir Putin took over. Putin, Tishkov today declares, is finally realising his, Tishkov's, *rossiiskii* nation project.[3] Tishkov has published several books in which he declares that the *rossiiskii* nation (*natsiia*) or the *rossiiskii* people (*narod*) – he uses the two concepts interchangeably – is already an established fact (Tishkov 2010, 2011, 2013). No need for any Russian D'Azeglio after all, then. Indeed, Tishkov pushes the genesis of the *rossiiskii* nation far into the past: both the Romanov state and the Soviet Union were nation-states, he has insisted (Tishkov 2010: 7). The fact that the official name of this nation has undergone alterations over time and in the communist period was referred to as 'the Soviet people' should not confuse us: the main thing is that also in its Soviet version this was a supra-ethnic concept. With this approach, all modern states would qualify as nation-states, irrespective of their state ideology or cultural consolidation.

ETHNIC CORE NATIONALISM

Tishkov's civic nationalism, however, does not seem to carry the day in Russia. In Putin's second presidential term (2004–8) ethnonationalism, previously a fairly marginal phenomenon even in the Russian nationalist movement, increasingly came to the fore (Popescu 2012). Writing in 2009, Alexander Verkhovsky (2010: 89) claimed that 'neither civic nor even imperial, today's Russian nationalism is instead almost exclusively ethnic'. This may be an exaggeration, but the tendency Verkhovsky identified was obviously correct. The leading nationalist organisation at the time was the Movement against Illegal Immigration (DPNI). Although DPNI's programme in many respects reflected a multinational stance, for instance by supporting the reintroduction of a nationality entry in Russian passports, it also specifically demanded that the Russian (*russkii*) people should be recognised as the 'state-bearing' or 'state-forming' (*gosudarstvoobrazuiushchii*) nation in the Russian Federation, 'the people which has created this state and which makes up the majority of the country's population' (*Programma DPNI* 2009).

In December 2010, DPNI was banned by the Russian authorities – only to re-emerge as one of two founding organisations in a new movement, Russkie, which explicitly calls itself an 'ethno-political association'.[4] As former DNPI leader Aleksandr Belov-Potkin explains:

> With the dissolution of the Soviet Union a national reawakening took place among all ethnic groups in the country, but most markedly among the Russians since their ethnic identity had been very weak. A new nation is being born today, a new identity, a new self-understanding. I myself was raised with a Soviet identity, but my son has a very different identity, an identity as a Russian. The empire disappears as a distant historical memory.[5]

In Russkie former DNPI members collaborate with former members of the Slavic Union (*Slavianskii soiuz*), another banned organisation. The Slavic Union had several neo-Fascist features, but in contrast to similar organisations in past decades, like

Pamiat and Russian National Unity, it was oriented towards Russia and not the former Soviet Union.

The new ethno-national current in Russian nationalism includes also various parties and personalities who represent pro-Western and pro-democracy leanings. This is particularly true of the large segment increasingly referred to as 'the national democrats'. They are a loose group that includes both thinkers who stress the importance of ethnicity and those who are more concerned with democracy (see Kolstø 2014). In the former category we find Aleksandr Sevastianov, who has declared: 'national democracy is democracy within the framework of the nation. And I emphasise time and again that *nation* in this context means the *ethnonation* and nothing else' (Sevast'ianov 2013: 203, emphasis in the original). This view is rejected by most other leading national democrats who insist that in a future Russian nation-state full democratic rights can and shall be extended to all citizens irrespective of ethnicity.[6] This is possible, they say, since ethnic Russians make up the vast majority of Russia's population, more than 80 per cent; this will guarantee the national quality also of a fully democratic Russian nation-state. The demographic predominance of ethnic Russians is a result of the collapse of the USSR. Commenting on this epochal event Sevastianov waxes lyrical:

> For our country the pseudoimperial epoch of development is now coming to an end. Having lived for three centuries in an internationalistic empire Russians suddenly find themselves in new realities, in a mononational state, a state in which Russians make up almost 9/10. This is truly a good fortune! (Sevast'ianov 2010: 139)

Even if it was hard to accept the dissolution of the unitary state at the time, explains Sergei Sergeev, managing editor of the journal *Voprosy natsionalizma* and another leading ethnonationalist theoretician, this momentous turning-point in history must be regarded as a blessing in disguise (Sergeev 2010: 236).[7] Such ideas have led the ethnonationalists into a bitter struggle with the Eurasianists and other empire nostalgics, whom the national democrats call '*impertsy*'. According to Konstantin Krylov, the leader of the National-Democratic Party (2011: 3) the conflict between these two groups has reached a level of 'open hatred' and 'a war of extinction'.

In this fierce ideological battle the ethnonationalists can note several defections from the *impertsy* camp to theirs. Sergeev confesses that he himself had been deluded by Eurasianist ideas, before converting to ethnonationalism. Remarkable is the change of heart among some former leaders of the National Salvation Front. For instance, Ilia Konstantinov, identified by Vera Tolz (1998: 272) as the mastermind behind the establishment of the Front, now sympathises with the ethnonationalists. Konstantinov remains a member of one of the smaller empire-saving parties but that is primarily for the sake of old friendships.[8] Also Viktor Alksnis, a former leader of both Soiuz and the National Salvation Front, has shifted sides. In an article tellingly entitled 'Farewell Empire! (At the dawn of a Russian Russia)' Alksnis admits: 'I have always been and will remain a person with an imperial mind-set and to me it has been painful to accept that my Great Empire Idea has died'. However, one must adapt to new realities, he writes: 'In Russia's transition from empire to nation-state . . . We must take into account the national interests of the state-bearing nation – the Russians' (Alksnis 2007: 42, 46). Thus, while in the 1990s the ranks of the National Salvation Front featured former 'culturalists' like Igor Shafarevich and Valentin Rasputin, now the tide seemed to have shifted in the opposite direction.

The threat against a genuine Russian nation-state, as the new ethnonationalists see it, does not emanate from the side of the *impertsy* only. They are fighting on two fronts, the other being the battle to dispel the illusions of Tishkov's civic nation-state model. Kirill Benediktov claims that the most important task for Russian nationalists today is to regain legitimacy for the concept *russkii* and to fight back the term *rossiiane* (*Russkii natsionalizm* 2010: 6). Aleksandr Khramov (2013: 229) criticises Tishkov for believing that in nation-building 'only the civic component is important – as if all citizens of Russia automatically make up a civic nation. In reality, without a common culture no self-identification as a nation is possible', Khramov insists. Sergeev (2010: 208) looks forward to the day when Tishkovianism will take its place in the graveyard of discarded scientific ideas – alongside Lysenkoism, which it allegedly resembles.

Krylov (2012) derisively calls the current Russian Federation *Erefiia* ('RF-iia'), while Pavel Sviatenkov claims that not only in the RSFSR but also in the Russian Federation the Russians have been deprived of a nation-state. For members of one of the smaller Russian ethnic groups, such as the Avars, it can make sense to say both that 'I am an Avar' and 'I am a *rossiianin*', Sviatenkov claims. In that case 'Avar' means ethnicity and *rossiianin* citizenship – 'but for a Russian, such a phrase is devoid of meaning' (Sviatenkov 2010: 3–4). Sviatenkov accepts that a common *rossiiskii* identity is possible, but on one indispensable condition only: '*if it is coupled to the recognition of a state status for the Russian people, Russia as the national state of Russians*' (2010: 6, emphasis in the original).

However, most Russian ethnonationalists will not be content with converting the present Russian state within its current borders into a Russian nation-state. They regard ethnic Russians in the 'near abroad' as members of the Russian nation, and demand that Russians who live in compact settlements outside Russia must be given the right to conduct referenda on unification of their territory with Russia. To justify this, Vladimir Tor, a leader of the National-Democratic Party, points to how German reunification was conducted in 1990: each of the German *Länder* of the former DDR was allowed to hold a referendum on joining the Federal Republic of Germany.[9] Contemporary Russian ethnonationalism, then, contains an element of ethnic irredentism. We may also note that Tor's recipe is strikingly similar to the method adopted by the Kremlin as the formal procedure for incorporating Crimea into the Russian Federation in March 2014.

Ethnonationalist rhetoric in the Russian leadership

Writing in April 2014 Igor Zevelev (2014: 3) has argued: 'even if ethnonationalism in Russia does not make up an organised political force, it is quite clear that its intellectual influence has been growing in recent years'. While most Russian ethnonationalists acknowledge that their impact on Russian public debate has been limited thus far, they note with satisfaction that some of their ideas and concepts are gradually seeping through the crevices of the Kremlin walls. However, it would certainly be an exaggeration to claim that Putin and his entourage have adopted ethnonationalism as their state ideology. Their messages are mixed bags of often-disparate signals; official documents and speeches draw on several, sometimes contradictory, discourses: Russian Federation-civic, Eurasianist and ethnonationalist. Documents signed by Medvedev generally promote a Tishkovian vision of the state. Medvedev regularly employs terms like *rossiiskii narod* and *rossiiskaia natsiia*, but rarely speaks of the *russkii narod* (see, for example, Medvedev 2008, 2009). As recently as in 2011 Medvedev declared: 'it is our task to create a full-fledged *rossiiskaia natsiia* in which the identity of all the peoples who inhabit our country is preserved' (*Ria Novosti* 2011).

Also documents signed by Putin sometimes contain expressions such as *rossiiskaia natsiia*, as with the December 2012 'State Strategy on Nationalities Policy for the Period through 2025' (*Strategiia...* 2012). This document had been drafted in the consultative Presidential Council on Interethnic Relations, where two prominent members – Valerii Tishkov and Vladimir Zorin – who both had served stints as minister in charge of nationality questions – take credit for having kept ethnonational phrases out of the final version. At one point, for instance, it had been suggested to include the concept of the Russian people as a 'state-forming nation', but this idea did not find its way into the published version.[10] However, the final version *did* refer to the Russian (*russkii*) people as 'the historically system-forming core' of the Russian state. 'Thanks to the unifying role of the *russkii* people... a unique cultural multiformity and a spiritual community of various peoples have been created' (*Strategiia ...* 2012). This was a far cry from Eltsin-era rhetoric.

In the run-up to the 2012 presidential elections Putin published a series of newspaper articles on various topics as part of his election campaign. One of these articles, 'On the national question', was on the face of it an attack on Russian ethnonationalism. Putin denounced 'thoroughly false talks about the *russkie's* right to self-determination'. The *russkie*, he declared, had exercised their right to self-determination long ago, by creating a polyethnic civilisation held together by a *russkii* cultural core. By dint of the fact that Russia continues to exist, the *russkii* people is therefore *gosudarstvoobrazuiushchii*, the 'state-forming' nation, in that state.

> Historically, Russia is not an ethnic state and not an American melting pot ... The Russian experience of state development is unique: we are a multinational society but we are one people ... attempts to preach the idea of a Russian 'national', monoethnic state contradict our thousand-year-long history. Indeed, it is the fastest path forward towards the destruction of the *russkii* people and *russkii* statehood. (Putin 2012b)

To a large extent Putin was here lashing out against a straw man, as few Russian ethnonationalists are in favour of a monoethnic state (Sevastianov being one exception). Instead, most ethnonationalists want the current Russian state to be regarded as an expression of '*russkii* statehood', with the Russian nation declared as 'state-forming'. Both of these terms were in fact used by Putin himself in his article. Two core tenets of the ethnonationalists had then, surprisingly, crept into official Kremlin rhetoric. Leading ethnonationalist theoretician Oleg Nemenskii (2012: 18) therefore chose to interpret Putin's message not as criticism, but as indirect acceptance of some of their main ideas. Nemenskii maintained that Putin's

> complete rejection of the previous attempt to establish a *rossiiskii* nation, together with his new accentuation of the Russian ethnic dominant element, represents a major shift in official discourse on nationality policy; V.V. Putin's article legitimises the Russian ethnonym in the official vocabulary. (Nemenskii 2012: 18)

The ethnonationalists take the very fact that Putin found it necessary to attack them as confirmation that the Russian leadership recognises the importance of the issues they raise.

Popular Russian ethnonationalism

From recent survey results Boris Dubin (2014: 15) claims the nationalism of the majority in Russia today is state-oriented and not ethnic. It is difficult to see how he draws that conclusion, since much of the survey results that he himself cites point in another direction. Thus, for instance, 66 per cent supported (more or less strongly) the slogan 'Russia for Russians (*russkie*)' while 61 per cent expressed negative attitudes towards people from the Caucasus and immigrants from Central Asia (Dubin 2014: 9, 12). The Romir survey conducted under the auspices of our project in May 2013 also confirmed that ethnocentric and xenophobic attitudes are strong among the Russian public. When we asked the same question about the slogan 'Russia for Russians (*russkie*)', we found slightly less support than Levada but still quite high: 59.3 per cent. Again, it should be emphasised that the meaning of the term *russkie* is in flux; in certain contexts it is understood as encompassing more than just ethnic Russians. When asked about this, 24.9 per cent of our respondents explained that to them *russkie* meant 'all citizens of the Russian Federation', while 30.0 per cent indicated 'mostly but not exclusively ethnic Russians'. Only 39.0 per cent meant 'ethnic Russians only'. The elusive quality of the word *russkie* must be taken into account in interpreting such survey results.

Even so, some of the responses in the Romir survey must be characterised as remarkably ethnocentric, even ethnocratic: for instance, as much as 73.9 per cent agreed 'fully' or 'basically' with the statement that 'Russians (*russkie*) ought to be given priority at appointments to higher positions in the state'. Even more remarkable was support for the view that 'the Russian (*russkii*) people ought to play the leading role in the Russian (*rossiiskii*) state': 47.4 per cent agreed fully, in addition to another 34.6 per cent who basically agreed. These attitudes are incompatible with a civic nation-state idea in which all citizens have equal opportunities.

These ethnocentric attitudes were accompanied in the 2013 Romir survey by deep scepticism towards migrants and other people perceived as culturally alien. A figure of 60.5 per cent of the respondents believed that Islam represents a threat to social stability and Russian culture, while more than half declared that Chechens, Chinese and Roma represent cultural values incompatible with the Russian way of life. A similar assessment was given to Kyrgyz (43.8 per cent), Tajiks 46.8 (per cent) and Azerbaijanis (44.3 per cent). These groups are heavily represented among the labour immigrants who since the early 2000s have been coming in increasing numbers to Russian cities (see Kosmarskaya and Savin, this volume). Further, 48.7 per cent believed that many migrants come not to do honest work, but to steal from Russians and to weaken the Russian people. Close to half opined that *all* migrants – not only those without proper work permits – should be deported back to their home countries, along with their children.

The great migration treks from Central Asia to Russian cities are a relatively new phenomenon, gaining momentum only after the differences in living standards between Russia and the southern tier of former Soviet republics began to widen drastically in the first decade of the 2000s. Exactly how many illegal workers there are in Russia is anybody's guess, with estimates varying from a few million to ten million or more. Actual figures, however, are less important for the new nationalism discourse in Russia than the perception, fed by Russian media, that the country is being inundated by people who are not only culturally alien but dangerous. Eurasianists and other state-focused nationalists have few solutions to offer. They want to integrate the former Soviet republics as much as possible with Russia, and would like to keep the borders open. The ethnonationalists, on the other hand, can capitalise on the new migrantophobia. Tellingly, in the early 2000s the most influential nationalist organisation was the Movement against Illegal Immigration. The new migration issue is clearly one important factor that can explain why the ethnification of Russian nationalism picked up speed after the turn of the millennium and not earlier.

Conclusions

In the Tsarist Empire, ethnic Russians were not dominant, demographically or politically. In the 1897 census the share of Great Russians in this state was only 44 per cent, and Russians did not enjoy any particular prerogatives such as privileged access to jobs in the civil service. Educated members of certain non-Russian groups, such as Germans and Poles, were far more likely to land attractive jobs in the state apparatus. Many Russians were no doubt proud to be subjects of the Tsar and identified with the state, but this was a dynastic state, and not 'their' 'nation-state' in any sense. Certain elements of a Russification policy were introduced in the final decades of the empire, but this affected the life of the non-Russians more than the Russians.

In territorial terms the Soviet Union represented a continuation of the Russian Empire. While the nationalities policy of the Bolsheviks differed radically from that pursued by the tsars, it was no more conducive to the formation of a Russian national identity. The federal structure of Soviet Union gave all the major non-Russian nationalities an ethnic homeland that bore their name and also to some extent their cultural imprint. In all Union republics and autonomous republics, education was available in the titular language, at least in elementary school if not necessarily at higher levels. Titulars were also overrepresented in top jobs in the republics, in the party and government structure (Hodnett 1979). All Soviet citizens carried with them at all times their internal passport in which their *natsionalnost* (read: ethnic identity) was recorded. This meant that also non-Russians living in other parts of the country, having a personally ascriptive identity that corresponded with one of the republics, would naturally identify with this federal unit.

All of this was different for the ethnic Russians. The first 'R' in the RSFSR was not *russkii* but *rossiiskii*, and this vast conglomerate republic was not intended to be or understood as a homeland for ethnic Russians. As a federation in itself with a large number of ethnically defined sub-units, RSFSR was in a sense a copy of the Soviet Union writ small; however, it lacked some basic attributes of Union republics, such as a separate party organisation or its own branch of the Academy of Sciences: it was felt that this would duplicate the respective Soviet structures and be redundant. Moreover, Russian-language schools and cultural institutions were available throughout the Soviet Union. For these reasons, Russians to a much larger degree than non-Russians came to identify with the USSR as a whole, not with any particular geographical area (Kolstø 1999). To be Russian was in a sense an unmarked quality, the opposite of being 'ethnic' (Brubaker 1996: 49). This was reflected also in Russian nationalism, which generally focused on state strength and state size. Hardly any Russian nationalists at the time would contemplate a truncation of state territory.

Only when the Soviet Union unravelled during perestroika did the RSFSR for the first time become a serious contender for the loyalty and identity of the ethnic Russians. But also in its new incarnation as the Russian Federation it was officially a multi-ethnic state and not a 'nation-state'. Tishkov made a resolute attempt to develop a civic Russian nation-state model – that virtually all Russian nationalists have found lacklustre and anaemic. Their alternative visions for a Russian state idea, however, point in two very different directions. On the one hand, quite a few still adhere to a statist or imperial nation concept; on the other, 'the new Russian nationalists' prioritise ethnic culture and the interests of ethnic Russians over state grandeur. Finally, some also try to combine an imperialist and an ethnic national idea, and end up with what I have here called supremacist nationalism. This means that in the post-Soviet debate on the future of the Russian national idea all four boxes in my typology of nationalisms are populated. Even so, some of them are more crowded than others and gain new recruits by interlopers from the other positions. The supremacists are a small and dwindling minority – certainly in the Russian population, but also among professed nationalists. This leaves three contenders fighting for the hearts and minds of the Russians, as well as for influence over the political leadership.

An ethnification of popular attitudes among the Russian public can be seen from opinion polls fed primarily by growing migrantophobia. For various reasons, the Russian state authorities for a long time hesitated to embrace the new ethnic rhetoric. For one thing, playing the ethnic card must be assumed to antagonise the non-Russian part of the population (see Alexseev, this volume). For the purposes of national consolidation, a civic nation idea seems more promising, and indeed elements of a *rossiiskii* nation concept are still evident in the speeches of Putin and particularly of Medvedev. However, if this idea does not stir any feelings and fails to attract people to the state, it cannot serve its purpose.

For the Kremlin, the benefit of Eurasianism is that it can provide ideological underpinnings for a foreign policy aimed at expanding Russian influence in the 'near abroad'. Symptomatically, Putin's pet project of an Eastern mini-European Union (mini-EU) that would include as many as possible of the former Soviet republics is called the Eurasian Union. However, this policy does not provide any answers to what a large and increasing number of Russians see as a major problem: the alleged inundation of Russia of 'culturally alien' migrants from other parts of the former Soviet Union. Precisely this problem, however, has swelled the ranks of the ethnonationalists.

With the annexation of Crimea, Putin has expanded the territory of the Russian state somewhat, a step warmly applauded by the Russian imperialists and Eurasianists. The justification for doing so he has to a considerable degree taken from the rhetorical repertoire of the ethnonationalists. In the process, Putin had, at least for the time being, managed to steal the thunder from both groups.

Notes

1. Even if Kohn did not use that term himself.
2. For other models of Russian nationalism, highlighting other aspects, see Yanov (1978); Carter (1990: 138–9); Tolz (1998); and Tuminez (2000).
3. Author's interview, Moscow, November 2013. When I later asked Tishkov whether he believed Putin's talk about a 'divided' Russian (*russkii*) nation undermined the *rossiiskii* nation-state concept, he denied that. Even after the recent annexation of Crimea, Tishkov was able to find statements in which the Russian president con-

tinued to use the *natsiia* concept in a supra-ethnic sense (e-mail exchange with the author, 24 March 2014).
4. See <http://rusnat.com> (last accessed 9 March 2015).
5. Author's interview, Moscow, October 2013.
6. Author's interview with Konstantin Krylov, leader of the National-Democratic Party, Moscow, October 2013.
7. This was also confirmed in author's interview, October 2013.
8. Author's interview, Moscow, October 2013.
9. Author's interview, Moscow, October 2013. In fact, while the German constitution allowed for referenda in the Eastern Länder before reunification, no such referenda were held.
10. Author's interview, Moscow, October 2013.

2

The imperial syndrome and its influence on Russian nationalism

Emil Pain

How to explain the continued presence of the imperial legacy in the political life of Russia, and its impact on Russian nationalism? This has been a focus of my research for more than a decade (Pain 2001, 2004, 2008, 2012). The combination of Russian nationalism and imperial consciousness is conducive to the development of a special phenomenon in Russia that may be called 'imperial nationalism'. That term may sound odd, at least to those within the Western academic tradition who are accustomed to examining nationalism as one of the factors confronting empires, as a factor involved in destroying the imperial system, but, in the Russian setting, an imperial nationalism that supports imperial aspirations really does exist, and has appeared more than once – recently manifesting itself boldly after the 2014 annexation of Crimea by the Russian Federation. The second decade of the 2000s had begun with political events that – it seemed to many – augured the replacement of imperial nationalism by a new (for Russia) anti-imperial Russian nationalism (Milov 2010; *Russkii svet* n.d.). Such hopes increased with the rise of the democratic opposition movement and the participation of Russian nationalists in the political protests that began in December 2011. The subsequent defeat of this new, anti-government, anti-Soviet Russian nationalism once again prompts reflection on the reasons for the stability of the imperial component in Russian nationalism – and, indeed, in contemporary Russian society as a whole.

In this chapter I take up some fundamental theoretical problems raised by such scholars as Sergei Gavrov (2004), Alexander Motyl (2004), Dominic Lieven (2005), Mark Beissinger (2005) and Egor Gaidar (2006) as a kind of extended conversation. These are primarily questions about the essence of empire, and the reasons for the reproduction or preservation of some imperial characteristics in the politics of post-Soviet Russia since the turn of the millennium. Here I propose a new theoretical construct – the 'imperial syndrome'. The bulk of the chapter focuses on the specific characteristics of the evolution of the idea of the nation and nationalism in Russia, from the end of the eighteenth century to the beginning of the twenty-first. Why did the European idea of the nation, which appeared in Russia influenced by the French Revolution, subsequently turn into an anti-Western concept of imperial nationalism? I also ask why the new, anti-imperial Russian nationalism in the end turned out to be so weak, as became evident after the annexation of Crimea in 2014. The chapter ends with an analysis of the political prospects for Russian nationalism.[1]

Nation and nationalism in Russia: Evolution of an idea

The term 'imperial nationalism' may sound odd because, in political theory, empire and the nation are treated as extreme opposites: the nation state is based on the principle of popular (in the sense of national) sovereignty, whereas the imperial type of state rests on the sovereignty of the ruler (Pain 2004). In Russia, however, the nation was long construed along entirely different lines, as synonymous with an ethnic community, and Russian nationalism was interpreted as organised groups voicing ideas of national egotism, xenophobia and great-power chauvinism. This understanding developed in Russia from the mid-nineteenth century onwards, based largely on the thinking of Vladimir Solov'ev. In polemics with later Slavophiles at the start of the twentieth century, this philosopher – so admired that he has been called the 'Pushkin of Russian philosophy' – expounded his extremely negative attitudes not only to nascent Russian nationalism but also to the idea of the 'nation' as such. Solov'ev saw the very 'principle of nationality' as 'the lowest principle', a manifestation of 'reaction' opposed to 'the rational course of history', a 'retrograde motion'; and nationalism (that is, ethnic nationalism), which protects this principle, as a deeply negative and destructive phenomenon. Further, in his view, nationalism arose as a result of efforts by separate peoples to distinguish themselves, to set themselves up in opposition to other peoples, to isolate themselves from others. Solov'ev was convinced that 'in this effort the positive force of national character (*narodnost*) turns into the negative force of nationalism' (Solov'ev 1901: 8–10). However, ethnic interpretations of the nation and of nationalism have not always been dominant in Russia. Other approaches had appeared almost a century earlier.

The Russian elite became aware of the civic nation concept, as reflected in the 1789 Declaration of the Rights of Man and of the Citizen in the late eighteenth century, hot on the heels of France. In this understanding, the nation is a community that supersedes the estates or classes; it is entitled to choose its representatives, and is the source of sovereignty ('the sovereignty of the people'). The revolutionaries of the nobility, later called 'Decembrists' after the 14 December 1825 uprising, defended this idea in various forms, demanding the limitation of autocracy in Russia (Nechkina 1982). The future emperor Aleksandr I (then heir to the throne) used it in this fashion in 1797, when he announced that when he became Tsar he would give Russia a constitution, and 'the nation will elect its representatives' (Miller 2012). However, the political events that took place from 1790 to 1830 radically changed the attitude of the elite to the essence of the nation, and to the very term 'nation'. If Aleksandr I ascended to the throne intending to give Russia a constitution from above in order to avoid a revolution from below, then his successor Nikolai I began his reign under pressure from the very revolution that his elder brother had wanted, but had not managed, to forestall. Moreover, the Decembrist revolutionaries demanded a constitution that would proclaim the sovereignty of the nation and its representatives. For the emperor, accepting the demands of the executed rebels was inconceivable. As the historian Aleksei Miller observes:

> After the Decembrist revolt and the Polish uprising of 1830–31, the former discourse about the *nation* and *national representation* as

an aim that was desirable but difficult to attain, gave way in official circles to a rejection of a constitution and to national representation being seen as inappropriate for Russia in principle. (Miller 2012, emphasis in the original)

From then on, the very term 'nation' was subject to censorship, above all because in the minds of the reading public it was constantly connected with national representation. It was replaced and supplanted by other similar, quasi-terms – and this was a major reason for its eventual demise.

On taking up office in 1833, Minister of Education Sergei Uvarov declared a formula that became famous: 'Orthodoxy, Autocracy, Nationality'. This triad was intended as the anti-thesis of the French Revolution's 'Freedom, Equality, Brotherhood', which in the minds of Russian conservatives of the early nineteenth century was inconceivable for the Russian people, with their 'special spirit' of devotion to Orthodoxy and autocracy (Vortman 1999). The main innovation in Uvarov's formula was the concept of nationality, or *narodnost*, from which the entire doctrine derived its name, 'official nationality'. By this was understood, first and foremost, Russia's devotion to its own traditions and original path, as opposed to Western models (a contemporary analogy is the concept of 'Russia's special path'). Within the framework of this doctrine, the idea of 'the nation' was regarded as a manifestation of 'free-thinking' and 'trouble-making', and the concept of *narodnost* was specifically contrasted with it. First, *narodnost* was identified as a Russian term, in contrast to the foreign *natsiia*, 'nation'. Second, as a concept it was devoid of any democratic connotations or connections with national representation: on the contrary, it reflects the paternalistic idea of the ruler's concern for his subjects. The ruler is the father of the people, and his devoted children piously revere their autocratic father. Such are the key ideas of the 'official nationality' doctrine (Vortman 1999).

Besides *narodnost*, *natsionalnost* was another term allowed by the censors and used in the 1830s to supplant the seditious term 'nation'. Count Petr Valuev, who became Minister of the Interior in the 1860s, had in the late 1830s frequented intellectual circles and written philosophical essays. One of these essays, 'Thoughts on nationality', outlined why it was necessary to replace the concept of 'nation', as a particularly politicised category, with the concept of *natsionalnost* (Fr. *nationalité*). This latter he presented as a native Russian concept, reflecting the specifics of the culture and rituals of the folk, understood in the way in which an 'ethnic community' is defined today – as a group of people linked together by ideas about a shared origin and with their own name for themselves (ethnonym) (Gershtein 1941).

Although the civic interpretation of the concept of 'nation' was eventually entirely supplanted, linguistically it lasted almost seventy years. The new, exclusively ethnic interpretation of the term appeared in Russia's political lexicon only in the mid-1860s. It had particularly negative connotations in the phrase 'national question', linked as it was with the perception of threats of national separatism in Poland and Ukraine (Miller 2012). With each passing decade of Russian history, the national problem became more ethnically coloured, increasingly being interpreted from an essentialist perspective, as a certain selection of characteristics bestowed by fate upon particular peoples ('ethnic nations'). From the end of the 1890s Russian Slavophiles in their arguments with Westernisers began to develop Uvarov's idea of fundamental and everlasting, pre-ordained differences between the Russian people and the nations of the West. According to the Slavophiles, 'the Russian people rejected the burden of popular representation in favour of everlasting autocratic monarchy' (Miller 2012). In doing so, the Slavophiles of the 1890s rejected the legacy of their predecessors, the Slavophiles of the mid-nineteenth century (like Aleksei Khomiakov, Konstantin and Ivan Aksakov, Aleksandr Koshelev and Iurii Samarin), who had opposed the doctrine of 'official nationality', which they saw as suffocating creative initiative ('soul-destroying despotism', 'an oppressive system'). The Slavophiles of the late 1890s and the early 1900s (Nikolai Danilevskii, Konstantin Leontiev, Vasilii Rozanov and others) developed the idea of Russia's special path. It was this cohort of Slavophiles that began to contrast the special national character of Russians (patient, thirsty for truth, spontaneous, warm, sincere, generous and inclined to *sobornost* – a preference for collective decision-making) – with a generic image of the Western mentality.

The latter they regarded as always and intrinsically self-interested, greedy, deceitful and coldly frugal (Tsimbaev 1986). These later Slavophiles harnessed the concept of the nation – as an ethnic phenomenon permanently grafted to the body of the Russian people – to preserve autocracy and imperial power.

Within this circle of later Slavophiles an ideological movement arose whose adherents began to see themselves as 'Russian nationalists' – and who were also defined as such by outside observers. In this author's opinion, several of the major generic characteristics of Russian nationalism have maintained their significance from the end of the nineteenth century to the present day:

- *essentialism* – the idea that there are special, eternal cultural qualities of the Russian people that distinguish them fundamentally from other peoples, in particular from the peoples of Western Europe. The West always functions as the constituting 'Other' in relation to Russian nationalism;
- *defensive imperial character* – from the start, Russian nationalists saw the service of autocracy and the preservation of empire as vitally important goals for their political activity. As the central point of their political programme, the first legal party of Russian nationalists that emerged in 1905 expounded that 'the Union of the Russian People ... establishes as its sacred, immutable duty to make every effort to ensure that the land won by the blood of our forefathers remains an eternally inalienable part of the Russian state. All attempts to dismember Russia, by whatever means, will be decisively and absolutely eliminated';[2]
- *the principle of the political domination of ethnic Russians* – a merging of the idea of protecting the empire with a reciprocal requirement for preferential rights to be accorded ethnic Russians within that empire – to the ethnic Russian people, the ethnic Russian nation: 'Russia for the Russians'.

Thus, the idea of the nation first appeared in Russia at the end of the eighteenth century as a sign of the enlightened sector of society's expectation of revolutionary change. Its first advocates, the Decembrists, who promoted the idea of the nation as a source of constitutional order, could on that basis be deemed 'civic nationalists'. However, while these first Russian 'nationalists' defended the value of popular representation, by the start of the twentieth century nationalism had degenerated into a highly reactionary political force, defending autocracy, Russia's imperial structure and the ethnic, religious and social inequality of its inhabitants. Nationalism based on these principles took shape conceptually and organisationally in the Russian Empire in the 1900s, and then – after a temporary embargo during the Soviet period – was revived in the post-Soviet Russia of the 1990s, initially as a political force opposing the then-officially proclaimed ideas of modernisation, liberalism, federalism and tolerance. Since the turn of the millennium, imperial nationalism has become a political fellow-traveller of the Russian authorities. However, as noted above, there were clear signs of an entirely new Russian nationalism in the wave of fervent political protest in 2011/12.

The rise and fall of the 'new' (national democratic) Russian nationalism, 2010–14

The characteristics of this current in nationalism were revealed as clearly as if in a laboratory experiment. Indeed, many of them were deliberately constructed as a contrast to traditional Russian nationalism.

ANTI-IMPERIAL NATURE OF THE NEW NATIONALISM

According to one popular theorist of the 'new' nationalism, Konstantin Krylov, Russian nationalism's transition from an imperial to a national ideology emerged quite recently: 'For a start, Russian nationalism proper is essentially a new phenomenon. I measure its history from around the first decade of the 2000s' (*Nazdem.info* 2010). Russian nationalism was conceived as imperial, and in the movement that, according to Krylov, was groundlessly termed Russian nationalism, until the late 1990s almost 'everything boiled down to fantasies of "how we can make good the empire"'. The national democrats demonstrated their rejection of the imperialism traditionally associated with Russian nationalists, and declared their belief that, in political terms, consistent nationalism is the opposite of imperial ideology, which asserts not the sovereignty of the people, but the dominion of the sovereign. Nationalism, as Krylov notes, 'considers the state of secondary value. The country exists for the people and not the people for the country' (*Nazdem.info* 2010). Rejecting the idea of empire and rethinking the role of state and society has already led several Russian nationalists to reject not only imperial inclinations, but also support for an autocratic, authoritarian model of governance. 'When the Soviet state fell apart', Krylov observes, 'all ideologically committed Russian forces sided with the communists. And as a result, they could not produce anything except a "red–brown fusion"' – which, in Krylov's opinion, also led the 'Russian party' to disaster. Today the situation has changed radically, he holds, and the idea that 'nationalism and democracy are practically the same thing' is growing in strength (*Nazdem.info* 2010).

Rejection of traditional statism, opposition to the authorities, demands for democracy

Open opposition to the current government became a defining feature of the new Russian nationalism. Almost all Russian nationalist ideologists have spoken out against the authorities: the authorities have been accused of persistent repression of the Russian nationalist movement and of the entire Russian nation; of a failure to pay attention to the problems of the Russian majority; and of a reluctance to fight the influx of migrants into cities. Russian nationalists had made similar complaints to the authorities even back in the USSR (Mitrokhin 2003), but in the Soviet period these accusations from nationalists were not associated with demands for democratisation. By the end of the first decade of the 2000s, however, there were signs that the sum total of uncoordinated protest moods within elite Russian nationalism was coming together in a single stream of sorts, on the basis of which a new variety of nationalism was being born: 'national democracy'. This stood in contrast to Russian nationalism's traditional and basic branch – the 'national imperial', sometimes also referred to as 'national patriotic'.

The first sign of what would later be called the 'democratic turn' of Russian nationalism was the formation of an anti-Soviet platform at its heart. A clear example was the creation of a separate anti-Soviet column in the 2012 'Russian March'.[3] After this, in their speeches many nationalist leaders increasingly began to repudiate not only Stalinism, but also authoritarianism as a political principle. As a result, the politics of the Russian national democratic movement took centre stage, and swiftly attracted the attention of observers. It was precisely their leaders who in the opposition demonstrations in Moscow in 2011–13 formed the core of the nationalist wing under the banner of 'for fair elections'. The historian Elena Galkina has identified the following key differences between national democrats and those whom she calls 'national patriots': '*Natsdems* [national democrats], as a rule, in a very emotional fashion accuse Soviet Russia of destroying the peasantry and the tradition of self-government, and of a tendency to suppress Russian ethnicity in national politics, of the *diktat* of the state and of totalitarianism' (Galkina 2012: 83). Today these accusations are directed at the Russian Federation, seen as the direct successor to the Soviet Union. The leaders of the National Democratic Party – Konstantin Krylov, Vladimir Tor, Rostislav Antonov, Aleksandr Khramov and others – have adopted this position. In some respects Valerii Solovei, the leader of the party New Force, holds similar views.

The ideas of Egor Prosvirnin have evolved at the junction between national democracy and the opposing autocratic-imperial model of nationalism. Prosvirnin is the founder and active leader of the trendy nationalist Internet project *Sputnik i Pogrom*,[4] and one of the most controversial figures in the Russian nationalist sphere. In his programmatic writings he rages against the Soviet communist regime, likening it to night-time ('amidst the clear Russian day suddenly the dark communist night fell') (Prosvirnin 2012). He devotes considerable attention to the necessity of democratic changes for the good of ethnic Russians: 'We view the Russian national democratic rule of law-based state as our ideal ... with economic life based on the principles of the rule of law and free competition' (Prosvirnin n.d.; see also Prosvirnin 2014a). All this draws Prosvirnin close to the national democratic tendency in Russian nationalism. That said, the anti-liberal rhetoric of most texts on *Sputnik i Pogrom*, with ideas of territorial revanchism and expansionism, makes Prosvirnin kin with the ideology of the bulk of imperial nationalists.

Rejection of traditional anti-westernism, imitation of western models of nationalism

Marlene Laruelle (2014b) identifies yet another peculiarity of the national democratic movement – the consistent references to the experience of Western right-wing parties, particularly with regard to the struggle against illegal migration and the integration of Russian nationalism's ideologemes into a Europe-wide context. In orienting themselves towards Western models of nationalism, the ideologists of the National Democratic Alliance of Aleksei Shiropaev and Ilia Lazarenko have gone further than most. They denounce not only the Soviet period, but also the imperial legacy of the Romanov era. They and their supporters call for a review of contemporary federal relationships in the Russian state and the creation of Russian republics within it (Shiropaev 2011). Of all the organisations, only the National Democratic Alliance shows a significant shift from ethnic nationalism towards civic nationalism. Lazarenko has publically called for the alliance to reject the fundamental requirement of Russian ethnic nationalists:

> We in no way call for the proclamation of the [ethnic] Russians as the state-forming nation in Russia. In our opinion, Russia must go the way of the European Union and consequently form a single community with it. In fact this is our sole option for the future. Everything else seems to me a completely blind alley. (Lazarenko 2013)

All the individuals mentioned, and the various ideological streams of national democracy they represent, may be categorised under the rubric of 'anti-regime (*nesistemnyi*) nationalism'. This differs from the popular, predominant pro-regime (*sistemnyi*) nationalism in the emphatic efforts of anti-regime nationalists to overcome the nostalgia that most Russian nationalists feel for the Soviet era. In the thinking of ethnic Russians, Soviet identity always severely impeded the development of ethnic Russian consciousness. Even during the twilight of the Soviet era, in 1986, 78 per cent of Russians considered themselves 'Soviet' and only 15 per cent identified as 'Russian' (Arutiunian 1999: 165). Soviet popular culture was a culture of authoritarian consciousness, and thus also contrary to the values of the national democrats.

The difference between traditional Soviet imperialists and those representing the new national democratic wing was thrown into sharp relief in the winter of 2013/14 with the Ukrainian political opposition events on the Maidan in Kyiv. A significant section of the national democrats supported the protesters on the Maidan. The National Democratic Alliance did so most consistently. One of the leaders of this organisation, Aleksei Shiropaev, called the events in Kyiv 'an anticolonial, democratic, European (in terms of civilisational vector) revolution' (Shiropaev 2014). In his opinion, the world was witnessing a European country freeing itself from an Asiatic empire. Russian nationalists in the National Democratic Party evaluated the Maidan events more cautiously, but they too did not hide their support, seeing them, above all, as evidence of the significant political role of ethnic nationalists in Ukrainian society. Accordingly, one of the leaders of this party wrote a 'Panegyric to Maidan' (Tor 2013). Such actions clearly showed that Russian national democrats were in opposition to both the authorities and the mass of Russian nationalists, who viewed Maidan extremely negatively, as a pro-Western movement.

After Crimea was annexed by Russia, however, the ranks of the Russian nationalist opposition quickly began to thin out. Prosvirnin, for example, who until then had voiced scathing criticisms of the Russian state authorities, openly supported the government's actions during the Crimean crisis and joyfully welcomed the union of the peninsula with the body of Russia. In one text on his website he commented on his change of stance: 'And the fact that Putin, after ten years of surrendering Russian interests at every turn, has suddenly remembered that Crimea is Russian land, is basically great . . . it would, to say the least, be strange to berate Putin for having begun to fulfil part of our programme' (Prosvirnin 2014b).

Of the few, small nationalist groups that have grown bold and displayed opposition tendencies, the most noticeable has been the above-mentioned National Democratic Alliance, which was always a minority even among the sparsely populated ranks of the national democrats. Even in the national democratic movement's most active period, its theorists noted that the final and most difficult task would be to free Russian nationalism from Soviet imperial ideology (*Nazdem.info* 2010). After the annexation of Crimea, it seems that even the national democratic elite of Russian nationalists have been unable to vanquish the dominant Soviet imperial stereotypes.

'The imperial syndrome' and how it was activated

World history provides various examples of 'reverse waves', that is, periods of retrograde movement and political reaction (Huntington 2003). In this respect the history of Russia, with multiple attempts at modernisation alternating with protracted periods of political reaction, cannot be deemed unique. Aleksei Kara-Murza has effectively described this process of going round in circles for the Russian reforms of the nineteenth and twentieth centuries: reforms began with efforts to

> draw close to the civilisation of the West – thereafter the reforms get 'bogged down', are overcome by 'costs', and gradually acquire the traits of pseudo-reforms. Finally, harsh advocates for restoring statism and extreme nationalists take centre stage on a wave of nostalgia for former imperial might and, albeit in name only, societal unity and clearly defined identities. (Kara-Murza 1999: 41)

Indeed, that same logic of reoccurring processes can be seen in Russia at the beginning of the twenty-first century. The epoch of Mikhail Gorbachev and Boris Eltsin (late 1980s–early 1990s) was marked by Russian efforts to draw close to the West, 'to return to the family of civilised nations', as it was put at the time.[5] From the turn of the millennium (with Vladimir Putin's ascent to power) a new course was set: in contrast to the 1990s, when the October Revolution of 1917 and the very emergence and existence of the Soviet Union were considered a catastrophe for Russia, the collapse of the USSR was declared the 'greatest geopolitical catastrophe'.[6] More recently, the most significant indicator of political stagnation has been clearly manifest: the absence of any notions among society of future social and political prospects. This is recognised even by circles close to the government establishment. Vserossiiskii tsentr izucheniia obshchestvennaia mneniia (VTsIOM) manager Valerii Fedorov, for example, stated in 2012 that the Russian public consciousness was characterised by 'apathy, disorder and vacillation', a preoccupation with basic survival and a 'sometimes fairly artificial' return to 'archaic, patriarchal values', intentionally opposing the values of modernisation (quoted by Sabitova 2012). The political manifestations of 2011/12 were public efforts 'from below' to break out of this stagnation, but they were quickly quashed by the Russian authorities, which moved to counterattack. To this end, the authorities subsequently made use of the Ukrainian events in late 2013/early 2014 (Maidan). With the entanglement of Russia in the crisis around Ukraine in spring 2014, the authorities attempted to create a semblance of a new political vision out of the hatred for a common enemy (Maidan/Ukrainian nationalists/the West) generated by Russian agents of mass propaganda. This took on clearer shape after the annexation of Crimea – no longer simply an open directive to revise the results of the collapse of the USSR, but with practical steps to realise this strategy.

Russia's turn to such politics took shape at the very start of the 2000s and was noted by many scholars. My own publication in those years was one of the first (Pain 2001), soon followed by other authors (Gudkov 2002; Dubin 2003a; Gavrov 2004; Motyl 2004). Many researchers turned to the phenomenon of the 'imperial legacy' in seeking to explain the latest disruption of the political modernisation process and the failure of democratic transformation in Russia. Alexander Motyl, for example, noted that the fundamental obstacle on the path to democracy 'of Russia and her neighbours is not bad politicians, making stupid decisions, but the institutional yoke of the imperial and totalitarian past' (2004: 174–5). While agreeing with him about the significance of the influence of the 'imperial legacy' on Russia's contemporary development, I should also underline where we disagree. In my opinion, it does not make sense to contrast 'bad legacy' with 'bad politicians', not least because the actions of such politicians generally also lead to the return or revival of remnants of the imperial heritage. Moreover, the metaphor of 'legacy' does not tell anything about its contents. I propose the following characteristics, conveyed by the category 'imperial syndrome', with three basic elements: imperial order, imperial body and imperial consciousness.

The *imperial order* is the political regime of the empire. 'The empire', notes Dominic Lieven, 'is by definition the antipode of democracy, popular sovereignty and national self-determination. Power over many peoples without their consent – here is what distinguished all great empires of the past and what all sensible definitions of this concept propose' (2005: 79). Mark Beissinger's interpretation of empire is very similar: 'an illegitimate relationship of control on the part of one political community over another or others' (2005: 68). Similarly, Egor Gaidar considers the most important trait of an imperial state to be its political regime: specifically that *'imperium* – state power – dominated in the organisation of daily life' (Gaidar 2006: 18). The formula 'power without the consent of the people' need not mean that this power is based exclusively on force: it only refers to the fact that the will of the citizens and of their associations – territorial communities, for example – are not significant for the functioning of the imperial order.

Power without the consent of the people means the sovereignty of the sovereign (Lat. *imperator*) in contrast to the sovereignty of the people in nation states. A good indicator of imperial order is the governance of the country's provinces with the help of deputies (satraps, procurators, voevodas). Depriving those who live in Russia's regions of the right to choose their governors, as happened in 2004, is a way of restoring imperial order – and this was a decision made exclusively by the machinery at the top, not based on any legitimate procedures that showed the will of the people in regard to these changes.[7] Restoring governance by a sort of Persian satrap or Russian voevoda was based on the same references to Russian national tradition used back in the days of Count Uvarov and his concept of 'official nationality'.

The *imperial body* is the territory of the country, divided into regions that are not culturally integrated with one another and that preserve historic traces of colonial conquest. These are visible, above all, in areas of compact settlement of colonised ethnic communities, whose elites still employ their own discourse of opposition – 'Russia versus us' – regardless of whether these peoples had their own state system in the past. However, it is not only territories where ethnic minorities predominate that are part of the 'imperial body' – Russian regions are also part of it: in fact, everything that is called a 'subject [constituent entity] of the Russian Federation'. In reality, these are deprived of their political subjectivity and integrated on the basis of administrative compulsion, 'the power vertical', and not by voluntary agreement and a conscious interest in integration. Today, the imperial principle of *retaining territory* has become canonised in Russian politics. In his annual address to the Federal Assembly, Putin called the *'retention of the state* over a vast space' Russia's thousand-year-old spiritual feat (Putin 2003, italics added).

And finally, there is *imperial consciousness*. This includes an intricate complex of traditional stereotypes of popular consciousness – for example, a self-understanding based on being subjects (a non-civic consciousness) – that preserves stable statist values, hopes for 'a wise tsar' and 'a firm hand', and also imperial ambitions.

In my opinion, the elitist variety of 'imperial consciousness' is above all connected with the geopolitical essentialism that arises in two interrelated notions: first, that of a special Russian civilisation eternally preserved in the 'Russian soul'; and second, that of Western civilisation presenting a continual threat to Russian civilisation. This old idea, familiar since the beginning of the nineteenth century, has from the mid-1990s again become popular in elite circles, leading them to draw the same conclusion as Count Uvarov did in the nineteenth century: that one needs a strong ruler, an emperor, as a defence against external enemies. After the collapse of the USSR, overtones of horror began to predominate in accounts of life in Russia and the plight of the Russian people, even among enlightened and sincere people, like the renowned Soviet historian of philosophy Arsenii Gulyga, who now claimed: 'We are on the edge of a precipice.' In the Soviet period Gulyga had been considered practically a dissident, but now he expressed aspirations of reviving the imperial doctrine of 'official nationality' (Gulyga 1995: 45). The idea of fundamental differences between the interests and values of Russia and those of the West, and the need to reanimate imperial order to ward off Western threats, has been developed to an even greater extent by professional propagandists such as, for example, the theatre director Sergei Kurginian.

Richard Wortman has argued that only two tsars in the Romanov dynasty, both of whom had personal grievances against Westernisers, based their policies on the mythological national uniqueness of Russia, and, on that basis, set them against the political models of the West (Vortman 1999). These two figures were Nikolai I after the Decembrist uprising, and Aleksandr III after the murder of his father by terrorist-Westernisers. Not contesting this, since what happened in the past is clearer to the historian, we may note that also Putin, from the very beginning of his leadership in Russia to the present day, has relied on that same mythology. In 1999, when the idea of 'catching up with the West' still dominated, Prime Minister Putin advocated what was in many ways a different approach, underlining the country's uniqueness:

> Russia will not quickly become, if she ever does, a second version of – let's say – the USA or England, where liberal values have deep historical traditions. Over here, the state, its institutions and structures, have always played an exceptionally important role in the life of the country, of the people ... For Russians a strong state is not an anomaly, but the originator and primary motivating force for change. (Putin 1999)

Putin wrote this while still a subordinate of Eltsin. On becoming head of state, he began increasingly openly to develop the idea of civilisational differences between Russia and the West, citing the philosopher Ivan Ilin, the direct successor of the intellectual tradition of the later Slavophiles. These ideas are most fully reflected in Putin's programmatic speech 'Russia: the national question' (Putin 2012b).

Not only are all the elements of the imperial syndrome interdependent, they also provide mutual stability, acting as preconditions for the reproduction of the entire construction. Here let me mention only a few aspects of this interdependency:

First, as long as the 'imperial body' remains, fears about its destruction will persist. Such fears became widespread after the collapse of the USSR, which, judging by the research of sociologists at VTsIOM, the majority of Russians still consider the most important and painful event of recent years (VTsIOM 2002: 19). The presence of national republics within Russia is a reminder that the USSR's fate could be repeated in Russia.

Second, as long as there are fears that the imperial body can be destroyed or captured by internal or external enemies, hopes of a 'firm hand' and 'wise tsar' also multiply. These stereotypes, in turn, are used as grounds for the restoration and strengthening of centralisation – in other words, the imperial order. Putin, in particular, based the introduction of federal districts in May 2000 (Zamiatin and Zamiatina 2000), and later the necessity of replacing elected governors with appointed ones, on the need to combat separatism.

Third, the size of the imperial body engenders 'great-power' ambitions. According to the Eurasianists, whose ideas have now become increasingly popular in Russia, a country possessing the largest territory on earth cannot but have a special geopolitical role in the world, cannot but claim the status of a Great Country: 'Geography as destiny', as their famous formula puts it (Dugin 1997).

The various links in the chain imperial body/imperial consciousness/imperial power can activate one another in many ways. Here I outline only the aspects connected with the restoration of 'imperial consciousness', which, in my opinion, is not inherent in the public consciousness of the entire population, or even in the Russian mentality. Imperial consciousness comes to life only when interested political forces – acting, moreover, under favourable conditions, as when people are tired of reform – consciously activate and reconstruct it.

In 1992–4, political forces that Kara-Murza has called 'tough state-restorers and extreme nationalists' appeared on the political stage (Kara-Murza 1999: 41). During this time they promoted a triune demand: 'the return of the USSR', 'the unification of the divided Russian people' and 'the defence of Russian compatriots, abandoned to the whims of fate' in the newly independent states. Gennadii Ziuganov, leader of the Russian communists, appealed bombastically to the feelings of Russians: 'Without the reunification of the currently divided Russian people, our state will not rise from its knees' (Ziuganov 1994: 22). These fiery speeches did not resonate with the public consciousness, however. Sociological surveys in 1993 did not reveal even the slightest regret over the collapse of the country or desires for its re-unification among Russians. Only 16 per cent of those surveyed, for example, declared that their lives were significantly connected with other republics of the former USSR. Moreover, actual connections with other republics were less significant for Russians than for respondents of other nationalities, many of whom probably were immigrants from other republics of the former Union (Pain 2004: 75). Only 9.3 per cent of Russians and 12.9 per cent of representatives of other nationalities declared that they perceived 'a commonality with the people and history of the [Union] republics'. Even simple interest in the territories beyond the boundaries of Russia was then low. The greatest interest was in Ukraine, but even Ukraine attracted the attention of a minority only – a mere 21 per cent of Russian respondents (Pain 2004: 75).

The Congress of Russian Communities appeared in 1993, and aspired to turn the many millions of diaspora Russians in the new states – the former republics of the USSR – into a powerful political force, an instrument of Russian irredentism, in other words, for the unification of 'the Russian world' around Russia. And what was the result? It was nothing resembling Hungarian irredentism (for example, the annexation of North Transylvania during the Second World War); Greek irredentism (*enosis*); or Romanian irredentism ('Greater Romania'). Nothing even faintly reminiscent of the strength displayed by these irredentist movements appeared on the territory of the Commonwealth of Independent States (CIS). In theory, irredentism is considered one of the clearest signs of imperial nationalism and imperial mass consciousness. In the 1990s, then, these characteristics were more manifest among the nationalities mentioned above than among the Russians.

It is safe to say that, until the mid-1990s, the 'tough statists' and 'extreme nationalists' cited the 'will of the people' without the slightest grounds for doing so. At the beginning of the 1990s, 60 per cent of those questioned by sociologists under the leadership of Iurii Levada considered the West a model to emulate, in terms of its political system, market economics and way of life (Dubin 2003a: 137). Time passed, however, and by 1995 the difficulties of the transition period were increasingly making themselves felt. People grew tired of reforms and of the mistakes in the implementation of these, and the public mood began to change. The positive image of the West began to erode only in the mid-1990s – but by 2000, survey responses from the previous decade were turned upside down. In 2001, 67 per cent of respondents in Russia considered the Western mode of organising society to be 'to some extent' inappropriate for Russian conditions and contrary to the lifestyle of the Russian people (Dubin 2003a: 150).

Reconstructing imperial consciousness in stages: From Soviet to imperial

The socio-economic changes in Russia during the 1990s were less markedly radical than in, for example, Poland or the Baltic states – at least the branch structure of Russia's economy and the composition of its management changed less. However, for the aforementioned neighbours of Russia, the psychological pain from the shock of changes was assuaged by the desire to join European structures. For the sake of this independent and important aim, it was felt that one could endure discomfort and surmount growing pains. In Russia there was no such defence mechanism in people's consciousness; a move towards Europe was not an aim in itself: on the contrary, this idea depended on several others. Attitudes to socialism and to the USSR played the most important role in the acceptance of Westernising reforms. In 1989–92 more than half of all Russians surveyed agreed with the statement that 'socialism has led us up a blind alley' (Pain 2004: 73). About the same share of respondents had answered similarly in Poland in the 1980s, but there such sentiments were better protected: museums of socialist life worked to preserve them, and Andrzej Wajda's films and practically all Polish literature contributed to suppressing the desire to return to socialism. In Russia there was nothing similar, and by 1995 a different thesis had gained currency – 'Socialism was not really that bad; its leaders were bad' – and by the early 2000s its leaders too had been rehabilitated.

The changing attitudes towards the image of Stalin are telling. In the second half of the 1980s, when nationwide sociological surveys began to be conducted in the USSR, Stalin did not feature on lists of outstanding figures, and was constantly subject to severe criticism in the perestroika media. In 1991, in the new, post-Soviet Russia, public attitudes towards him only worsened. At that time less than 1 per cent of those asked by VTsIOM thought Stalin would still be remembered after ten years. The overwhelming majority of respondents were sure that he would soon simply be forgotten. However, this prognosis did not come true; less than ten years later, VTsIOM noted that a public opinion poll placed Stalin at the head of the list of 'the most outstanding heads of the Russian state of all time' (Dubin 2003b). Moreover, in third place came Iurii Andropov, the communist leader of the USSR 1982–4, and before that head of the KGB for many years. Just like Stalin, Andropov was perceived in Russian public consciousness as a strong authoritarian administrator – an 'iron hand' (Dubin 2003b).

After ten hard years, adjustment to a new social and economic environment had engendered among Russians the habitual Soviet mental stereotypes that linked stability exclusively to an authoritarian ruler. Even more important, these paternalistic stereotypes were foisted on the public by the Russian political elite, which not only morally rehabilitated Stalin but even promoted him. A few examples will suffice. For the fifty-fifth anniversary of the victory over fascism on 9 May 2000, a memorial tablet was unveiled in the Kremlin in honour of the heroes of the Second World War.

The list included Stalin's name. A jubilee medal issued in the same year bore a portrait of Stalin. In his congratulatory speech on Victory Day 2000, President Putin addressed his compatriots as 'brothers and sisters', echoing the radio broadcast that Stalin made to the Soviet people on 3 July 1941. Finally, in television commentary accompanying the same celebrations in 2000, the film director Nikita Mikhalkov called for the town of Volgograd to return to its former name, Stalingrad (Dubin 2003b). In 2002 VTsIOM, then directed by Iurii Levada, published a Festschrift marking its fifteen years of work, reflecting on social changes in Russia since 1987. It turned out that, in 2002, for the first time in fifteen years of sociological monitoring, respondents evaluated the collapse of the USSR as the most important and dramatic event of this entire period (VTsIOM 2002: 199).

In the wake of changing views on socialism and the Soviet Union, ideas about Russia's enemies were swiftly altered as well. In the USSR the West had been seen not only as a geopolitical opponent, but indeed as a class enemy with whom compromise was impossible – class opposition, according to Marxist doctrine, is intrinsically antagonistic. The only period in which the political elite of the USSR, and then Russia, proclaimed the slogan of a return to the 'family of civilised nations', 'to Europe', was from the late 1980s to the early 1990s. Public moods then supported this policy actively. The idea 'Why look for enemies, if the root of our misfortune lies within us?' dominated, but with the return of the Soviet element in Russian culture, Soviet stereotypes also began to reawaken in the public consciousness. Fears, phobias and images of the enemy were the first to return. In 1991 only 12 per cent of those asked considered the West (above all the USA) their enemy; by 1994 this figure had risen to 41 per cent, and by 1999 to more than two-thirds of those surveyed, 65 per cent (Gudkov 2002: 132–3). Moreover, in 2014, after the events in Ukraine, the main body of Russians expressed almost total enmity towards the West. A Levada Centre survey conducted on 18–21 July 2014 showed that 74 per cent of respondents – the highest percentage ever recorded by the centre – described their attitude towards the USA as 'bad'; almost two-thirds of those surveyed (60 per cent) had negative feelings towards the countries of the European Union (Levada Centre 2014d). More than half of those surveyed (52 per cent) explained Ukraine's aspiration to draw closer to the EU thus: 'Ukraine has become a puppet in the hands of the West and the USA, who are pursuing an anti-Russian policy' (Levada Centre 2014e).

In popular consciousness, the growth of a phobia about the West is not connected with the revival of Soviet traits in Russian life. Russians explain the changes with reference to the incompatibility of Russian and Western civilisation: 'So we changed, became a democracy, and the West still does not like us – that shows their innate Russophobia.'

First, Soviet consciousness returned (in the late 1990s), and then, the idea of empire was gradually rehabilitated in its pre-Soviet version. The fact of the matter is that in the Soviet Union the term 'empire' had held entirely negative connotations. Terry Martin, an authoritative historian of Soviet nationalities policies, has provided documentary evidence to support his conclusion that 'Lenin and Stalin understood very well the danger of being labeled an empire in the age of nationalism'; therefore, Soviet leaders never referred to the USSR as an empire (Martin 2001: 19). And to this day the rulers of contemporary Russia stubbornly call it a federation, although it increasingly displays the characteristics of an imperial system. From school, the Soviet people have had it instilled in them that an empire is 'bad', a 'prison of the peoples' and a regime against which the great Lenin struggled, and that imperialism is the final stage in the decay of capitalism. Thus, the rehabilitation of the term 'empire' at the beginning of the twenty-first century seems all the more surprising.

It is noteworthy that in the year 2000, several publishers chose to issue novels written within the anti-utopia genre (prose in the style of George Orwell, illustrating contemporary life in the shape of future events) devoted to Russia as an empire (see Divov 2000; Gevorkian 2000; Krusanov 2000; van Zaichik 2000). The interest in the anti-utopia genre, which is sometimes called a 'coded language' genre, is telling in itself. There was no demand for such literature in Russia in the Gorbachev and Eltsin era. On the contrary, after many years behind the 'iron curtain', the post-Soviet public was hungry for the truth, and cast themselves over literature that depicted real problems. The most popular current affairs journalism had been that of Iurii Burtin, Vitalii Korotich, Nikolai Shmelev and Iurii Cherednichenko, among others. Now, just as in the Stalin era, it became necessary to once again codify one's thoughts about contemporaneity.

Moreover, it is surprising that these novels, all published in 2000, give premonitions of Russia's imminent return to an imperial system. In Eduard Gevorkian's *Age of Scoundrels*, Russia is openly portrayed as an empire; in others we find imagined names such as the 'Slavic Union' (Oleg Divov's *Culling*), 'the Horde-Rus empire' (Kholm van Zaichik's *The Case of the Greedy Barbarian*) or 'the Empire of Hesperia', the capital of which is called Moscow (Pavel Krusanov, *The Angel's Bite*). The period in which the action takes place in these novels varies: in Gevorkian's novel it is 2014; in others it is less specific, like the first two or three decades of the current century. A little later, in 2006, the anti-utopian writer Vladimir Sorokin released *The Day of the Oprichnik*. According to Sorokin, this book is a warning about the fate that awaits Russia if it continues on its current political course. Its action takes place in 2027, in a Russia fenced off from the rest of the world by the Great Russian Wall, like the wall that surrounded the medieval Chinese Empire, effectively symbolising Russia's current (2014) isolation in the world. In all these novels the writers convey their fears in the face of impending totalitarianism. They sensed the changes in Russian society earlier than the sociologists – above all, the popular demand for the stereotypes of imperial consciousness, which were purposefully activated from the end of the 1990s and are now widely exploited for the self-preservation of the authoritarian forces and the reanimation of the imperial syndrome. One of the heroes in *Age of Scoundrels* expounds Russia's national idea in 2014 thus: 'Only a large country can conquer its enemies in the future.' Then the hero corrects himself: 'Not large, but great . . . A great country is made by great people . . . A great ruler musters great people.' I am not sure whether President Putin has read these lines, but his famous slogan 'Russia will either be great, or she will not be at all' is certainly a generalisation of popular stereotypes.[8]

In the political discourse of the 'national patriotic' or 'red–brown' forces in Russia – of Aleksandr Dugin, Aleksandr

Prokhanov, Mikhail Iuriev and others – it became fashionable to use the word 'empire' to denote the grandeur and order of the Soviet past, and the desired changes for the future, only towards the end of the first decade of the 2000s. In fact, it was business advertising that worked the hardest – and succeeded the most – in popularising 'empire'. By its efforts, the motifs of empire gradually entered into popular culture and thence into popular consciousness. In many regions of Russia the most popular brands of Russian vodka are called 'empire' or 'imperial'. In various Russian airlines, business class has been renamed 'imperial' class. The term 'empire' has become a symbol of something very good, turning up in phrases like 'imperial taste' and 'imperial spirit'. Empire is lauded on the stage, in the cinema, in literature. In the film world, empire almost always looks attractive, 'beautiful', sometimes even 'glamorous', like Tsar Aleksandr III's parade of soldiers on the Kremlin's Cathedral Square in Nikita Mikhalkov's film *The Barber of Siberia* (1998). Imperial style has begun to dominate also in architecture and urban construction.

As soon as the imperial consciousness that was reconstructed and activated became established, it began to display significant influence on political life, generating demand for a type of popular political figures and their discourse. Reconstructed traditionalism combined with the relatively stable particularities of the country's geography, agriculture and cultural traditions – all this has influenced the reproduction of the 'imperial syndrome' that, to a certain extent, now shapes the course of political creativity in Russia, making the reproduction of imperial traits in the politics of the country highly probable.

The political prospects of Russian nationalism

In the conditions of Russia's current stage of development, with its stormy re-traditionalisation and almost total unity between the authorities and Russian (imperial) nationalists, questions arise about the fate of this movement. At least two scenarios for a changed role in Russia's political life are, in theory, possible.

First, there is the possibility of the fading of Russian nationalism, its complete dissolution in the general mass of post-Soviet advocates for the reconstruction of the USSR. Today imperial nationalism is becoming not only a political fellow-traveller of the authorities, but also its ally. Imperial nationalists greeted Russia's annexation of Crimea with great enthusiasm, and all disagreements with the authorities were set aside. With this ideological rapprochement with the authorities, the specifics of imperial nationalism and its attractiveness for potential adherents are disappearing, which may lead to the nationalist movement losing members. It is now possible for many of them to realise their political ambitions under the current authorities, without having to call themselves nationalists – as noted, a term with extremely negative connotations in Soviet times. Since the Russian press, with unprecedented vigour, began to cover the regime change in Ukraine as a 'nationalist' and 'fascist' revolution, negative perceptions of the term 'nationalism' have only grown.

However, the nationalist elite will not allow Russian nationalism to disappear completely, or be dissolved into the general mass of those who support a great state and the revival of the USSR. The leaders of the extremely thin national democratic stream of Russian nationalism understand well the fundamental difference between nationalism and imperial ideology and politics. These leaders are unlikely to abandon their principled positions utterly, even in conditions where a significant portion of this movement's representatives supported the authorities over the 'Crimean question'. Nationalists of this category are not set to play fellow-traveller with the authorities for long. A socio-economic crisis is ripening in Russia, for domestic reasons as well as due to the country's increasing international isolation. All this has already begun to give rise to a new political polarisation, which will only increase. In these conditions, greater pressure from the authorities on all autonomous ideological groups, including the national democrat organisations, is an entirely plausible scenario. Furthermore, the opposition of the latter is predestined by the inevitable growth in demand for slogans like 'defence of Russians in Russia'. The Russian authorities have more than once announced their right to protect Russians beyond the country's borders, but the position of Russians in many of the Federation's republics is clearly no better than it was in the former Ukrainian

Republic of Crimea. There are increasing demands to protect the rights of Russians to representation in the organs of power and to protect the Russian language in the educational system of Tatarstan, for example (Suleimanov 2012). These demands come primarily from national democratic-type organisations. In the North Caucasus the national democratic-type party New Force has been promoting human rights with regard to ethnic Russians. Not only is its opposition stance in this region not weakening, it is becoming stronger. Further aggravation of inter-ethnic tension connected with the influx of migrants and the plummeting levels of tolerance in Russian society will also provoke the national democratic movement to further opposition.

The second scenario is a new upsurge of Russian nationalism as the leader of the imperial great power movement and a political rival to the current authorities. Here I refer not to the marginal movements of national democrats, but the nationalist majority – the imperial nationalists. Today the 'Donbas militias' are extraordinarily popular with Russians. VTsIOM data from July 2014 show that the overwhelming majority of survey respondents (85 per cent) perceive the militias positively 'to some extent', whereas only 8 per cent relate to them negatively and 7 per cent neutrally. Furthermore, 89 per cent of respondents are sure that Ukraine is violating the rights of Russians and Russian-speaking citizens, and that militias should protect them (VTsIOM 2014b). The ideology of the militia leaders is typical of imperial nationalism of the Soviet type. The possibility cannot be ruled out that militia leaders, especially those like Igor Strelkov (Girkin), could head a movement of national imperial forces and even pose a threat to Putin. As of autumn 2014, the name 'Strelkov' could be found on social networking sites as often as the name of 'Putin' (Nepogodin 2014).

However, it seems more likely that events will unfold differently, and that, once again, the Russian authorities will be able to redirect the rise of imperial nationalism for their own purposes. In fact, the authorities have always managed to destroy the large nationalist organisations that over the years have aspired to lead and unite nationalist parties and movements in Russia. In the 1990s this was Pamiat, then the Russia-wide patriotic movement

Russian National Unity (RNE). The authorities managed to divide, decapitate and make the Nazi skinhead movement illegal at the turn of the millennium, and, by 2011, the Movement against Illegal Migration (DPNI). The nationalists have not been able to overcome the ideological splits and disagreements between various currents within nationalism: between left and right wing, red and white. Opposing the unauthorised nationalist movement are the pro-authorities forces, organised from above, with the Russian mass propaganda machine on their side, now mobilised to conduct a 'cold war'. No one from the imperial nationalist forces is currently able to compete politically with Putin, whose approval ratings after the annexation of Crimea have grown to nearly 90 per cent. Today Putin is, in fact, developing the idea of 'official nationality', in conjunction with the idea of Russia's special path and the concept of protecting 'the Russian world' (*russkii mir*) on the territories that once comprised the Russian Empire. In a situation of exacerbated public prejudices about the eternal enmity of the West towards Russia, Putin would appear to be the only real defender of the people.

Thus far, all this has strengthened the popularity of the Russian leader among the Russian public. At the same time, Russia is growing more isolated in the world. This may be a repetition of a historical lesson that Russia has gone through without learning. On ascending the throne, Nikolai I attempted to use the doctrine of 'official nationality' to fend off the ideological influence of Europe. In my opinion, it is indeed remarkable that, almost two centuries later, the Russian authorities are dealing with the actions of the opposition (who may also be called 'Decembrists' after the December manifestations in Moscow 2011) by using methods similar to those adopted in the nineteenth century after the first Decembrist uprising. The similarity concerns not so much the application of some form of repression against political opponents, as the appropriation of the opposition's slogans and – more importantly – the falsification of these slogans – the substitution of the opposition's ideas with something that looks the same but is essentially contrary in principle. In place of the idea of *nation* advocated by the Decembrists, Nikolai I's cabinet presented the doctrine of *official nationality*; in 2014 the presidential administration disarmed the Russian nationalist opposition with a second issue of 'official nationality', specifically support for the idea of 'the Russian world', which served as the ideological basis for annexing Crimea and all-round support for the Donbas separatists – albeit unacknowledged – from official Russia. But we should remember how the government of Nikolai I ended – in Russia's defeat in the Crimean war of 1853–6. It was after this defeat that Aleksandr II's great reforms began in Russia.

If history allows the possibility of a second edition of 'official nationality' in Russia, then it may also allow the possibility of seeing it crash a second time – this time not in military failure, but in economic disaster. If in the mid-nineteenth century the law of serfdom fell, then in the twenty-first century, it is authoritarianism that must retreat, or fall.

Notes

1. The current publication was prepared as part of the NEORUSS project, and simultaneously continues a series of publications emerging from large-scale, collaborative research conducted during 2012–14. The research was conducted by colleagues, postgraduate fellows and students at the National Research University – Higher School of Economics in Moscow, Russia under my supervision, and with academic input by Galina Nikiporets-Takigawa (Cambridge University, UK). Project methodology is outlined in the team's co-authored article (Pain et al. 2013).
2. See the programme of the Union of the Russian People, available at <http://krotov.info/acts/20/1900/1906anti.html> (last accessed 10 April 2015).
3. The manifesto of the anti-Soviet column in the 2012 'Russian March' is available at the website of the Russian Imperial Union-Order at <http://legitimist.ru/sight/politics/2012/09/manifest-antisovetskoj-kolonnyi-na.html> (last accessed 10 April 2015).
4. See the website of *Sputnik i Pogrom*, available at <http://sputnikipogrom.com> (last accessed 10 April 2015).
5. This formula, in one form or another, was repeatedly used by President Eltsin: for example in 1992 when it was announced that Russian missiles would not be aimed at the USA, in 1993 when a friendship treaty was signed with Poland, and – finally – in January

1994 during President Clinton's visit to Russia, when the Russian leader announced that the confrontation with the West had catastrophic consequences for Russia and it should be ended once and for all, returning Russia 'to the family of civilised nations' (Torkunov 1999: 56).
6. On 25 April 2005, in an address to the Federal Assembly, Putin called the collapse of the USSR 'the greatest geopolitical catastrophe of the 20th century' (Putin 2005).
7. In September 2004 President Putin initiated changes to the way in which heads of executive power of federal subjects were to be selected, proposing to appoint governors and heads of republics by a decision made in the relevant regional legislative bodies on the President's recommendation, instead of their being elected by the regional population. On Putin's orders, the relevant legislation was drafted in the shortest amount of time and passed already in December 2004 (see Baberina 2010).
8. This phrase is constantly repeated as Putin's, but it is attributed to Putin in the words of someone else. At the Worldwide Russian People's Council in Moscow, 13–14 December 2001, Aleksandr Dugin said: 'The words of our President are close to the heart of each one of us: Russia may be either great, or not be at all' (see Itskovich 2002).

3

Radical nationalists from the start of Medvedev's presidency to the war in Donbas: True till death?

Alexander Verkhovsky

This chapter examines the evolution of the radical wing in Russian nationalism, from the early days of Dmitrii Medvedev's presidency in 2008 to the war in the Donbas region that started in 2014.[1] 'Russian nationalism' is an extremely broad concept (see Laruelle 2009a); there is no such thing as one unified movement of Russian nationalists. However, in the context of an authoritarian regime and the general weakness of political movements, we may note one important distinguishing criterion: relations with the authorities. This enables us, for the purposes of discussion, to separate those nationalists who oppose the authorities from those who support them. This chapter deals only with the opposition sector, so organisations like Motherland (*Rodina*) and the People's Assembly (*Narodnyi Sobor*) are not examined here.[2]

The opposition sector is also diverse. Here I will focus on those groups and organisations that are characteristic of it, which means excluding from the analysis those currents that, while undoubtedly interesting, are not typical. First, I will not be examining groups and organisations representing the 'old nationalism' of the 1990s, because these groups are becoming steadily less active and do not play any special role in the movement as a whole.[3] Second, I will not be considering those groups that are primarily Stalinist, and nationalist only as a secondary consideration, like the followers of Colonel Vladimir Kvachkov. Eduard Limonov's followers also clearly keep themselves apart from the nationalist movement. Third, I exclude from the analysis here all national democratic currents – not because they are not part of the nationalist movement (they are), but because they differ significantly from the main sector and are notably fewer in number (in terms of various numerical indicators). National democrats clearly have their own, emergent path, and it would be a mistake to examine their dynamics and potential together with the rest.

Who, then, makes up the mainstream, if we exclude those enumerated above? We are left with those groups who, as of 2013, were somehow connected with the Russians (*Russkie*) movement or the Russian All-People's Union (*Rossiiskii obshchenarodnyi soiuz*) (ROS), some individual organisations, as well as various autonomous groups – usually youth groups – that do not associate themselves with these well-known political organisations although the latter are forever wooing them. Many, but far from all, of these groups call themselves 'autonomous nationalists' (*natsional-avtonomy*), 'national socialists' or similar. They are typically oriented towards various neo-fascist ideas and racist violence. This chapter thus focuses on those who participate in the 4 November 'Russian March', excluding the national democrats. I refer to them as 'radical nationalists', simply to demarcate them from the rest, who are either less clearly nationalist or more moderate in their methods or their aims.

I have chosen 2008 as the starting point – not primarily because of the change of president, but, as I will return to below, because this proved to be an extremely significant year on several parameters of greater importance for radical nationalists than the change of president in itself. Similarly, the war in Donbas is a major landmark in the development of the radical nationalist movement, so it cannot be avoided in this chapter. However, since that war is not yet over, the consequences for radical nationalists are not yet entirely clear.

In 2007 I wrote about how the Russian nationalist mainstream had come to take the place of the 'old nationalism' (Verkhovsky 2007a). To sum up briefly: in the middle of the first decade of the 2000s a fairly powerful movement emerged, and one very different from the nationalism of the 1990s. Instead of being motivated by nostalgic visions or the like, it focused on the ultra-simplified idea of building a new, ethnically pure (or, at the very least, ethnically hierarchical) Russia in place of the lost empire. It built on violence from the streets, and on the aggressive racism of the neo-Nazi skinhead movement, although the skinhead sub-culture as such was already going out of fashion. The present chapter explores how the movement has evolved since then, whether it has a future and, if so, what sort of future that may be.[4]

2008: Setting the scene

According to SOVA Center for Information and Analysis data, hate crime peaked precisely in 2008; we reported 116 murder victims in that year alone. However, active police work against the gangs committing these crimes had also been expanding at the same time – or, more accurately, had begun to do so back in 2007. For several years, the number of people sentenced for these crimes grew steadily, with arrests numbering in the hundreds, in stark contrast to the situation in previous years.[5] Racist violence escalated until 2008 – and then, just as swiftly, began to decline.

Organised battles between radical nationalists and youth from the Caucasus had already passed their peak by 2007; on the whole, the street war with 'antifa' (antifascist) fighters had supplanted the street war with the 'Caucasians' (*kavkaztsy*). For some years, this war – conducted most actively from 2007 to 2009 – absorbed significant resources of the ultra-right sector's militant groups.

In about 2008 the sector itself became fully 'equipped', developing its own businesses, legal services, support systems for those arrested and so on. This made it possible for members to confine almost all their social contact to within the sector, and to view society at large – not just 'ethnic enemies' – with increasing scepticism.

It was in 2008, too, that antifascists faced the greatest number of genuine threats from neo-Nazis. The terrorist component of neo-Nazi violence directed against political opponents and the authorities also expanded, including the activities of the Combat Organisation of Russian Nationalists (*Boevaia organizatsiia russkikh natsionalistov*) (BORN) (see Kozlov and Tumanov 2014;

Novaia gazeta 2014). Explosives were increasingly used. Not only did neo-Nazis kill 'antifa fighters', their opponents in the street war, they even murdered a federal judge. Arson and bombing attempts against police stations became commonplace. There was no discernible abatement of these activities in 2009 and 2010, but thereafter they declined steeply.[6]

In late 2007 and early 2008, the National Socialist Society (*Natsional-sotsialisticheskoe obshchestvo*) (NSO) of Dmitrii Rumiantsev and Sergei Korotkikh, which until then had been expanding fast, fell apart under pressure from law enforcement agencies. The NSO, an organisation that had been a sort of model result of the neo-Nazis' near-total impunity, had combined energetic political activism with no less energetic murder. The collapse of the NSO showed young radical nationalists that it would be impossible to combine these activities in the years to come. Some became disillusioned, and some opted for politics instead of violence, but it would appear that the majority chose violence and took secrecy more seriously.

That is not to say that political activities were divorced from violence. In 2008, for example, an activist of the 'political' Movement against Illegal Immigration (DPNI) blew himself up while preparing explosives in his flat. Among the organisations in focus here, it would appear that the separation of politics and violence has not been entirely accomplished to this day.

As for organised politics, almost no genuine patrons of the radical nationalists remained in the new State Duma elected in December 2007, so the hopes raised by collaboration with the Motherland bloc were dashed. At the same time, pro-Kremlin youth movements – primarily the Moscow region Locals (*Mestnye*) – began a campaign against 'illegal migrants', quite reminiscent of DPNI's early activities. The top–down tactic of 'intercepting slogans' was coupled with backstage manoeuvres aimed at reducing support for the then-leading ultra-right organisation, DPNI, to benefit Russian Image (*Russkii obraz*), an organisation no less radical but that presented itself as apolitical (Horvath 2014). Russian Image attracted a sizeable portion of the radical youth core from the DPNI in 2008. The politics of manipulating the nationalist arena continued in this fashion until November 2009.

For its part the DPNI set up a broad coalition that included Aleksei Navalnyi's group and the remnants of Andrei Saveliev's party Great Russia (*Velikaia Rossiia*), created one year earlier, as well as Konstantin Krylov's Russian Public Movement (*Russkoe obshchestvennoe dvizhenie*) (ROD), then the national democrats' most notable initiative. Although the coalition soon withered away, this highlighted the division of radical nationalists into those who publically declared their opposition and those who did not (it is hard to see Russian Image activists as being truly loyal). The DPNI itself continued to be dogged by internal crisis, due largely to the transformation of the movement into a more politicised and centralised structure. The movement, for several years the undisputed leader of the visible part of the nationalist sector, now went into decline.[7]

Methodological approach

The radical nationalist movement combines political activity and violence, but it is more convenient to explore these two types of activity separately, since – for the most part – different individuals take part in them and, accordingly, different dynamics emerge. It is also important to take into consideration the relations of the movement as a whole with the authorities, since in an authoritarian system this parameter is of great significance for any movement.

Here I identify three measurements – level of political activity, violence, and relations with the authorities. These are interdependent, so it would be most correct to examine precisely these interactions across every time period. That approach has already been tested in SOVA Center for Information and Analysis publications, however, so here I will explore the dynamics of the three lines of enquiry in sequence instead, only occasionally referring to their interaction.

The Ukrainian crisis, escalating into violence since February 2014, has greatly impacted on radical nationalists (Al'perovich and Yudina 2014b). Therefore I begin by examining these three lines from 2009 up to early 2014, and then offer a provisional summary of more recent changes.

Relations with the authorities

In not allowing radical nationalists to compete in the parliamentary elections of 2007, the federal authorities set a course of suppression, although obviously not of total repression. First, there were fairly large-scale arrests of those involved in racist violence, many of whom were sentenced to significant periods of imprisonment. In part this led to a reduction of violent activity, in part to such groups going underground and to their separation from political movements. Although the number of arrests dropped over time, the impact of this strategy was still being felt up until at least 2013. As the bulk of radical nationalists are members of groups inclined to violence, the movement as a whole saw this policy as a 'declaration of war'. This raised the temperature of anti-government feelings within the sector.

Second, the political movements – especially the largest, the DPNI – were also subjected to significant pressure. No political activists were imprisoned, but the sense of their being unpunishable evaporated: the authorities progressed from a suspended sentence given to the DPNI leader, Aleksandr Belov, in 2009, to a ban on the DPNI as an extremist organisation in 2011. The aim was to marginalise an entire stream of Russian nationalism. The evident pointlessness of participating in the DPNI and similar organisations led to a drop in numbers and to attempts at political manoeuvring by their leadership (see below).

Third, alternatives were created for radical nationalists who wanted to break away from the groups that had come under pressure. Structures connected with Russian Image provided the main alternative, and many of the more radical neo-Nazi youth groups (that had at that point embarked on marching together as the 'black block') went for this alternative. However, it was also possible to join the pro-Kremlin 'youth movements', and some radical nationalists apparently saw this as an opportunity to infiltrate the regime (Kozhevnikova 2010). The arrest of Nikita Tikhonov in November 2009 revealed the extent to which the radicalism of Russian Image was unacceptable to the authorities, and hence, this alternative was curtailed. At the same time, pro-Kremlin youth groups stopped being used as a soft alternative to the DPNI. Thus, suppression became the only strategy – at least until 2013 (see below).

The riot on Moscow's Manezhnaia Square on 11 December 2010 marked a turning point in the authorities' relations with radical nationalists. The fact that riot police (OMON) could not disperse a crowd of about 3,000 (my estimate) radical nationalists and football hooligans, right under the very walls of the Kremlin, evoked serious concern. Although it remained unique in terms of size, this event prompted the federal authorities to undertake not only a series of police operations and populist gestures, but also to formulate a more intelligible and, importantly, stable position. Recent years have seen a whole series of official announcements, concept papers and programmes, which – despite the unavoidable eclecticism – have at least established a basic position. Not only do the authorities reject any radical nationalism, they also pit their own variant of statist 'civilisational' nationalism against ethnic (including Russian) nationalism. Although not set out in detail, the basic shape of the confrontation is clear: the political nation must unite around figures and ideas proposed by the authorities, and not around ethnic or any other communities that may arise and/or be manifested independently of them (Verkhovsky 2014a).

There were also less significant political manoeuvres, especially in the pre-election period of 2011 (see, for example, *Novorossiia* 2011). Dmitrii Rogozin's return to politics became the most important event. He simultaneously resurrected the Rodina party and re-established contacts with the nationalist movement. In the end, however, representatives of the movement were not allowed real access to the elections, whether through Rogozin or via DPNI channels, and the strategy of marginalising radical nationalists continued. Since then there have been some episodic exceptions to this trend, like inviting the known neo-Nazi Maksim (Tesak) Martsinkevich to participate in a television programme as a 'warrior against paedophilia', but these have not developed into a general tendency – not least since radical nationalists took part in the protest movement (see below).

The events of 2013 proved considerably more serious – specifically, the totally unexpected anti-migrant campaign conducted over several months on federal television channels (see

Hutchings and Tolz, this volume), and by several regional administrations, including those of Moscow and St Petersburg. Although in Moscow this could be ascribed to mayoral elections, there were no elections in St Petersburg. What is significant is not just that the police began to bring criminal charges against non-citizens far more often,[8] but how and to what extent this was conveyed to the public. The campaign led to an unprecedented rise in ethno-xenophobia in society (Levada Centre 2013c).

Radical nationalists responded with their own activities, both large-scale political events and direct action in the form of 'raids' (such raids were, and are to this day, conducted even by the pro-Kremlin Motherland). The campaign was effective in promoting radical nationalists in the mass media, forcing the authorities to take additional steps to restrict over-zealous 'helpers' in the struggle against 'illegal migration' (Al'perovich and Yudina 2014a). Importantly, the anti-migration campaign appeared to call into question the declared goal of supra-ethnic political consolidation, and thereby the grounds for opposing radical nationalists. It is difficult to say whether this is the reason why the campaign was eventually wound down by the end of autumn 2013.

However, with the beginning of the mass political mobilisation against the West and the 'Kiev junta' (the new authorities in Ukraine after the ouster of Viktor Yanukovych), the impact of the anti-migrant campaign was completely smoothed over. The new propaganda campaign led to maximum political consolidation around the Kremlin, to the detriment of nationalist ideas: in spring 2014 ethno-xenophobia declined sharply, as did support for ethnic nationalist slogans, including slogans about the need for introducing a visa regime for citizens of Central Asian countries (Romanov and Stepanov 2014). One may, of course, question the specific data collated in response to these or other surveys, but there can be no doubt that, for the majority of the population, the foreign policy conflict and patriotic enthusiasm connected with the annexation of Crimea eclipsed the previous year's priorities for some time. As of the time of this writing (summer 2014–winter 2015), the theme of political unity has again come to dominate the discourse of the authorities and those groups loyal to them, only now in a more militant form. And again there is some ambiguity as to what this national unity means – that is, whether the struggle is being waged for 'the Russian world' (*russkii mir*) (the establishment of transborder cultural and political unity with Moscow's allies), or for the ethnic Russians. Consequently, national unity must also be understood as relating to 'Russian civilisation' – but with clear ethnic undertones.

Is it possible to say how this has impacted upon policies in relation to the radical nationalists? As yet, no. Despite the abundance of new laws, various declarations and a deluge of propaganda, there has been very little clarity within Russian domestic politics in general since the beginning of the Ukrainian political crisis. Very tentatively, it may be suggested that the authorities' policy in relation to radical nationalists has returned to basically the situation of late 2012/early 2013 – that is, to the state of play that existed after the collapse of the protest movement but before the start of the anti-migrant campaign.

The dynamics of violence

All political organisations that may be deemed part of the radical nationalist movement are connected with racist violence, either historically or currently. The most obvious examples from the early 2000s are the National Socialist Society, which combined politics and violence almost openly; and Russian Image, which had a sort of military wing in the shape of the above-mentioned BORN. The radical nationalist leaders themselves have said more than once that they do not any longer resort to violence, whatever the nature of their militant pasts – undeniable pasts, in the case of such leaders as Dmitrii Demushkin of the Slavic Union (*Slavianskii soiuz*) (SS) and Dmitrii (Shults) Bobrov of the National-socialist Initiative (*Natsional-sotsialisticheskaia initsiativa*) (NSI). More important is that the *activists* in their organisations clearly do resort to violence (SOVA Center for Information and Analysis 2012, 2013a), and there are no visible boundaries between the 'peaceable' radical nationalists and the 'warriors'. However, it is also true that most such crimes are committed by members of 'autonomous' groups that are not part of any political organisation. In any case, the use of violence is very important for radical nationalists – a fact they do not attempt to hide, judging from their enthusiasm for public lessons in knife fighting, paramilitary gatherings and the like.

Under serious police pressure, the level of racist and neo-Nazi violence began to fall from 2009 onwards, while violence against political opponents (as opposed to 'aliens' and the homeless), began to decline two or so years later. This shift may be explained by a certain disillusionment among militant groups with their usual practice of racist attacks. Simply put, they have gradually come to realise that beatings, even murders, of 'aliens' have no impact on the pace of migration or on government policies, or even on public opinion – such methods will not bring the 'white revolution' any nearer. However, it would be erroneous to see their goals as simply the venting of personal xenophobic emotions and hooligan tendencies, as this sector also has a fully defined political aim ('Podlinnaia istoriia . . .' n.d.).

Political terror is a more effective method of radicalising the Russian majority, and this argument is essentially the one used by members of the People's Will (*Narodovoltsy*) (*RAC 14* 2008). That said, it is almost impossible to find groups that could organise serious attacks on representatives of the authorities: such activity involves a higher degree of risk, and – even more challenging – a greater facility for conspiracy. Despite idle talk of the attractions of terrorism, this method of revolutionising the masses has not advanced significantly enough to instil optimism in radical nationalists.

Since at least 2002, efforts have been made to turn criminal incidents – the participants of which are described in ethnic terms ('Russians' or 'non-Russians') – into local disturbances with the potential for wider revolutionary development. Since the riots in Kondopoga in 2006, there have been multiple efforts to deploy this same scenario – several each year – and nationalists have not yet abandoned this tactic.[9] Occasionally, riots are pulled off, whether with the participation of nationalist activists or not. More often, however, the 'Kondopoga technique' fails to work. By 2009 the enthusiasm that Kondopoga generated among radical nationalists had faded notably. Even where disturbances did occur, they failed to raise the level of revolutionary fervour locally, or in the country as a whole.

One solution could be to seek support from the significant share of the citizenry who, while not fully ideologically committed, are nevertheless inclined towards racism and violence. However, these people have not yet allowed themselves to be mobilised in sufficient numbers. On Paratrooper Day (2 August), for example, every year the usual hooligan violence is accompanied by several attacks clearly motivated by racism, but the ultra-right have not managed to derive any advantage from this.

Greater potential may lie in organised football hooligans. Ultraright ideas and racist tendencies are widespread among them, and their gangs are well-organised structures, surpassing communities of Nazi skinheads and similar groups in terms of 'fighting strength'. But the football hooligans have kept apart from ultra-right organisations: they value their independence and apolitical nature, and do not particularly respect nationalists as street fighters. Of course, many fans are involved in various nationalist groups in a personal capacity, and there are some fairly ideologically minded, racist groups of fans. Moreover, many 'Russian fans' may unite against fans of clubs from the North Caucasus, but this does not mean that they are managed by radical nationalists (Tarasov 2010).

For a while, at the end of 2010, it seemed as if this may change. The death of an ultra-right Spartak fan, Egor Sviridov, in a street fight mobilised both the ultra-right and the fans. The result was the 11 December demonstration on Manezhnaia Square, which swiftly degenerated into attacks on passers-by and pitched battles with OMON. The mass participation of fans, and the fact that these battles under the very walls of the Kremlin resulted in a draw, raised hopes that larger meetings would soon gather and the 'white revolution' would finally come to pass. Young groups of autonomous Nazis created an informal '11 December movement', which aimed to repeat the Manezhnaia scenario in the hope that things may develop in that direction. That has proved impossible, however: the police have maintained control over Moscow – and the nationalists have not yet managed to mobilise the fans en masse even once.

This does not mean that the fans are incapable of acting as an organised force – also in relation to incidents that the nationalists and their sympathisers attribute to 'ethnic criminality'.[10] During 2011, however, radical nationalists' hopes of harnessing the energy of racist fans for their political ends dropped to their ordinary, low, level.

The protest movement, which began in December 2011 and continued actively for about a year, turned out to be almost unconnected with violence. Various radical groups, also nationalist ones, made attempts to turn protests into attacks on the police or to provoke police violence, but generally with scant success. The use of force by radical nationalists – more accurately, by the Russkie movement – also proved fruitless in disputes within the opposition (Al'perovich and Yudina 2013).

The majority of radical nationalists did not get involved at all in the protest movement, although they of course monitored it. It is easy to imagine that, in these circumstances, the opposition's lack of political success throughout the whole of 2012 can only have reinforced the perception that political action could not conquer the authoritarian 'anti-Russian regime'. If force is the only thing that the regime understands, then the problem is simply from where to harness such force.

The radical nationalists may have hoped, of course, that the 2012 year of protest would give a jolt to the customary political indifference of ethnic Russians (referred to as 'sheep' in the most radical circles, for their passive failure to defend their 'national interests' or 'national pride'). Although the radical nationalists did not manage to enlist new supporters directly on Bolotnaia Square and Sakharov Prospect, dissatisfaction spread wider than the circle of participants in protest marches and meetings. It seemed reasonable to hope that this public dissatisfaction could turn towards the ideal, converting a (democratic) 'revolution of white ribbons' into a (racist) 'white revolution'. Indeed, 2013 did see an unprecedented number of local riots along Kondopoga lines. The political climax came with a pogrom conducted not in the provinces, but in the Moscow suburb of Biriulevo-Zapadnoe. This could have been read as the start of the long-awaited ethno-nationalist mobilisation (Pain 2014).

The authorities took the situation seriously, however, and managed to extinguish this mobilisation. First, in every case the authorities somehow engaged with the participants, even if only symbolically: in other words, they attempted to reduce dissatisfaction. Second, in an effort not to embitter the participants, they took hardly any repressive measures against those who had engaged in rioting with racist overtones. Third, perhaps even more importantly, the public mood is heavily influenced by television propaganda,[11] and the curtailment of the anti-migrant campaign on television significantly reduced the likelihood of further pogroms. And, finally, since December 2013, the events in Ukraine have increasingly occupied broadcasting time and preoccupied the citizenry, including the nationalists – diverting attention away from mobilisation, even on the local level. Take the last riot of 2013 that followed the 'Kondopoga script', the December pogrom in Arzamas (see SOVA Center for Information and Analysis 2013b): it was practically ignored by the mass media, even by radical nationalists themselves. Moreover, with the exception of an incident with fans in the Moscow region of Pushkino, there was not a single incident of this type in 2014.

It would appear that the 'white revolution' has been postponed yet again. This does not mean that racist violence has stopped, though. In fact, street attacks in the traditional form even increased slightly in 2013/14, related to a distinct decline in police competence in dealing with these matters.[12] However, many radical nationalists now consider this type of violence ineffectual (Tikhonov 2011).

The various forms of what may be termed 'semi-legal' violence are quite a different matter. What is meant here are activities that involve force, but that may be openly presented as actions defending the public good, and even claimed to be carried out in partnership with law enforcement agencies. Such practices – in the form of street patrols, for example – were well-known even in the 1990s. At an early stage, the DPNI carried out raids on the homes of 'illegal migrants' together with the police. But this practice was then simply one among many. Now, in the context of a severe police crackdown on 'traditional' racist violence and the failure of political actions, raids of various types came to be seen by many as the most promising type of activity.

Raids – mostly carried out on the workplaces and living quarters of those considered to be migrants – were attractive because they were aggressive without being dangerous. They required little risk-taking by leaders or ordinary participants. Some managed to work closely with the police and migration services, some less so, but, either way, police tolerance was significantly higher than in cases of ordinary violence. Raids could be advertised, and were often covered on television as well as in film clips distributed via the Internet, becoming a powerful way to attract supporters as well. Raids did not have to be directed against migrants only: in 2012 the 'hunt for paedophiles' – led by Martsinkevich – gave the 'raid movement' a powerful boost. Raids were also conducted against 'spice' dealers (those selling quasi-legal smoking mixes), a target shared with pro-Kremlin youth groups. The widespread anti-gay campaign at the start of 2013 was swiftly reflected in attacks on lesbian, gay, bisexual and transgender (LGBT) activists, with the police remaining remarkably tolerant.

It is important to note that the rise in such activities came from the 'grassroots', beyond the main radical nationalist organisations. The initiative was taken in 2011 by new groups such as Igor Mangushev's Bright Rus (*Svetlaia Rus'*)[13] and the Moscow Defence League (*Liga oborony Moskvy*) of Daniel Konstantinov;[14] in 2012, Martsinkevich's neo-Nazi Restrukt! took the lead. (The spread of the latter movement was halted only in 2014, when the police arrested the chief activists.) The authorities' anti-migrant campaign was picked up by radical nationalists, with a massive increase in the number of raids. Open attacks on traders in the streets, known as 'Russian cleansing', also began. This practice developed in an especially tempestuous fashion in St Petersburg until the arrest of Nikolai Bondarik in October 2013.[15] New types of youth movements, like Aleksei Khudiakov's Shield of Moscow (*Shchit Moskvy*), came into the limelight in 2013.[16] Eventually, the main radical nationalist organisations set up their own 'raid projects' – the Russkie movement, for example, call their project 'Guestbusters'.

Thus, a more organised alternative to the current leaders of the radical nationalists has begun to take shape. What is noteworthy here is not so much the competition between these groups and their leaders as their finding a form of activity that can simultaneously satisfy the most active core members, who are highly inclined to violence, and the mass of potential supporters, who as yet view the radical nationalists with clear mistrust and, in doing so, not unduly provoke the law enforcement agencies.

The first half of 2014 showed that raids are not becoming more widespread – perhaps again because of the distraction provided by Ukraine, but possibly for other reasons. All the same, this particular type of action has retained its attractiveness and potential. Broadly formulated: raids, or other forms of limited violence, have more potential than efforts to instigate pogroms or simple backstreet murders, because the public is more accepting of them – as a rather unusual, but nevertheless necessary, form of civic activism.

One serious problem remains: the organisers of this limited violence need to become acceptable to a significant number of citizens. In spring 2013 the large-scale NEORUSS survey revealed that while one-quarter of the respondents held that Russians usually beat up migrants 'because they deserve it', less than 20 per cent disagreed with the suggestion that groups such as Russian National Unity (*Russkoe natsional'noe edinstvo*) (RNE) or skinheads should be banned. At the same time, 45 per cent felt that 'it is necessary to support armed Cossack formations and similar patriotic groups and patrols'.[17] Of course, the citizenry may know as little about skinheads as they do about Cossacks, but they clearly believe that there exist unacceptable 'very radical' nationalists who are unconnected with the authorities, and acceptable 'not very radical' nationalists and other types of groups who maintain links with the authorities and may use violence but without going to extremes. This means that, although radical nationalist raids may not yet have real popular support, radical nationalist or other sorts of populist movements may gain political weight in the future by combining political activity with this sort of limited violence.

The evolution of political structures

Three ever-present factors impact upon the development of the radical nationalists' political structures. First, these structures maintain close links with the militant sector of radical youth groups. Radical nationalist political leaders consider breaking away from these groups to be an extremely risky strategy, as that would raise the serious issue of who, then, would actually support them. Second, they have to establish relations with the authorities in such a way as to avoid being crushed by them, but without appearing to be puppets, as viewed by potential supporters. Accusations that leaders have 'caved in' or 'sold out' are common in any radical opposition group, so it is essential to make sure that such impressions do not spread. Third, they have to broaden the social base somehow, and that will involve learning to appeal to the man in the street and not only the committed, ultra-rightist warrior.

It is no easy task to take all these factors into account, so the political trajectories of prominent nationalist leaders are understandably less than direct. Since 2008 the DPNI, together with the national democrats, has firmly positioned itself in the opposition. During the same period, Russian Image has combined apolitical rhetoric with sheltering militants, whereas the respectable and 'mature' Russian All-People's Union has attracted younger, more radical activists to its leadership and core membership.

At the same time, in an effort to present themselves as not too radical, and to network more widely with potential new participants, all radical nationalist organisations take part in a broad range of initiatives that are not entirely political, but may be ecological, charitable or preservationist. Moreover, after some ten years, a wave of 'civil rights activism' is developing, by which the ultra-right understand the protection of their foot soldiers, including those sentenced or accused of serious violent crime.[18] There is also a political angle to 'the defence of the rights of the Right'. Since 2009 the radical nationalists have increasingly presented themselves as defenders of freedom of speech (although their 'prisoners of conscience' are, in fact, most often sentenced for violence), and this has become a means of drawing closer to the liberal opposition.

Since Russian Image's indirect support from above came to an end in late 2009, their competition with the DPNI has lost its former dynamism. Things reached such a pass that in September 2009 these organisations signed a joint declaration together with the Slavic Union, National-socialist Initiative, various national democrats and even a few 'old nationalists' – Stanislav Vorobev's Russian Imperial Movement (*Russkoe imperskoe dvizhenie*) (RID) and Aleksandr Turik's Union of Russian People (*Soiuz russkogo naroda* (SRN) (*DPNI 2010*). It is notable that this declaration invoked democracy and civil rights, and not the usual nationalist ideas. The discrediting of Russian Image meant that the intended coalition never materialised,[19] but the approach to coalition building is significant in itself. Radical nationalists would like to be accepted by the liberal opposition as equals, albeit special ones.

The pre-election period of 2011 presented further opportunities in this respect. New criminal and civil proceedings were instigated against the DPNI, the Slavic Union and the Russian All-National Union (*Russkii obshchenatsional'nyi soiuz*) (RONS), making it possible for them to present themselves as 'victims of the regime'. Nationalists outstripped liberals and communists in terms of the size of their public demonstrations, in the capital and in most large cities. Talk about the growth of ethno-xenophobia became increasingly widespread.[20] These factors led various political groups to view the nationalists as the most credible opposition sector. Contacts and even joint actions between nationalist groups and the liberal opposition multiplied. However, against the backdrop of continuing rhetorical support for the 'Manezhka' by nationalists of all persuasions, this collaboration looks rather dubious. In the course of 2011, the most important nationalist forces decided on their political trajectory. Here I will outline only the main aspects of this regrouping.

The main radical nationalist forces disassociated themselves from the national democrats (although maintaining friendly relations) and created the Russkie movement as a coalition involving the DPNI, the Slavic Force (*Slavianskaia sila*) (the successor of the now banned Slavic Union), the National-socialist Initiative, the Russian Imperial Movement, the Union of Russian People and Georgii Borovikov's Russian Liberation Front 'Pamiat' (*Russkii Front Osvobozhdeniia 'Pamiat'*).[21] True, the National-socialist Initiative and the Russian Imperial Movement also joined the Russian Platform founded by the national democrats – but, in the end, the Platform fell apart and the national democrats opted for the path of party building, which ruled out associates like the National-socialist Initiative. Thus the Russkie movement have remained de facto the main political union and face of radical nationalists.

Sergei Baburin's Russian All-People's Union chose to go it alone, and since December 2011 has more often come out against the protest movement than for it. In 2012, with the liberalisation of legislation relating to political parties, the Russian All-People's Union managed to reclaim registration swiftly, in contrast to the other radical nationalist organisations that have remained unregistered to this day (Verkhovsky and Strukova 2014). Since then, the party has made efforts to regain respectability. As a result, its political trajectory has been entirely separate from that of the Russkie movement, and the Russian All-People's Union has become part of pro-Kremlin nationalism – like the resurrected Rodina party, only even weaker. It is difficult to say who of the grassroots radical core still remain in the Russian All-People's Union, but the leadership once again looks like a group of 'old nationalists', united in their loyalty to the authorities.

The Russkie movement, in contrast, have played an active role in the protest movement from the very beginning, together with the national democrats. The most obvious result of this policy has been a marked shrinkage of support for the radical nationalist movement's political wing among the main body of their grassroots militant allies. At the large anti-regime Moscow protest marches during the winter of 2011/12, nationalists, including national democrats, usually numbered about 500 people – some ten to twelve times fewer than at Moscow's 'Russian March',[22] and on average 50 to 100 times fewer than the overall number of participants.

By participating in the protest movement, the nationalist elite lost almost all grassroots support: not only did ordinary activists not want to march alongside liberals and leftists themselves, they also described those who did so in extremely negative terms. Repeated efforts to organise independent opposition events such as that of 6 May 2012 failed to heal this schism or deliver any positive results.

In the united opposition that evolved in the context of the protest movement, the nationalists – with their clearly limited support – could occupy a position of sorts thanks solely to some of the liberal and leftist leaders (like Aleksei Navalnyi and Ilia Ponomarev). The latter have made every effort to secure nationalists in the opposition leadership via the 'ideological quota' mechanism. Evidently the belief widely held elsewhere in the opposition that the nationalist leaders represent mass ethno-xenophobic tendencies – that many opposition activists consider impossible to disregard – also worked in the nationalists' favour.

The clear division between radical nationalists and national democrats has also been maintained within the protest movement. At the first Citizens' Council of the opposition, formed in January 2012, the ten representatives of the nationalist 'curia' were divided from the start into two equal sides: the 'national liberation' and the 'national democratic' factions.

Have the nationalists influenced the general direction of the opposition and its position in society as a result? I doubt it. Their only real achievement is the 11 February 2013 resolution of the Opposition Coordination Council, on the need for a visa regime for the countries of Central Asia (except Kazakhstan). It should be noted, however, that protest meetings beyond Moscow have been smaller, and the proportion of new participants considerably lower, so here the proportion of nationalists and their role may prove more significant than in the capital. The proportion of nationalists was particularly high in St Petersburg because the highly effective National-socialist Initiative and Russian Imperial Movement are based there, and because the local branch of Limonov's Other Russia shows strongly nationalist tendencies.

However, even in St Petersburg, nationalist opposition activity has gradually faded away, in parallel with the general decrease in opposition fervour. As far as can be judged, at the close of this period of active protest, radical nationalist political organisations have not managed to strengthen their support base, whether in terms of new protest participants or in terms of radical nationalist youth. Groups that opposed the protest movement in every way, like the Russovet coalition or the Great Russia Party, have also notably failed to achieve anything in this respect.

As a result, radical nationalists have begun to distance themselves from the politics of the united opposition. The summer 2013 Moscow mayoral election campaign saw the opposition's greatest political success, with more than a quarter of the vote going to Navalnyi. This campaign split the radical nationalists: the Moscow Russkie movement supported Navalnyi (together with the national democrats), while the main St Petersburg leaders (Nikolai Bondarik, Dmitrii (Beshenyi) Evtushenko and Maksim Kalinichenko) shared the opinion of the majority of radical nationalists: one cannot vote for a 'liberal'. However, very few activists spoke out on either side.

Moreover, this distancing of the radical nationalists from the opposition basically coincided with the beginning of the anti-migrant campaign. That meant that activist fervour could now be deployed on 'home ground'. We have noted the attempts of the radical nationalists to attach themselves to spontaneous riots, and the great surge of 'raid initiatives' among the most diverse organisations, old and new. Radical nationalists have also conducted a range of meetings, for instance the 'Day of Russian Wrath', held on 13 April 2013 in ten towns – a record for this kind of new networked action. From July to September there were many meetings 'against ethnic criminality', often in the form of 'people's assemblies'. In other words they were not coordinated. They did not descend into rioting, but in recent years the very format of 'assemblies' would indicate that this is a possibility.

On 13 October the Russkie movement helped local residents organise a 'people's assembly' in the Biriulevo-Zapadnoe region of Moscow, which snowballed into the most politically significant public disturbance of the year. However, at least equally significant was the appeal by local radical nationalists to which local residents and, importantly, militant kindred spirits from the

Moscow-wide ultra-right youth sector responded. With the simultaneous participation of several hundred bellicose neo-Nazis and several thousand local inhabitants, OMON could not suppress the riots.

This turn of events strengthened hopes among Russian nationalists that they may seize the initiative from the weakened opposition movement and, if not actually have a revolution, then at least manage to enter the main political arena. In the week following 13 October, efforts were made in Moscow and St Petersburg to prolong the disturbances. Record numbers of people attended the 4 November 'Russian March' in 2013 – more than in any year since the event was established. The march also reached its furthest geographic spread, being held in forty-seven towns (although the most significant leap, from thirty-two to forty-five towns, had taken place one year earlier). In Moscow numbers were slightly higher than those attained in 2011,[23] and in St Petersburg the march turned into a pogrom in a market, with other attacks as well.

However, the impression of a stable rise in radical nationalist fervour proved deceptive. As noted, the stream of Kondopoga-like events suddenly dried up, and the public disorders in Arzamas in December were practically ignored by nationalists – although the curtailing of the anti-migrant campaign in the mass media should not have impacted upon them, in contrast to the broad mass of ordinary citizens. In fact, after 4 November 2013, all enthusiasm swiftly evaporated.

During the winter of 2013/14, meetings 'against ethnic criminality' were already fading away, and even the number of raids was beginning to fall. Not all traditional networked activities have been declining, however. Although in 2014 the 'Day of Heroes'[24] was held in just half as many towns (nine) as in 2013, 'Russian May Day' attracted about the same number of participants and was held in about the same number of towns as the year before. Still, on the whole, measured by the standards of recent years, radical nationalist political activity has been less marked since the end of 2013. And the 'Russian March' on 4 November 2014 gathered half as many participants in Moscow as in previous years, and it was perceived as a great failure. Why is this so?

To some extent, the explanation may lie in the simple fact that all activists have been very occupied with the events unfolding in Ukraine. Although the thesis that Russian nationalists were simply 'hypnotised by the screen' seems inadequate, the degree to which this holds true testifies to the less than impressive political quality of the movement.

Police pressure has also played a part. The arrest of Bondarik (and the earlier house arrest of Evtushenko) notably reduced the activity of radical nationalists in the more dynamic St Petersburg, where – in contrast to Moscow – the practice of combining political and violent action had become firmly established. Just how easily repression can control radical nationalist structures indicates how unprepared for effective action they actually are.

Thus, even in the favourable conditions of 2013 the radical nationalist movement demonstrated only very weak signs of growth. This had also been the case up to December 2011, when they clearly dominated the opposition; and in the period in which they participated in a wider social movement in 2012. Any growth has been primarily a matter of geographic spread. There has been almost no research on the makeup of activist groups in various towns across Russia, but it may be assumed that the 'Russian March' and 'Russian May Day' attract the same sorts of groups in the new towns as in the old. The radical nationalists have not managed to qualitatively expand support for their movement.[25] There are at least three reasons – other than pressure from the authorities – for this.

First, youth groups inclined towards violence still provide the grassroots and mass membership of the movement. It is specifically these groups, visibly characterising the 'Russian March', which remain the face of Russian nationalism in the eyes of the public. Statistically, there is good reason for this. In terms of style, this sort of political force is not compatible with the moderate ethno-xenophobic inclinations of the general public.

Second, the most successful radical nationalist methods thus far have been diverse types of 'Kondopogas', 'Manezhnaia riots' and 'Russian cleansing' – but such disturbances definitely do not generate public sympathy. Most people respond badly – or at least with suspicion – to the use of force in politics. And radical nationalists are less skilled in applying other methods.

Third, people prefer to trust the government or the organisations mandated by them to deal with the struggle against 'illegal migration', as with any other problem – and not 'amateur' groups, least of all groups in opposition to the government. For all the criticism of the authorities, the Russian public still relies on them. Of course, this third factor is not a perennial fixture; arguably, neither is the second. Moreover, changes can happen fairly swiftly, and they are always unexpected, so hope yet remains for the radical nationalist leaders.

Concluding remarks: The 'Ukrainian question' and the future of the radical nationalists

Considering the situation as of 2014, it seems highly likely that the attention of radical nationalists – like that of any politically active Russian citizen – has been focused the whole time on what is happening in Ukraine. Beginning with the confrontation on Hrushevskiy Street, Ukrainian events evoked nationalist hopes of a 'white revolution' in Russia: Maidan could be interpreted as a positive example, especially if the role of the Right Sector was exaggerated. Since then it has become clear that relations between the new authorities in Kyiv and the Ukrainian ultra-right still face many twists and turns. It is too early to say what will be made of all this in the Russian ultra-right camp.

The move from a phase of conflict involving opposition to the authorities to a phase of conflict along lines that may be interpreted as 'Ukrainian-Russian' in the Ukrainian crisis presented Russian nationalists with a serious dilemma. If the opposition sector of nationalists steadfastly supported Maidan, very serious disagreement was bound to arise. Here I will not even attempt to outline this debate (see Al'perovich 2014), but will focus briefly on the division among radical nationalists.

The 'Russian Spring' – the annexation of Crimea and the military actions against Kyiv taken in the Donbas region – garnered support from organisations such as the Russian All-National Union, Russian Imperial Movement, National-socialist Initiative and various smaller groups of the 'Black Hundreds' type, together with pro-Kremlin nationalists, the National Bolsheviks and the majority of national democrats. The classic 'imperial' paradigm, which basically does not recognise the existence of the Ukrainian nation, has been used by some (like the Russian Imperial Movement) in this context. Alternatively, an 'ethnic conflict' with Ukrainians may be emphasised. Either way, opposition activists have not stopped thinking of the Russian government as 'anti-Russian'. Consequently, they expect the 'Russian uprising' in the Donbas to activate a Russian 'national rebirth' in Russia.

However, many radical nationalist political leaders have spoken out against the 'Russian Spring'. This includes almost the entire leadership of the Russkie movement in Moscow and in St Petersburg, the neo-Nazi movement Restrukt!, as well as individual activists from movements and groups that otherwise support the 'Russian Spring'. This position is also based on denying or minimising the conflict between Ukrainians and Russians, and in general the distinction between them. These activists see the Ukrainian revolution as the first step in a general nationalistic revolution against the 'anti-Russian regime'. The clear majority of autonomous radical nationalists have adopted this position. Opponents of the 'Russian Spring' differ only on whether to support the Ukrainian side,[26] or to maintain a position of neutrality, seeing both sides as 'puppets of Zionism' or something of that sort.

To some extent, military as well as political differences are the result of these arguments. A fair number of nationalists have gone to fight on the separatist side, and some on the opposing Kyivan side. As yet the information available on the makeup of these fighting forces is too fragmentary to permit analysis of the impact that specific organisations are having on military action.[27] Various news reports make brief mention of many organisations, but it is usually impossible to discern whether these glimpses relate to individual initiatives or the active involvement of those organisations per se: it is not unusual for activists of organisations whose leaders clearly condemn participation to go and join the fighting.

Politically, what is important here is precisely institutional presence: at stake is who may capitalise politically on their war effort.

RADICAL NATIONALISTS: TRUE TILL DEATH?

Thus far, it seems to be decidedly less-prominent organisations that have dispatched warriors, such as Aleksandr Barshakov's dimly remembered Russian National Unity (participating as Barshakov's Guard) and the National Liberation Movement (*Natsional'no-osvoboditel'noe dvizhenie*) (NOD), led by United Russia deputy Evgenii Fedorov.[28] One thing is certain, however: the Russians fighting in Ukraine include people with very different viewpoints, and the majority of them are not connected with any sort of nationalist organisation. Even less is known about those who have left to fight on the Kyivan side. Neo-Nazis make up a significant proportion,[29] if not the majority, but very different types of people are also to be found there. When – and if – these fighters return to Russia, they may well play some sort of role in redirecting these highly diverse radical currents. Judging by the information available as of this writing, those groups and currents that currently dominate the radical nationalist sector will not gain anything from this process. Indeed, they may even lose out.

As a whole, Russian nationalists appear to be in a fairly awkward situation: depending on their positions on the 'Ukrainian question' they are either hanging on the tail of support for the course President Putin has set, or they must oppose the overwhelming patriotic majority, which is a scary and – most likely – unprofitable stance to take. This may also explain the drop in their activity. Most importantly, this situation seems set to last for some time yet – which suggests that, in terms of their influence on society, radical nationalists have a gloomy future ahead.

This does not mean, of course, that Russian nationalism has no future in Russia. Despite the current drop in support for its ideas and ethno-xenophobic prejudices, this level will probably soon rise again once the war in Donbas is over. And populists of the most diverse kinds will undoubtedly manipulate these prejudices, 'skimming the cream' from the discourses and even some practices developed by radical nationalists. However, today's radical nationalists themselves have already become superfluous in this respect.

The radical core, particularly the youth, has not disappeared, and may even have expanded – the Ukraine crisis and everything accompanying it having legitimised the use of force. However, recent years have shown that the most diverse groups of radical nationalists, from the most marginal to the almost respectable, are incapable of broadening their support base. They are simply competing with one another for the same people. The methods used to involve potential supporters – be it weightlifting, 'Russian runs' or other such gimmicks – have all proven ineffectual.

It would be a mistake to think that radical nationalists do not have enough prominent leaders. Their leaders are not bad at all, and manage to satisfy the demands of those groups that promoted them. What is lacking, then, is not 'supply' but 'demand' – not methods and leaders, but a new generation of grassroots activists. When a new grassroots emerges, as happened at the end of the 1990s and the early 2000s, it will doubtless promote new leaders.

Judging by the experience of recent years, the majority of today's leaders – from the famous heads of the Russkie movement to the leaders of local neo-Nazi gangs – have little chance of promoting their ideas more widely. They are also not going to change these ideas, which are firmly rooted in the Western tradition of 'White Power' and only partially in the Russian nationalist tradition. They will have to leave the stage (gradually or suddenly, depending on what happens), as did most of the 'old' Russian nationalist leaders of the 1990s. True, many of these older leaders have hung on to prominent positions to this day, and the generational change will not be total this time round either – but it may be that the notably lower intellectualism of the radical nationalist movement of the 2000s will not allow today's leaders to adapt to changes to the same extent as the previous generation.

Notes

1. This chapter was prepared during the summer of 2014 and early winter of 2015, in the heat of military hostilities; hence, it does not address the entire period of this war.
2. This chapter assumes reader familiarity with the main actors and circumstances of the Russian nationalist movement. For further information about many present-day organisations, see Kozhevnikova and Shekhovtsov (2009).

3. There are only two exceptions of note: Igor Artemov's Russian All-National Union (*Russkii obshchenatsional'nyi soiuz*) (RONS), which has managed to remain active and to play a significant role in the movement to this day; and Sergei Baburin's Russian All-People's Union (*Rossiiskii obshchenarodnyi soiuz*) (ROS), which at the beginning of the period under study regained an active role, thanks to an infusion of new forces. Its opposition tendencies may be considered moderate, however.
4. The chapter draws significantly on the reports prepared by my colleagues at the SOVA Center for Information and Analysis, and I am grateful to them for their analyses of a huge body of information. Galina Kozhevnikova was the main author of these reports until her death in 2010; since then Nataliia Iudina and Vera Alperovich have assumed that function. All reports may be accessed on the SOVA Center for Information and Analysis website, available at <http://www.sova-center.ru/racism-xenophobia/publications> (last accessed 1 March 2015), and are also published in the SOVA Center for Information and Analysis's annual collections, available at <http://www.sova-center.ru/books> (last accessed 1 March 2015). In this chapter I will confine myself to a few citations.
5. Detailed statistics on hate crime and related convictions may be found in the appendices to every major SOVA Center for Information and Analysis report. At the time of writing, the most recent is Al'perovich and Yudina (2014b).
6. The facts relating to violence are outlined only briefly here, as this analysis is based on SOVA Center for Information and Analysis reports and also on Verkhovsky (2014b), to which the reader is referred.
7. Jumping ahead a bit, I should add that this decline did not result in the emergence of a new, undisputed leader, although at the time Russian Image clearly had pretentions in this regard (see Kozhevnikova 2009).
8. According to figures from the Prosecutor General (available at <http://crimestat.ru/offenses_chart>, last accessed 1 April 2015), the number of crimes committed by non-citizens rose by 10 per cent in 2013, although it decreased before and after. The increase was even more marked in Moscow and St Petersburg: 36 per cent and 34 per cent, respectively. It seems clear that these figures reflect fluctuations in police practice and not in criminality.
9. All substantive incidents of this sort are described in SOVA Center for Information and Analysis annual reports.

10. At the time of writing, the most recent pogrom conducted specifically by young football fans took place in the Moscow region of Pushkino on 15 May 2014.
11. This relationship has been analysed by sociologist Aleksei Levinson (Levada Centre 2014c). For further details about this particular campaign, see Tolz and Harding (2015).
12. Law enforcement agencies have been investigating fewer and fewer incidents of violent racist crime, and more and more cases of hate propaganda, making racist violence once again less risky. This increasing distortion has been described in detail in Al'perovich and Yudina (2013, 2014a, 2014b).
13. Prior to this, Mangushev was coordinator of the Orthodox movement Supporters of St George! (*Georgievtsy!*), especially notorious for its unsuccessful efforts to attack gays. During the war in Donbas Bright Rus has been busy supplying 'humanitarian aid'.
14. Konstantinov was soon arrested on a murder charge, which most civil rights activists consider unfounded.
15. This veteran of the radical nationalist movement and member of the Opposition Coordination Council is charged with organising a provocation by means of inflicting bodily harm.
16. Before this, Khudiakov participated in the equally violent raids of the 'Youth anti-narcotics special forces' of the Young Russia movement. He was briefly arrested after a brawl during a raid on an immigrant hostel. Khudiakov was taking part in pro-Russian action in Donbas in the spring of 2014.
17. Data from a Romir survey of 1,000 respondents across Russia and 600 in Moscow in May 2013, at the request of the international academic project 'Nation-building, nationalism and the new "other" in today's Russia, NEORUSS'. It should be noted that there is significantly more xenophobia in Moscow than in Russia as a whole, and the gap between support for theoretical 'skinheads' and theoretical 'Cossacks' is even greater than the average.
18. Aid to 'prisoners on the right' is a rapidly developing field in need of serious scrutiny by researchers.
19. Ilia Goriachev and some other activists gave the investigators the testimony needed in the trial of Nikita Tikhonov and Evgeniia Khasis, and the publication of these protocols led to Russian Image being stonewalled in radical nationalist circles.
20. Although the level actually remained relatively stable from 2000 until 2012 (Levada Centre 2013c), the theme of 'interethnic con-

21. At the time, this group, a direct successor of Dmitrii Vasilev's National-patriotic Front Pamiat, appeared to be a typical militant youth group, if stylistically somewhat exotic. The leader of the Russian Liberation Front 'Pamiat' and several other people were later convicted to several years' imprisonment for criminal violence.
22. The sole exception was the February 2012 march through Iakimanka, with in the region of 800 to 900 nationalists. In many other cases they numbered significantly less than 500.
23. Counting all nationalist 'marches' on that day. In 2012 the 'Russian March' was notably weaker because the radical wing was unwilling to march together with leaders participating in the general protest movement.
24. The 'Day of Heroes', 1 March, is dedicated to the Pskov paratroopers who died in battle in Chechnya in 2000.
25. If we exclude the Navalniy phenomenon, it would appear that national democrats have not managed to either – but that is beyond the remit of my chapter.
26. See, for example, the site of the WotanJugend group, available at <http://wotanjugend.info> (last accessed 1 April).
27. Marlene Laruelle (2014c) has estimated the number of fighters despatched to Donbas by the nationalists at in the region of 100 to 200. The SOVA Center for Information and Analysis considers that there are more, even not taking Cossacks into account.
28. The National Liberation Movement is as yet little studied, but this movement is undoubtedly nationalist. Judging by its current activities, it may be seen as part of the radical wing, although it is impossible to call it part of the opposition (Strukova 2014).
29. There is a lot of journalistic evidence; see, for example, Nikulin (2014).

4
Russian ethnic nationalism and religion today

Anastasia Mitrofanova

This chapter examines the ideology and the political practice of Russian ethnic nationalists, exploring religio-ideological trends in contemporary Russian ethnic nationalism and assessing their potential. By Russian ethnic nationalists, I refer solely to those individual authors, parties and movements who hold the self-determination of Russians as an ethnic group as a central element of their ideology and political programme. Thus I do not deal here with political movements that are not nationalist but that borrow from the nationalists various popular ideas or political slogans at odds with the basic ideology of that party or movement.

Ethnic nationalists do not acknowledge that it is possible or necessary to create a civic nation that unites different ethnic and racial groups within Russia. For them, the Russian Federation is an alien state, dominated by a minority that oppresses the majority – akin to the South African system of apartheid. Nationalists often call Russia '*Rossiianiia*' or '*Erefiia*' ('RF-iia'), stressing that they are not patriots. For nationalists, the word '*rossiianin*', a citizen of the Russian Federation, as opposed to '*russkii*', an ethnic Russian, is an insult, and '*tozherossiianin*' ('also-a-Russian-citizen') is a scornful label for non-Russian ethnic groups.

Russian ethnic nationalism and religion in historical perspective

Ethnic nationalism is a relatively young ideology in Russia. Political thought in Russia has always focused on the relationship between the state and Orthodox Christianity. Until the beginning of the nineteenth century, the historical role of the Russian people was rarely questioned. As John Anderson notes, in the first quarter of the nineteenth century, Slavophiles were the first to focus more on the roots of religion in the 'national psyche' (2012: 209). Slavophiles barely distinguished the 'people' from the 'state': 'they all took the view that Orthodoxy was in some sense core to the very identity of Russians as a people and Russia as a state' (ibid.). At that time the Russian people were divided into social classes with differing legal status, so the foundations for ethnic nationalism had not yet been laid.[1] The idea of a civic nation, borrowed from the West, was unacceptable to conservatives, but was to become the hallmark of the liberal and social-democratic camp.

At the start of the twentieth century, the 'Black Hundreds' ideology emerged. This became a step on the way to ethnic nationalism, since the Black Hundreds sought the formation of a Russian state, rather than imperial expansion (Stepanov 1992). However, the Black Hundreds were still closely linked with the traditions of Russian conservatism, which was state-centred and religious, whereas ethnic nationalists severed the connection between the Russian people and the Russian state, admitting the possibility of personally opposing the state. This kind of Russian ethnic nationalism emerged only after the revolution of 1917. It developed in the diaspora and was a part of the dissident movement in the USSR, but only after the beginning of *perestroika* was it possible to propagate ethnic nationalism openly.

In the final years of the USSR and immediately after its collapse, various conglomerates took shape that united people of diverse ideological orientations under the common name of 'Russian nationalists'. Important here were the Pamiat Society, which arose at the end of the 1980s, and Russian National Unity (RNE). Almost all long-standing members of today's nationalist movement began their activities either in Pamiat or in RNE (the RNE leadership also emerged from Pamiat). Then even larger super-conglomerates of 'red-whites' (the Russian National Council under General Aleksandr Sterligov and the National Salvation Front) emerged in the early 1990s, joined by nationalists, imperialist patriots and Soviet patriots, giving rise to the name 'national patriots'. People with incompatible ideological positions were united in their hostility to the Russian authorities and their desire for regime change. These national patriots represented not so much a set of organisations as a milieu consisting of individuals and small groups, connected by a network in virtual and real space (for information on some of these individuals and groups, see Verkhovsky and Kozhevnikova 2009).

Sergei Lebedev, a scholar and also a participant in the national patriotic movement of the 1990s (he was a member of the Russian National Council), writes that at that time 'the defence of Orthodoxy' was one of the shared characteristics common to all national patriots, even atheists (Lebedev 2007: 472). Alexander Verkhovsky (2007a: 11) also observes the 'obligatory' presence of Orthodoxy in the political doctrines of 'serious nationalists', at least until after the turn of the millennium. This was due partly to the legacy of conservative thought of the past, and partly to the mass public interest in Orthodoxy in the first post-Soviet decade. The profusion of neophytes with high expectations created the illusion among nationalist ideologues that identification with Orthodoxy in particular would help to attract more supporters. Pamiat, for whom Orthodoxy was an ideological prop, played a role in this. This was the first nationalist organisation to gain Russia-wide media coverage, although it was consistently depicted in a negative light. For a long time new organisations, whether consciously or not, copied the ideology of Pamiat, including their emphatic adherence to Orthodoxy. Some of the nationalists liked the fact that by doing so they were maintaining a link with the Russian conservative tradition. Others, conversely, wanted to be more contemporary, turning to the experience of the European right-wing.

Soon after the turn of the millennium, 'true' Russian nationalists began to demarcate themselves from those in the national patriotic sphere more appropriately called 'statists' or 'patriots', using nationalist rhetoric. The 'true' nationalists seek an ethnically homogenous state of Russian people: they do not want to preserve the Russian Federation, still less to resurrect the Soviet Union or the Russian Empire. Patriots, by contrast, are ready to sacrifice the 'special position' of the Russian majority in the name of preserving and increasing the territory of the state. The transformation of the rhetoric, and in part also the nature, of the ruling regime led the patriots to adopt a natural – for them – position of supporting the government, which in their eyes now appeared suitably (if not entirely) Russian and national. Among the nationalists, one section was busy consolidating the citizens of Russia, and became civic nationalists, extremely loyal to the authorities. 'True' nationalists, in contrast, strengthened their opposition to the regime, which they hitherto had deemed weak and unworthy of serious opposition.

Ethnic nationalists had been a minority among the broad array of 'national patriots' in the 1990s. Lebedev (2007: 453, 450) refers to them as 'low-profile', 'outsiders in the national patriotic movement' and even 'a ghetto'. The process of demarcation created the illusion among nationalists themselves that a completely new ideology now had appeared.

The political demarcation between nationalists and patriots was accompanied by a religious demarcation. Statist patriots preserved their traditional orientation towards Orthodoxy. Ethnic nationalists split into three basic groups, to be examined separately in detail below: (1) Orthodox nationalists, who may belong to the Russian Orthodox Church or to uncanonical religious organisations; (2) contemporary Slavic pagans (neopagans); and (3) secularists: those who consider religious questions unimportant and do not advertise their religious affiliation (if they have one).

Orthodox Christianity and Russian nationalism

Orthodox organisations and activist writers who publicly proclaim their adherence to nationalism comprise a discrete section of the nationalist movement. Among the organisations, the most important are the Union of Russian People and various similarly named structures that appeared as a result of the splintering of this organisation as well as the Union of Orthodox Banner-bearers; among activists Konstantin Dushenov, editor of the newspaper *Rus Pravoslavnaia* (Orthodox Rus), the politicians Iurii Ekishev, Boris Mironov (and his wife Tatiana) and Andrei Saveliev, and the publicist Mikhail Nazarov. The position of Orthodox nationalists in the nationalist sphere has always been difficult and ambiguous, and their ideological principles indistinct.

It is not Orthodox doctrine that presents nationalists with the greatest difficulty, since they freely adapt it according to their aims, but the necessity of belonging to the Church and participating in liturgical life. Since this necessity is spelt out in the Creed and in Holy Scripture, Orthodox nationalists cannot avoid the 'Church issue'. The average person can call him or herself Orthodox without partaking of the sacraments of the Church, but Orthodox nationalists study their ideology, they read and think, and as a result are aware that identifying oneself as an Orthodox Christian means having a life within the Church. The main problem for Russian nationalists is their critical and even hostile attitude to the Orthodox Church that ministers to the area in which they live.

In order to understand the attitude of Orthodox nationalists towards the Russian Orthodox Church, we must examine the official ecclesiastical position on issues that concern nationalists, relating to the people, the state and the Church.

THE RUSSIAN CHURCH IN THE RUSSIAN WORLD

The official position of the Church is not the same as the position adopted by its individual or group members, clerical and lay.[2] All possible ideological tendencies, from complete universalism (*uranopolitizm*)[3] to racist ethnic nationalism, are unofficially represented. None of these tendencies is the official one. The position of the Church is reflected in the articles and speeches of the Primate (the Patriarch of Moscow and All Rus), representatives of synodal departments and the other governing bodies that guide the Church.

Following the 1917 revolution, groups that insisted on separating the concept of the Russian (*rossiiskoe*) state from that of the Russian (*russkii*) people first appeared in the Church: among members of the 'catacomb church' (True Orthodox Christians) and of the Church Abroad. The ecclesiastical majority remained loyal to the traditional approach of Russian conservative thought, asserting that there was an unbreakable link between people and state. That said, the former link between the Church and state established in the synodal period was not, of course, restored.

With the collapse of the USSR, it became necessary for the Russian Orthodox Church to rethink the issue of patriotism. In the 'people or state' conundrum the Church did not side unilaterally with the state. The Church did not consider it appropriate to 'shrink' to the boundaries of the Russian Federation and function as an ideological support to this state. Civic nationalism is therefore not characteristic of the Church, which is patriotic but not inclined to support any state action. This is reflected in the Bases of the Social Concept of the Russian Orthodox Church, where, at least in theory the possibility of civil disobedience is recognised.[4]

The state would like to use the Church to legitimise its politics and to strengthen the civic nation. At the same time, it has not tried to take any significant steps towards meeting the needs of the Church.[5] The Church insists on having its own agenda, and although it acts with caution, instances of opposition between the Church and the state have multiplied in the post-Soviet period. One of these concerns the fate of the Orthodox parishes of Abkhazia and South Ossetia. Even though Moscow recognised the independence of the two republics, the Russian Orthodox Church continues to insist that they are located on the canonical territory of the Georgian Church; supplications by clerics and laity have not changed this position (Matsuzato 2009, 2010). Parishes in Crimea have likewise remained under the jurisdiction of the Ukrainian Orthodox Church of the Moscow Patriarchate, although this region has now been included in the Russian Federation. In terms of domestic politics, we may recall the Church's struggle for the 'Fundamentals of Orthodox culture' as a mandatory school subject: the state eventually decided to introduce a course on the 'Fundamentals of religious cultures and secular ethics', in which the 'Fundamentals of Orthodox culture' is one of five options that parents (not the school) may choose from.

The independence of the Church from the state does not mean that its official position has become ethnic Russian nationalism. Names such as the Russian (*Russkaia*) Orthodox Church and the World Russian (*Russkii*) People's Council can be misleading,[6] as they suggest an ethnic narrowness that is alien to Orthodox Christianity. In reality, only the Moscow and Constantinople Patriarchates do not aspire to create ethnic parishes abroad – the remaining local Churches usually minister to ethnic diasporas. Only these patriarchates conduct missionary activity beyond the boundaries of the historical Orthodox realm: in China, Thailand, Pakistan and elsewhere. The ethnic diversity of the Russian Church grows with the opening of new parishes: local residents unconnected with Russian culture become parishioners.

In contrast to the ethnic nationalists, the Russian Orthodox Church does not consider immigrants from other cultures a threat to the Russian people. On 19 April 2013, the Church signed a cooperation agreement with the Federal Migration Service and went on to create a diocesan system for facilitating linguistic and cultural adaptation of migrant workers. As official spokespersons have announced more than once, this work with immigrants is not a missionary effort to bring them to Orthodoxy[7] – although individual clerics and lay members may, of course, insist on the need to catechise immigrants.

Despite the fact that the Church through its activity thus has proven its negative attitude to ethnic nationalism, the use of the phrase 'the Russian world' (*russkii mir*) can cause confusion if interpreted as an indicator if not of ethnic, then of 'imperial', ecclesiastical nationalism. Theoretically the concept of 'the Russian world' allows such a possibility, but the Church uses this phrase in its own way, and over the past few years it has imbued 'the Russian world' with increasingly broad content.

Until 2009, the Church did not use the concept 'the Russian world'. In a 2008 article by Father Georgii Riabykh (the later Abbot Filipp Riabykh; see below), ideas of 'civilisational diversity', of a 'multi-polar world' and 'civilisational originality' are evoked in a discussion of Orthodox civilisation (Riabykh 2008:

25). Apparently on the basis of similar publications, Verkhovsky came to the conclusion that 'beyond the territory of the USSR the Russian Orthodox Church claims a flock which is exclusively Russian in cultural and ethnic terms', and that the ecclesiastical understanding of unique and segregated civilisations is close to that of Samuel Huntington (Verkhovsky 2007b: 178, 180). Father Georgii Riabykh (2008: 30) cites not ecclesiastical but state circles on the concept of 'the Russian world', the aim of which is to unify the Russian-speaking diaspora. The diaspora does indeed look like a closed and isolated version of an Orthodox civilisation. However, the Church swiftly rejected this approach, perhaps because the unity of Orthodox civilisation is up for debate (Mitrofanova 2004).

Patriarch Kirill first began talking about 'the Russian world' from an ecclesiastical perspective on 3 November 2009, at the Third Assembly of the Russian World, where he suggested the widest possible interpretation of all of the concepts raised – the 'Russian Church' (*russkaia tserkov'*), the 'Russian culture' (*russkaia kul'tura*), even 'the Russian language'. Abbot Filipp (Riabykh),[8] elaborating on the Patriarch's position, stressed that the debate was not about Russian ethnic identity (*etnos*) but about the spiritual-cultural tradition that every local church creates. According to Abbot Filipp, tradition suggests shared spiritual centres, shared shrines and specific traits in ecclesiastical life – for example, the Old Style calendar that unites people belonging to 'different ethnic and national cultures' – and that the sources of such tradition may be located outside of Russia (for example, the Kyivan Caves Monastery) (quoted by Sokolov 2010). 'With such an understanding of the Russian world, we depart from a narrow ethnic perception of the Russian Church itself, too. In this light the Russian Church is the Church of the multinational Russian world, and not of the Russian ethnic group', he explained (ibid).

Confirming the unacceptability of ethnic nationalism, Patriarch Kirill did not confine himself to praising the 'unique *russkaia* civilisation' and did not call for its isolation. He declared:

> We need to be even more clearly aware of the uniqueness of the Russian way of life and to reproduce it not only in countries where

Russian culture dominates, but to testify to it far beyond its boundaries, especially in conditions of contemporary human civilisation's spiritual and moral crisis. (*Ofitsial'nyi sait Moskovskogo patriarkhata* 2009)

Patriarch Kirill's suggestion that the Russian way of life be presented (and even reproduced) worldwide clearly goes beyond Huntington's theory of original and exclusive civilisations that are unable to comprehend one another. In ecclesiastical understanding, Russian civilisation is valuable not so much because of its uniqueness as because its values and principles are deemed to be universal, and can be disseminated beyond the realms of 'the Russian world'. If uniqueness were the only issue at stake, one may agree with the phrase 'civilisational nationalism', suggested by Emil Pain (2007; see also Verkhovsky 2014c: 74). However, the ecclesiastical approach is not nationalist, but universal. Nationalism – ethnic or civic – suggests exclusivity, a closed nature, the maintenance of strict boundaries between 'us' and 'them'. One can hardly talk about 'nationalism' when the values of a specific civilisation are freely promoted to more or less the entire rest of the world.

The universalism of the ecclesiastical approach emerged even more clearly during Patriarch Kirill's speech at the World Russian People's Council in 2013. Despite a preliminary remark about the uniqueness of the Russian civilisation, the Patriarch stressed that 'the value of any civilisation lies in what it brings to humanity ... As a country and a civilisation, Russia has something to offer the world' (*Ofitsial'nyi sait Moskovskogo patriarkhata* 2013). Here the universal cultural mission of Russian civilisation is clearly in harmony with the universal mission of the Church to save humanity – that would be impossible if the Church accepted Huntington's theory of isolated and hostile civilisations.

Thus, on the official level the Russian Orthodox Church does not promote nationalist concepts – neither ethnic, nor imperial, nor civilisational. The Church does not ethnicise, but universalises, going beyond – theoretically and practically – not only the borders of the Russian Federation but also the borders of its canonical territory. Since the idea of 'the Russian world' is not of ecclesiastical origin, it may also be that, with time, the Church will stop using this phrase and develop another that better reflects its universal approach.

Hence, nationalists – ethnic and civic – can be only marginal within the Church. Nevertheless, there is a layer of nationalists for whom affiliation to Orthodoxy is important, for personal reasons. These individuals develop a variety of strategies that allow them to unite two apparently incompatible outlooks on the world. The simplest strategy is to join various uncanonical Orthodox jurisdictions (or to create such jurisdictions) where it is easier to hold non-standard opinions. More complex strategies involve the endurance of separate nationalists and even whole groups as members of the Russian Orthodox Church. Before turning to each of these variants, let us examine the shared ideological foundations of Orthodox nationalism (Mitrofanova 2005; Verkhovsky 2005a, 2005b).

The ideology of Orthodox nationalism: A general overview

Orthodox nationalists trace their ideological biography to the works of Metropolitan Ioann (Snychev) of St Petersburg and Ladoga. From 1992 to 1995 Konstantin Dushenov – the best-known representative of Orthodox nationalism, a retired submarine officer and one of the original leaders of the Union of Orthodox Brotherhoods – worked as his aide (according to Dushenov, as press secretary).

A starting point for Orthodox nationalism is its rejection of the contemporary world, which is perceived as having abandoned God and fallen under the sway of the Antichrist. Orthodox nationalists hold that the special mission of Russia and the Russian people is the preservation of the Orthodox enclave in a decaying world. The Russian people and their state (not any Russian state, but specifically a state of the Russian people) are the *katechon*, 'the one who withholds', keeping back the collapse of the world and the establishment of the rule of the Antichrist (see Dushenov 2006).

There is an idea about the Russians as a chosen people, of the uniqueness of their fate. The Russian people acquire special worth not only as the preserver of the true faith, but in and of itself, independently of formal confession of faith. 'Russia and the Russian people are a sort of holy ark, in which God's Revelation is preserved', Dushenov declared (*Portal-Credo.ru* 2005). 'Russian' and 'Orthodox' are equivalent concepts for nationalists. Dushenov came to the conclusion that

> the doctrine of Russian Orthodox nationalism is an inalienable part of the religious doctrine of the Church. Every Christian is now simply obliged to be a Russian Orthodox nationalist. And the enemies of this doctrine are the enemies of the Mother Church and our Lord Jesus Christ. (Dushenov 2006)

Orthodox nationalists also tend to be pro-monarchist. A phenomenon has emerged in their midst that their opponents contemptuously refer to as '*tsarebozhnichestvo*' – worshipping the tsar in place of Christ (Orthodox nationalists themselves consider this epithet insulting, and do not use it). The source of this concept is the nationalist idea of the Russian people's collective guilt for the sin of regicide: the Russian people are not only God's chosen people, but also a great sinner nation. The sins of the Russian people were on such a terrible, cosmic scale that they could be redeemed only by the voluntary, sacrificial death of Nikolai II and his family.

The tsar and his family are indeed venerated as saints by the entire Russian Orthodox Church. But the Church considers the forms of veneration that have developed among Orthodox nationalists uncanonical, and even heretical. The latter paint uncanonical icons of Saint Tsar Nikolai, depicting him with a halo that contains the form of a cross, like Christ (Bodin 2009). The nationalists have also developed their own version of eschatology. They hold that, through repentance, Russia will receive a new tsar, who will conquer the Antichrist and prevent him holding sway over Russia (see Zemtsov 2012). The Orthodox nationalist ritual of 'the whole nation's repentance' – in other words, the repentance of the Russian people for the sin of regicide – has become widely known. Group repentance is conducted with diverse participants and in various places. Particularly well-known is the 'rite of repentance of the whole nation', conducted at the monument to Tsar Nikolai in the village of Taininskoe in the Moscow region.[9] A similar ritual is also conducted each year in Nizhnii Novgorod, where Prince Dmitrii Pozharskii and the merchant Kuzma Minin levied their militia against the Polish invaders in the early seventeenth century.

Most Orthodox nationalists share these ideological directions to a greater or lesser extent. These directions do not accord with, or accord poorly with, Orthodox doctrine and the official position of the Church, which makes life within the Russian Orthodox Church problematic for the nationalists. Nevertheless, the Church has been relatively lenient towards them, although their views and activities (especially the introduction of uncanonical icons and rituals) have attracted criticism from the hierarchy and ecclesiastical press. By contrast, nationalists themselves are often hostile towards the 'official church'. Their negative views of the Russian Orthodox Church are not just a result of the absence of indicators of ethnic nationalism in the Church's stance, but also because of its collaboration with the ruling regime. Orthodox nationalists – like all nationalists – see the secular authorities in Russia as being ranged against the Russian people and Orthodoxy (as 'godless', and a 'power not from God'). In reality it is almost impossible for an Orthodox believer to be an implacable opponent of a governing regime: the requirement to obey the authorities is set out in Holy Scripture (for example, Romans 13: 3–4). However, the catacomb milieu, with its complete rejection of all secular authority and weakened liturgical life, had an enormous influence on Orthodox nationalists in the early 1990s, and continues to have so (see Beglov 2014). There is nothing surprising in the fact that Orthodox nationalists often do not want to be members of the Russian Orthodox Church, or split off from the Church at some point in their lives.

ORTHODOX NATIONALISTS OF ALTERNATIVE JURISDICTIONS

Until the reunification of the Russian Orthodox Church and the Russian Orthodox Church Abroad (ROCA) in 2007, Orthodox nationalists generally aligned themselves with ROCA communities. This allowed them to remain within an apparently canonical church and simultaneously to avoid cooperating with the Russian authorities. After the reunification of the churches, uncanonical structures that did not want to be reconciled with the 'Soviet' Church and split away from the ROCA became popular with nationalists.

One example is the 'Russian (*Rossiiskaia*) Orthodox Church' (RosOC), which appeared in 2006. Iurii Ekishev, a well-known nationalist politician from Syktyvkar, had been a member of this community since about 1998, when it was still part of ROCA. Previously he had been a parishioner of the Russian Orthodox Church, but had left this because of its cooperation with the 'godless authorities' and its reluctance to call for an armed uprising (Kuzmin 2011: 257). Ekishev's successor as head of the nationalists in the Komi Republic, Aleksei Kolegov, is proud of the fact that he occasionally cooperates with the Syktyvkar diocese of the Russian Orthodox Church, but he considers its priests unable to motivate people to protect Orthodoxy. He holds a higher opinion of the RosOC priests Ekishev has introduced him to:

> [young people] like the fact that they [the RosOC priests] say: we have to protect ourselves. And these photographs there: a priest bearing arms. That's normal for them. They all have weapons, they have all possible kinds of sports activities ... They are clearly different from the Moscow Patriarchate. If we could only show this sort of priests on television ... But instead we show a priest sitting by the fire, drinking tea.[10]

It has also been reported in the media (although this is currently impossible to verify) that Colonel Vladimir Kvachkov of the People's Militia of Minin and Pozharskii has joined the RosOC (Chelnokov 2011).[11] Kvachkov's deputy in the People's Militia was Ekishev; after Colonel Kvachkov was arrested for the second time in 2010, Ekishev remained the sole leader of the People's Militia. According to the *New Times*, while in prison Kvachkov announced, 'I transferred to the jurisdiction of the RosOC and took communion there' (*Newsland.com* 2011).

Another jurisdiction that emerged as a result of splits in the ROCA is the ROCA-A led by Bishop Agafangel (Pashkovskii) and with its centre in Odessa. Orthodox nationalist Mikhail Nazarov was a member of this jurisdiction. The well-known publicist Egor Kholmogorov, who calls himself 'a Russian nationalist and an Orthodox fundamentalist', at one time belonged to another splinter group emerging from ROCA, the Russian (*Rossiiskaia*) Orthodox Autonomous Church (ROAC), which has its centre in Suzdal. At the time of this writing, however, Kholmogorov has returned to the Russian Orthodox Church (see also Kholmogorov 2008).

Other than ROCA splinter groups, nationalists may join the Russian Old Believers and the Old Style jurisdictions of other local churches that reject cooperation with the authorities. In extreme circumstances, there remains the possibility of independently creating an uncanonical structure. Bishop Diomid (Dziuban) of Anadyr and Chukotka – the author of several open letters accusing the hierarchy of the Church, and even Patriarch Aleksii himself, of heresy and cooperation with an anti-people regime – was defrocked in 2008 by the Russian Orthodox Church. After his dismissal Diomid created a virtual structure, 'the Most Holy Governing Synod', which a section of the Orthodox nationalists joined. It is worth noting that in his open letters Diomid did not articulate any sort of nationalist ideas: in other words, what nationalists find attractive is probably his implacable hostility to the 'official church'. Nationalists themselves deduced from Diomid's phrases about the 'anti-people regime' that he was denouncing 'non-Russian' authorities. Schema-priest-monk Rafail (Berestov), to whom we will return to below, swiftly spoke out in support of Diomid on the grounds that 'the government of Russia is not Russian. It does not follow a Russian ideology' (Rafail [Berestov, R.] 2008).

ORTHODOX NATIONALISTS IN THE RUSSIAN ORTHODOX CHURCH

The Orthodox nationalists who remain in the Russian Orthodox Church, doomed to the difficult combination of belonging to the Church and continuously criticising her actions, are bordering on schism. Aleksandr Zhuchkovskii, for instance, who writes in the journal *Voprosy natsionalizma* (Questions of Nationalism), stresses that 'I am Orthodox by confession, I am a member of the Russian Orthodox Church' (Zhuchkovskii 2014: 33). At the same time, the position of the Church on the 'Russian question' does not suit him:

> Members of the Russian Orthodox Church should be in the first ranks of the Russian March, and in discussions with the authorities the ecclesiastical leadership should be strict lobbyists for the introduction of a visa regime with the countries that send migrants alien to our culture and religion. Instead, unfortunately, we observe the contrary. (Zhuchkovskii 2014: 42)

Before his arrest in 2010, Dushenov was an especially ambiguous figure, disseminating openly anti-Church materials while remaining a member of the Church. This bewildered even those individuals who shared the views of Orthodox nationalism, such as Leonid Simonovich-Nikshich:

> I don't entirely understand Konstantin Dushenov. His newspaper [*Rus Pravoslavnaia*] often speaks from a theoretical position which Karl Marx founded and considered the most important during his lifetime. This thesis is called: criticism of everything that exists. And so that is how it turns out. He criticises absolutely everything and everybody. Why? What sort of criticism? Not necessary criticism, but creative activity and help to the weak. As it is said, 'and mercy to the fallen is called for', as one not entirely stupid person wrote. But where is this mercy? Not mercy, but some sort of awfulness. We attack everyone and everyone is bad. And what sort of people are we, then?[12]

Simonovich-Nikshich stressed that the Union of Orthodox Banner-bearers, of which he is the leader, belongs to the Church:

I say clearly to you: we are not *edinovertsy* [an Old Believer group in communion with the Moscow Patriarchate], not Old Believers, not catacomb Christians, not True Orthodox Church, not Church Abroad, neither those nor any others of their huge number of offshoots. We are the Russian Orthodox Church of the Moscow Patriarchate, headed by the Most Holy Patriarch Kirill.[13]

Due to the specific administrative structure of the Church, which allows individual parishes considerable independence, it is possible to be an adherent of nationalism and simultaneously a member of the Russian Orthodox Church. An Orthodox believer who is inclined towards nationalism can find a parish where his views will be considered dogmatically acceptable (although this may mean he will need to travel a great distance to participate in the liturgical life of this parish), and a group of Orthodox nationalists can create such a parish.

The above-mentioned 'tsar-worshippers' (*tsarebozhniki*), for example, created a parish around the priest Roman Zelenskii, who, until he was dismissed in 2008, served in Leningrad oblast and ministered to several nationalist monarchist organisations such as the Society of Zealots for the Glorification of the Royal Martyrs. Father Roman's parishioners were (and perhaps remain) notable figures of Orthodox nationalism – such as the singer Zhanna Bichevskaia and her husband, the poet and composer Gennadii Ponomarev. Before he was dismissed, Father Roman conducted the liturgy according to the pre-revolutionary service book, including prayers for the Emperor, and during the Prothesis he would cut a piece from the offertory bread for the Tsar – practices not in use in the contemporary Orthodox Church.[14]

Parishes may also be more abstract, when believers are 'spiritually fed' by some cleric at a distance, reading his publications on the Internet or frequenting mass meetings (not church services). There is a number of politically active 'wandering clerics', who are not registered with any particular church or monastery, and who are sometimes without clear jurisdiction. They write books and articles, and organise meetings with their virtual flock. Notable here is schema-priest-monk Rafail (Berestov), brother of the famed and highly respected cleric, medical doctor and philanthropist Abbot Anatolii (Berestov). Father Rafail speaks out against the church hierarchs extremely harshly, considering them 'riddled with heresies' (*Novorossiia* 2010). Despite his advanced years (he was born in 1932), he travels around the world meeting with believers. Such practices allow Orthodox nationalists to remain within the Russian Orthodox Church, despite not trusting its hierarchy and holding dogmatic ideas that are not Church-approved.

Elements of nationalism existed in the ideology of many Orthodox political organisations and activist writers in the 1990s. However, after two significant events – the defrocking of Bishop Diomid in 2008 and the sentencing of Dushenov in 2010 under Criminal Code Article 282 Part 2 (incitement to hatred and enmity on the grounds of nationality, origin or religion), nationalism has been reduced to a marginal ideological tendency in the Orthodox sphere. The majority of Orthodox believers are aware that nationalism leads one into opposition with the Church and into conflict with the authorities. Few Orthodox nationalist organisations have survived until today, and the majority of visible Orthodox nationalists have either moved into the camp of 'patriots' (Kholmogorov, Dushenov), or are no longer Orthodox (Aleksei Shiropaev). Verkhovsky notes that toward the middle of first decade of the new millennium, the official position of the Russian Orthodox Church became closer to that of Orthodox civil society movements (that is, as one can deduce from his text, to *nationalist* movements), but explains this as a result of the hierarchy's inclination towards the ideology of these movements (Verkhovsky 2007b: 173). In my opinion, the reverse is the case: the views of one-time radical nationalists have grown closer to the official position of the Church, at least on the most important questions. Today, Orthodox nationalists represent an obsolete, archaic element of the nationalist movement, left over from the early 1990s. Many concepts that have been abandoned by contemporary Russian nationalism – anti-Semitism, for example – are retained in the ideology of Orthodox nationalism.

Pagans

The neopagan tendency has existed in Russian nationalism at least since the 1970s, but for a long time was openly propagated only by individual, marginal figures.[15] In the 1990s pagans were represented by isolated groupings of like-minded people, who had neither organisational structures nor media access. Operating within these networks were well-known nationalist ideologists and activists who either did not belong to any of the groups or moved between them, like the artist Aleksei Shiropaev and the publisher Viktor Korchagin. After the turn of the millennium, a pagan cluster formed around the Russkaia Pravda publishing group, including Aleksandr Aratov, Vladimir Istarkhov and Vladimir Avdeev. The wider pagan milieu now includes individuals as well as organisations such as Vadim Kazakov's Union of Slavic Communities of the Slavic Native Faith.

Most (but not all) pagans prefer to define their religion as a 'native' faith, and themselves as 'native believers' (*rodnovery*). In order to qualify as a community of native believers (specifically, in order to join Kazakov's Union of Slavic Communities of the Slavic Native Faith) a group must have no less than seven members with Slavic names, a pagan priest and a place for feasts, and conduct no less than four feast ceremonies a year (*Opredelenie* ... 2012). The Internet is the main means for establishing links between pagan organisations. These non-virtual, politicised organisations are often paramilitary in nature, offering or facilitating instruction in the martial arts, use of firearms and sports training. Many of them are formed around Slavic-Goritsa martial clubs (for example, the Sviatogor Centre of Old Russian Warfare and Military Culture in Kaluga, the Trigora Club in Petersburg and the Svarog and Rus Clubs in Moscow).

A basic problem for Russian native believers is that they have no living pagan tradition to lean on. Their leaders acknowledge that what they see as the Russian national religion seriously suffered under a thousand years of Christianity, so most of it has to be 'reconstructed' or created anew. Theorists cite the awakened memory of the ancient sorcerers (*volkhvy*) as a source of knowledge about indigenous Russian religion. One elder of Russian paganism, Dobroslav (Aleksei Dobrovolskii), named the 'revelations of Mother Nature herself and inherited memory' as a source, for example (Dobroslav 2010: 78). Moreover, much of the theory and practice of pagans is taken from Orthodoxy, with appropriate changes. Orthodox publications, for example, are issued with the blessing of bishops, while the neopagan newspaper *Russkaia Pravda* comes out 'with the blessing of Magus Ratebor of the Holy Rus'. The popular theory that there is one 'Vedic religion' for all pagans (Istarkhov 1999: 10) is also reminiscent of Orthodox Christianity, where the autocephalous churches make up the Universal Church. Noting the pagans' paradoxical proclivity for Church Slavonic, archaic scripts and the like, Andrei Beskov writes that 'a game on grounds which are foreign to them and native to the Russian Orthodox Church clearly cannot lead to success for the neopagans' (2014: 20).

In the absence of a single tradition, each pagan group may have its own worldview and rituals, since the communities are relatively isolated from one another. In this chapter I am not concerned with the religious life of all neopagans in Russia today, but with that sector of the nationalist movement that sees public adherence to paganism an integral part of their ideology. These nationalists – occasionally for utilitarian reasons – hold that paganism is the best religion for the Russian people because it can allow them to find strength, to protect themselves from 'foreigners' and to create their own state. Contemporary paganism attracts those nationalists who consider Christianity to be the religion of the weak. In his popular book *The Blow of the Russian Gods*, pagan theoretician Vladimir Istarkhov writes: 'Russian ... paganism, in contrast to Christianity, raised proud, brave, life-celebrating, strong in spirit, independent personalities, people of honour and dignity' (Istarkhov 1999: 190).

Ultimately, it is not important how specific nationalists practise paganism, or indeed whether they practise it at all. It is equally unimportant how sincerely they believe in pagan doctrines, since for nationalists paganism is part of ideology. Beskov proposes distinguishing 'ultranationalists, using pagan symbols only for decoration', that is, to attract the attention of potential participants or the mass media, from 'spiritual individuals, preoccupied with spiritual searching' (2014: 16). One is, however, unlikely to find such clear-cut 'ideal types' in practice: a 'spiritual individual' and a nationalist may coexist in one person.

Neopaganism is not only a political movement, but also a relatively insular sub-culture, with its own language, dress code and rules of behaviour. Native believers strive to use 'Slavic' names of the month in place of Latin ones (*stuzhen'* instead of January, *liuten'* instead of February), for example, or to replace foreign words with 'Slavic' equivalents (*svetopisi* instead of *fotografii*, *izvedy* instead of *interv'iu*). As a rule, native believers undergo a kind of 'baptism' and adopt 'pagan names' – Aratov took Ogneved (from *ogon'*, fire), for example. Radicals insist that native believers must always wear Slavic tunics and head-bands. Appropriate shirts can be bought on neopagan websites, or a pattern downloaded for sewing at home. However, most neopagans wear special clothes only for religious feasts, and politicised neopagans are less likely to dress in such clothing. Concerned with 'respectability', leaders of political movements wear normal shirts and ties. Vladimir Avdeev, for example, explains:

> I have undergone pagan initiation, I have a sacred pagan name. I have all of this. But I do not play these games, I do not run around with a little ribbon round my forehead. I go around in a suit and tie like a normal European person. (Belov 2005)

We should also bear in mind that not everyone can afford to dress in accordance with the specific demands of this sub-culture.

In Russian nationalism the pagan sector is not so much marginalised as closed off. The pool of potential neophytes is probably almost exhausted and neopagan organisations are unlikely to grow significantly. The native believer sub-culture (with costumes, pagan names, sacrifices and so forth) most likely scares off new recruits to the nationalist movement, so nationalist leaders who strive for mass participation prefer not to advertise their affiliations with native belief. Many pagans also emphasise that they are not opposed to the secular state, and that paganism in particular 'can exist and develop perfectly well in a secular society' (Valkovich 2014: 106). Thus, there seems to be no insurmountable wall between pagans and secularists (see below). As for relations between pagans and Orthodox nationalists, however, these are significantly worse than in the early 1990s, although not everywhere.

Secularists

There were practically no secular Russian ethnonationalists until about a decade ago. Nationalism indicated religiosity – either Orthodoxy (according to tradition), or paganism, which functioned as 'anti-Orthodoxy'. Religious arguments were a regular feature of nationalist organisations and often led to schisms. Observing this, some nationalist leaders stopped drawing attention to religious questions and talking openly about their personal religious affiliation. The designation of a given section of the nationalist movement as 'secularists' does not mean that its adherents do not have a personal religious faith and/or do not practise any religion; personally they may be practising or non-practising adherents of a religion, generally Orthodox Christianity or native beliefs. It is rather that, for secularist nationalists, religion is not an important issue worth mentioning in ideological and political documents.

One of the first secular nationalist organisations was the Slavic Community of St Petersburg, led by Roman Perin. In an interview, Perin explained the reasons for his then-innovative approach to creating the community thus:

> We have an Orthodox section ... We have a Vedic section ... We prioritise the ethnic over the religious, the class and the political ... Creating the community, I was convinced that if society is divided any further now, that if we contribute to this, if even the patriots themselves are going to invest their strength in division, then this will end in tragedy ... The first year was really difficult. There were scandals, arguments, emotions. We even had to expel people from the community, those who particularly distinguished themselves by scandal-mongering. But then everything calmed down.[16]

The same position is discernible in an interview with a member of the community's council, Igor Kovalev:

> From experience I can say that, on the whole, it is not truth that is generated by controversies, but rather strained relations ... Incidentally, the Slavic Community Charter forbids conversations about religion, because it is no secret that there are Orthodox people, atheists, and a pre-Christian Russian culture. Therefore the Charter of our community forbids these conversations, at least within the confines of the community.[17]

The leadership of the National Great Power Party of Russia has adopted a similar view on religious arguments. Party co-chair Aleksandr Sevastianov explained his position thus:

> Firstly, any discussion on religious issues is categorically forbidden in the Party. And secondly, our basic thesis may be expressed like this: we protect Russians regardless of their religious affiliation and convictions. Recently I defended the convinced pagan Korchagin in court and saved him from the gallows, and I also offered my services as defence lawyer to Mikhail Nazarov, who is the most Orthodox of the Orthodox. This is my principled, firmly-held position.[18]

Nationalist leaders have also recognised that excessive attention to Orthodoxy frightens away new participants rather than attracting them. Nikolai Lysenko, the creator of one of the first ethnic nationalist organisations – the National Republican Party – spoke out in support of secular nationalism back in 1992:

> In its traditional hypostasis Orthodoxy is unlikely to preserve its former role as a fundamental ideological foundation in the future: more than 70 years of Soviet society without religion could not pass without leaving a trace. Today Russians are a people with an almost entirely secularised, worldly mentality. (Lysenko cited in Lebedev 2007: 456)

This theme has subsequently been repeated by most of the secular nationalists, even if they personally practice some religion or other. Aleksandr Zhuchkovskii, for example, writes that '*en masse* the Russian majority is not religious and even less churched', citing the 2 per cent of people who are church-goers 'according to sociologists' (Zhuchkovskii 2014: 41). The same idea is developed by Moskovskii gosudarstvennyi institut mezhdunarodnykh otnoshenii (MGIMO) professor Valerii Solovei and his sister Tatiana in their book *Nesostoiavshaiasia revoliutsiia* (The Revolution that Didn't Happen):

> The ideologeme of Orthodox monarchy, the hope for a churching of Russian society and the reanimation of traditional values are *vox clamantis in deserto*. At the very least, these ideas are completely unsuitable for the purposes of mass political mobilisation. (Solovei and Solovei 2009)

Although the main arguments in favour of secularism always were and remain pragmatic, promoting secularism has also acquired a value in itself for these nationalists and become one of their few ideological positions. Still, secularists may use religious rhetoric for their own ends – most often Orthodox, since that attracts more supporters than, for example, paganism and allows them to appear more 'respectable' in the eyes of the authorities. To give an example: the Komi-based nationalist organisation Frontier of the North is presented as secular, although its symbol is a cross and the website includes the heading 'Orthodoxy'. The membership is made up of pagans, Orthodox and non-religious people. Aleksei Kolegov, the organisation's leader, does not deny that the use of Orthodox symbols and rhetoric is instrumental:

> A person can, for example, say that 'I am Orthodox', and apart from a cross [round his neck] not wear anything. Here is an option 'to protect Orthodoxy'. That is, coming into the organisation there is an option to protect Orthodoxy against the construction of mosques, the Islamisation of the North, to protect Orthodox land. To protect Orthodoxy, Orthodox Christians, an Orthodox town from invasion by sectarians. To protect, let's say, Orthodox people from the propaganda of homosexuals.[19]

Secularists often pass through a period of personal religious searching, and then, not finding a tradition that suits them, develop their own individual religious practices. Sevastianov, for example, gives the following account:

> I was an Orthodox Christian, I got baptised when I was 24 years old ... But for ten years I was beset by questions about the Orthodox Church, to which [the Church] didn't give me satisfactory answers. I gradually moved away from Orthodoxy and now don't consider myself a Christian, although I consider very many Orthodox rituals effective, necessary and I carry them out.[20]

In her blog, the nationalist poet and activist Marina Strukova describes a period of religious searching: 'Christianity was always alien to me, I do not even know why. From 2001 until 2007 I considered myself a native believer. Then I took up Judaica' (Strukova 2013a). She is studying Hebrew and reports positively on Judaism:

> Jews consider only Jews as neighbours. For Christians it is everyone. The Christian interpretation is striking, but unrealistic – like, for example, requiring every person to be able to fly into space or compose a symphony – not everyone is capable. Judaism is realistic. (Strukova 2013b)

Another source of the secularists' indifference to religion is their anti-immigrant sentiments. According to Lebedev (2007), one of the ideological innovations of the secular nationalists is 'the image of the main enemy' not in the shape of Jews or Freemasons, but in culturally alien migrants. This innovation was first articulated by Nikolai Lysenko. Some secularists, like Perin's Slavic Community of St Petersburg, continued to focus on the Jewish theme – which is why, perhaps, they did not achieve national reach. However, the anti-Semitic constructs of the nineteenth and twentieth centuries (the Jewish-Masonic conspiracy, the 'Elders of Zion' and so on) have now practically disappeared from the nationalist lexicon.

Nationalists oppose not only Muslim migrants, but also Christians, such as Georgians, Armenians, Ossetians, and Abkhazians. However, the fact that the majority of migrants happen to be Muslims (if only culturally) predetermines the anti-Islamic orientation of secular Russian nationalism. Nationalists associate Islam with religion in general, and so they see religiosity as a source of backwardness and 'obscurantism'. If immigrants are religious, nationalists suggest, then those who stand against them are obliged to be rational people of the world.

In an article about the 15 April 2013 terrorist attack on the Boston Marathon, carried out by the Chechen Tsarnaev brothers, Mikhail Pozharskii, co-chair of the National Democratic Alliance, subjects not only Islam but also religion in general to criticism (Pozharskii 2013). In his opinion, there is a gulf between the consciousness of the 'civilised person' and that of the 'conventional Tsarnaev, the product of a traditional, religious society'. According to this representative of secular nationalism, Islam is the quintessence of all that is negative in every religion: 'Of all world religions Islam is the most militant and aggressive', he writes, but sees others as being no better: religiosity is an indicator of 'intellectual degradation', 'impenetrable archaism' and 'psychosis'. Being non-religious is part of the secularists' emphatic adherence to 'European' values (see also Mitrofanova 2012).

Until recently, the secular segment of ethnic nationalism was a marginal phenomenon, but today it is the most dynamic part of the movement. It is here that new (relative to the 1990s) ideas, organisations and leaders are appearing. Secularists are internationally active on a broad scale, and master new forms of propaganda – for example, through social media (Orthodox nationalists are more likely to maintain blogs than to be active on Facebook and Vkontakte). One example of this is of the young – in terms of age (born in 1986) and length of time in the movement – political publicist Egor Prosvirnin. When he created the site *Sputnik i Pogrom* in 2012, he had already become a significant figure among Russian nationalists. Prosvirnin is just as active on social networks. The high-quality artistic work on *Sputnik i Pogrom* has no equivalent among other nationalist sites or ordinary web publications in Russia.

Concluding remarks

Since the collapse of the USSR, Russian ethnic nationalism has developed in an increasingly fragmented fashion, also as regards questions of religion. Secular nationalism is the only religio-ideological trend that is evolving in contemporary Russian nationalism. It is in this sector that new ideological concepts, clusters and leaders are emerging. The leadership of the neopagan and Orthodox nationalist sectors has remained practically unchanged since the early 1990s: Shiropaev, Mironov, Saveliev, Simonovich-Nikshich and others remain active in the movement. No new organisations are being formed, and new methods of communication and visual propaganda are not being adopted. The ideological foundations of both neopagan and Orthodox nationalism were fully elaborated by the 1990s or even earlier: today the likelihood of new ideas appearing in these sectors is so slim that it would be fair to speak of ideological stagnation.

The secularists' advantage over pagans rests in their practically unfettered potential to attract new participants and sympathisers to the nationalist movement. The neopagan wing of nationalism has probably exhausted any potential social base and will probably not grow any further. As compared to the Orthodox nationalists, the secularists enjoy the advantage of avoiding internal conflicts and specific difficulties linked with ecclesiastical life. Orthodox nationalism is a relic of the 1990s, and its adherents are declining in number, as many former Orthodox nationalists have joined the ranks of the 'patriotic statists' – even Dushenov, who until his arrest had been an implacable opponent of the authorities and called for armed insurrection.

Declared secularism does not mean that activists from this sector of the nationalist movement do not have their own religious convictions and/or practise religion. Further, secular nationalists may even use religious rhetoric in order to attract supporters or to make a good impression on the authorities. For today's ethnic nationalists, secularism is not an ideological stance but a populist device.

Notes

1. On the formation of the nation in Russia, see Tolz (2001).
2. Lay members are those people who identify themselves with the Russian Orthodox Church and confirm this identification with more or less regular communion in its churches.
3. Uranopolitans, 'citizens of the Heavenly Kingdom', represent a current within the Russian Orthodox Church that rejects the importance of patriotism. Their spiritual leader was Father Daniil Sysoev (assassinated in 2009).
4. The official English translation is available at the website of the Department for External Church Relations of the Russian Orthodox Church, <http://www.mospat.ru/en/documents/social-concepts> (last accessed 15 January 2015).
5. On the political influence of the Church, see Papkova (2011); Curanovic (2012); Knox and Mitrofanova (2014).
6. The World Russian People's Council (WRPC) is an annual forum of the Orthodox community, founded in 1993.
7. See, for example, interview with the Chair of the Synodal Department for Church-Society Relations, archpriest Vsevolod Chaplin (Aleksandrova 2014).
8. At the time, Abbot Filipp (Riabykh) was Deputy Chair of the Moscow Patriarchal Department for External Church Relations. Currently he heads the Representation of the Russian Orthodox Church at the Council of Europe.
9. The event's official site is available at <http://chin-pokayaniya.ru> (last accessed 15 January 2015).
10. Author's interview, Syktyvkar, 2 November 2013.
11. Information that Antonii (Orlov) of the RosOC blessed Kvachkov and Ekishev in their political struggle was published in Ekishev's blog, which has later been blocked by a ruling of Russian authorities.
12. Author's interview, Moscow, 3 June 2009.
13. Author's interview, Moscow, 3 June 2009.
14. The Prothesis is the preparatory part of the Divine Liturgy during which the priest cuts fragments of the prosphoron (offertory bread) in commemoration of living and dead members of the Church. Since there is no longer an Orthodox Tsar in Russia, a fragment for his commemoration is naturally not cut (see Zemtsov 2012).
15. On the origins of Russian paganism, see Pribylovskii (2002); Shizhenskii (2010); Shnirel'man (2012).
16. Author's interview, St Petersburg, 14 September 2005.

17. Author's interview, Moscow, 3 October 2006.
18. Author's interview, Moscow, 25 December 2006.
19. Author's interview, Syktyvkar, 2 November 2013.
20. Author's interview, Moscow, 25 December 2006.

5

Everyday nationalism in Russia in European context: Moscow residents' perceptions of ethnic minority migrants and migration

Natalya Kosmarskaya and Igor Savin

This chapter examines how ordinary residents of the Russian capital relate to the sharply increased influx of migrant workers to Russia, and to Moscow in particular. For several decades now, Western academics have scrutinised cross-border migration to Western European countries through the prism of local residents' perceptions. However, far more attention has been paid to the problems of the migrants themselves than to the attitudes of the host populations.

Similarly in Russia: despite the growing volume of academic literature on diverse aspects of the lives of migrant workers,[1] efforts at viewing this issue through the eyes of the host population are fairly rare. Well-established centres for the study of public opinion (Fond 'Obshchestvennoe mnenie' (FOM), the Levada Centre and others) periodically conduct large-scale surveys nationwide or within specific regions, and the collated 'percentages' are then commented on, above all in the press and online media,[2] as well as in social media. Less often are such 'official' surveys, or surveys conducted by teams of researchers, analysed in academic literature (see, for example, Leonova 2004; Tiuriukanova 2009; Grigor'eva et al. 2010). There are practically no studies that for comparative or analytical purposes draw on Western experience of studying public attitudes towards migrants, and employ the conceptual approaches used in these works to explain the reasons for various public sentiments.

Instead, research on perceptions of migration in Russia consists overwhelmingly of works of a polemical-conceptual nature, in which – from a constructivist position – the authors analyse and criticise discursive practices widespread in Russian society (see, for example, Karpenko 2002; Malakhov 2007, 2011; Shnirel'man 2008; Regame [Regamey] 2010; Demintseva 2013). These discourses have an alarmist character – employing concepts of 'territorial ethnic balance', 'ethno-cultural safety', 'critical share of immigrant population', 'ethnic criminality' and the like – thereby furthering the ethnification of social relations and the growing migrantophobia among the populace.

Russian academics have taken the same approach to foreign experience as well. Instead of approaching Western works as concrete sociological studies, they have tended to focus on the specificities of the production of ethnically 'charged' discourses, and on how the authorities and various sectors of civil society in Western countries oppose the discursive and actual practices of discrimination against ethnic minority migrants (see Malakhov 2004; Mukomel' and Pain 2005; Osipov 2013).

For all the significance of the above-mentioned Russian research, we feel there is a gap between the still-prevalent 'view from above' (conceptual-discursive) and the 'view from below' (concretely sociological). To our knowledge, there has been hardly any literature in Russia in which the attitudes of local residents towards migrants have been studied on the micro-level by qualitative sociological methods (various types of interviewing, participant/non-participant observation).[3] Here we mean the attitudes of *ordinary citizens*, specifically, and not a particular section of society – football fans, young extremist gangs, various representatives of (un)organised nationalist opposition groups, and so forth.

In essence, what we know may be reduced to a simple conclusion that is repeated, in various formulations, in publication after publication: 'Xenophobic attitudes have spread through all levels of Russian society ... xenophobia is primarily projected at representatives of migrant minorities non-traditional to a given location' (Mukomel' 2013: 199, 200). Many aspects of our theme remain unclear: what selection and hierarchy of factors engender negative attitudes towards migrants? How do these negative attitudes manifest themselves, also within specific socio-demographic groups? Are there regional specifics? And, finally, do 'locals' relate differently to migrants of different ethnocultural backgrounds?

This chapter attempts to fill these lacunae, analysing material from Moscow. We begin with a comparison (to the extent that available quantitative data allow) of the situation in Russia with that of countries in the West. Then we turn to how factors 'responsible' for the negativity towards external labour migrants identified in Western research work in a Russian/Moscow context. To ensure a firm footing for the analysis, we use large-scale quantitative data (the 2013 NEORUSS survey), and our own qualitative research on the attitudes of Muscovites to migrants and migration.

We start by assuming that the two methods are complementary; one of our main aims is therefore to show how, in comparison with respondents' answers to closed survey questions, unstructured interviews may illuminate and deepen our understanding of the issue under study – and perhaps also serve as a source of alternative interpretations. Here we should recall certain inadequacies of large-scale surveys. Amandine Regamey, for example, has highlighted the 'magic of negativity' in the interpretation of results. In particular she notes:

> According to Levada Centre survey data, in November 2009 . . . 35 per cent 'probably or definitely related negatively to the fact that one increasingly encounters workers from various countries of the near abroad on Russian building sites' . . . This being the case, the use of survey data to demonstrate xenophobic 'sentiments' is extremely problematic, since an even greater percentage of respondents (44 per cent) relate to this fact neutrally. (Regame [Regamey] 2013: 362)

Furthermore, surveys often require people to respond to ideas and convictions that may be alien to their way of thinking, in form or content. Alexander Verkhovsky has expressed this concern – that we share – in commenting on the results of the 2013 NEORUSS survey. Evaluating its results as a whole, he notes: 'The survey creates the outward appearance of a fully developed agenda of Russian nationalism, which the majority of the population supports.' However, after citing several concrete figures, he concludes:

But it is time to express a most important reservation: the views and suggestions supported by citizens in mass surveys are very often not their convictions, not part of their political views – they are uncoordinated responses to the questions unexpectedly posed by an interviewer. Such surveys do not reveal how serious or stable citizens' views are, what role those views play in their worldview as a whole. (Verkhovsky 2013)

In contrast, qualitative research – especially that based on interviews without such 'unexpected' formulations – is better able to show how people formulate their judgements, and which logical links, made by the respondents themselves, contribute to this process. Here we find more habitual, routine ways of thinking. Of course, qualitative methods also have their inadequacies and limitations. Our preference for 'soft' methods here is not motivated by any faith in their infallibility, but is a reaction to the clear dominance of surveys in the study of our topic – in Russia, survey data (in the form of information on 'percentages' of support for one conviction or another) are almost the sole source of information available about ordinary people's perceptions concerning migrants and migration.

Let us briefly explain our qualitative research methodology. The empirical basis is formed by thirty-two interviews conducted with Muscovites from November 2013 to June 2014.[4] The average interview lasted in the region of sixty to eighty minutes. By 'Muscovites', or the 'host population', we mean people who have lived in Moscow for at least five to seven years, and who have permanent registration, accommodation and work there. Although our 'sample' is not statistically representative, we have sought to balance interviewees as regards gender, age, educational level, social status and area of residence.

Set against those respondents who have lived in the capital since the Soviet period (or were born here) our sample also includes a group of eight individuals who have arrived relatively recently from various regions of Russia or from former Soviet republics. Since Moscow is the most dynamically growing urban area of Russia, it attracts not only persons from the dominant ethnic groups of those countries of the 'near abroad' from which migrant workers come:

also Russian-speaking residents of the former Soviet republics continue to arrive (although this flow was especially large in the 1990s, and has declined significantly since then) – as do Russian citizens from across the regions of the Russian Federation.

In principle, compared with questionnaires, the genre of interviews is better suited for levelling out the impact of public and political discourse on respondents' state of mind, although one is unlikely to achieve this fully. The wording of closed questions is often deliberately constructed around opposing extreme positions and can thus have a rather provocative nature; moreover, such questions may contain formulations drawn from the mass media. We chose a very 'soft' approach: we did not declare in any way our interest in the theme of migration and associated topics, and there were no direct questions about this.[5] We described ourselves as researchers of the lives of ordinary people in Moscow – their perceptions of change, their views on the difficulties they face and possible ways of overcoming them.[6]

From the end of 2013 to autumn 2014, one of the authors participated in a pilot project to develop a model for integration through daily interaction between migrants and residents of specific housing estates in various areas of Moscow. He was able not only to record the comments of migrants and local residents, but also to observe their behaviour and mutual contact. Material from this participant observation supplements the empirical base of the work reported here.

Anti-migrant sentiments in Russia and in the West: A tentative comparison

Being situated 'within' Russian discourse about migration and migrants creates a strong impression of the exceptional nature of the Russian experience – 'exceptional' in a negative sense. However, the many academic publications about attitudes to migrants in other countries seem to indicate that Russia is not so unique here after all.[7]

Indeed, some authors note the universality of the phenomenon under scrutiny: 'denigration of individuals or groups based on perceived differences, i.e. xenophobia, is arguably a part of everyday life around the world. Xenophobic attitudes are not new, nor are they likely to disappear in the near future' (Hayes and Dowds 2006: 458); 'studies from around the world show that the public generally hold negative perceptions of migration and migrant workers' (Tunon and Baruah 2012: 149); 'as immigration continues, conflicts and integration problems between the native population and foreigners will persist. These problems should be regarded as "normal" problems of an open society and should not be dramatized' (Böltken 2003: 253). Others propose existential explanations. As Roger Waldinger writes:

> The turn of the twenty-first century has brought a world of mass migration, but this is a reality that the residents of the rich democracies do not like. Often wanting foreign workers, but having much less taste for foreign people who settle down, the residents of the rich democracies want their national communities maintained . . . Keeping membership restricted is of strategic value, especially when the place in question is a wealthy society that attracts the poor. Selfishness is not the only motivation at work; however, the idea of the national community, understood as a broad, family-like group of people responsible for taking care of one another, but *not* everyone outside the circle, is also an ideal . . . governments do what their people want, making strenuous efforts to control movements across the border. (Waldinger 2010: 58, 42, emphasis in the original)

Attention is also paid to the interconnection between migrantophobia and the growth of political radicalism:

> During the last two decades, opposition to immigration has become increasingly politicized in many regions of Western Europe . . . It is no exaggeration to claim that the extreme right, for the first time since the Second World War, constitutes a significant force in established Western European democracies at both the local and national level. (Hayes and Dowds 2006: 455, 456)

Further: 'Right leaning political parties tend to promote stricter policies toward immigrants and reinforce negative stereotypes concerning immigrants being a threat to economic and cultural stability' (Rustenbach 2010: 68). Based on a comparative analysis of material across many European countries, Moshe Semyonov and colleagues note: 'Research conducted across European countries reveals strong and mostly negative sentiments toward foreigners and immigrants ... Immigrants often are viewed as a threat to economic success, to national identity, and to the social order' (Semyonov et al. 2006: 432).

As regards the dynamics of negative attitudes to ethnic minority migrants, the process is seen as developing in waves (see Böltken 2003; Semyonov et al. 2006). The results of elections to the European Parliament in May 2014, when support for far-right parties grew markedly in many European countries, seem to indicate a phase of intensifying anti-migrant sentiments.

In comparing the European and Russian situations, it is important to identify what phase of the migration cycle each specific country finds itself in. If the history of immigration to a country is relatively recent, and the population is consequently not yet accustomed to the presence of a significant number of ethnic minority migrants (and this is the case for Russia), there comes a swift growth in anti-migrant sentiments – that subsequently slows down (Semyonov et al. 2006: 429, 430).[8] Initially, the host population also typically exaggerates the number of migrants: 'In the early phase, inflated perceptions of threat may lead to a sharp rise in anti-foreigner sentiment. Later, however, many of these perceptions become more realistic, and the sentiments toward outsiders, although negative, level off and become stable' (Semyonov et al. 2006: 445). On the local level, the length of time the foreigners have been resident is a central factor in explaining the dynamic of negative attitudes: Have they lived there for a long time? Are their numbers increasing? If so, the host population is less inclined to support integration.[9] We return to the issue of the number of migrants, with regard to the specific situation in Moscow, below.

We view the situation in Russia as comparable with that in Europe also as regards various quantitative indicators (the 'percentages' presented in Western literature). Here we are not talking about literally comparing specific figures, but about comparing general trends in collective consciousness. Our data allow us to compare three important aspects of perceptions of migrants: (1) Does the host country need migrants? (2) Is a growth in crime seen as connected with migration? (3) Does migration represent an ethno-cultural threat?

According to the 2013 NEORUSS survey data, 51.3 per cent of respondents in Moscow (52.8 per cent in Russia as a whole) agree or somewhat agree with the opinion: 'Russia really needs migrants, because they take on low-paid but important work that Russians are now reluctant to do'. Another 46.8 per cent of Muscovites disagree with this statement (41.8 per cent in Russia in general). Hence, a slight majority among respondents recognises that migrants are needed. In response to different wording, however – 'Given the population decline in Russia, more migrants are needed in order to avert a deficit in the workforce which may endanger the country' – the majority now denies that migration is a positive factor in the development of the economy: only 25.5 per cent of respondents in Moscow (and 31.8 per cent in Russia) agreed, while 64 per cent of the Muscovites (and 59.5 per cent in the all-Russian sample) declared themselves 'against' or 'somewhat against' this opinion.[10]

Based on a survey conducted in 2003 by the International Social Survey Programme that included all developed countries, Roger Waldinger has carried out a comparative analysis, studying the attitudes of the part of the population that belongs to the 'third generation [of immigrants] or more' (Waldinger 2010: 45). He concludes that 'in both France and the US, only a minority of ethnic majority respondents agreed that migrants were good for the economy' (ibid.: 54; see also 44). Furthermore, he cites the following data: 67 per cent of US respondents and 72 per cent of French think that there should be fewer migrants (ibid.: 48).

For the most part, however, the reluctance in both Russia and other countries to host large numbers of migrants is not explained by economic reasons. In answering a question posed in the NEORUSS survey about the significance of threats associated with migration, for example, only 15.7 per cent of respondents in Moscow (and 8.1 per cent in Russia) linked such threats primarily to 'a destabilisation of the Russian economy'. Apparently, the position on 'economic issues' was influenced by other fears evoked by migrants, the most important of which were the threats of 'terrorism or banditry' (25 per cent in Moscow and 30 per cent in Russia), and 'illegal residency' (24 per cent in Moscow and 13.5 per cent in Russia).

One of the fears shared worldwide is connected with crime, which allegedly increases with migration. As a small experiment, one of the present authors asked five sociologists what country was being talked about in the following quotation: 'There is a widespread impression that migrants are disproportionately responsible for crime; and legislation may be introduced that has little impact on crime rates, but stifles migrants' freedoms and rights. It is therefore important that attitudes should be informed and based on fact rather than on misinformation or misinterpretation'. All responded confidently that, naturally, the subject was contemporary Russia – whereas in fact the quotation begins 'in many countries' and is taken from an English-language article in which attitudes to migrant workers worldwide are subject to comparative analysis (see Tunon and Baruah 2012: 151).

As to quantitative evaluations, in France, for example, only 'a minority' do not agree that 'immigrants increase crime' (Waldinger 2010: 54).[11] In Australia, over the period 1998 to 2007, 49.1 per cent of 'white' residents agreed with a similar statement (Bilodeau and Fadol 2011: 1095). In the USA in 1997, 43 per cent of those surveyed agreed that migrants 'significantly increase crime', although, by 2006, this share had dropped to 33 per cent (Tunon and Baruah 2012: 156). In the NEORUSS survey, 48.7 per cent of respondents in the all-Russian sample (and a full 74.1 per cent of those surveyed in Moscow) agreed that 'many migrants come to Russia not in order to work honestly, but to steal from Russians and weaken the Russian people', whereas 42.7 per cent disagreed with this statement. However, that the survey uses stronger and rather provocative wording here should, we feel, be taken into account.

There is a clear analogy in the degree to which migration is perceived as an 'ethno-cultural threat' to the host society and its (variously conceived) values. In France a majority of respondents agreed with the statement that immigrants' ideas and culture do not improve the country (Waldinger 2010: 54). In the USA, public opinion was divided as to the influence of migration: there were about as many respondents who saw migrants as a factor that strengthens American society as those who saw them as a threat to traditional American values (Tunon and Baruah 2012: 151).

What, then, of Russia? Choosing among the various responses to the statement 'the ethnic diversity of the Russian population strengthens our country', 57.1 per cent of the NEORUSS respondents in Moscow (56.6 per cent in Russia) said that it 'in some respects strengthens, and in some respects weakens' Russia; 30.4 per cent in Moscow (22.1 per cent in Russia) felt that ethnic diversity weakens the country; whereas 10.1 per cent of respondents in Moscow (11.3 per cent in Russia) agreed that ethnic diversity 'strengthens our country'.

Of particular interest are data about various host-societies' perceptions of Islam and Muslims – considered an especially difficult issue for Russia. Pieter Bevelander and Jonas Otterbeck's work on young people's attitudes towards Muslim immigrants in Sweden also includes data on other countries. Thus they report that a 2006 study found that about 30 per cent of respondents in Switzerland displayed Islamophobia, and, similarly, 20–25 per cent of respondents in Germany (Bevelander and Otterbeck 2010: 409). In Sweden, according to a nationwide survey, in 2005 and 2006 39 per cent and 37 per cent of respondents respectively felt that the number of Muslims entering the country should be restricted (ibid.: 408). In the Netherlands – according to a 2007 study – 54 per cent of young respondents expressed negative attitudes to Muslims (ibid.: 409). Here one should take into account that young people are generally far more tolerant than older generations (see below). In Moscow, 30 per cent of the NEORUSS survey respondents 'agreed entirely' with the rather provocative statement 'Islam is becoming a threat to social stability and Russian culture'; a further 43 per cent 'agreed somewhat'.

Thus, even a swift glance at the comparative data on attitudes to migration allows us to draw distinct parallels between Western and Russian experience. This makes it appropriate to use conceptual approaches originally developed by Western academics for understanding the reasons for migrantophobia and xenophobia, in analysing the Russian situation.

How do factors influencing perceptions of migrants 'work' in Russia?

In Western research on the causes and manifestations of migrantophobia, two groups of fundamentally different factors are usually identified as independent variables, hypothetically influencing the position of the local population.

The first group of factors is contextual, or structural: these factors describe the state of the society in which the individual or group lives, and to which s/he belongs. The number/proportion of migrants (index of threat) and the economic situation in the host country (index of competition), measured by growth/fall in gross domestic product (GDP), unemployment levels, regional development levels and so forth, are often tested out as potential 'provokers' of negative attitudes to migrants (see Semyonov et al. 2006; Rustenbach 2010; Bilodeau and Fadol 2011; Careja and Andres 2013).

In comparing the Russian and Western situations, however, we are mainly interested in the second group of factors: characteristics of the individuals themselves. Generally, socio-demographic indicators are tested for influence on negative attitudes towards migration: age, sex, education level and social status (availability of work; level and dynamics of income). Political orientation is also seen as a factor. There is almost no disagreement over its influence: in various countries, holding right-wing political views is highly likely to be accompanied by negative attitudes to migrants (see Rustenbach 2010; Waldinger 2010; Bilodeau and Fadol 2011; Careja and Andres 2013). The human capital explanation is also frequent. Education levels are linked to anti-migrant sentiments: people with higher education are usually found to be more tolerant (Bilodeau and Fadol 2011: 1092, 1104; Rustenbach 2010: 56, 66; Careja and Andres 2013: 383).

Regarding age, for various reasons, older people are seen as holding more negative attitudes towards migrants (see Careja and

Andres 2013; Martinović 2013). As for gender, some authors discuss the influence of gender within the framework of the concept of 'cultural marginality'. It is suggested that women, like members of other (potentially) discriminated-against groups (members of religious minorities, children of mixed marriages), view migrants more positively. However, not all researchers support this hypothesis.

Similarly, the relationship between migrantophobia and various indicators of the socio-economic position of individuals is also open to debate. Several works fail to find significant relationships, and have also shown that respondents do not conceive of migration in terms of 'economic competition' (see, for example, Hayes and Dowds 2006; Escandell and Ceobanu 2009; Rustenbach 2010; Waldinger 2010; Bilodeau and Fadol 2011; Careja and Andres 2013).

No specific questions about potential economic competition from migrants were posed in the NEORUSS survey. According to the interview materials, respondents are not particularly preoccupied with this issue. Their comments reveal why there is no sense of competition for workplaces between Muscovites (as well as newcomers from the other regions of Russia) and labour migrants: this hinges on the division of labour that has arisen in the city, entirely in line with the international pattern: 'Because of the size, age, education and skills of the native population, there is a demand for migrant workers in specific jobs and sectors. These are mostly low-skilled and labour-intensive jobs – often classified as 3D: dirty, dangerous and demeaning' (Tunon and Baruah 2012: 152).

Noting this factor, respondents stress the different motivations of Muscovites and 'migrants':

I. Some people think that migrants take work away from Russians. Do you agree with that?
R. If Russians worked in those lines of work for that money, then nobody would take anything away because there would be no positions open. But a Russian who thinks he's mighty clever won't go to work . . . won't go to work for 15 thousand [roubles] to mix concrete on a building site, to carry bricks or work as a fitter-welder . . . Better

to do nothing at all than to go [to that sort of work]. But a migrant worker can work from morning till night and at weekends, because he has an aim, and the aim is achieved only by hard work, not only by learning, but by working hard overtime. But a Muscovite doesn't need this. 'Ding! – five o'clock, and it's home time. It's hardly a matter of life and death if they sack me, I'll find something else. Or mum and dad will keep me.' (Man, aged 63, higher technical education, security guard in a private company)

Also important here is the particular socio-psychological atmosphere in a large city with high standards of living and a range of possibilities:

I. Have you thought about why local residents don't want this [sort of] work?
R. It's simply that social status is really important for us. For a start, being a Muscovite is already a pretty significant status for a person. Moscow is a motivational town; you see how luxuriously people can live, and you want to somehow copy that. People are aspiring upwards, and such lowly jobs, even if they were well paid, no one would take them.
I. And if someone is retired, without great pretensions?
R. When you're on a pension there are other options – for example, go to [work in] a museum. Here physical labour is considered a relic of the past, now we have intellectual labour, and everyone aims, above all, at that. (Woman, aged 24, higher education, manager in the education sector)

The connection between the economic status of the respondents and their attitudes to migrants does not emerge very clearly from the NEORUSS survey results. It is evident from the responses to a majority of questions that people who worked part-time took stances that were slightly harsher in relation to migrants – but it is difficult to detect any unambiguous tendency, as the numerical differences were small. Similarly, the better-educated respondents were not always distinguished by greater tolerance. As regards age, younger people more often displayed greater tolerance, especially students (with some exceptions) – a trend observed elsewhere as well.

Thus, the results of the Moscow survey did not demonstrate a clear-cut relation between anti-migrant sentiments and the socio-demographic characteristics of respondents. This 'diffusion' of results agrees quite well with the findings of Western researchers. There is, however, one exception: the gender factor. In almost all questions, Moscow women displayed more negative attitudes towards migrants – whereas Russian women on the whole displayed greater tolerance. The most sweeping, but hardly sufficient, explanation is an argument *a contrario* – that in Moscow, as a developed contemporary metropolis, the idea of the 'cultural marginality' of women simply does not apply. That said, the question of whether women from other Russian regions consider themselves 'marginalised' also remains open. On the whole, as regards whether non-acceptance of migrants is dependent on socio-demographic factors, the survey gives somewhat fuzzy and contradictory results. The results may, however, be supplemented and clarified with the help of interview materials that can reflect the specificities of the particular Moscow context (see below).

Apart from socio-demographic factors, there are also individual factors of a different nature. For researchers of inter-group/interpersonal relations, personality characteristics (attitudinal factors) are important. These are manifested on the level of trust towards people, readiness to live in a multi-ethnic environment, to interact with people of different races and cultures. The hypothetical link between these factors and perceptions of migrants is tested in terms of concepts such as social contact, social exposure and interpersonal trust.

Contact between migrants and Moscow residents

Important among the many social theories seeking to explain the growth of migrantophobia in Europe is 'contact theory' (Hayes and Dowds 2006: 456). It holds that interaction itself, in various ways (living as neighbours, friendship – and, even more, marriage – with migrants) creates more tolerant perceptions of migrants among the host population (see Böltken 2003; Escandell and Ceobanu 2009; Bevelander and Otterbeck 2010; Martinović 2013).

The qualitative research conducted by the present authors does not contest the main propositions of contact theory. Those of our interlocutors who had extensive experience of interaction with migrants demonstrated a more balanced and welcoming position towards them. Among local community activists (property owner councils, local veteran councils and so forth), the most active in all integration initiatives were people who due to their professional service or life circumstances had lived and interacted with people from Central Asia and the Caucasus – the regions from which most migrants to Moscow come.

Here we are concerned with positive or neutral contact. However, even if an individual's experience of interaction with migrants has been not solely positive, it still helps him or her to regard migrants with greater equanimity, neither idealising nor demonising them. One respondent who himself had come to Moscow from Kazakhstan, for example, sees migrants not as a 'scary mob' but as people who are obliged to work in a different social setting:

> Personally I don't have any complaints against anyone; I understand them, they have to feed their relatives back at home, earn something for themselves. Of course, 80 per cent of these people are honest and hardworking, who don't even imagine how people here are conning them, they are forced to accept that, without even thinking. But 20 per cent and even more come to commit fraud, engaging in various illegal activities . . . (Man, aged 53, secondary education, driver)

The criticism expressed is rooted not in the very presence of migrants or their having some sort of characteristics that the respondent finds unpleasant, but in concrete situations that involve certain 'migrants' and 'local inhabitants' in connection with, for example, supervising markets, wholesale vegetable trade and so on (see below for further details). The denunciation of illegal activities is not extended to all migrants.

People who have no contact with individuals from other cultures demonstrate a different attitude. One respondent empathises with street cleaners who live under difficult conditions: 'I feel bitterly sorry for them, although I don't respect this nation, all Asia . . . nor the Caucasus . . . I've never been there' (Man, 66 years old, secondary education, retired, now watchman). Here empathy is expressed by overcoming the barrier of a personal attitude to migrants as fundamentally alien, since there is no personal experience of interaction that could allow 'them' to be perceived as oneself or 'one's own'.

Personal interactions can significantly influence, even change, attitudes to migrants. We know of cases where residents who initially opposed a 'foreign' café in their building changed their attitudes to the establishment and the people (for example, from Uzbekistan) after having been invited to participate in regular events at the café, and came to recognise these people's right to work in the neighbourhood.

In the case of repeated or lasting positive contact, a person perceives 'others' not as an undifferentiated mass, but as specific individuals, with idiosyncrasies and individual reasons for behaviour. Where there is no such foundation, a negative contact may influence the next interaction with migrants. A person becomes more sensitive to information that 'confirms' the already formed negative attitude than to information that may contradict and destroy this schema. One of our interviewees displays such a chain of inference. Negative experiences of being neighbours to a family from Azerbaijan ('a crazy amount of yelling, the children yell, these blokes yell . . .') led to the respondent's more general conclusion about migrants as a whole: 'They are noisy, and it's impossible to reach agreement with them. They give the impression that we are guests of theirs . . .' (Woman, aged 35, secondary education, hairdresser).

In the absence of personal experience of interaction, external factors become increasingly important: the dominant assessment of migrants in the public sphere, rumours and fears. Then information is accepted uncritically, further deepening people's negativity, even when they cannot explain this. For example, one respondent admitted that 'a person of Slavic appearance and a Tajik evoke completely different emotions in me'. However, she was unable to recall a single incident in which she, or those close to her, had experienced rudeness or aggression from a migrant. Speculating on why she has such views, she concludes: 'It is because they are different ... they look different, they came to our country, they came illegally, they are after something.' This respondent does not know what they are after, or how to distinguish 'legal' from 'illegal', and confesses that it is precisely the inexplicability of her feelings towards migrants that makes her feel most stressed (Woman, 28 years old, secondary education, manager).

It is well known that negative information about migrants may be used to manipulate public consciousness for political ends – for example, to mobilise the conservative part of the electorate. This happens in Europe (see, for example, Escandell and Ceobanu 2009; Bevelander and Otterbeck 2010), as well as in Russia, a recent Moscow example being the 2013 mayoral election campaign.

During the implementation of the project 'Integration through daily interaction', one of the authors also encountered managers of companies that attract migrants, for example, to work in the housing and public amenities sphere, who were not interested in their directly interacting with the neighbourhood residents: 'Our Tajiks have no need of integration', declared one of the lower-level supervisors of such a company.

It is highly likely that such a reaction is evoked not by any subconscious dislike of interaction between Muscovites and, say, street cleaners, but by fear of losing the monopoly on the organisation of employees' social contacts, a monopoly that allows them to keep the migrants' conditions of engagement, accommodation and so forth in the dark. The non-transparent procedures by which these companies are selected as service providers, the absence of mechanisms by which residents may control budget expenditures set aside for construction and so on, are well known. However, regardless of what is the basis for such strategies, they lead to alienation and opposition between local residents and the migrants who are busy providing public amenities – they coexist in the same housing estates, but inhabit parallel worlds, having no occasion to interact.

Similarly, there is a dearth of information about the contribution that migrants make to the construction of the new residential blocks, the social, cultural and educational institutions that

Moscow needs, and their contribution in providing public amenities. This is especially important where construction is underway in close proximity to residential areas: on a daily basis, local residents observe dozens of strangers, talking in an incomprehensible language, near their homes, for reasons which are unclear to them.

The sharpest reaction to such a situation expressed during the interviews occurred when a respondent related how she was standing on the street with a friend when the work shift ended: 'we froze, because it was just like a plague of locusts, when you open the cupboards and some sort of black cockroaches rush out. They were all dressed the same, in stain-resistant black. They have a traditional, local style; these hats, pushed to the back of the head ...' (Woman, aged 30, higher education, philologist). Such identification of migrants with insects is clearly offensive. However, this sort of imagery arises in situations where local residents do not connect the activities of migrants with themselves or their world in any way, because they have no information about where 'these people' – who do not resemble 'us' and who were not 'here' earlier – work, and what work they are doing.

Among our respondents, especially the younger ones, some doubts about the desirability of living next door to migrants were explained not by the characteristics of 'migrants as a whole', but by the potential difficulties that people accustomed to living in small families may experience living near to populous communities. This circumstance, in itself neutral, may become a source of hidden and often unconscious anxiety about some neighbours, including migrants. For example, one respondent answered a question about whom she would not want to live near (in the same building, on the same floor) thus: 'Probably, first of all, alcoholics, drug addicts, naturally. I also wouldn't want Tajiks, who settle themselves as a whole collective farm' (Woman, aged 45, higher education, doctor).

Another respondent says: 'I probably have an image of exactly such a flat, rented out to a whole brigade, sleeping in shifts on mattresses. I wouldn't want such a flat near me' (Woman, aged 50, higher education, designer). Interestingly, in responding to a clarification question about whether these features were connected with the fact that these people had arrived fairly recently, the respondent answered with conviction that it was connected to their culture (or rather, lack thereof) – without directly identifying migrants as people without culture.

From the answers to this question it becomes clear that the majority of respondents do not especially aim at excluding migrants from the pool of potential neighbours. Alcoholics, drug addicts and noisy people evoked far more hostility. However, migrants often accompany the latter in the 'blacklist' of undesirable neighbours, are unwittingly associated with them and, consequently, assume a share of the unfavourable images and associations. Here is a typical answer:

> I wouldn't want, first of all, to live with those who create a great deal of disturbance, who, for example, hold drunken concerts at three in the morning, so that the whole building jumps. It doesn't matter to me who's in there, what nationality. Be they Turks, Mongolians, be they from Sicily. People may be quite different – that's even, on the contrary, interesting. When everyone's the same, sorted by type, that's also hard. (Man, aged 57, higher education, university teacher)

Another example shows how negative impressions may be created in people who have no distinct anti-migrant orientation:

> Naturally [I wouldn't want to live with those], who are migrants, who have many relatives. That goes without saying. It may seem more or less a normal family, but there's noise, commotion, visitors constantly. They don't have [families with] few children. Noise, visitors constantly. On different floors, but it's stressful, all the same. I don't have other aversions. Absolutely no aversions based on ethnic features, and the same for educational qualifications. When there is noise and commotion from six until midnight, it's already inevitable ... Only for that reason. I wouldn't even have known them, if they had behaved quietly. (Man, aged 63, higher technical education, security guard in a private company)

It is likely that if the respondents had interacted with migrants in some way, they would have perceived them less as a source of disturbance and more as ordinary people with individual characteristics. In turn, the migrants themselves (and the researchers) may link this apprehension towards 'newcomers' with already developed anti-migrant sentiments, and draw conclusions about an unfriendly environment for migrants. If, however, there were regular contacts between local residents and migrants, spontaneous or organised, involving them in some sort of communal activity with neighbours connected with community safety, resolving communal problems, creating a space for shared leisure, this could create the basis for reducing migrantophobia and surmounting negative stereotypes about 'migrants in general'.

Our material, however, suggests the presence of selectivity in the views that Muscovites hold about various migrants. One criterion is ethno-cultural. Thus, for example, in a focus group organised by one of the authors and consisting of young male Muscovites from one housing estate, participants demonstrated differing attitudes to migrants from Central Asia and from regions of the North Caucasus. Briefly put, the presence of migrants from Central Asia in Moscow did not bother the participants, since they had come to work, that is, to be 'like us', and did not display arrogance. But '*kavkaztsy*' (people from the Caucasus), participants felt, wanted to be 'above us' and to 'humiliate us'. As Russian citizens they have certain rights, and they use them in order to command a special position, according to the focus group participants. But 'Tajiks' come in order to earn that same status 'that we have'.

The second criterion is social status. Respondents who talked about their close relationships with migrants (neighbours, a daughter's girlfriend and so forth) stressed that these people – despite having come from countries in Central Asia and the Caucasus – are 'just like us' (as to the length of time having lived in Russia, having a stable position and a respected profession and so forth). This topic, which touches on the important issue of the relationship between ethnic and social divisions in post-Soviet societies, requires further investigation.

Contextual factors according to interview findings

We mentioned above that in Western literature certain general characteristics of the socio-economic system, reduced to formalised, measurable form, are used as independent variables potentially impacting upon public attitudes to migrants. In analysing the interview materials, we found that in Moscow the theme of migration (migrants) is also wrapped in 'context'– but here this 'context' has a different meaning: the topic of migration arises, and is accompanied, interpreted and understood by respondents in connection with other, more general, themes. Moreover, judging by the persistent presence of such themes in many interviews, by the length of time spent considering them, as well as by the degree of emotion accompanying them, we see these themes as in fact more significant for our interlocutors than the migrants themselves and everything connected with the latter. The answers to the NEORUSS questions eliciting an evaluation of the sociopolitical system that has developed in Russia provide a conceptual 'bridge' to understanding what really worries our respondents. People displayed a high level of consensus in their dissatisfaction. For example, 72 per cent of Moscow respondents agreed with the statement, 'Those in power are indifferent to what is going on for people like me.' Further, 70 per cent agreed that the participation of ordinary people in elections does not change anything (few of the questions related to migration as such received this level of support).

Respondents were able to express their dissatisfaction freely in interviews, and specific matters that vexed people emerged: these included corruption and the shady business connected with this; schemes for recruiting illegal labour; malpractice by bureaucrats and police; and also the ineffective work of social, housing and utilities services. Migrants invariably featured in discussions of these themes – because they embody these 'sore points' of Muscovite/Russian social life; they are an irritating or distressing reminder of them. Evidently Moscow, with its many specificities – the variety of legal and illegal forms of economic activity; the enormous volume of financial and also personnel resources, including 'imported' ones; as well as the city's recently revitalised programmes for construction and improvements – represents a showcase.

Narratives in which 'migration' is inserted within the context of 'corruption' are present in many interviews, usually constructed in one of two ways. The first of these goes as follows: some socially significant urban problem or other is being discussed, then the respondent shifts over to the topic of migration, which is seen as a 'natural' and expected continuation of the long-established unfortunate situation (from generalisation to case). For example, in discussing why the roads cannot be repaired in a way so that they would remain in good condition for many years:

> R: That's no good for the boss who runs this construction and repair company. He gets paid once for the road and that's it. And then what? So, every year he dashes here and there, repairs, takes money. The roads are bad, the Moscow government pays. And there is no replacement. The business is shared. He's well established here, he has connections, naturally, in that same government of Moscow. The mechanism works well . . .
> I. There is a solution, but it is difficult to implement . . .
> R. This whole structure is built on unskilled labour [implying the work of migrants, who predominate in this business]. And political will is needed to bring it down. But they sympathise with their own, and these are their own. (Man, aged 63, higher technical education, security guard in a private company)

In the second type of narrative, the observation/opinion of the respondent about migration and migrants 'unfolds' further in a more general evaluation of some socio-political problem (from case to generalisation). For example, discussing the problem of 'rubber flats'[12] and the terrible conditions in which migrants live:

> R. In order to live like that . . . around 3,800 for that place . . . A Kyrgyz woman rented a flat for herself there. . .
> I. And then sublets it?
> R. Then she gathers her countrymen and settles in. Agrees with the landlord that she would live there, around 30,000 a month in rent, and if 18 people at 3,800? Here the mafia are already organising . . . The

cops see everything, know everything. You see it on the television – every day they are locked up, and people still continue to pay for protection . . . what is it with these people? (Man, aged 66, secondary education, retired, now watchman)

In analysing narratives of 'corruption' a further element also requires attention. All respondents, from business people to teachers, from elderly pensioners to yesterday's students, clearly picture the schemes for recruiting migrants that enrich the many participants in this structure: 'And they are brought here for this, to be defrauded and line the pockets [of those who bring migrants]' (Man, aged 66, secondary education, retired, now watchman).

Migrants are seen as 'embedded' (not by their own volition) in this system, which arose long before they appeared. Moreover, usually nobody blames the migrants themselves. So, for example, the respondents who related attempts to get work – either by themselves or by acquaintances – and had been unsuccessful because they were Muscovites and not migrants (who could be paid less), blamed the established system for this: 'Every Muscovite wants to work officially, but now no one wants to employ you officially, [there's] a lot of tax, really a lot' (Woman, aged 35, secondary education, hairdresser).

Besides corruption, the second 'background factor' that is often intertwined with the theme of migration and defining attitudes towards the latter fits within the concept of 'defended neighbourhood theory' (Bevelander and Otterbeck 2010: 407). During periods of rapid changes in local living conditions (at city, microregion or estate level), people lose the sense of habitualness, of being comfortable in their living environment. These changes have at least two constituents: the transformation of the built environment, and the appearance of a multitude of new people to whom they have not grown accustomed. The fragment of an interview below shows how both themes are interwoven in the consciousness of the respondent, a resident of one of Moscow's satellite towns:

I. And what has changed, as regards appearance, generally?
R. Of those people there is practically no one left . . . and now, you yourself know, what sort of people are there.

I. Is that good or bad?
R. I don't like it.
I. Why?
R. I'm no opponent of the friendship of peoples, but it gets on my nerves because I have lived in this town all my life. All this has happened in front of my eyes. All this entire development . . . I don't like the unregulated development all over town. (Man, aged 50, secondary education, driver)

In the industrial metropolis of Moscow, traditions of 'neighbourliness' (*sosedstvo*), local support and cooperation are generally long gone. This is why, when a multitude of 'others' appears, Muscovites find in this a visible embodiment of the collapse of the 'old world'. In fact, that world disappeared much earlier, during the fundamental socio-economic transformation of post-Soviet times – but before the phase of active labour migration commenced, there were not that many visual proofs of its absence. It seemed if everybody around was 'our people', things were peaceful. Now it seems that many of the surrounding people are 'not ours', and this has become disturbing.

Concerning the 'quality' of migrants (that is, their 'otherness'), mention should be made of a central aspect that relates to the bulk of interviews as a whole: We find that the ethno-cultural specifics of migrants concern respondents considerably less than the socio-political 'context' of the problem of migration. Practically none of the interviewees mentioned Islam of their own volition; no one commented on 'alien culture' in the context of 'threat'. They basically talked, in quite general terms, about the appearance of a multitude of strangers in the city, who talk (often loudly) in an incomprehensible language among themselves and on the telephone, and who listen to loud music. That bears little relation to the ethno-confessional specifics of migrants, or to ethnic culture as such.

The 'quality' of migrants (in this context) is closely intertwined with the question of their 'quantity'. Researchers have already noted that local residents' perception of migrants is influenced by the fear that 'we have a lot of migrants', irrespective of their actual numbers (that is, as a perceived threat) (see Böltken 2003:

236, 237; Escandell and Ceobanu 2009: 64–5). Thus, in Moscow, according to the NEORUSS data, about 60 per cent of respondents consider that, where they live, more than 40 per cent of the population are migrants. This incredible figure derives from fears, aggravations and fatigue – stemming, in the first instance, from difficulties in adapting to the breakdown of one's accustomed environment; second, from the lack of information about the reasons for the concentration of migrants in particular places and about their role in the development of the town; and lastly, because Moscow is a giant, overfilled metropolis (many interviewees talked about this).[13]

Seen in this light, the greater apprehension displayed in the NEORUSS survey by Moscow women towards migrants becomes more understandable. Judging by the interviews, such an attitude is not usually accompanied by consciously anti-migrant frames, but boils down to a feeling of insecurity in situations where there are large groups of migrant men nearby – say, in an empty street or remote corner of a market. Moreover, on clarification, it appears that such feelings of fear may also be engendered by encountering a crowd of 'Russian' men. However, the chance of meeting a large group of non-migrant ('Russian') men united by some factor or other is not so great in Moscow – military units, football matches and bikers' rallies are not on the list of places the average resident visits every day. But as a result of their not resembling anything that the women are familiar with, migrant men are already united as a notional 'crowd' in the minds of these women.

Concluding remarks

An understanding of Russian society as continuously changing, among other things, as a result of migration, is only starting to form. This can be seen in the absence of a stable public consensus about migrants and their role and place 'among us' – and is why, in our opinion, various contradictions emerge in the answers to some survey questions. It can also be seen in a lack of tools, practices and initiatives that could facilitate mutually enriching contacts between different people living in Russia.

The mental unpreparedness of society to accept the new daily reality gives rise to anxiety among the population. From this stems the readiness to import images and formulations from the mass media and sociological surveys into the models they use for describing the world; and the readiness to respond to any appealing declaration, also if provocative or contradictory. In ordinary life, such things are quickly forgotten, disappearing into passive memory; people are perplexed to find feelings that they themselves would classify as xenophobic arising in them. However, these feelings emerge either as a result of negative personal experience, producing a readymade explanation for the situation, or due to the necessity of participating in discussions initiated by others – for example, when answering survey or interview questions. In such cases, people discover (sometimes to their surprise) pre-formulated answers to questions they would not have posed themselves in everyday life.

We could call this state of public consciousness 'manifest xenophobia'. Most categories presented by the infosphere to describe social surroundings build on the opposition between different types of 'us' and 'them', whereas in daily life, the agency of these categories is very limited indeed. Many Muscovites may thus choose survey answers that seem to testify to their concern about the threat that migrants, Islam and so on represent to Russian culture, to society and the economy – even though they do not see this threat in the real-life migrants whom they observe around themselves every day.

Notes

1. This literature, in our opinion, still falls seriously short and contrasts starkly with the socio-economic and ethno-cultural significance of the problem of migrant workers in Russia today.
2. Such texts are quite numerous. Some participants in the NEORUSS project have, for example, reflected on the results of the survey of Moscow residents commissioned as part of the project (Filina 2013; Verkhovsky 2013).
3. There are several works based on research conducted with the help of ethno-psychological tests (see, for example, Lebedeva and

Tatarko 2007; Tatarko 2009), but the specifics of these tools make it difficult to compare the results of such studies with those of other research conducted on the micro-level.
4. We postponed the start of interviewing for as long as possible after the Moscow mayoral elections (6 September 2013) in hopes of minimising the effect on informants of the various forms of alarmist anti-migrant rhetoric employed in the election campaign.
5. Here we drew on the experience of Rogers Brubaker and colleagues (2006), who studied – via interviews and focus groups – various manifestations of ethnicity in the lives of ordinary people, taking as an example the daily cooperation of Hungarians and Romanians in Transylvania. As Brubaker notes, 'we avoided asking directly about ethnicity, or signalling a special interest in ethnicity'. He cites Thomas Hylland Eriksen: 'If one goes out to look for ethnicity, one will "find" it' (Brubaker et al. 2006: 15). If ethnicity is only one, far from exclusive, means by which people may interpret and understand social reality (ibid.), in our opinion migrantophobia and xenophobia may be treated in a similar fashion. Therefore 'prompts' are inappropriate.
6. 'Indirect' questions were posed about matters potentially connected with migration, and that could lead to it (transport problems, social services, personal safety, street cleaning, public amenities), but without 'prompts' from the interviewer.
7. Again we stress that we are talking about the attitudes of ordinary citizens. As regards other aspects of nationalism and xenophobia – their manifestation in politics and ideology, in the mass media and public discourse and in the ranks of different (in)formal organisations and groups; as well as the forms and scale of opposition to xenophobia in civil society – in all this a specific 'Russian' character is notable, and indeed is the object of scrutiny in this book.
8. The example of contemporary Russia may be indicative of how foreign policy factors can impact on the level of everyday nationalism. A series of public opinion polls conducted in spring/summer 2014 recorded the declining popularity of anti-migrant views among Russians, influenced by events in Ukraine (see Opalev 2014; Tumanov 2014). However, this conclusion will need to be confirmed by further monitoring of the situation and analysis of new data.
9. For a study of these processes in the case of Germany, see Böltken (2003: 239). As to the dynamics of migrant population numbers, Western research, to our knowledge, does not say anything about

what happens in case this number falls swiftly. Under the economic crisis in Russia of 2014–15, migrants from the 'near abroad', facing 'inflation' of their currency remittances, have started to leave for their home countries. However, it is still unclear whether this trend will produce a serious and lasting (non-seasonal) reduction in the numbers of labour migrants in Russia, or what regions may be most affected. It is also difficult to produce estimates of possible correlation between this trend and the level of migrantophobia in different parts of the country.

10. The inconsistencies in respondents' positions are notable also in the fact that, for example, together with support for the idea of 'the necessity of migrants', almost the same percentage (53.3 per cent) fully or somewhat agreed that 'migrants – legal and illegal, and their children – should be sent back to their former homes' (42.5 per cent did not support this idea, fully or somewhat). The pragmatism of respondents, who understand that the demographic situation in Russia demands an influx of supplementary workforce, is thus coupled with an emotionally coloured and unmotivated (in the question, no explanation is offered) desire 'not to let them in'. We return to this peculiarity in respondents' views in the concluding part of the chapter.
11. Waldinger writes only of 'majority/minority', without giving concrete figures.
12. Flats whose owners illegally register and/or accommodate dozens of migrants.
13. The reluctance of respondents to live in close proximity to multiple-family neighbours who are potentially noisy is also aligned with this aspect (see section on contact between migrants and Muscovites above).

6

Backing the USSR 2.0: Russia's ethnic minorities and expansionist ethnic Russian nationalism

Mikhail A. Alexseev

Rossiiane. It was a word that Eltsin had trouble pronouncing, particularly after indulging in inebriating festivities, yet he clung doggedly to it in public statements, to reassure the ethnic minorities they belonged in the Russian state just as much as the majority ethnic Russians (*russkie*) did. Putin enunciated the word clearly and smoothly after arriving in the Kremlin in late 1999. But in March 2014, the month Russia annexed Crimea from Ukraine, Putin switched over to *russkie* when addressing the joint session of Russia's two houses of parliament. Crimea was now 'a primordial *russkaia* land', its key port of Sevastopol – 'a *russkii* city' and Ukraine's capital Kyiv – 'the mother of *russkie* cities' (Putin 2014a). The annexation of Crimea was accomplished, Putin asserted, to defend the 1.5 million *russkie* there from the pro-EU protesters who had swept away Ukraine's Moscow-leaning government in February 2014. With the guards behind him sporting an updated version of the Imperial Russia regalia, Putin signed into law Crimea's annexation, signalling his resolve to expand Russia's territory and dominance in the former Soviet space under the banner of ethnic *russkii* nationalism (see Aridici 2014 for a review). Commenting on Putin's vision, his spokesman Dmitrii Peskov said: 'Russia (*Rossiia*) is the country on which the Russian [*russkii*] world is based' and Putin 'is probably the main guarantor of the safety of the Russian [*russkii*] world' (Coalson 2014).

Although Russia's militarised intervention in Ukraine thrust it into the media limelight, the conceptual shift to *russkie* had been institutionalised and promoted earlier, when Putin returned to the Kremlin in early 2012. In a programmatic newspaper article on national identity, Putin claimed that Russia was a unique multi-cultural civilisation. This civilisation was based, he argued, on centuries of coexistence among ethnic groups along with the recognition of a special consolidating and leading role of ethnic Russians. 'The core and the binding fabric of this unique civilisation', he wrote, 'are the *russkii* people, the *russkaia* culture' (Putin 2012b). In essence, Putin was proposing a non-Marxist re-packaging of the Soviet principle that ethnic Russians should play a leading role in the process of the 'merging and getting closer' (*sliianie i sblizhenie*) of all ethnic groups. In the new version, this applied to the ethnic groups in the Russian Federation – but potentially also those in its 'near abroad' – with the Russian language as 'the language of interethnic communication'.

This shift raises a question – important both politically and theoretically: Could Putin's turn to ethnic Russian great-power nationalism alienate Russia's ethnic minorities, if not spark off anti-regime protest among them? To what extent may Putin's expansionist rhetoric re-animate among them common memories of imperial and Soviet-era oppression? To what extent may it ignite grievances about the diminution of political status of ethnically non-Russian republics under Putin's 'power vertical' – followed by encroaching restrictions on the use of languages other than Russian, particularly in government and public life, in the predominantly ethnically non-Russian territories of Russia? Ethnic minorities not only comprise about one-fifth of Russia's settled population as well as the majority of an estimated 2.5 to 7 million labour migrants (Bessudnov 2014),[1] they are also heavily concentrated in geopolitically sensitive areas of the Caucasus and down the Volga River to the Central Asian borderlands. Even if latent, their grievances, if sizeable, could serve as a prospective constraint on Putin's expansionist policies.

In particular, we may ask whether Putin's ethnic nationalist turn would face backlashes in Tatarstan, a territorial home to more than 2 million Tatars. The latter are Russia's largest ethnic minority, numbering more than 5.5 million throughout Russia. How may they respond, given the not so distant history of discrimination, repressions and horrific, murderous wholesale deportation of the ethnically related Crimean Tatars under Stalin? Top regional analysts at the Radio Free Europe/Radio Liberty Tatar-Bashkir Service – its director Rim Gilfanov and senior correspondent Merkhat Sharipzhan – in fact raised this and related questions on the air in April 2014.[2]

As yet, these concerns would appear misplaced. Putin has faced practically no ethnic minority backlash over his Ukraine policy since the autumn of 2013. No survey or other systematic data on the issue have been available, but the reputable Levada Centre poll of 20–23 March 2014 showed that 88 per cent of Russia's population (+/– a sampling error of 3.4 per cent) backed what the questionnaire described as 'Crimea's joining of Russia'. Only 6 per cent of those surveyed opposed it (Levada Centre 2014b). In a telephone 'megasurvey' of 48,590 Russians in eighty-three provinces, conducted on 14–16 March 2014 by the independent but government-loyal Public Opinion Foundation (FOM) and the Kremlin-run VTsIOM service, 91 per cent of the respondents supported, and only about 5 per cent opposed, Crimea's annexation. In all but one of the predominantly non-Russian ethnic republics (Bashkortostan, Chuvashia, Dagestan, Ingushetia, Kabardino-Balkaria, Karachaevo-Cherkessia, Mari El, North Ossetia, Tatarstan and Tyva) residents polled in the megasurvey supported Crimea's annexation at about the same rate as residents of Russia did on average, plus or minus three percentage points. The sole exception was Chechnya, where support was somewhat lower – yet, at 83 per cent, still overwhelming. In all republics the number of those who opposed the annexation was within about 2 per cent of the Russian average (FOM 2014; VTsIOM 2014a).[3]

Meanwhile, Putin's approval rating in Levada polls surged from 61 per cent in November 2013, the month the pro-EU protests erupted in Ukraine, to 80 per cent in March 2014, when Russia annexed Ukraine's Crimean Peninsula. By June 2014, Putin's approval climbed to 86 per cent. And by May 2014 the number of Russians saying they were willing to participate in public anti-government protests had sunk to an all-time low of 14 per cent.[4]

In Tatarstan, challenges to the Kremlin on Crimea have been mostly restricted to the separatist blogosphere. Some public protests took place in Tatarstan in the spring of 2014. However, they were, symptomatically, not over the predicament of Crimean Tatars, but against land development along the Volga River that infringed on summer cottage (*dacha*) smallholders. In a twist, the anti-development protesters compared the allegedly corrupt local officials to Ukrainian and US governments and asked Putin to protect them. In formulating their claims, the protesters referred to the United States 'fragmenting other countries, while ignoring the voice of Crimea residents who decided to leave Ukraine'. This was hardly a sign that the Tatarstan public had lost confidence in Putin over Ukraine policy (Biktimirova 2014).

Among Tatarstan's Internet users who search Google, according to Google Trends, interest in the term 'Crimean Tatars' (*'krymskie tatary'*) spiked more so than elsewhere in Russia in March 2014, but then dropped down to statistically insignificant numbers – faster, in fact, than it did in Moscow and St Petersburg (see Figure 6.1). Tatarstan residents exhibited no measurable increase in interest for the term 'deportation' that could have indicated rising fears of discrimination and oppression against non-Russian minorities. The Google search volume for the leading Tatar nationalist groups – the Azatlyk Union of Tatar Youth, the Milli Medzhlis and the All-Tatar Public Centre – generally remained below the level registered by Google Trends. The exception was a moderate rise in searches for 'Azatlyk' in March 2014, but it was lower than the spike in early 2013 (long before the Ukraine crisis and the only other measurable spike since the data became available in 2004).

Theory puzzles

The question of ethnic minority support for ethnic majority nationalism illuminates important knowledge gaps. Mainstream theory schools of intergroup relations – the largely instrumentalist 'group threat' approach (sociology) and the largely constructivist 'social identity' approach (psychology) – hold that minorities may both support or oppose majority nationalism. In other words, neither approach is diagnostic outside further specification. Instrumentalists could argue, based on the seminal work of

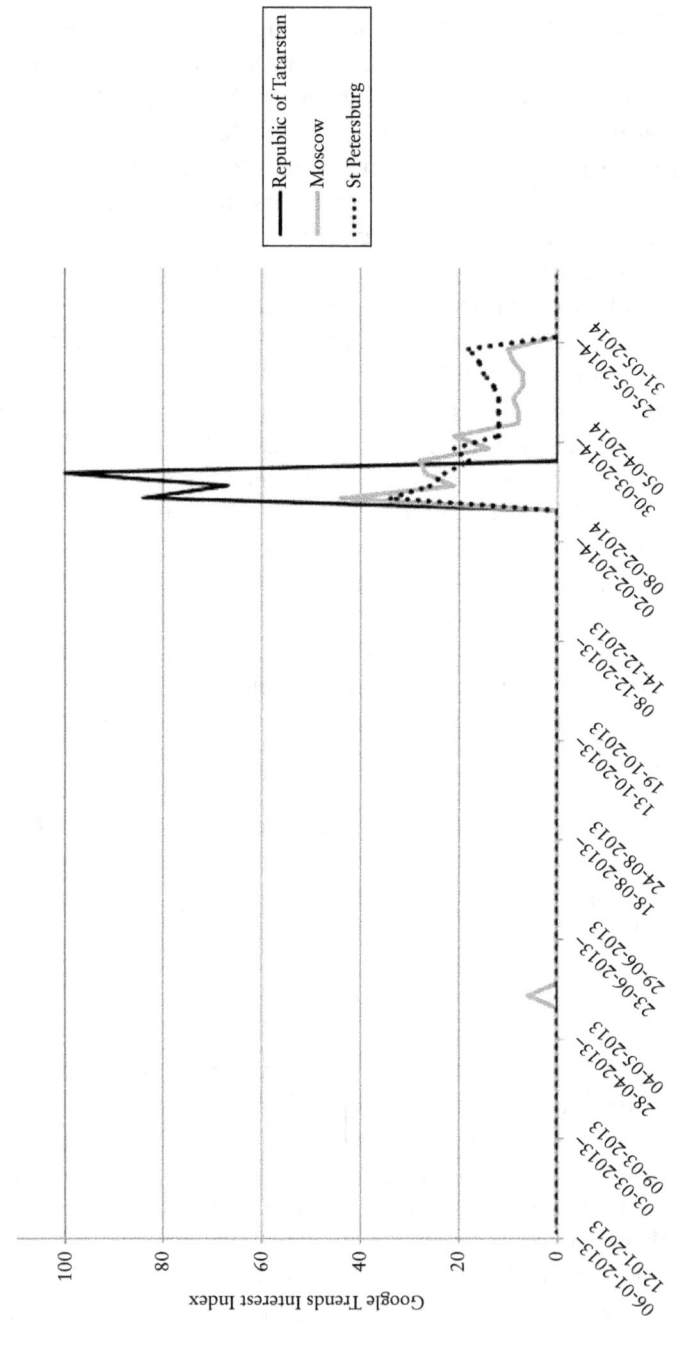

Figure 6.1 Search frequency on Google for the term 'Crimean Tatars' in the Russian language in Tatarstan and the cities of Moscow and St Petersburg (January 2013–June 2014)[5]

Herbert Blumer and scholars who further developed his approach (Blumer 1958; Bobo and Hutchings 1996; Fetzer 2000; McLaren 2003), that Russia's expansion into predominantly ethnic Russian territories of the former Soviet Union poses a threat to the ethnic minorities' group position. The incorporation of new ethnic Russian populations – as in the case of Crimea – means that, collectively, ethnic minorities become less numerous relative to ethnic Russians. Ultimately, this diminution of status would mean diminution of bargaining power for finite state-controlled resources (Blumer 1958). The sense of threat to group position could also be aggravated by fears of labour market competition if the newly acquired territories of a hypothetically expanding state are seen as poorer, prospective migrant-sending areas (Olzak 1992). That could apply to concentrated ethnic Russian settlements in Ukraine, including Crimea. If this logic stands, then we would expect ethnic minorities to oppose Russia's enlargement.

Yet, the same instrumentalist logic may also predict – when extrapolated to expansionist majority nationalism – that threat to their group position would induce ethnic minorities to be more loyal, not less, to the rulers of the expanding state. Formal models and case studies have demonstrated that individuals identify with a group if they care about the status of that group (Shayo 2009), and that individuals assess the payoffs of siding with ingroups or outgroups – including ethnicity versus nation – based on gains from their social environment (Laitin 1998; Sambanis and Shayo 2013). Therefore, the more the perceived status of one's group diminishes, the more individual members of the minority groups may be drawn to compensate with a stronger expression of loyalty to the majority. In other words, they could draw more on their loyalty capital to offset the reduction of their material leverage capital. This would, for example, be the logic of a religious outsider seeking acceptance in a Catholic society by behaving as if she were 'holier than the Pope'. In fact, rigorous analysis of voting behaviour shows that voters systematically support candidates of ethnic groups other than their own in precincts where the candidate's ethnic group is more numerous (Ichino and Nathan 2013). More broadly, in ethnic politics, this response would be consistent with the logic of defection under uncertainty about group identity among individuals facing a collective action problem (see Hale 2008: 62–80). With regard to the central question of this study, that would entail a defection from ethnic minority groups or the weakening of minority group loyalty and claiming a stronger loyalty to the majority group within a state under uncertainty about the effects of Russia's territorial expansion on intergroup relations.

The instrumentalist approach also yields mutually exclusive predictions regarding support for incorporating both Slavic and non-Slavic republics of the former Soviet Union into some form of Russian dominion (most plausibly, a Eurasian Union or a reformed Commonwealth of Independent States – a USSR 2.0, so to speak). The threat to group position theory may, on the one hand, predict that ethnic minorities would oppose such an expansion, fearing more intense intra-minority group competition. With more minorities in the Russian domain, minority group competition for the second-best status is likely to increase. In research on immigration and conflict this logic plays out when the most hostile responses toward immigrants come not from the ethnic majority group in a receiving state, but from ethnic minorities whose proportion in the population is just above the estimated proportion of ethnic minorities represented by migrants (Bergesen and Herman 1998). This competition would be enhanced by minority elites vying to be 'the most favoured lords' – a privileged status giving them greater access to the central government (for example, Moscow) and more protected 'lordship' in minority-populated regions than that enjoyed by other minority elites (Laitin 1991). The institutional legacies of the 'most favoured lord' politics have been pronounced in the post-Soviet area (Cooley 2005).

On the other hand, the instrumentalists could also predict the opposite, if they feel that the privileged position of the dominant ethnic Russians (and Slavs) would be reduced in a larger entity and minority groups may form alliances among each other to increase their bargaining position vis-à-vis the majority on specific issues. From this standpoint, Russia's incumbent ethnic minorities may value the opportunity to form coalitions with other minorities versus the majority more than they may fear the cost of competing with other minorities, as the majority controls key resources. Formal models show that this propensity for minority coalitions is enhanced by the ethnic minorities' sense of vulnerability to the divide-and-rule policies of the ethnic majority government (Lichbach 1995; Lichbach and Weerasinghe 2007). This logic applies particularly in centralised ethnic majority political systems where the centre becomes the object of ethnic group competition (Horowitz 1985). It is not necessarily that minorities would form durable, institutionalised coalitions, but they would compete harder against the ethnic majority and form instrumental issue-based intergroup alliances. The reasoning here would resemble the logic of mobilise-more-against-the-leader – as observed in sports when teams play harder against higher ranked opponents than against similarly or lower ranked opponents.

The constructivist/social identity approach also begets mutually exclusive predictions regarding putative minority support for Russia's expansion to some form of either a Slavic Union or a 'USSR 2.0'. The logic of intergroup bias is that ingroup pride begets outgroup prejudice, intolerance and hostility (Tajfel 1970; Tajfel and Turner 1986; Postmes and Branscombe 2010). This is the logic of ethno-centrism (Levine and Campbell 1972). Faced with increasing majority ethno-centrism, minorities would have stronger fears about their identity security (Seul 1999) or even survival (Waever et al. 1993; Theiler 2003). Thus, the symbolic enhancement of an already dominant outgroup position under a Slavic Union scenario – as with Putin's ethnocentric emphasis on ethnic Russian culture as the 'core and the binding fabric' of the Russian state – would also heighten the sense of threat among Russia's ethnic minorities to their identity security. If so, we would expect ethnic minorities to oppose expansionist ethnic majority nationalism.

And yet, in the case of Russia's expansion, the same social identity logic may also mitigate the majority–minority intergroup bias. In social psychology, the sense that the heterogeneity of one's group decreases relative to others has been linked to a diminishing sense of outgroup threat (Falomir-Pichastor and Frederic 2013; Ommundsen et al. 2013). Minority groups may view the territorial expansion of their state as potentially diluting majority outgroup cohesiveness and therefore decreasing their ingroup heterogeneity relative to the majority ethnic group. In that case, we would expect the sense of identity threat among Russia's ethnic minorities to decline as the Russian territorial domain expands. Minorities would then be less likely to oppose expansionist majority group nationalism. This dynamic seems plausible even regarding expansion into ethnic-Russian populated territories, given debates in Russia as to whether, after nearly a quarter century of the dissolution of the Soviet Union, those ethnic Russians who stayed in the former Soviet republics have retained a sufficiently Russian identity to count as 'full-fledged' (*polnotsennye*) *russkie* (Karavaev 2008). Hypothetically, the same logic would also reduce opposition among Russia's ethnic minorities to Russia's territorial expansion into all of the former Soviet Union – in which case, the symbolic value of common superordinate minority identity relative to the existing ethnic Russian majority identity would increase.

Conversely, the same constructivist/social identity logic of relative group heterogeneity could also be used to argue that Russia's ethnic minorities would oppose an expansion toward a USSR 2.0. This is because, under such a scenario, minority groups would have to deal with new outgroups – other ethnic minorities – within a state. By extension, any inter-minority coalition or alliance (that is, their superordinate group identity as minorities versus the ethnic Russian majority) would be more heterogeneous and therefore more threatened by and hostile to the majority group.

It may be tempting to conclude that these conflicting theoretical interpretations, on balance, mean that ethnic minorities would support expansionist ethnic majority nationalism about as much as ethnic majorities would themselves. Such a conclusion, however, would be under-specified and therefore theoretically infertile. The workings and effects of specific causal processes would be conflated in an indeterminate fashion, and the knowledge gaps would remain.

These theory controversies warrant new empirical probes and tests to improve our understanding of nationalism and intergroup relations in general. The present study takes this path with a detailed analysis of custom mass opinion surveys from Russia on nationalism and ethnic relations.

The data and the measures: Pre-Ukraine crisis opinion baseline

Publicly reported regular opinion surveys in Russia – based on randomised national population samples – typically aggregate into silence the voices of ethnic minorities. In Russia, the Levada Centre, FOM, Romir and other reputed polling agencies, as well as the Kremlin-run VTsIOM, tend not to report the differences between ethnic Russian and ethnic non-Russian respondents.[6] This includes their regular political and socioeconomic monitoring polls, as well as the Ukrainian crisis and Crimea annexation surveys noted above.

Moreover, paradoxical as it may appear, surveys conducted at the time of Russia's actual territorial expansion are unlikely to provide the data necessary to differentiate majority from minority support for such policy. The Kremlin's patriotic, pro-*russkie* media barrage since late 2013 created a context that has made it practically impossible to tease out long-held durable preferences of respondents from the spur-of-the-moment, media- and peer-pressure induced responses in the atmosphere of patriotic fervour. As former US President George W. H. Bush discovered, patriotism-inflated popularity can ebb quickly – after hitting 89 per cent after the Gulf War in February 1991, his approval ratings plummeted to 29 per cent in July 1992.[7] Furthermore, as regards research design, lack of variation on the outcome variables of interest means that the 2014 surveys on Crimea's annexation and Putin's leadership and related issues offer little usable data for systematic comparison of ethnic minority and ethnic majority views.

Fortunately, survey data from shortly before the Ukraine crisis are available to investigate social bases of support among Russia's ethnic minorities for Putin's leadership and Russian expansionist nationalism. With the surveys conducted just a few months before the Ukrainian crisis, the data are likely to capture relatively recent yet probably durable public preferences in Russia, while offering enough variation on key variables to enable theory-relevant inferences to be drawn.

This analysis uses the polls that Russia's Romir agency, respected especially for its business and marketing surveys, carried out from 8 to 27 May 2013. The polls were part of the 'Nation-building, nationalism and the new "other" in today's Russia (NEORUSS)' project. Four surveys were conducted based on representative multi-stage probability samples of adult residents of the Russian Federation (N = 1,000 respondents) and, separately, the cities of Moscow (N = 600), Krasnodar (N = 600) and Vladivostok (N = 601). In the Russian national sample, respondents were selected from fifty-eight out of eighty-three provinces in key population clusters of all eight federal districts of the Russian Federation (including the North Caucasus district).[8] The sampling error margin was approximately +/− 3 per cent. City polls followed identical sampling procedures, resulting in approximately the same non-response rate and the margin of sampling error of about +/− 4 per cent. In each poll, all responses were obtained from face-to-face interviews.[9] The data from these four polls were merged and parsed into two sub-samples.

The grouping variable for the sub-samples was the respondents' ethnic self-identification. The interviewers gave respondents the opportunity to identify with any number of ethnic groups. The overwhelming majority picked only one. The largest number of coded self-identifications was three, in the order given by respondents. All respondents answered this question. The first sub-sample consists only of respondents in the four polls whose first-listed ethnic self-identification was non-Russian (N = 180): 24 per cent among these listed Tatar, 22 per cent Ukrainian, 10 per cent Armenian and 17 per cent belonging to various ethnic groups from the Caucasus or Central Asia.[10] The second sub-sample (N = 2,219) consisted solely of respondents who identified themselves exclusively as ethnic Russians – minus a random sub-set of respondents from Krasnodar. The under-sampling in Krasnodar corrected for the only significant discrepancy in the regional distribution of respondents between the ethnic Russian and non-Russian sub-samples – namely, that the proportion of ethnic Russians interviewed in Krasnodar relative to other locations was about twice as high as that of the non-Russians. Hence, using a random number generator in the Statistical Package for the Social Sciences (SPSS), about half of ethnic Russian respondents in the Krasnodar sample were excluded. This improved the correspondence between the two sub-samples on the distributional properties of socio-demographic indicators. The independent samples t-test showed that age, sex, education level and household income among respondents, as well as the size and location of the sampling units – in fact, all socio-demographic control measures available – were about the same between the sub-samples, and corresponded closely with Russian averages. The results remained constant with equal variances assumed and not assumed, indicating that the difference in sub-sample size had no significant effect on sub-sample means.[11]

The design was quasi-experimental. Ethnic identification was the independent variable, generated by sub-sample selection. In the language of experimental research, the ethnic non-Russian sub-sample was the 'treatment group' and the ethnic Russian sub-sample the 'control group'. Additional control variables – held constant as the t-tests showed – were socio-demographic characteristics of respondents and sampling units. The five dependent variables were territorial state identity preferences, ethnic and civic pride, voting preferences, economic valuations and responsiveness to Putin's statements. To rule out the selective measures bias, the analysis included all survey questions under these topics.

Territorial state identity preference was measured by the question asked in all four NEORUSS polls: 'In the course of history, the borders of states sometimes change. Where do you think the borders of Russia should be – where they are now, but without the Muslim republics of the North Caucasus (response value = 1); exactly where they are now (value = 2); where they are now but with the addition of the former Soviet Slavic republics of Ukraine and Belarus (value = 3); or where the borders of the former Soviet Union were (value = 4)?' In addition, the third and the fourth responses were recoded as dummy variables (0 = not selected, 1 = selected) measuring support separately for the Slavic Union and USSR 2.0. The reference to 'Slavic' in the first item is a hypothetical proxy measure of predominantly ethnic identity motivation. The reference to 'Soviet' in the second item is a hypothetical proxy measure of non-ethnic (civic) identity motivation (see Table 6.1 for descriptives). The 'without the North Caucasus' option implies agreement with Russia's territorial contraction. But since only one answer could be chosen, this does not rule out a latent preference for expansion to other parts of the former Soviet Union or elsewhere – merely that the exclusion of the North Caucasus was seen as a priority.

Ethnic and civic ingroup pride was gauged with two survey questions asked as a cluster in all four NEORUSS polls: 'How proud are you of your ethnic identity?', followed by 'And how proud are you to be a citizen of Russia?' Responses were on a standard four-point agreement/disagreement scale with 1 = agree completely and 4 = disagree completely. The rationale for using both measures was to contrast state/institutional identity commitment and ethnic/non-state group identity commitment, both within and between the sub-samples.

Voting preferences were measured with two questions. The first one, included in all polls, asked: 'Did you vote in the Russian Federation's presidential election on 4 March 2012? If yes, for which candidate did you vote?' Only one answer was allowed. Responses were recoded into two variables – a dummy for voting for Putin in 2012 (0 = no, 1 = yes) and a dummy for voting in 2012 (0 = vote, 1 = no vote). The second question was: 'If a presidential election in Russia were held today, for whom would you vote?' Only one answer was allowed. Responses were recoded into two variables – a dummy for the intent to vote for Putin in 2013 (0 = no, 1 = yes) and a dummy for voting intent in 2013 (0 = vote, 1 = no vote). This question was asked in the national survey only.

Economic valuation was operationalised as a five-point scale based on responses to the question asked in all four NEORUSS polls: 'Do you feel that in the past 12 months the state of the Russian economy has become much better, somewhat better, has not changed, become somewhat worse, or much worse?' Valuations of this kind are likely to be particularly diagnostic of Putin's approval ratings as president, given the importance that Putin has attached in his public statements to his leader-

Table 6.1 Comparison of means test between ethnic Russian and non-Russian respondents in 2013 NEORUSS surveys on select outcome variables[12]

	Ethnic ID	N	Mean	Std Deviation	t-test for Equality of Means	
					Equival variance assumed	Equival variance not assumed
Q35. Support expansion of Russian territory to all of Ukraine and Belarus (0 = no, 1 = yes)	Russian Non-Russian	2,060 166	0.218 0.193	0.413 0.396	0.44	0.424
Q35. Support expansion of Russian territory to all of the former Soviet Union (0 = no, 1 = yes)	Russian Non-Russian	2,060 166	0.255 0.337	0.436 0.474	0.021*	0.032*
Q8. How proud are you of your ethnic identity? (1 = very proud to 4 = not at all proud)	Russian Non-Russian	2,151 171	1.530 1.440	0.643 0.605	0.097	0.081
Q9. How proud are you to be a citizen of Russia? (1 = very proud to 4 = not at all proud)	Russian Non-Russian	2,138 168	1.650 1.580	0.735 0.687	0.258	0.232
Q73. Voted for Putin in 2012 presidential election (0 = no, 1 = yes)	Russian Non-Russian	1,357 91	0.654 0.703	0.476 0.459	0.342	0.329
Q73. Did not vote in 2012 presidential election (0 = voted, 1 = didn't vote)	Russian Non-Russian	1,906 159	0.303 0.434	0.460 0.497	0.001***	0.002**
Q20. Would vote for Putin as president now (May 2013) (0 = no, 1 = yes)	Russian Non-Russian	645 60	0.501 0.467	0.500 0.503	0.614	0.617
Q20. Would not vote if presidential election was held now (May 2013) (0 = would vote, 1 = wouldn't vote)	Russian Non-Russian	755 78	0.146 0.231	0.353 0.424	0.047*	0.09
Q74. Do you think in the last 12 months the Russian economy improved or got worse? (on a scale from 1 = much improved to 5 = much worsened, 3 = no change)	Russian Non-Russian	2,038 163	3.050 3.010	0.856 0.846	0.54	0.536

Note: Significance levels are marked ***, if $p < .001$; **, if $p < .01$; and *, if $p < 0.05$.

ship as promoting Russia's economic growth. In fact, Putin's initials based on his first, middle and last names (VVP) have been frequently evoked in mainstream (that is, Kremlin-sanctioned) Russian media's economic discourses referring to the identically sounding Russian abbreviation for GDP (VVP).

Responsiveness to Putin – a proxy for Putin's capacity to change the public's views on social and political issues – was assessed with a split-sample experiment embedded in the questionnaires used in Moscow, Krasnodar and Vladivostok. A random selection of half of the respondents in these polls were asked: 'Let us now talk a little about ethnic relations in Russia. Do you believe the ethnic diversity of Russia's population strengthens or weakens our country?' The remaining half of respondents were asked the same question, but after a different introduction: 'Putin claims that the ethnic diversity of Russia's population strengthens our country.' Responses were coded as 1 = 'strengthens', 2 = 'somewhat strengthens, somewhat weakens' and 3 = 'weakens'. The interviewers rotated these versions of the questions, so if one respondent was asked the original question, the next respondent was asked the same question, but with a Putin cue.[13]

For all these variables, frequencies were computed to examine substantive similarities and differences on the issues of interest between the ethnic Russian and non-Russian sub-samples. The statistical significance (that is, the likelihood of occurrence due to chance alone) was assessed with independent-samples t-tests and, in the split-sample experiment, with one-sample t-tests. Additional tests controlled for differences in sub-sample size.

The results: Minorities no constraint on Russian expansionism, despite latent grievances

The principal finding was that ethnic identity had limited effects. Ethnic non-Russian respondents were almost as likely as ethnic Russian ones to support Russian territorial expansion to include all of Ukraine and Belarus (Slavic Union); they were about equally proud of their ethnic identity and Russian citizenship, about equally likely to have voted for Putin in 2012 and in 2013

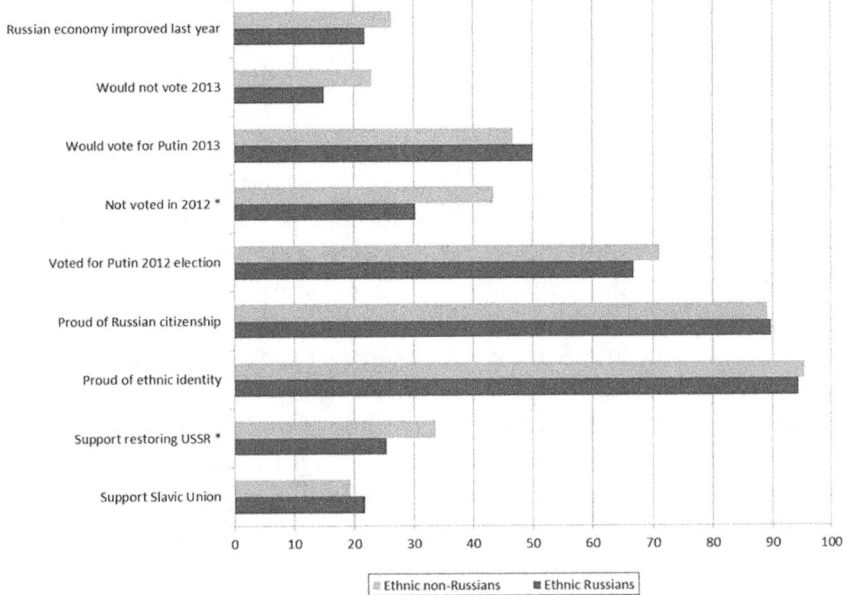

Figure 6.2 Preferences for Russian territorial identity, ingroup pride, political preferences and economic valuations among ethnic Russian and non-Russian respondents in the 2013 NEORUSS surveys (percentage of all respondents who answered the question)[14]

Note: *Statistically significant (non-randomly related) in the independent sample t-test

as well as to abstain from voting in 2013, and to believe that the Russian economy had been improving over the previous year (see Table 6.1 and Figure 6.2). This conclusion is based on the p-significance values in the independent sample t-test with SPSS 21.0, with equal variance between the sub-samples not assumed.

Two differences between sub-sample means were statistically significant. Ethnic non-Russians were more likely than ethnic Russians to support Russian expansion to the entire territory of the former Soviet Union, but were also less likely to have voted in the 2012 presidential election. Descriptive statistics offer additional insights on the likely prominence of these views in the general population and on intergroup differences on key issues of interest in absolute terms.

BACKING THE USSR

Paradoxical as it may seem, in absolute terms the ethnic non-Russian respondents – more so than ethnic Russian respondents – wanted to see Russia's territory expand. Prompted by the introductory statement that state borders may shift in the course of history and asked where they believed Russia's borders should be, 47.3 per cent of the ethnic Russian and 53 per cent of the non-Russian respondents preferred expansion.[15] Even though the additional t-test showed that this difference was not statistically significant, in absolute terms support for expansion trumped support for the status quo. Another 36.7 per cent of the ethnic non-Russians and 38.1 per cent of the ethnic Russians said they felt Russia's present borders should remain as they now are. A minority of respondents opted for excluding the republics of the North Caucasus from Russia while keeping other borders the same – about 10 per cent of ethnic non-Russians and 14.5 per cent ethnic Russians (Figure 6.3). That option, however, probably reflects a strong ethnic exclusionist preference consistent with ethnic Russian nationalism, given that the question specifically mentioned only the Muslim republics of the North Caucasus as areas to be excluded from Russia. In the context of media-frenzied ethnic nationalist fervour, these respondents could plausibly support Putin's expansionist ethnic nationalism. However, whether or not they do so is empirically indeterminate with the existing data.

A concurrent nontrivial and counterintuitive finding is that almost as many ethnic non-Russians as ethnic Russians –19.3 per cent versus 21.8 per cent of respondents, respectively – backed the idea of Russia expanding to the size of a 'Slavic Union' of Russia, Ukraine and Belarus (Figure 6.3). This distinction was not statistically significant. However, ethnic identification mattered significantly within the non-Russian sub-sample. Since a large number of ethnic non-Russians were Slavs (Ukrainian and Belorussian), an additional test checked if their views differed systematically from those of the non-Slavs. They did. A Slavic Union was favoured by only 12.2 per cent of the Tatars (N = 41) and 11.1 per cent of the respondents who identified with an ethnic

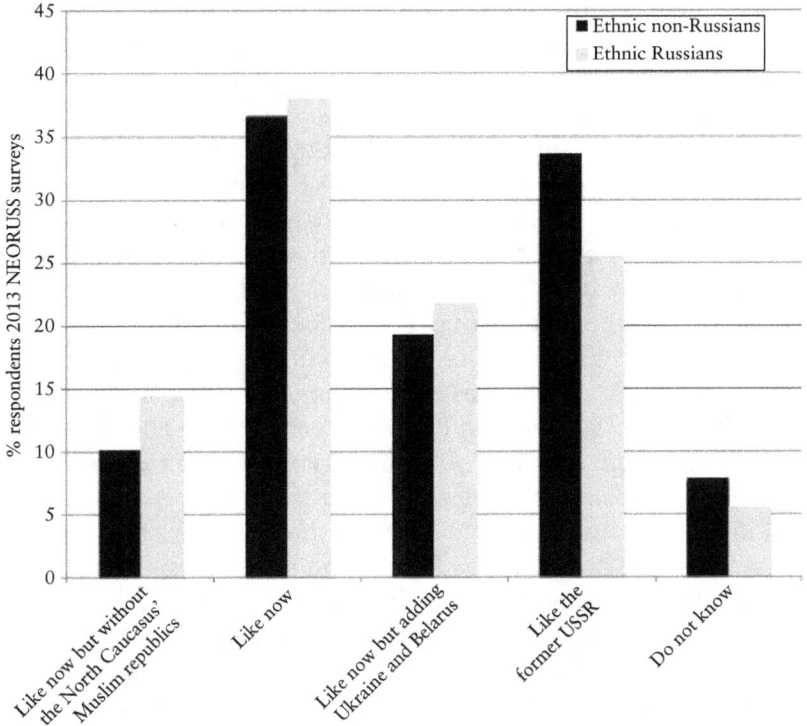

Figure 6.3 Russia territorial identity preferences in the 2013 NEORUSS surveys among ethnic Russian and non-Russian respondents

group hailing from the Caucasus or Central Asia (N = 36) – but was favoured by 34.2 per cent of the Ukrainians (N = 38). The difference between the Slavs (N = 45) and the non-Slavs (N = 121) on this question was statistically significant. Still, it is also notable that almost two-thirds (65.8 per cent) of the ethnic Ukrainians surveyed and four out of seven Belorussians opted not to support the Slavic Union. The difference-of-means tests on Slavic versus non-Slavic views within the non-Russian sub-sample, however, are not as substantively reliable as those on the views between the Russian versus non-Russian sub-samples, given the small n within the sub-sample for specific ethnic groups. The same goes for one other result evident from this comparison: that support for the

Slavic Union within Russia was stronger among Russia's non-Russian Slavs than among ethnic Russians. If this tentative finding holds, it means that ethnic irredentist motivations trumped ethnic expansionist motivations among the respondents.

The most important substantive finding from these tests is that significantly more ethnic non-Russians (33.7 per cent) than ethnic Russians (25.5 per cent) wanted Russia's borders to encompass all of the former Soviet Union. Large in absolute terms, this difference is also statistically non-random. Within the non-Russian ethnic sub-sample, intergroup differences were smaller than on support for the Slavic Union, even though support for expansion to a USSR 2.0 was this time stronger among the non-Slavs than among the Slavs – namely, 31.7 per cent among the Tatars and 42.7 per cent among those identifying with an ethnic group from the Caucasus or Central Asia versus 23.7 per cent among Ukrainians. About 36 per cent among the non-Slavs and 26.7 per cent among the non-Russian Slavs supported Russia's expansion to a USSR 2.0. However, these intergroup differences were not statistically significant. On the whole, it appears that among the ethnic non-Russians, the idea of the imagined or idealised Soviet 'condominium', for all its flaws and controversies, has retained a significantly stronger allure than among the ethnic Russians.

Proud Rossiiane

Ethnic non-Russians emerged just as proud as ethnic Russians of their ethnicity and Russian citizenship. In both sub-samples, approximately 95 per cent of respondents expressed pride in their ethnicity and approximately 90 per cent in being Russian citizens (that is, *rossiiane*) (Table 6.1). The breakdown between respondents who said they were 'very proud' of their ethnicity and citizenship and those who said they were 'more proud than not' was about the same between the sub-samples. On the whole, the data show that Putin in 2013 could tap into Russian patriotism for support almost equally among ethnic Russians and non-Russians alike.

Backing Putin

While indicating they were generally less likely to participate in elections, ethnic non-Russians said they were about as likely to vote for Putin as president as were ethnic Russians (Figure 6.2). Among ethnic non-Russians who said they voted in the 2012 presidential election, some 71 per cent said they voted for Putin – slightly more than among the ethnic Russians, with 67 per cent. Stated willingness to vote for Putin if elections were held at the time of the survey in May 2013 declined, but at about the same rate between the sub-samples. Some 47 per cent of ethnic non-Russians and 50 per cent of ethnic Russians from among those who said they would vote in 2013 opted for Putin. These percentage-point differences in 2012 and 2013 voting preference between sub-samples were not statistically significant. The decline in the number of respondents willing to vote for Putin from 2012 to 2013 was statistically significant among ethnic Russians and non-Russians alike – indicating no systematic difference in voting preferences.

We should note that ethnic non-Russians were more likely to abstain from voting in 2012. In the NEORUSS surveys, more than 43 per cent of ethnic non-Russians said they did not vote in 2012, compared to some 30 per cent of ethnic Russians. The difference is statistically significant and may indicate latent tensions between Putin's government and Russia's ethnic minorities – assuming that *not* voting is an expression of alienation or grievances.[16]

However, this issue hardly poses a political threat to the Kremlin. First, the scale of estimated non-participation was low. It was certainly nowhere near the scale of the Crimean Tatars' boycott of the 'referendum' on Crimean independence that was set barely two weeks following the Russia-led military takeover of the peninsula in March 2014 – a boycott, which despite tensions, failed to stop the Russian annexation. Second, the finding actually indicates that even if they develop grievances against the regime, Russia's ethnic minorities are more likely to express them by withdrawing from politics, not by marching on the Kremlin. Third, the difference on the intent to vote in 2013 between non-Russians and ethnic Russians was not statistically significant when controlling for sub-sample size (Table 6.1). Finally, economic valuations remained positive across the sub-samples, indicating that ethnic minorities had no special economic grievances that may undermine their support for Putin. Some 77 per cent of ethnic Russians and non-Russians alike felt the economy was just as strong or stronger than one year previously. Ethnic minority respondents, in fact, had a somewhat more optimistic economic outlook in absolute terms, with more of them – 26.4, compared to 21.9 per cent among ethnic Russians – saying the economy was improving (Table 6.1).

Responding to Putin: A caveat from the split-sample experiment

Ethnic non-Russians were systematically more responsive to Putin's political messages than ethnic Russians – but not necessarily the way Putin would approve. In the split-sample experiment embedded in the surveys in Moscow, Krasnodar and Vladivostok, the number of ethnic Russians who said ethnic diversity strengthens, partly strengthens and partly weakens, or weakens Russia was practically the same, regardless of whether the question was asked with or without a prompt saying Putin believed diversity strengthened Russia: the Putin cue simply had no effect. This was not the case among ethnic non-Russians, where the Putin cue had a sizeable and statistically significant effect – a mere 0.1 per cent probability that the difference between the Putin-cue and no-Putin-cue results was due to chance alone.[17]

However, the Putin cue resonated negatively among ethnic non-Russians. After hearing that Putin said that diversity strengthened Russia, fewer non-Russians agreed with that statement than without the prompt. The Putin cue reduced the percentage of non-Russians who believed diversity strengthened Russia by almost a fifth – from 32 to 26 per cent in absolute terms. The ethnic non-Russians in this test responded as if they mistrusted Putin: it was as if Putin said one thing, he meant the opposite, or if he proposed a course of action, the best bet would be not to follow it.[18]

Substantively, such a response poses a challenge to the Kremlin – although hardly a pressing or sizeable one. In the final count,

Table 6.2 Responsiveness to Putin's message that ethnic diversity strengthens Russia in a split-sample experiment, 2013 NEORUSS surveys in the Russian Federation and the cities of Moscow, Vladivostok and Krasnodar

	RUSSIAN		NON-RUSSIAN	
	No cue	Putin cue	No cue	Putin cue
	(N = 1,467)	(N = 592)	(N = 122)	(N = 42)
Strengthens	10.3	11.0	32.0	26.2
Partly strengthens, partly weakens	62.3	62.8	55.7	59.5
Weakens	27.4	26.2	12.3	14.3

Note: In the 'no cue' sub-sample, respondents were asked if they believed ethnic diversity strengthened, somewhat strengthened and somewhat weakened, or weakened Russia. In the 'Putin cue' sample, the same question was prefaced with the statement: 'Putin claims that ethnic diversity strengthens Russia . . .'

similar to non-voting, the negative effect was small in absolute terms. The percentage of respondents apparently swayed by the Putin cue was marginal relative to the total sample size.

Theoretical significance: Prospective group status within dynamic state identity

Ethnic identity matters to the extent that the state identity is at stake. Ethnic non-Russians were significantly more likely than ethnic Russians to support the expansion of Russia to the entire territory of the former Soviet Union. Ethnic Ukrainians and Belorussians were significantly more likely than ethnic non-Slavs and ethnic Russians to support incorporating into Russia the entire territory of Ukraine and Belarus. The study design ruled out that these differences could be ascribed to socio-demographic factors – age, sex, income, education and location or size of the settlements where respondents resided. Furthermore, the comparison-of-means tests ruled out that these differences were a likely by-product of differences in ingroup pride (ethnic or civic), socio-tropic economic valuations (that have been shown to significantly affect intergroup tolerance), or political preferences (electoral support for Putin). It is also unlikely that support for Russia's territorial identity was a by-product of a somewhat larger, although statistically significant, self-reported non-voting rate among ethnic non-Russians in the 2012 presidential election.

The results offer important insights into the theory puzzles that set the stage for this analysis. They are twofold. First, the tests help to rule out the causal arguments that predicted no difference or less support among ethnic non-Russians for Russian territorial expansion to a USSR 2.0, as well as the causal arguments that predicted no difference or less support among non-Slavs than among Slavs and Russians for Russia expanding to a Slavic Union. In other words, ethnic identity was found to matter in intergroup status reassessment. From the instrumentalist/group threat perspective, this means that the logic of intergroup competition may not apply to *inter-minority* competition, and the logic of incentives for defection from minority ingroups to majority outgroups ('holier than the Pope' effect) may not be as potent as may be expected when the intergroup boundary is ethnic. From the constructivist/social identity perspective, the findings suggest that when intergroup boundaries run along minority–majority lines, group homogeneity (or 'entitativity') is not as important as the theory may predict – whether what is at issue is the assessment of minority ingroup homogeneity or majority outgroup homogeneity. In other words, status does matter in intergroup identity evaluations. Status and identity are likely to be relational; they provide interactive motivations. But how are they related or do they interact?

This is what the second insight from the empirical analysis is about. It brings in the state – a distinct political science contribution to the study of intergroup relations. It suggests that instrumentalist (status) and constructivist (identity) motivations are themselves contingent on perceived state power and institutional design. The Russian case is uniquely suited for exploring the impact of the latter, because it is part of a region where interstate borders have been disputed and in flux and, in many respects, not readily imagined as permanent, given how fast the Soviet Union collapsed and how long the legacies of its unresolved border issues lasted. We should recall the thousands of miles of still non-demarcated borders among the former Soviet republics and unrecognised self-proclaimed states within them (such as Transnistria/Moldova or Abkhazia/Georgia). Thus, the question about where the borders of Russia should be actually tapped into real-world preferences that varied meaningfully among respondents. This ensured variation on theory-relevant dependent variables. It is not surprising that previous studies of intergroup relations could not assess the role of the state in the same way. In Western Europe and North America, where most of this research has been conducted, states have been institutionally and territorially stable at least since the Second World War. Replicating the NEORUSS question on Russia's territory preference would entail unthinkable, unrealistic questions, such as whether respondents in France may want the borders of their country to include the entire empire of Charlemagne, or whether Austrians would want to restore the borders of the Hapsburg Empire. And whatever variations such questions may produce, they would mean little in terms of one's ethnic group identity or status, since few (if any) respondents would actually believe that restoration of these empires could be feasible. Not so in Russia, with its indeterminate and explicitly or implicitly contested borders.

Thus, social identity becomes a significant motivation for ethnic minorities when identity applies to the state. The key idea here is *state identity*. It becomes critically important in shaping intergroup relations when state identity is uncertain or debated or re-imagined or desired to be changed – that is, when state identity is *dynamic*. Since the state must be sovereign in international relations and sovereignty means the exercise of legitimate coercive power within a defined territory, state identity must, by default, be territorial identity. And this, in turn, means that territory is also a proxy for the understanding of *how* this coercive power should be exercised – how it is to be policed, what the rules of policing are and, hence, what kind of government governs the territory. However, in the context of dynamic state identity, imagining specifically what these government institutions may be and projecting their effects is probably too complex an endeavour for the average person (and survey respondents). They most likely derive their preferences from cognitive and emotional shortcuts.

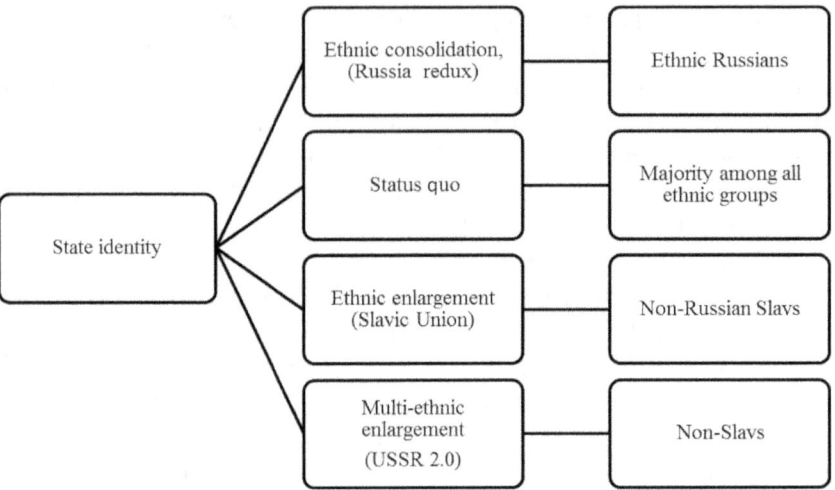

Figure 6.4 Dominant preferences for Russia's state identity across ethnic groups in the 2013 NEORUSS survey.

Note: Groups listed in the right-hand column are based on percentages of responses, within ethnic groups, to the question on preferred Russian borders and tests of statistical significance

Ethnic identity is one of the strongest shortcuts of this kind, being 'an especially useful uncertainty-reducing device' in the context of group politics (Hale 2008: 40–7). The present analysis has further shown how ethnic group identification decisively shapes preferences when individual group members consider, project or *prospectively* evaluate their status or group position within the context of changing or uncertain – that is, dynamic – state identity.

These prospective group status valuations under dynamic state identity are modelled in Figures 6.4 and 6.5. The first figure maps out the feasible state identity choices available in the contemporary Russian context and links them with a distinct pattern of state identity preferences among ethnic sub-samples of NEORUSS survey respondents. The status quo (Russia within the borders at the time of the survey) was the preference indicated by more respondents than any other option across all ethnic groups (see Figure 6.3). Preferences for other state identity options diverged.

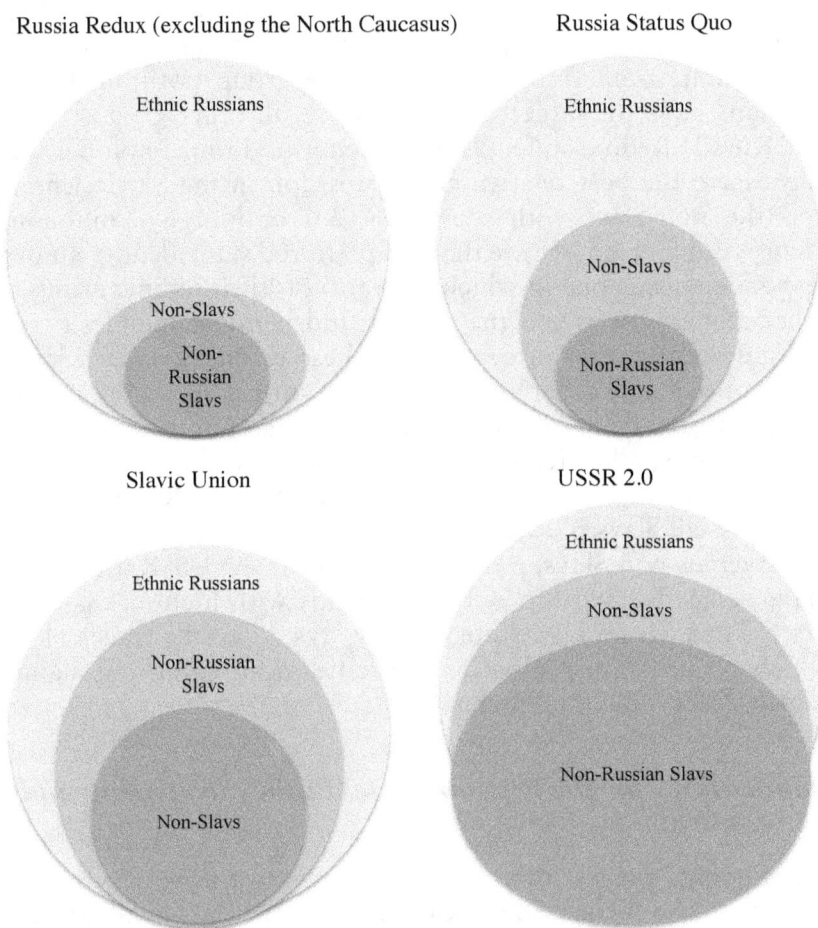

Figure 6.5 Prospective group status in four Russia state identity scenarios

The 'Russia Redux' option (same borders but without the Muslim republics of the North Caucasus) got the strongest support from ethnic Russians. The Slavic Union option (Russia incorporating Ukraine and Belarus) got the strongest support from ethnic non-Russian Slavs (Ukrainians and Belorussians). The USSR 2.0 option was backed most strongly by the non-Slavs – of whom the largest groups were ethnic Tatars and Armenians.

Figure 6.5 shows the logic of prospective status valuations. The relative size of each group is approximate, but this is immaterial, for the important thing here is relative group position. Ethnic Russians have the largest size relative to all other groups under the Russia Redux state identity scenario. Ethnic non-Russian Slavs have the best relative group position in the Slavic Union, and the non-Slavs with the USSR 2.0 option. By combining Figures 6.4 and 6.5, we see that the preferred state identity among respondents was one in which the ratio of 'their' ethnic group to other ethnic groups was the highest. Independent samples t-tests for statistical significance validated these results. For the 'Status Quo' option, all differences of means among the three groups were statistically insignificant, as expected. For the remaining three options, all differences between high and low group means were statistically significant: for 'Russia Redux' – Russian versus non-Russian Slavs $p = .031^*$; for the Slavic Union – non-Russian Slavs versus non-Slavs, $p = .006^{**}$; and for the USSR 2.0 – non-Slavs versus Russians, $p = .023^*$ (groups with high means listed first). Thus we see how state identity lays down the tracks along which group status valuations become meaningful and significantly affect individual preferences.

Implications for the Russian state, Putin's leadership and nationalism

The findings suggest that Putin's expansionist policy in the territories of the former Soviet Union under the banner of Russian nationalism and triumphalism over the annexation of Crimea from Ukraine – as paradoxical as it may seem – is unlikely to alienate a significant number of Russia's ethnic minorities. Three indicators are the most telling. First, Russia's ethnic minorities were just as much in favour of Russian territorial expansion as were the ethnic Russians. The distinction between the ethnic non-Russian Slavs and non-Slavs within Russia, however, suggests that support for Russian nationalist expansionism – and, specifically, on expanding into Ukraine – would be stronger among ethnic minorities if framed as part of rebuilding a USSR 2.0 than creating a Slavic Union (if anything, due simply to the fact that Russia has a larger non-Slavic population than a Ukrainian and Belarussian population). The bottom line on Ukraine is that incorporating Ukraine into Russia or into a Russia-led interstate union would get strong support among ethnic Russians and non-Russians alike.

Second, pride in Russian citizenship was just as high among ethnic non-Russians as it was among ethnic Russians. The ratio of pride in ethnicity over pride in citizenship was the same across these groups. This means that, fundamentally, Russia's ethnic minorities could be just as patriotic and support Putin's Ukraine policy just as adamantly as the ethnic Russian majority. Their pride in Russia hardly needs a boost of nationalist, patriotic fervour. It was so high already in 2013 that there was hardly any room for expanding.

Third, support for Putin as president appears basically strong among ethnic non-Russians. While voting preferences may change quickly, the surveys find – importantly – that Putin can bank on an overwhelming sense among ethnic minorities that the Russian economy has been doing well and has good prospects. This sentiment was shared with ethnic Russians, and is typically a strong indicator of support for incumbent politicians. Moreover, the data show that even those ethnic non-Russians who may be wary of or protest against the rise of Russian chauvinism or the resurgence of Soviet legacies of ethnic minority discrimination and oppression are most likely to do so in silence.

In a twist that favours Putin's rule, not only has territorial expansion in the former Soviet space a solid basis of support among ethnic non-Russians: it also appears to be reducing exclusionist sentiments among ethnic Russians that had remained consistently strong for more than a decade. Moderately reliable VTsIOM polls found that support for the slogan 'Russia for Russians' (*Rossiia dlia russkikh*) dropped to 38 per cent in May 2014 compared to 50 per cent in September 2013. Over the same period, support for Russia as a multi-ethnic state rose to 57 per cent from 44 per cent (Rustamova 2014). This would indicate that territorial expansion – or institutional expansion entailing greater Russian influence over former Soviet territories – may pay a double dividend in reducing both majority ethnic intolerance and minority ethnic grievances domestically. In order for these effects to last, however, such expansion would have to be long-term, piecemeal and cumulative. With these opinion trends – as well as the understanding that patriotic opinion rallies may not be durable – the Kremlin gets an added motivation to carry out expansionist policies in the former Soviet Union, so as to boost the longevity of Putin's rule – indeed, well beyond 2024, if desired. If Russia's ethnic minorities turn into a 'fifth column' it is more likely to be one helping Putin build up a USSR 2.0, not one aimed at subverting his expansionist designs.

Russia's expansion into Crimea in 2014 is a telling case, a demonstration par excellence of the logic of dynamic state identity. It relates to all three options for Russia's state identity change. First, it could be supported as ethnic consolidation. The Crimean population is predominantly ethnic Russian – about 59 per cent in 2001 self-identified as ethnic Russians and 77 per cent as predominantly Russian-language speakers. This would arguably resonate with the sense of ethnic group dominance among Russia's ethnic Russians (80.6 per cent in 2010)[19] and support perceptions that the annexation of Crimea sustains the group position of ethnic Russians while increasing the territory and population of their state – a clear gain.

Second, the annexation of Crimea could be viewed as a step toward a Slavic Union and receive particularly strong support among Russia's ethnic non-Russian Slavs. This perception could draw on the interaction of ethnic and institutional dimensions of group identity. Ethnically, the Crimean population in 2001 was 24.4 per cent Ukrainian and 1.5 per cent Belorussian – a significantly larger non-Russian Slav share than in the Russian Federation. This Ukrainian ethnic identity was reinforced institutionally, with Crimea being part of the Soviet republic of Ukraine since 1954 and of independent Ukraine since 1991. This means that Russia's ethnic Ukrainians could regard the inclusion of Crimea's Ukrainians as boosting not only their numbers but their institutional leverage as well.

Third, the annexation of Crimea may be viewed as a long-term process leading toward USSR 2.0. Typical secondary-school history education in Russia since the Soviet period has presented the initial incorporation of Crimea into the Russian Empire in 1783 as a glorious moment in history that paved the way for Russian expansion to Eastern Europe, the Caucasus and Central Asia. In the large historical picture, the collapse of the Soviet Union reversed those territorial gains. Russia's post-Soviet borders resemble its pre-Crimea eighteenth-century borders. The annexation of Crimea could thus trigger a sense of the tide of history turning back in Russia's favour. These considerations – as well as the fact that non-Slavic Crimean Tatars comprise 12 per cent of Crimea's population – could boost support for the annexation of Crimea among Russia's ethnic non-Slavs who in 2013 backed expansion to a USSR 2.0. The non-Slavic population factor, however, means that support among ethnic non-Slavs for a putative expansion into the overwhelmingly Slavic Eastern Ukraine would hinge on historical-institutional understandings, that is, on how strongly they may associate the concept of *Novorossiia* with a path toward the 'USSR 2.0' option.

These considerations indicate that Moscow is likely to enjoy strong baseline support for territorial expansion among Russia's ethnic minorities regardless of how long the patriotic euphoria over Crimea lasts. However, the degree of support among specific groups of ethnic non-Russians will probably depend on the nature of such an expansion – territorial (through annexation or accession to Russia) or institutional (through Russia-dominant entities like the Eurasian Union). Persistent support across all ethnic non-Russian groups is more likely if territorial acquisitions occur first in predominantly Slavic areas and are seen as part of a longer-term institutional expansion toward the 'USSR 2.0'.

Notes

1. With reference to the data provided by Russia's Federal Migration Service.
2. Radio Free Europe/Radio Liberty Podcast, 'Russia's Looming Tatar Problem', 4 April 2014, available at <www.rferl.org/content/podcast-russias-looming-tatar-problem/25321627.html> (last accessed 17 July 2014).
3. The number of respondents was 723 in Bashkortostan, 504 in

Chechnya, 511 in Chuvashia, 717 in Dagestan, 502 in Ingushetia, 529 in Kabardino-Balkaria, 505 in Karachaevo-Cherkessia, 504 in Mari El, 513 in North Ossetia, 830 in Tatarstan and 306 in Tyva.
4. See the Levada Centre's 'Indeksy' [Indices], available at <www.levada.ru/indeksy> (last accessed 17 July 2014).
5. Based on the Google Trends frequency index, scaled to the top value = 100 at the highest peak in the chart. Source: <http://www.google.com/trends/explore?q=%D0%B4%D0%B5%D0%BF%D0%BE%D1%80%D1%82%D0%B0%D1%86%D0%B8%D1%8F#q=%D0%BA%D1%80%D1%8B%D0%BC%D1%81%D0%BA%D0%B8%D0%B5%20%D1%82%D0%B0%D1%82%D0%B0%D1%80%D1%8B&geo=RU-TA%2C%20RU-MOW%2C%20RU-SPE&date=1%2F2013%2018m&cmpt=geo> (last accessed 23 March 2014).
6. Based on examination of published reports of all surveys on agency websites matching the keywords or tags 'Ukraine' and 'Crimea' as well as regular (weekly, biweekly or monthly) monitoring surveys.
7. Gallup, official website, available at <http://www.gallup.com/poll/116677/presidential-approval-ratings-gallup-historical-statistics-trends.aspx> (last accessed 10 August 2014).
8. Excluding Chechnya and Ingushetia in the North Caucasus and six regions in the Russian Far North, where marginally small populations and remoteness made access infeasible.
9. The non-response rate was about 81 per cent. Principal reasons for non-response were inability to access the residence (6 per cent), no residents at home after three visits (30 per cent), the randomly selected household member was not at home (26 per cent), refusal to participate in the interview after opening the door (27 per cent) and refusal to complete the interview (9 per cent). When the first randomly selected respondent could not be reached, the same multi-stage random sampling procedure was used to find an alternative respondent. Interviewers re-did about 4 per cent of the interviews after post-survey peer quality control by phone or the examination of questionnaires. Additionally, about 5 per cent of the interviews were re-done after quality control by regional supervisors.
10. Of these, eight respondents (4.4 per cent) gave their second identification and two respondents (1.1 per cent) their third identification as ethnic Russian. Given the small size of the ethnic minority sub-sample, these respondents were retained.
11. A methodological appendix with these tests results is available on request.

12. The Welch–Satterthwaite method was used to compare means, assuming the sub-samples did not have equal variance. The results show that violating the equal variance assumption had no effect on the estimation of which between-the-sample differences of means were statistically significant.
13. The rotation was 100 per cent randomised. Interviewers were not set quotas in terms of socio-demographic categories. The difference in experimental (N = 41) versus control (N = 121) group size is a by-product of this random selection, given the small proportion of ethnic non-Russians in the total sample. Comprising just 4.5 per cent of the total sub-sample in the three polls (N = 1,800) it is consistent with the sampling error margin for each poll.
14. Excluding the 'don't knows' and refusals.
15. Excluding the 'don't knows' and refusals to answer the question, with valid N = 166 (non-Russian sub-sample) and N = 2,060 (ethnic Russian sub-sample).
16. Differences between Slavs versus non-Slavs in the ethnic non-Russian sample were not statistically significant.
17. Based on a one-sample t-test.
18. One other split-sample experiment with a Putin cue was conducted in the Krasnodar survey, on support for the political slogan 'Stop feeding the Caucasus!', popular in Russia's predominantly ethnic Russian regions at the time of the survey. About half of the randomly selected respondents from the sample were given a prompt that Putin had condemned the slogan. The prompt had practically no effect, whether among ethnic Russians or non-Russians. The full results are not reported here, because the ethnic non-Russian sub-sample was small – with valid N = 20 for the no-cue question and N = 17 for the Putin-cue question.
19. State Statistics Committee of Ukraine, government website, available at <http://2001.ukrcensus.gov.ua/eng/results/general/language/Crimea> (last accessed 10 August 2014); Federal'naia sluzhba gosudarstvennoi statistiki (n.d).

7
Rallying 'round the leader more than the flag: Changes in Russian nationalist public opinion 2013–14

Mikhail A. Alexseev and Henry E. Hale

From May 2013 to November 2014, Russia's domestic and international environment underwent a tectonic shift. As hundreds of thousands of ordinary citizens in neighbouring Ukraine rose up against the Moscow-backed and increasingly authoritarian government of Viktor Yanukovych and ultimately ousted him in early 2014, the Kremlin and the media it controls ratcheted up anti-Western rhetoric, dramatically increased its use of nationalist themes, and even employed military force in a sudden operation to annex the Ukrainian peninsula of Crimea and its port of Sevastopol, which Ukraine had since independence rented out to the Russian Black Sea Fleet. The Kremlin then expanded its activity with a separatist insurgency in parts of eastern Ukraine. The Russian state, after almost a quarter century of retreat and recovery, finally appeared to be striking back to restore what many Russians saw as its rightful place in the world.

Theories of nationalism indicate that such events would have a profound effect on Russia's national and state identity among the general public – particularly given the intense use of state-backed symbolic politics (Suny 1993; Billig 1995; Kaufman 2001), the invocation of emotive mythology and rhetoric (Breuilly 1993), the direct contestation of state borders (Brubaker 1996), the putative need to respond to invasive international influences (Greenfeld 1992), the mobilisation of nationalist collective action (Hechter 1995; Wintrobe 1995), and changing social categorisations (Horowitz 1985). With these factors suddenly becoming more prominent during 2013 and 2014, one would expect significant shifts in support among the Russian public for various 'institutionalized forms of [nationalist] inclusion and exclusion' (Wimmer 2002: 9) – that is, attitudes as to which groups to include or exclude from the nation or the state. Indeed, there is a significant literature that argues state leaders often anticipate such upswells of nationalist and patriotic sentiment and sometimes even launch wars precisely in order to generate 'rally-around-the-flag' effects that can squelch dissent and boost support for a leadership whose popularity is flagging (see Levy 1989).

In this chapter, we analyse findings from two nationally representative surveys, one conducted in May 2013 and the other in November 2014, designed to investigate the extent to which these unexpected and earth-shaking events altered how Russian citizens think about themselves in terms of ethnicity, nation and state. Some findings are striking and corroborate theory-based expectations: well over four-fifths of those surveyed welcomed the incorporation of Crimea into Russia, and support for Russian President Vladimir Putin surged half again. Other parts of the story, however, would indicate that further nuancing is required in the kind of change we attribute to the wild events of 2014. As regards many kinds of nationalist thinking, the increase was actually rather slight; and some aspects of Russian nationalism, including support for further territorial expansion, actually declined after Crimea was annexed. Moreover, we also discern strong indications that the 'rally-around-the-leader' effect may not be long-lived. Members of the public have remained deeply concerned about economic problems that have only grown worse since the crisis, as well as about other problems that the wave of patriotism has not actually resolved. The crisis, then, seems to have successfully diverted attention from these other problems without effecting the kind of social transformation that could benefit the regime in the longer run. What we find appears to be much more a contingent 'rally-around-the-leader' effect than a potentially enduring 'rally-around-the-flag' effect.

The 2013 and 2014 NEORUSS surveys

Our data come primarily from two surveys carried out by Russia's well-established and respected Romir polling agency as part of the University of Oslo's 'Nation-building, nationalism and the new "other" in today's Russia (NEORUSS)' project. The first survey included a nationally representative sample of 1,000 respondents interviewed face-to-face from 8 May to 27 May 2013, selected through a five-stage random sampling design.[1] This questionnaire was created and administered before any of the participants could have had any inkling of the major crisis that was to come so soon, but it was nevertheless designed to measure the extent of a wide range of nationalist attitudes in Russia.

After the outbreak of the 2014 crisis, it was decided to conduct a new survey that would replicate most of the questions from 2013 so as to see what had changed, supplemented with a new set of questions about attitudes to the ongoing crisis. This new survey was carried out from 5 November to 18 November 2014, according to the same methodology, except that it included 1,200 instead of 1,000 respondents, an increase possible thanks to the availability of funding.[2]

The sections that follow discuss the central findings, beginning with attitudes to the Ukraine crisis itself, followed by an examination of what has changed in the interim between the two surveys. We also draw on evidence from before 2013, where appropriate, including a 2005 survey organised by one of the present authors that asked some of the same questions included in the 2013 and 2014 surveys.[3] All surveys were conducted in every federal district of the Russian Federation, with standard quality controls by mail and by phone.[4]

Perceptions of the Ukraine crisis

The bulk of the population have fallen – hook, line and sinker – for some elements of the Russian state media's version of events. One of these concerns depictions of the post-revolutionary leadership in Ukraine, which by the time of the survey had held presidential elections in May 2014, won by Petro Poroshenko,

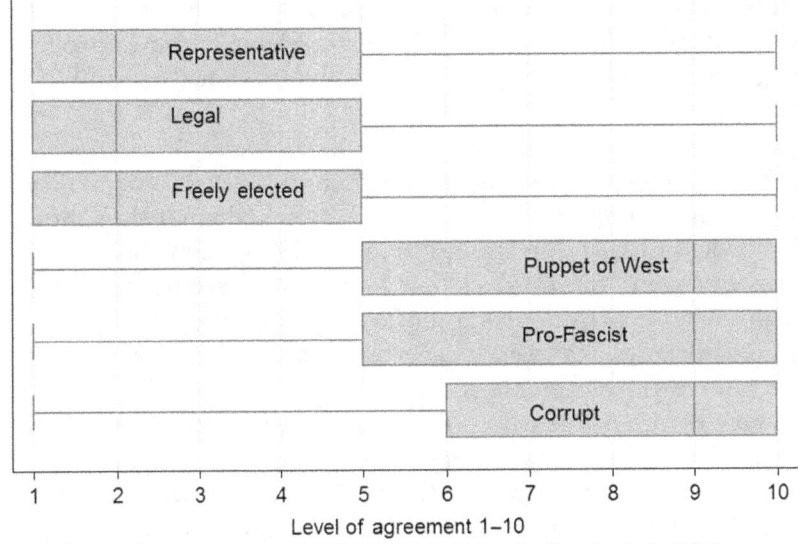

Figure 7.1 Agreement that the current Ukrainian leadership is ...

and parliamentary elections in October 2014, producing a coalition government led by Arsenii Yatseniuk as prime minister. These elections – held across Ukraine except for the annexed Crimea and parts of Donetsk and Luhansk provinces occupied by anti-government forces – were held with extensive international monitoring and were certified by the Organisation for Security and Co-operation in Europe (OSCE) as free and fair (OSCE n.d.). Figure 7.1 uses a box plot to represent patterns of answers when Russians were asked in November 2014 to say how much they agreed or disagreed that the Ukrainian leadership could be characterised in different ways. The boxes represent the range of positions taken by the middle 50 per cent of the respondents and the vertical line inside each box indicates the median view. As can be seen, respondents quite definitively rejected the ideas that the Ukrainian leadership was legally in power, that it in fact was representative of the people and that it had been freely elected. Instead, they were generally in agreement that Ukraine's current leadership was not only corrupt, but simultaneously a 'puppet of the West' *as well as* 'pro-fascist'. These are themes that have featured very strongly in Russian television news programming, reinforcing findings by other scholars that Russian TV has had a significant influence on popular discourse in Russia about Ukraine (Cottiero et al. 2015).

The respondents also display a striking disregard for the legitimacy and viability of Ukraine as a state. Asked what they thought the borders of Ukraine should be, only 17 per cent favoured the status quo ante, the borders that had been internationally recognised as those of independent Ukraine after the USSR's demise and had been guaranteed by Russia in a 1994 treaty. All others who gave a response asserted that Ukraine should be smaller in one way or other. Nearly a third (29 per cent) thought Ukraine's borders without Crimea were most appropriate; another 17 per cent favoured lopping off all Russian-majority territories; an additional 15 per cent held that the Donbas should not be part of Ukraine; and 12 per cent replied that the only part of Ukraine's territory that should remain in the Ukrainian state was the western Ukrainian regions that were not part of the USSR as of 1930. Furthermore, more than a tenth (11 per cent) held that Ukraine should not be an independent state at all.

In line with this view of Ukraine's illegitimacy, respondents tended to see the current events as having more to do with Ukrainian domestic politics than with international forces. Asked to rate the extent to which the Ukrainian conflict could be characterised in various ways on a scale of 1 to 10, respondents were significantly more likely to say that it was primarily a domestic conflict among Ukrainian political forces (mean response 7) than that it represented a struggle between different countries (mean response 6) or different civilisations (mean response 5). Also consistent with the narrative dominant in Russian television reporting is that respondents overwhelmingly (61 per cent) believed it would be impossible for Ukraine to join both the European Union and a Russian-led Eurasian Union; they thought Ukraine faced a zero-sum choice between the two integration projects. Only 13 per cent felt that Ukraine could have the best of both worlds.

Other evidence, however, indicates that the respondents had only inconsistently internalised the Kremlin's narrative about the Ukraine crisis. For one thing, although the Kremlin has waged a ponderous diplomatic campaign to prevent Ukraine and other countries from taking further serious steps on the path to EU integration, the vast bulk of Russians do not think that Russia should be interfering in these countries' sovereign choices. Asked how Russia should react to the possibility of Ukraine, Moldova, Georgia and Armenia joining the EU, at least two-thirds of the respondents in each case thought that Russia should do nothing, neither helping nor hindering this prospect. There was only a small minority, well under a third of the survey population, who thought that Russia should be doing something to stop these countries from EU accession. Similarly, asked what Russia should do in its relations with Ukraine, 44 per cent opposed any kind of Russian interference – more than the combined total who wanted Russia to help Ukraine elect a pro-Russian government (27 per cent), to divide up Ukraine (12 per cent) or help it join the Eurasian Union (4 per cent). A very small minority (3 per cent) even wanted Ukraine to be assisted in joining the EU.

Similarly, respondents appeared to have no clear understanding of the geographic concept of 'Novorossiia' that forces allied with the Kremlin have been promoting. As Marlene Laruelle has detailed, this concept – until very recently a relatively obscure term referring to regions of Ukraine that were incorporated into the Russian Empire mostly in the eighteenth century and that in the Soviet period contained a significant percentage of primarily Russian-speaking people – has been newly politicised as a way of driving an identity wedge between these people and the rest of Ukraine (Laruelle 2015a). The 2014 NEORUSS survey, however, reveals that when people are asked what it is and given a list of possible answers to choose from, few agree on exactly what it refers to. (See Table 7.1.) For example, while 16 per cent correctly identified Novorossiia as referring to all of the regions of Ukraine along the Azov and Black Seas, the most common answer was that it referred to the same thing as the Donbas (30 per cent), most likely reflecting the Donbas rebels' proclamation of a 'Novorossiia' in the areas they control.

Table 7.1 'What is Novorossiia?'(per cent)

About the same thing as the Donbas	30
All of the regions of Ukraine along the Azov and Black Seas	16
The Black Sea coast of Ukraine	13
The Black Sea coast of Ukraine plus Moldova and the Black Sea coast of Russia	7
All Azov and Black Sea oblasts of Ukraine plus Moldova	5
Do not know what Novorossiia is	28

A 'rally-around-the-leader' effect

Turning to changes in patterns of public opinion from May 2013 to November 2014, we detect an impressive 'rally-around-the-leader' phenomenon, especially as to presidential popularity, as can be seen in Figure 7.2. Asked for whom they would vote if presidential elections were held on the day of the survey, and given a list of prominent political leaders who are often discussed as potential candidates, 40 per cent of all respondents in 2013 declared they would vote for Putin, compared to 7.4 per cent for the second-place candidate, the veteran populist-nationalist Vladimir Zhirinovskii. By November 2014, the share of those who would choose Putin had skyrocketed to 68 per cent, with Zhirinovskii still second but now netting only 4.4 per cent of the hypothetical vote.[5] These Putin gains came at the expense of nearly every other potential candidate and drew in many who had previously said they would not vote at all, had indicated that they were undecided or had refused to answer. This corroborates research by other survey agencies, such as the Levada Centre, which observed a significant jump in Putin's ratings in connection with the March 2014 annexation of Crimea and the president's speech announcing and justifying that move (Balzer 2014).

Our study cannot tell us how solid or deeply felt this surge in support for Putin is. It is also possible that by 2014 some people may have become more reluctant to reveal their true presidential preferences to pollsters than they were in 2013, and named Putin just to be on the safe side. Possibly supportive of such an interpretation is that not only did the share of respondents who

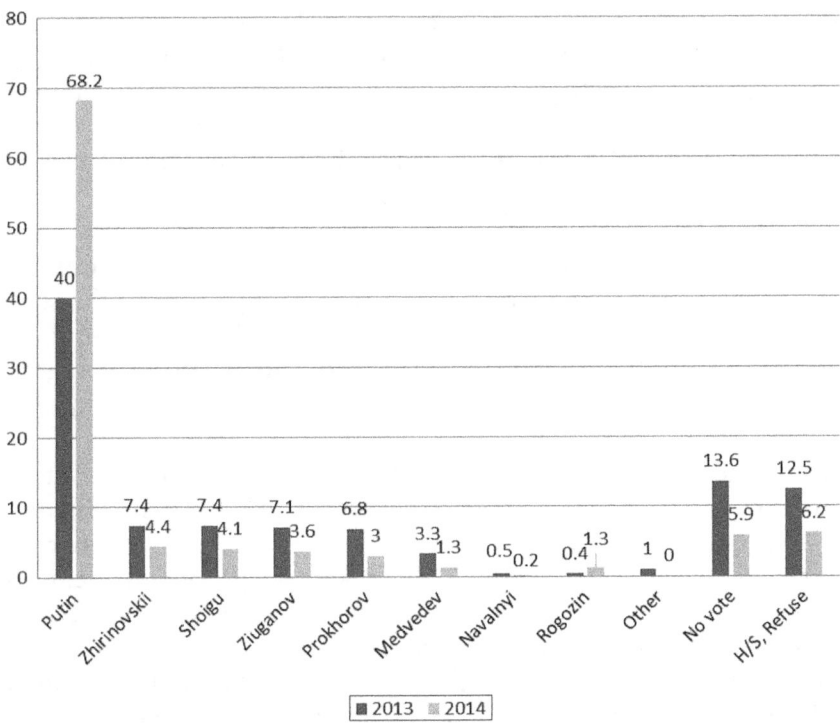

Figure 7.2 'If presidential elections were held today, for whom would you vote?' (estimated percentage of entire adult population)

said they would vote for Putin now go up, but so did the share who said they had voted for Putin *in 2012*. In the 2013 survey, 39 per cent said they had voted for him in the 2012 presidential contest, whereas by 2014 a whopping 59 per cent claimed they had cast their vote for him. This need not reflect fear, however: there is a well-known tendency for people to self-identify with winners after the fact, so the surge in people's self-reported earlier support for Putin could also reflect the simple desire to align themselves, vis-à-vis the survey interviewer, with the highly popular winner. In any case, what we find is clearly evidence of a massive 'rally-around-the-leader' effect of some kind or other.

There is some evidence that this rally-around-the-leader effect is also something of a more general 'rally-around-the-political-system' effect. Both the 2013 and 2014 NEORUSS surveys asked respondents to rate 'the political system that exists in our country today' on a scale from 1 to 10, where 1 was 'very bad' and 10 was 'very good'. While 4–8 per cent in both surveys said that they could not give an answer, among the rest we can note a dramatic change during the period in question. In May 2013, the average score was 3.3, decidedly on the negative end of the spectrum. By November 2014, the average assessment had shifted all the way to 6, making the mean score positive instead of negative. And, of course, the political system is widely understood to be dominated by the individual figure of Putin.

The NEORUSS surveys show that this rallying effect extended from general positive feelings toward Putin and his political system to views as to how competent he is in handling issues related to nationalism. Both the 2013 and 2014 NEORUSS surveys asked Russians which among the potential presidential candidates listed in Figure 7.2 would be best able to deal with issues related to Russia's national identity. Strikingly, in May 2013, only 14 per cent named Putin, a mere 5 per cent more than named Zhirinovskii (9 per cent). In fact, the combined total who selected other potential candidates was markedly greater than the share who chose Putin himself; moreover, a clear majority either found the question too hard to answer (27 per cent) or explicitly volunteered that there was no difference among the candidates (another 27 per cent). By November 2014, however, the share of those who named Putin had more than doubled to 34 per cent, leaving Zhirinovskii in the dust with just 4 per cent and Communist Party leader Gennadii Ziuganov a distant second with 5 per cent. The combined share of respondents who either felt unable to say (18 per cent) or who perceived no difference among potential leaders (28 per cent) was still greater than those who named Putin, but this was now a minority and the surge in the perception of Putin's competency on this issue is impressive. The survey also finds evidence that perceptions of Putin's competence on nationalist issues had grown more broadly: a similar question on the issue of immigration from Central Asia, the Caucasus and China found that the share of Russians who singled Putin out as 'most competent' rose from just 15 per cent in May 2013 to 32 per cent in November 2014.

Do these notable jumps in pro-Putin feelings reflect equally large leaps in nationalist sentiment in Russia, as would happen if the 'rally-around-the-leader' effect were more fundamentally a 'rally-around-the-flag' effect? This question is discussed in the following sections. We begin by examining issues of ethnic pride, and then turn to whether Russians see their state in mono-ethnic or multi-ethnic terms. Next we examine issues of interpersonal tolerance and prejudice, followed by consideration of differences that Russians perceive between themselves and other ethnic groups. Interestingly enough, here we find far greater continuity than change: the increase in nationalist sentiment is nowhere near the scale of the surge in pro-Putin feelings.

Ethnic pride and privilege: Enduring valuations

Despite widespread reporting of a rising tide of ethnic Russian nationalism in the immediate aftermath of the annexation of Crimea (see, for example, Marten 2014; Levada Centre 2014b), the NEORUSS surveys find no significant rise in ethnic pride from May 2013 to November 2014. Indeed, pride in one's ethnicity – or, in the language of post-Soviet states, 'nationality' – has remained highly stable throughout the period covered by the surveys we consider here and going back to at least 2005. In 2005, 2013 and 2014, more than half of the respondents – 55, 53 and 56 per cent, respectively – said they were 'very proud' of their ethnic identity, and some 35–40 per cent in each survey said they were 'mostly proud'.[6] These changes are well within the combined sampling error of the surveys. Considering that approximately 90 per cent of respondents in the 2013 and 2014 surveys identified themselves as ethnic Russians, one may have expected the share of those who said they were very proud of their nationality to increase markedly in 2014. After all, the overwhelming majority of Russians enthusiastically supported the annexation of Crimea, and protection of ethnic Russians there from the putative threat of a 'Ukrainian fascist junta' in the wake of the successful Euromaidan revolution was a strong message that the Kremlin disseminated through mainstream media. Yet, the general public seems to have resisted these impacts, or perhaps any such impacts were short-lived and had dissipated by November 2014. Of course, one reason for this is that Russian pride was already quite high before the dramatic events of 2014. What we seem to have been witnessing in 2014, therefore, is less a surge in Russian nationalism than an activation of sentiment that was already there, but now became directed toward support for the Kremlin.

Indeed, almost all of the numerous other indicators of ethnic nationalism considered in the NEORUSS surveys have remained relatively stable. One is the number of respondents who say they support the slogan 'Russia for [ethnic] Russians' (*Rossiia dlia russkikh*). This slogan hinges on the linguistic distinction between two terms both typically translated as 'Russian' in English: *russkii* tends to imply a specifically ethnic category whereas *rossiiskii* is a more civic concept that explicitly unites the whole range of ethnic groups historically associated with the Russian state.[7] It is noteworthy that the official name of Russia, the Russian Federation, uses the term *rossiiskii*. Thus the call 'Russia for ethnic Russians' suggests a move away from a more civic to a more ethnically exclusive Russia. Overall, the surveys reveal that 63, 64 and 66 per cent of respondents express complete or partial support for the slogan in 2005, 2013 and 2014, respectively. The share of those completely endorsing the slogan also remained stable – at 31, 27 and 33 per cent. The increase from 2013 to 2014 lies within the combined sampling error margin. Similarly, support for other ways in which ethnic Russians may deserve a privileged group position in Russia has also remained fairly stable. About three-quarters of respondents in 2013 and 2014 believed that top government jobs should go primarily to ethnic Russians – with about 39 and 40 per cent, respectively, supporting this idea fully. In 2005, about 80 per cent of respondents agreed with this privilege for ethnic Russians, with 48 per cent supporting it fully – so, if anything, such exclusivist sentiment has declined over the past decade. Additionally, in both 2013 and 2014 about half of the respondents fully supported the idea that ethnic Russians must play the leading role in the Russian state, and about 82–84 per cent backed it at least partially. Again, the pattern seems to be one of scant increase in such nationalist sentiments in connection with the 2014 events – but such sentiment was already quite high to begin with and had long been so.

Attitudes also remained largely unchanged from 2013 to 2014 when respondents were asked if they supported granting all migrants unconditional permanent residency rights (admitting them all to Russia) or if they were in favour of having all migrants deported – legal and illegal and their children – from Russia. Given that most respondents see migrants as representing non-Russian ethnic groups, these questions de facto measure public support for ethnic inclusion and exclusion. About 23 per cent of the respondents fully supported wholesale deportation of migrants in 2013, and 24 per cent did so in 2014. The share of those who 'agreed somewhat' with deportation rose from 24 to 27 per cent. Once again, these slight increases, separately or in sum, are statistically insignificant. It is possible that they were part of a more substantial, slow-moving long-term trend. In 2005, deportation was supported fully by 22.5 per cent of respondents and partially by 21 per cent. Thus, total support for deportation rose from 43.5 per cent in 2005 to about 51 per cent in 2014, which is unlikely to be due to sampling error alone. However, if this is the case, we may well be dealing with an enduring trend and not a sharp fluctuation resulting predominantly from the nationalist-patriotic mobilisation over developments in Ukraine. Views on inclusion show a near-identical pattern. No significant change was observed from 2013 to 2014. When asked about admitting all migrants as Russian residents, about 9 per cent of respondents agreed fully and 22 per cent agreed somewhat in 2013, whereas 7 per cent agreed fully and 23 per cent agreed somewhat in 2014. Anti-migrant nationalism was already very high to begin with and did not experience a particularly noteworthy surge in 2014. Thus while the Levada Centre found that tolerance of migrants actually increased somewhat as part of a general euphoria immediately following the Crimean annexation (*Polit.ru* 2014), our study indicates this was at most temporary, and was neither substantial nor robust.

Moreover, the stability we observe did not reflect only those questions on which hard-line sentiments dominated Russian opinion. For example, a clear majority of respondents continued to see inter-ethnic relations in their province, city or town as 'rather good than bad' – close to 56 per cent in 2013 and 58 per cent in 2014. Approximately the same share perceived these relations as very good (12 per cent and 15 per cent, respectively) or very bad (8 per cent and 6 per cent, respectively). And in both years just over a third of the respondents considered Russian civilisation to be unique – neither Western nor Eastern – a subject treated in Marlene Laruelle's chapter in this volume.

State identity: Slightly stronger and slightly more inclusive

Unlike the case with ethnic pride, we do find that pride in Russia as a multi-ethnic state has risen, although on a scale far smaller than the rise in support for Putin. Thus a greater share of respondents in 2014 (52 per cent) than in 2013 (44 per cent) said they were 'very proud' to be Russian citizens. The eight percentage point increase is outside the margin of error yet not particularly impressive, given the scale of events that had occurred in the interim. The proportion of those who said they were more proud than not to be citizens of Russia remained about the same – 44 per cent in 2013 and 42 per cent in 2014. Russians were very proud of their state in 2014, but they had already been very proud of it prior to the Ukrainian events.

Accompanying this finding, we can note a growing sense among the Russian public that the strength of the state in which they invest so much pride does not depend on ethnic Russians alone – even though attitudes toward diversity per se and other ethnic or religious groups did not necessarily improve. The NEORUSS surveys assessed these views with the question: 'Do you believe the ethnic diversity of the population strengthens or weakens Russia?' In 2013, 13 per cent of the respondents said that diversity strengthened Russia while 25 per cent averred that diversity weakened it. In 2014, more than 22 per cent saw diversity as a boon, and only about 16 per cent called it a liability for Russia. The share of respondents who held that diversity had mixed effects remained the same, at about 60 per cent. To an extent, the decline in perceptions of diversity as weakness may be seen

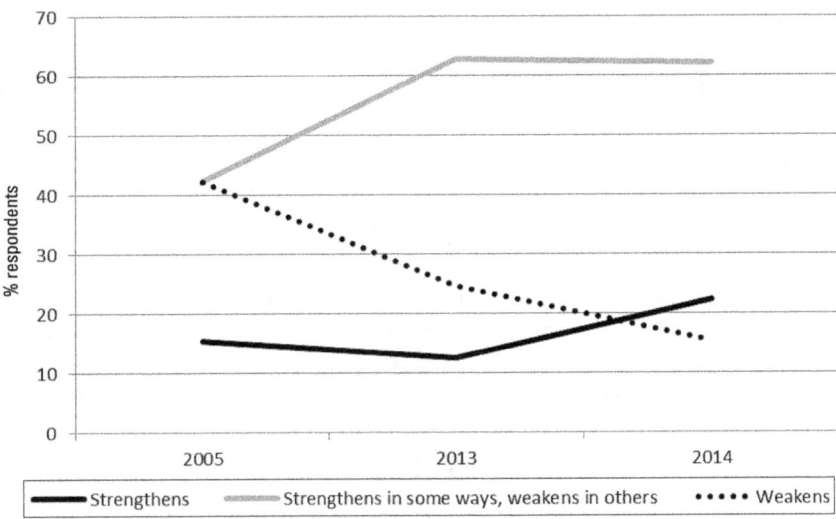

Figure 7.3 'Do you believe the ethnic diversity of the population strengthens or weakens Russia?' – based on nationwide survey samples from 2005, 2013, and 2014

as part of a longer trend: about 44 per cent of the respondents in the 2005 Levada Centre survey felt ethnic diversity weakened Russia. However, the change from 2013 to 2014 was greater if pro-rated by year. Moreover, not only did the perception that diversity weakens Russia decline, but the perception that diversity strengthens Russia increased. In 2005, just about 16 per cent of respondents held that view, as against more than 22 per cent in 2014 (see Figure 7.3).

Similarly, respondents in 2014 more than in 2013 had a broader concept of 'Russians' as a social category (*russkie*). In 2013, a plurality of respondents (42 per cent) said that only ethnic Russians ('Russians by nationality') could be considered *russkie*. But about 32 per cent of respondents then said that while *russkie* referred predominantly to ethnic Russians, it could include others, and another 27 per cent understood the term to refer to all people living in the Russian Federation regardless of ethnicity. In 2014, the order of preferences switched. The share who believed that the term *russkie* referred to all citizens of

Russia regardless of nationality remained relatively steady at 29 per cent. But the share of those who saw it as referring solely to ethnic Russians fell to just 30 per cent, while the proportion of those who understood it as referring primarily but not exclusively to ethnic Russians leapt to 41 per cent. By late 2014, then, well over two-thirds of those surveyed indicated that the term *russkii* was not *necessarily* ethnically exclusive. This is particularly noteworthy since many observers have cited Putin's striking use of the term *russkie* in his dramatic March 2014 speech justifying the Crimea annexation, in claiming that the Kremlin had shifted to seeking a more ethnically exclusive basis of its legitimacy (see, for example, Marten 2014).

The specific finding in the previous paragraph, then, underscores that not all Russians are likely to interpret Putin's claims to Crimea as reflecting a purely ethnic conception of the Russian state. In fact, Putin appears to be playing on the same conceptual ambiguity that the Kremlin has long used in its nationality policy (Shevel 2011). The larger finding of this section, accordingly, is that the Russian state came to inspire greater pride at the same time as it became more multi-ethnic in Russian eyes, even in light of Putin's Crimea speech.

Publicly acceptant, privately selective

Opinion trends discussed so far indicate that, even though ethnocentric and xenophobic views remained strong, respondents generally became more publicly acceptant of ethnic diversity in Russia as a state and a nation from May 2013 to November 2014. At the same time, we also find that when it comes to the inclusion or exclusion of specific ethnic groups in respondents' private lives, acceptance levels waxed and waned selectively. In particular, it emerges that the Kremlin's demonisation of Ukraine's Euromaidan protests and its leadership – a discourse that frequently portrays anti-Russian 'fascism' as a major strain in Ukrainian public opinion – has had a palpable effect on the private lives of Russians concerning relationships with Ukrainians, despite Kremlin rhetoric that has attempted to portray a good Ukrainian population as victimised by a violent, even genocidal junta.

One window on this public–private dichotomy can be gained by asking Russians how they feel about members of their family marrying migrants of different ethnic categories – with the important proviso conveyed to respondents that these prospective in-laws have the same income level as that of the respondent's family.[8] Interesting enough – and going against the rising sense that ethnic diversity strengthens more than weakens Russia – was a significant increase in the percentage of respondents who saw ethnicity as an important factor in the choice of a marriage partner for one's relatives. In 2013, these respondents comprised 77 per cent of the sample and in 2014, 86 per cent.

On the whole, respondents remained averse to their relatives marrying representatives of other ethnic groups coming from outside their region or outside Russia. On a scale of 0 (least acceptable) to 10 (most acceptable), the overwhelming majority of respondents who thought ethnicity did matter picked the bottom three options, indicating strong rejection of such marriages. Figure 7.4 presents the combined percentages opting for 0, 1, and 2 on the scale for different ethnic groups, calculated among the 77–86 per cent of the sample who felt that ethnicity mattered for marriage. With most of these groups, the level of negative attitudes was about the same in 2014 as in 2013. While Figure 7.4 shows a slight shift in the direction of greater tolerance for most groups, the only such shift that is outside the margin of sampling error was that regarding ethnic Georgians, and that change is still under 10 per cent.

The most striking change that Figure 7.4 reveals is the spike in rejection of migrant Ukrainians as marriage partners. In May 2013, Ukrainians joined Belarusians – who both share a common Slavic identity with Russians – as by far the least rejected ethnic out-group for marriage. By 2014, the share of respondents who believed that ethnicity mattered for marriage and also believed that Ukrainians were 'highly unacceptable' rose by nearly fourteen percentage points from about 28 per cent in 2013. Opposition to marrying similarly Slavic Belorussian migrants, however, remained about the same, so this change cannot be said to reflect a broader separation of Russians from other Slavic categories more generally.

THE NEW RUSSIAN NATIONALISM

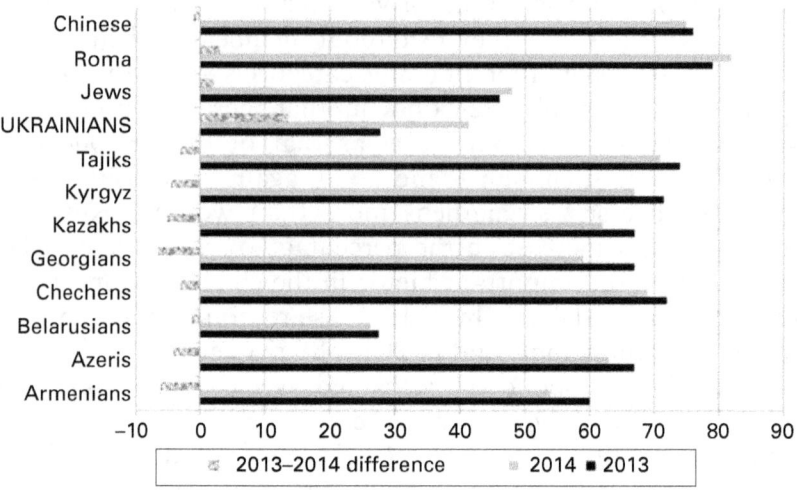

Figure 7.4 Share of respondents who strongly opposed their family members marrying migrants belonging to ethnic groups other than their own

Note: 'Don't know' and 'refuse to answer' responses have been excluded from the denominator of the calculations here. The number of 'don't knows' and refusals differed within only a few percentage points by ethnic group in both years. The proportion of those who said ethnicity did not matter for marriage was constant and has thus been omitted from the denominator; respondents who chose that option were not asked their views for each specific group. In total, these data excluded from the denominator made up about 28 per cent of the sample in 2013 and about 20 per cent in 2014.

It would strongly appear that the Kremlin's repeated emphasis during the ongoing Russia–Ukraine conflict that Ukrainians and Russians are 'fraternal peoples' – a favourite term used to evoke the idea that these ethnic groups share a common state from Kievan Rus to the Soviet Union and deserve to stay together politically – was outweighed by months of the Kremlin's publicly demonising Ukraine's protesters and government as 'fascist' and more generally by the negative coverage of events in Ukraine. Significantly fewer respondents in 2014 than in 2013 wanted migrant Ukrainians to be 'fraternal' or otherwise related as family. These findings may actually understate the real rise in intolerance levels regarding Ukrainians: the NEORUSS survey questions concerned only Ukrainians who were migrants and at the same income level as the respondents, but presumably those Ukrainians who chose to migrate specifically to Russia rather than to other parts of Ukraine to escape the conflict were among the most Russian-oriented migrants, those most likely to be viewed favourably by Russian respondents. The fact that unwillingness to have Ukrainians marry into the family increased substantially even for this particular Ukrainian population, then, suggests that it may well have increased more regarding Ukrainians who are not migrants and who have lower income levels. Our survey also finds that relatively few people actually report having much significant contact with relatives and friends in Ukraine; 64 per cent say that they have no friends or relatives of any kind, or even acquaintances, in Ukraine. Geopolitical perceptions seem to have trumped the essentialist 'fraternal people' rhetoric.

The dynamic of out-group acceptance – when we look at respondents who chose 8, 9 and 10 on the intermarriage acceptability scale for migrants – is also consistent with this interpretation. For most ethnic groups in 2013, the proportion of such respondents was less than 5 per cent (Azeris, Chechens, Georgians, Kazakhs, Kyrgyz, Tajiks, Roma and Chinese) or just under 10 per cent (Armenians and Jews). The two exceptions were Belarusians and Ukrainians – migrants from each group were considered highly desirable for marriage by about a third of respondents. These views remained about the same (within the sampling error margin) in 2014. Ukrainians were not among the groups for which the pattern of most positive responses changed; people who were the very most favourable to Ukrainians in 2013 tended to remain favourable in 2014. This means that strongly exclusionist views of Ukrainians increased primarily among those whose answers in 2013 had been somewhere mid-range on the NEORUSS survey scale. A separate question indicates that while Russians became less willing to intermarry with Ukrainian migrants, they were generally tolerant of Ukrainian refugees from the conflict coming to Russia; only 12 per cent would favour having Russia's borders closed to them, while 51 per cent felt they should be aided and their return to Ukraine facilitated.

Interestingly, the greatest changes from 2013 to 2014 regarding potential intermarriage with migrants involved Belarusians and

Jews: the number of respondents who viewed Belarusians as desirable went up from 33 to 40 per cent and those who viewed Jews as desirable rose from about 14 to 20 per cent. Why would positive attitudes toward Belarusians and Jews increase? The survey data as such do not offer definitive answers, but we can venture at least a speculative interpretation here. There is little reason to suspect that these shifts have resulted from any kind of change in how Russians understood the cultures or behaviour patterns of these groups, as no major events come to mind that may have changed longstanding public perceptions of any intrinsic properties of these groups in such a short period. A change in the geopolitical prism through which these groups are viewed, however, may account for this shift. One issue that could be examined further in this regard is the effect of the Kremlin's extensive use during 2014 of anti-Nazi, Great Patriotic War (Second World War) tropes to mobilise patriotic passions among Russians in support of its Ukraine policy. This mobilisation included the invocation of powerful emotive symbols such as the orange-and-black striped ribbons of the Order of St George – a decoration for exceptional valour in war, highly esteemed by ordinary Russians. A potent symbol of victory in the Soviet Union's Great Patriotic War of 1941–5, these ribbons became one of the principal identifiers of the Russian military operating without insignia and of their mercenaries and allies in Crimea and Eastern Ukraine, starting with their takeover of Ukrainian government buildings in February and March 2014. The Great Patriotic War trope may thus have increased the perceived affinity with Belarusians – notably since Nazi collaboration rhetoric with respect to Belarusians was absent or marginal in Soviet and post-Soviet Russia. And given the deeply embedded understanding of Jews as among the principal victims of the Nazis, the sense of affinity with them could have increased out of common perception of victimisation inspired by Russian media.

With many more respondents than before now seeing sharp negative lines dividing them from Ukrainians, what specifically was it that they understood as the chief sources of division? The 2014 NEORUSS survey added some new questions, asking Russians what they thought most unites the peoples of Russia and Ukraine and also what they thought most divides them.

CHANGES IN RUSSIAN NATIONALIST PUBLIC OPINION 2013-14

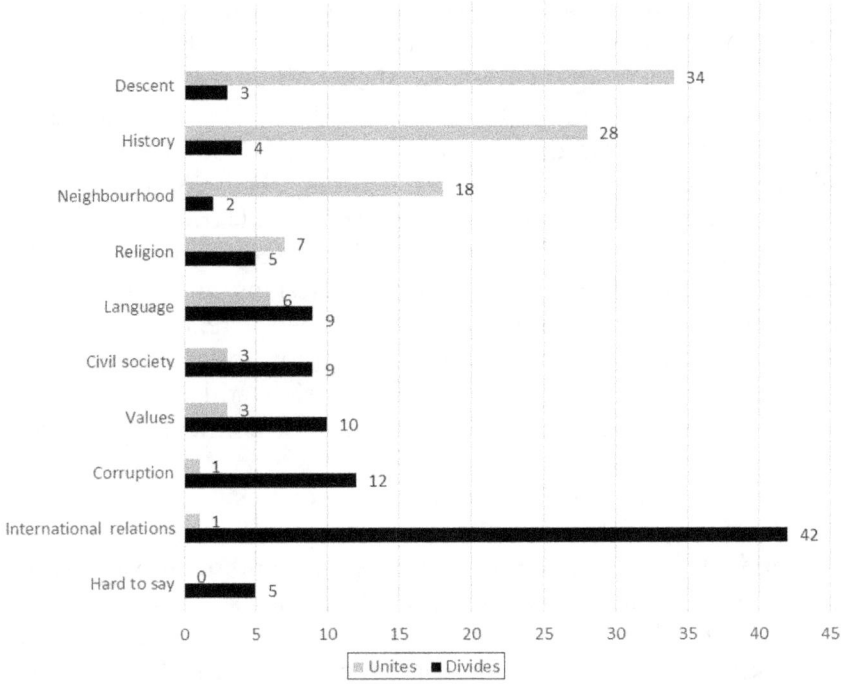

Figure 7.5 Factors singled out by the respondents as most uniting/dividing the peoples of Russia and Ukraine (per cent of total)

As can be seen in Figure 7.5, the respondents saw themselves as most united to Ukrainians by common history, descent and geography, placing relatively little emphasis on religion, values or language. The major source of division was international relations, mentioned by an impressive plurality of 42 per cent, and an interpretation firmly in line with the Kremlin narrative of a Western-backed puppet government bent on subduing Russia and the Russians. The second-most common answers were named by only 9–12 per cent, who indicated the divide with Ukrainians was sharpest on issues of corruption, values, civil society and language.

These views on what divides Ukrainians and Russians had little to do with the respondents' acceptance of Ukrainians as marriage partners for close relatives. With only one marginal exception, respondents who selected the most negative and the most positive three answers on the intermarriage desirability scale with Ukrainians cited roughly the same distribution of factors as most dividing and most uniting Ukrainians and Russians – in each case, closely matching the data reported in Figure 7.5. The exception concerns the role of corruption. Among the 393 respondents who strongly opposed a relative marrying a Ukrainian migrant of similar income level, 10 per cent indicated corruption as the greatest source of division between Russians and Ukrainians. But among the 272 who strongly favoured a relative marrying such a Ukrainian, the share citing corruption rose to 14 per cent. Although this was the largest difference, it still was relatively small, making it hard to read much social or political significance into this variation.

Also with only one exception, stated sources of unity between the Russians and Ukrainians were about the same among those respondents who selected the most negative and the most positive three answers on the Ukrainian intermarriage scale. In this case, however, the lone exception was more significant and thought-provoking: it concerns the idea of being neighbours. Among those most opposed to marriage with a Ukrainian migrant of similar income level, 27 per cent believed that being neighbours was the greatest source of unity between Russians and Ukrainians. Among those most favouring such a marriage, only 13 per cent held that view. While open to multiple interpretations, this finding suggests that the idea of being neighbours may not be as strong an argument for the Kremlin in favour of keeping Ukraine within Russia's sphere of influence as some may think, based on the survey results for all respondents.

Inclusion versus expansion

As Russian respondents expressed a growing sense that their state was strong enough to accommodate greater diversity on the inside, and could even draw strength from this diversity, their support for territorial expansion – which would entail incorporating diverse ethnic populations from outside the state – declined markedly. Basically, a significant proportion of the Russian public who supported Russia's territorial expansion in the past must have felt that expanding to Crimea was enough.

In both May 2013 and November 2014, respondents were given a prompt that state borders sometimes change in the course of history, and were then asked where they believed the borders of the Russian Federation should be. The share of those who said Russia's borders should remain the same increased sharply – from about 39 per cent in 2013 to 50 per cent in 2014 (not counting the 8–9 per cent who found it hard to say or refused to answer in each survey). The crucial difference, of course, is that after March 2014 'the same' implied the inclusion of Crimea into Russia. The proportion of respondents who preferred an expansion of Russia's territory – either bringing Ukraine and Belarus into a 'Slavic Union' or incorporating all territories of the former Soviet Union – dropped from 47 to 38 per cent. The 2013/14 period appears to have marked a turning point. In mid-2013, a larger and statistically significant proportion of respondents wanted to see Russia's territory expand than stay the same. In 2014, a larger and statistically significant proportion wanted Russia's territory to remain the same rather than expanding. Meanwhile, the share of respondents who preferred having the Muslim republics of the North Caucasus excluded from Russia remained about the same – indicating that xenophobic views (those who so deeply wanted an ethnically pure Russia that they would even accept territorial contraction as the price) remained relatively constant year on year. Figure 7.6 shows all response frequencies on this question in 2013 and 2014.

These findings indicate that views of Islam are not about territorial expansionism. After the annexation of Crimea, public preferences for expansion to a 'Slavic Union' or a 'USSR 2.0' went down, but views stayed the same regarding the exclusion of Russia's North Caucasian Muslim regions. This implies that ethnic/imperialist nationalist and xenophobic nationalist views operate with at least partially different perceptual logics. The NEORUSS survey data on Russians' views of Islam further support this idea. In particular, only a small change was observed when respondents were asked if Islam posed a threat to social stability and Russian culture. In 2013, about 66 per cent of the respondents agreed completely or partially that Islam posed such a threat, compared to 70 per cent in

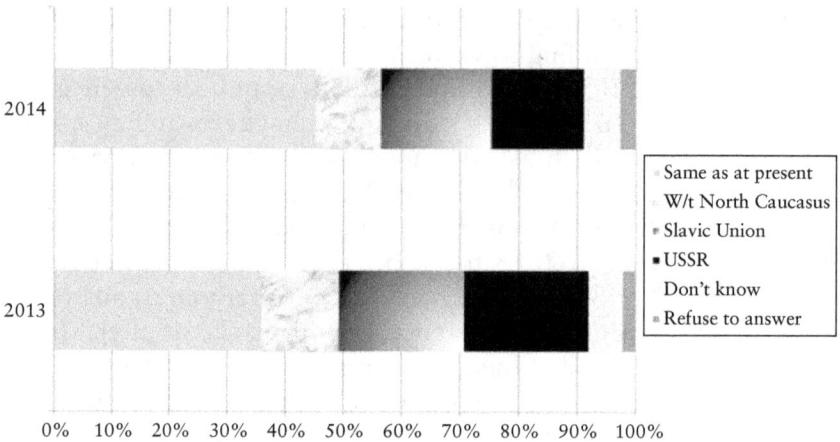

Figure 7.6 Preferences for the territorial boundaries of the Russian Federation

2014. The proportion of those who fully agreed with this proposition increased by fewer percentage points – from about 28 to 30 per cent. These changes are well within the combined margin of the sampling error of the two surveys.

The relative stability of perceptions of Islam as a social and cultural threat appears consistent with the relative stability of support for excluding the Muslim North Caucasus republics from the Russian Federation. The fact that support for Russia's territorial expansion dropped significantly after the annexation of Crimea while support for excluding the Muslim regions of the North Caucasus from Russia stayed the same indicates that the latter may hinge more on views of Islam as a threat.

Economic worries

While our findings overall would indicate less of a surge in Russian nationalism than a classic 'rally-around-the-leader' effect in Russian public opinion from May 2013 to November 2014, the NEORUSS surveys also support arguments that the rallying may be difficult to sustain (see Balzer 2014). This is most clearly evident in the realm of the economy. In May 2013, 19 per cent of Russians surveyed felt that the country's economy had improved in the preceding year, with the majority (54 per cent) opining that the economy had remained essentially stable and only 21 per cent judging it to have become worse. Eighteen months later, after the events in Ukraine discussed here, this had changed dramatically: a striking 55 per cent now said that the economy had gotten worse in the previous year, with just 9 per cent seeing improvement and 30 per cent no change. We note a similar shift in how people reported change in the financial situation of their own family in the twelve months preceding each survey: in 2013 some 19 per cent saw improvement, 60 per cent saw no change and 18 per cent perceived decline; by 2014, a full 45 per cent bemoaned their worsening personal financial well-being and only 8 per cent cited improvement, with 42 per cent sensing no change from the previous year.

More ominous for the Kremlin is that respondents appear to be linking these economic perceptions to the annexation of Crimea. Interestingly, 55 per cent agreed with the statement that the incorporation of Crimea has been 'too expensive', with only 36 per cent disagreeing. Of course, we must interpret this finding with caution since it could be interpreted in at least two ways. One interpretation is that 'too expensive' is understood as meaning 'not worth it'. Another is that the annexation is supported, but that it should not have cost Russia so much – for example, the West should have simply recognised Crimea as rightfully Russian instead of imposing sanctions that created an artificial cost that ought not have to be borne by Russia.

To check whether people were responding sincerely to this question, it was only asked directly of roughly half the sample, and the other half of the sample (randomly selected) were asked it in an indirect way that did not require respondents to state their views explicitly.[9] The indirect method, which is less precise but more likely to elicit honest answers, found that only 38 per cent agreed that the Crimean acquisition was too expensive. Interestingly, this at least raises the possibility that what people are reluctant to admit to a survey researcher in Russia is not that Crimea is too expensive, but that they actually believe it is worth the economic price. This would be consistent with the finding that the annexation remains broadly supported and Putin's ratings have skyrocketed even while Russians' views of economic performance have turned sharply negative.[10] In any case, our study uses multiple methods to establish that from 38 to 55 per cent of the population is unhappy with the economics of the Crimean annexation – and that, however one interprets it, does not bode well for the Kremlin on the road ahead.

Conclusions

Overall, our study indicates that Russia in the interim between our two surveys experienced much more of a 'rally-around-the-leader' effect than an upsurge in nationalism per se, although this is partly because Russian nationalism was already extremely strong prior to the Ukraine crisis and Crimean annexation. That said, the survey indicates certain specific, smaller-scale changes in the Russian nationalist landscape that are important to note. First, perceptions of ethnic as opposed to state identity underwent different sorts of shifts. While there was relatively little change in patterns of ethnic pride and xenophobia, people had become slightly (but only slightly) more proud to be associated with the Russian state, even as they increasingly viewed this state as multi-ethnic and became more positive to its diversity. Second, we noted a widening gap between public and private identity preferences, particularly with respect to 'defraternisation' with Ukrainians, despite Kremlin efforts to portray Ukrainians as a brotherly people who should be returned to the Russian fold. Third, our findings indicate that support for inclusion of diverse ethnic populations already present within a state may be inversely related to support for inclusion of new ethnic groups into a state through territorial expansion.

Above and beyond these nuances, we also observe that preferences for national inclusion and exclusion appear to be more entrenched and durable than may have been expected. On a considerable number of survey items, we have found surprisingly little change – surprising considering the surge of nationalist and patriotic rhetoric and symbolism that filled the state-dominated mass media following the successful ouster of Yanukovych by the Euromaidan protesters in Kyiv and Russia's swift annexation of Crimea in March 2014. Putin appears to have tapped into these sentiments, rather than engendering them through his actions and the Kremlin's public relations campaigns. Indeed, while many Russians internalised Kremlin-supported narratives about dangers of fascism, of Russophobia and of Western aggression emanating from Ukraine, they generally did not support Russia interfering in the foreign policy choices of Ukraine or other neighbouring countries.

In conclusion, we may venture to say that the patterns of public opinion found in Russia in 2013 and 2014 are largely consistent with 'diversionary theories of war', according to which leaders recognise that a short victorious war can bolster their short-run popular support and thus undertake such action in order to effect it (see Levy 1989). That said, the Russian evidence also suggests several interesting avenues for developing this line of theory in future research.

One such question is how long this effect is likely to last – a point central to its expected utility for state leaders. In the United States, for example, analysts with the Gallup polling organisation have estimated that, in the twentieth century, surges of public support for incumbent presidents related to foreign affairs and military action lasted an average of ten weeks (Hugick and Engle 2003). This is far shorter than the effects we have observed in Russia. One plausible explanation is that the duration of rallying effects may vary across political systems, with state media control, repression of opponents and agenda-setting power enabling them to last longer. Another, however, draws on comparative research on 'rallying' effects in public opinion related to conflict, some of which has found that conflict ties presidential popularity closely to nationalist identity, although this typically fades as other issues eventually come to the fore (Kam and Ramos 2008). This may imply that countries with strong and enduring nationalist sentiment prior to the war are more conducive to longer-lasting rallying effects, even though these effects are likely to fade as other issues again become salient. We may also speculate that regime type conditions the kind of rallying seen in the event of a short, victorious war: in pluralistic polities based on the rule of law and media freedom, the populace may be more likely to rally first and foremost around the flag – that is, impersonal, institutional symbols of their state and nation – while authoritarian countries governed (as the saying goes) 'by men, not laws' may be more likely to feature rallying first and foremost around the leader personally, a kind of rallying likely to prove more contingent since it would be less structurally grounded. Finally, we should also consider that both the political system and nationalist identity effects could be significantly affected by the nature and magnitude of the rallying events per se. The annexation of Crimea could be viewed as a tectonic geopolitical shift, as a turning point in the *long durée* of Russia's history, the regaining of territories lost due to the Soviet Union's collapse a quarter century earlier – something perhaps akin to the beginning of the 'gathering of Russian lands' after casting off the two-and-a-half centuries' rule of the Tatar-Mongols in the late fifteenth century.

In any case, Russia's leadership certainly appears to have tapped into a pre-existing deep well of nationalist sentiment that has translated into a large 'rally-around-the-leader' (more than 'rally-around-the-flag') effect, distracting people from problems that had previously led them to hold more negative perceptions of their political system, if not of the leader himself.[11] But, regardless of polity type, to distract is not to eliminate or solve. And the evidence indicates that the distracting action is associated in the eyes of a great many Russians with negative economic consequences that are 'too expensive'. As the Crimean annexation moves further into history, major problems loom for the Kremlin, problems that it has yet to find ways of resolving.

Notes

1. This sample size, drawn randomly from Russia's population of about 143 million, would typically result in a margin of sampling error of about 3.1 per cent with a 95 per cent confidence level, assuming that responses to a question are fairly equally split across response options. The sampling error effect would decline the more responses are skewed toward one of the options – for example, with this Romir NEORUSS sample, it would be as small as 2.5 per cent if the percentage of responses on a question were split 80–20. See

<www.surveysystem.com/sscalc.htm#one> (last accessed 5 April 2015).
2. Resulting in an estimated margin of sampling error of about 2.8 per cent with a 95 per cent confidence level, assuming responses to a question are fairly equally split across response options. See <www.surveysystem.com/sscalc.htm#one> (last accessed 5 April 2015).
3. The 2005 survey, conducted by the Moscow-based Levada Centre and commissioned by Mikhail A. Alexseev, involved 680 respondents and had an estimated margin of sampling error just under 4 per cent at a 95 per cent confidence level. For a description of survey methodology, data and results, see <http://www.rohan.sdsu.edu/~alexseev/migration_and_ethnic_conflict/data.html> (last accessed 5 April 2015).
4. Excluded from the sample in 2013 and 2014 were zones deemed to be in armed conflict (Chechnya and Ingushetia) and remote, sparsely populated areas of northern Siberia and the Russian Far East (Nenets, Khanty-Mansi, Yamal-Nenets, Kamchatka, Chukotka and Sakhalin). Altogether these omitted regions account for less than 4 per cent of the total population of the Russian Federation. Further, in 2005, respondents were not sampled in the insurgency-prone republics of Dagestan and North Ossetia. The non-response rate in these surveys was between roughly three-quarters and four-fifths – rather typical for industrially developed, predominantly urban societies.
5. The figures on presidential vote choice are calculated from randomly selected sub-samples of respondents: 553 in 2013 and 549 in 2014. This is because for the other half of the sample the question was differently worded, as part of a study on various factors that may influence presidential voting (Hale 2014).
6. To ensure that substantive results remain equitable over time, the missing data (including responses of 'hard to say' and refusal to answer) are excluded here and thereafter, unless otherwise stated. In general, this makes little difference for the figures reported. For ethnic pride, the missing data involved 3.5 per cent of respondents in 2005, 2 per cent in 2013 and 2.4 per cent in 2014.
7. However, in some contexts, the term *russkii* can also be interpreted more broadly, reflecting a certain ambiguity about ethnic categories inherent in the language that is also explored by the NEORUSS survey and discussed further below. There is strong reason to believe that the Kremlin actively exploits this ambiguity (Shevel 2011).

8. This was done to control for stereotypes associating certain ethnic groups with specific occupations and, by extension, their income and marital eligibility.
9. Specifically, a list experiment is employed that involves a random splitting of the sample into two parts. One of the two parts was given a list of four innocuous things with which average people may agree or disagree, and was asked only to give the number of things they agreed with on the list. The other part of the sample was given the same list plus one extra item, the statement that the incorporation of Crimea has been too expensive, and also asked to give the number of things they agreed with on the list. Importantly, respondents never had to say which of the specific items they agreed with; all that was recorded was the overall number of things they agreed with. The difference in the average number of items agreed with between the first and second parts of the sample amounts to a calculation of the percentage of the population agreeing that Crimea was too costly. More details are available from the authors upon request.
10. Previous research focusing on the pre-2013 period has found economic performance to be strongly linked to popular support for Putin (Colton and Hale 2009; Treisman 2011b).
11. Popular support for Putin was not considered low as of 2013, as our survey showed he was still outpacing potential rivals.

8

How nationalism and machine politics mix in Russia

Henry E. Hale

By some accounts, Russian politics is a realm of cynics, where everything is for sale, leaders rudely dismiss public opinion and politicians mainly pursue their own power and enrichment through a mix of repression and corruption (Gessen 2013; Dawisha 2014). In others, Russia's leadership is resolutely principled, driven at least in part by a nationalist goal of restoring Russian pride and recapturing the status and perhaps even the territory of the former USSR and Russian Empire before it (Aron 2008; Trenin 2014; Tsygankov 2014). If we assume that each perspective at least partly reflects at least some aspect of Russian politics, an interesting puzzle is framed. How precisely is it that these things fit together? In other words, how can a strong principle like nationalism play an important role in a political system where corruption is rife and elections are the preserve of the political machine?[1]

The present chapter argues that we must understand the logic of what I have elsewhere called *patronal presidentialism* in order to explain how and why Russia's leadership is likely to be influenced by ideas like nationalism. Patronal presidentialism refers to a constitutionally strong presidency that exists in a particular social context, one in which political collective action takes place primarily through extensive networks of personal acquaintance, networks that tend to give presidents 'informal' power that extends far beyond the authority formally stipulated in the constitution. It turns out that even when such presidents use manipulation, coercion and fraud to win such elections, they run significant risks of losing power when they lose popular support. For this reason, presidents like those in Russia have been very sensitive to public opinion. Nationalism comes into play here.

The relationship between nationalism and political support in Russia is not straightforward, however, and for this reason the Kremlin has generally treaded very carefully on this issue. In fact, this chapter argues that President Vladimir Putin up until 2014 largely avoided making nationalism a central element of his popular appeal. It was not entirely absent; it is just that other things were much more important and that nationalism was mobilised more actively by Kremlin opponents than by Putin himself. The annexation of Crimea represents a bold stroke that for the first time made nationalism a centrepiece not only of Putin's own authority, but of the political system's stability more generally. But even then this was only a certain type of nationalism, not of the ethnically exclusive kind and still limited in its spoken aspirations. Indeed, the ability of nationalism to play a central role in bolstering Putin's authority is highly questionable due to the fact that Russian nationalism is in fact divided, with Crimea itself being one of the few moves that Russian nationalists of nearly all stripes can enthusiastically support. The challenges that Russian nationalism (or more precisely, Russian nationalisms) pose for Russia's political system are thus likely to make themselves felt strongly in the years ahead despite the rallying around Putin personally that the Crimea operation produced.

Patronal presidentialism

It can be useful to understand Russian politics as taking place in a context involving high levels of *patronalism*. Patronalism refers to a social equilibrium in which people pursue their political and economic ends primarily through personalised rewards and punishments that are meted out through extended chains of actual personal acquaintance rather than organising this activity impersonally on the basis of broad principles such as ideologies or identities (Hale 2015). As a rule, patronalistic societies tend to be characterised by weak rule of law, high levels of corruption and low social capital.

Patronalistic collective action can be thought of as distinct from collective action based on what Benedict Anderson famously called 'imagined communities', or sets of people who see themselves as sharing something important that makes them a community even though this 'communing' does not take place face to face; people in an imagined community do not generally know one another personally and need not be connected by networks of personal acquaintance (Anderson 2006). Of course, for Anderson, the nation was the consummate imagined community. So when Ernest Gellner famously defines national-*ism* as political activities designed to make the nation coterminous with the state (or, in Michael Hechter's useful refinement, 'collective action designed to render the boundaries of the nation congruent with those of its governance unit'), we can understand nationalism as one form of collective action that is *not* based primarily on personalised rewards and punishments and *not* mainly through networks of actual acquaintance (Gellner 1983; Hechter 2000: 7). Nationalism, then, is decidedly non-patronalistic. This does not mean that highly patronalistic societies cannot experience nationalism, but it does mean that large-scale *mobilisation* primarily on the basis of nationalist ideals is likely to be the exception rather than the rule in such societies, and that any such mobilisation is more likely to occur through (and thus be limited by) personalistic networks.

Indeed, one of the chief features of politics in highly patronalistic societies ('patronal politics') is that the primary political actors in these societies are not formal institutions like 'parties' or 'parliament', but instead extensive *networks* of actual personal acquaintance that typically penetrate many such formal institutions at once. In Russia, the most important networks have tended to take three forms. One is a set of networks led by 'oligarchs', mega-rich private businesspeople who typically control not only vast economic holdings across the country but also 'political assets' in the form of their representatives in different political parties, regional or national legislatures, and even executive power as well as non-governmental organisations. The most visible examples in post-Soviet Russian history have included the networks of such figures as Vladimir Potanin, Mikhail Khodorkovskii, Oleg Deripaska and Roman Abramovich. Another is what may be called 'regional political machines', or networks that usually have their roots in regional executive power structures and that are regionally limited in scope but tend to have particularly thoroughgoing control over a wide range of economic, political and social resources in that territory. Classic examples from post-Soviet Russia's history include Iurii Luzhkov's Moscow political machine, and excellent contemporary examples include Ramzan Kadyrov's Chechnya machine and Mintimer Shaimiev's Tatarstan machine. Finally, some of Russia's most powerful networks have essentially operated out of different branches of the central Russian state, with the most prominent of course being the personal networks of Vladimir Putin himself. Putin's networks have tended to draw on people who became associated with him through his service in the KGB (such as Igor Sechin and Sergei Ivanov), through his time as a top figure in the St Petersburg mayor's administration (such as Dmitrii Medvedev), and others connected to him through more random personal ties (such as the Kovalchuk brothers). These networks include not only Putin's direct subordinates in the executive branch, but a wide range of figures placed in the worlds of business, party politics and civil society.

In highly patronalistic societies like Russia, whoever controls these sets of networks controls the country. The most important challenge for a president, then, is getting all of these different networks to work together in his or her support instead of working against him or her. The challenge is serious. If a society's most important networks refuse to obey the leader, that leader is in serious trouble. But when they are working together in support of a leader, that leader can be powerful indeed. In the latter situation, if the leader happens to hold the presidency under a constitution that gives the president a great deal of power, this leader wields not only this formal power but also the ability to influence politics in many other ways through his or her networks. For example, political parties he or she does not like can be starved of resources through the president's business networks. Politicians who challenge the president can find themselves subjected to all kinds of difficulties in their home districts, including harassing inspections or even prosecution at the hands of regional political machines. And media that publish material critical of the authorities can be sued by 'ordinary citizens' in the leader's network and found guilty of slander, extremism or other crimes by judges in networks that are aligned with the president.

This system of patronal presidentialism, where a president combines strong formal power with extensive informal power exercised through networks at the intersection of state and economy, can squelch political competition to a large degree even when most opposition politicians themselves are not actually arrested, directly threatened or killed. Indeed, these network-based resources largely enable patronal presidents to allow opposition figures and parties to exist and even run in elections while providing powerful weapons for defeating them in these contests. Patronal presidentialism thus underpins the existence of many *hybrid regimes*, systems that combine elements of democracy with elements of autocracy, allowing political competition but skewing that competition in favour of incumbent authorities.

The key to the stability of such systems is that the country's most powerful networks, and most importantly the 'elites' that dominate them, expect the president to remain in power long into the future. When they expect the president to be in power in the future, they have full confidence that the president will be in a position to carry out the threats or promises he or she makes today. But when they start to suspect that the president may not be in power beyond a certain point, they have reason to start to doubt that the president will be in a position in the future to follow through on promises and threats made today. And that leads them to think they are more likely to be able to get away with disobedience, which in turn makes them more likely to *be* disobedient. To wit, the networks in the patronal presidential system can become uncoordinated. And since the president depends on these elites and their networks to actually carry out his or her threats and promises, his or her ability to exercise authority can dissipate even before he or she actually leaves presidential office. In essence, the president can rather suddenly become a lame duck, unable to govern and incapable even of ushering a handpicked successor into office as his or her political machine falls apart.

One may question whether this is ever likely to happen since patronal presidents, one may suppose, rarely decide to give up their offices. But this can happen more frequently than one may think for a variety of reasons. Some fall ill, generating expectations of their future demise. Others reach prominent markers of old age, increasingly leading people to conclude that a succession is nearing. Still others face term limits. Even though many presidents attempt to have term limits overturned, some do not and others are unable to do so, meaning that so long as term limits are on the books, the president remains at a higher risk of becoming a lame duck when she or he is in his or her legally final term. And, finally, some presidents actually do decide not to run for reelection as president. For example, in 2004, Ukraine's President Leonid Kuchma attempted to usher a handpicked successor into office instead of running himself. In fact, even Putin opted to leave the presidency in 2008 and then in 2012 effectively forced his successor to leave office as he arranged his own return to the post.

The reference to Putin's 2008 succession makes clear the following point: a lame-duck syndrome is usually not by itself enough to provoke the disintegration of a robust patronal presidential system. Putin did experience significant turmoil in his political machine in the lead-up to that election, but it survived intact as he successfully guided Medvedev into the presidency (Sakwa 2011a). What we can say is that when a president becomes a lame duck, pressures are created for the discoordination of the system's major networks. But how (or whether) the networks will again manage to coordinate their activities is a separate question. Since what matters most for a network's power and wealth in a patronalistic society is connections, what each of these networks typically wants most is somehow to wind up on the winning side of any ensuing political struggle. And this essentially means trying to figure out which person is most likely to emerge as the next president. Complicating this process is that any one person's emergence as the likeliest next president depends on how many of the country's most powerful networks decide to support him or her. The succession competition, then, is essentially a kind of self-fulfilling prophecy: unless relations are irreparably spoiled for some reason, networks join the presidential contender they expect to be most likely to win, and their joining that contender in fact *makes* him or her more likely to win. This is, at root, a giant game of coordination, where the networks try to figure out which potential president the other major networks are likely to support and to make their choice accordingly. Of course, they may like some potential chief patrons more than others, but they want even more not to wind up on a losing side of the struggle, which could cost them power, resources and possibly even their existences if the winner proves hostile or wants to settle scores with prior opponents.

So what determines how the newly uncoordinated networks are likely to decide on who is likely to win? One thing that matters is the political machinery that each network wields. Networks that control the most resources are likely to be seen as favourites in the struggle, thereby attracting other networks and gaining more resources. But when a dominant presidential machine is disintegrating, the relative strength of the various networks within it is often unclear, and machine strength can dissipate rapidly if a network's allies or even members start to think it is unlikely to win.

Thus another factor is more important to the story being told in this chapter: when the winner of the succession struggle must consummate this victory by producing an official vote count in his or her favour against at least some sort of opposition on the ballot (even if this vote count does not have to be honest in any way), public opinion comes to play a crucial role in determining who elites see as most likely to win. This is true for several reasons. For one thing, it takes more effort and resources to falsify votes against a more popular rival, so the candidate that does need to organise less falsification has an advantage. In addition, if an official vote count turns out to be blatantly against what is widely believed to be prevailing public opinion, it becomes easier for the loser to rally supporters to the streets, making for larger and more threatening protests. Accordingly, suppressing the uprising becomes more costly for the falsifier the more committed the protesters are, and potentially so costly that troops may start to refuse to obey orders to carry it out. Popular support, in other words, is an important resource that can be wielded by patronalistic networks in battle. And this means that potential chief patrons who also wield popular support are more likely to be seen by other networks as likely winners, making these other networks more likely to join them, which in turn makes them seem still more likely to win. Patronalistic networks, therefore, tend to coordinate around patrons that have the most popular support, although primarily after a sitting president starts to be seen as a lame duck for other reasons.

The most successful patronal presidents thus tend not only to be popular, but also to pay intense attention to their standing in public eyes. Public support is a critical stabiliser of their regimes. When they wield it, the key networks in the president's system are likely to see defection to the opposition as particularly unpromising, as the president could likely win an election even if the political machine falls apart. But when they lose popular support, elites looking ahead to the future are more likely to start hedging their bets and to break rank when a crisis emerges, especially one linked to succession or other sources of lame duck syndromes. This has surely been the case for Putin, whose regime is known for its intense attention to his 'ratings' in public opinion (Treisman 2011a).

This, then, is where Russian nationalism has the opportunity to play its greatest role in influencing Russian state policy and rhetoric. The next question we must ask is to what extent *has* Russian nationalism played such a role? Has nationalism been a prominent source of the high public approval ratings that have been characteristic of Putin's time in high office, stabilising it? The sections that follow address this question, beginning with his rise to power to his late 2000s peak, then examining his regime's domestic political crisis in 2011–12, and concluding with a look at the period since that crisis.

The role of nationalism in Putin's political machine

This chapter's overarching argument is that while Putin has certainly sounded themes that fit under one definition or other of 'nationalist', as examined elsewhere in this volume, up until 2014 these were not the most important parts of his public appeal. If anything, Putin represented a relatively moderate voice on

Russia's nationalist spectrum, at least compared with available political rivals. The events starting in 2014 mark a major shift to a situation in which nationalist issues became central to Putin's public support. But these same events also reveal why Putin has been so reluctant to make nationalism the centrepiece of his public appeal: playing to nationalist sentiment is a risky strategy that threatens to divide his supporters more than unite them over the long- or even medium-term. For this reason, even when Putin gives nationalism more prominence in his rhetoric, he does so in an intentionally ambiguous way (Shevel 2011).

Before examining the role of nationalism in Russia's political system under Putin, it is important to elaborate on the Gellnerian definition of nationalism used in this chapter, with the term referring (as noted above) to collective action designed to promote the congruence between the governance unit and the nation. Importantly, the concept of 'nation' need not be defined in narrowly ethnic terms, but can also be based on 'civic' criteria, such as belonging to a particular state defined in terms of territory and institutions (Brubaker 1998).

With respect to Russian nationalism, this distinction helps us identify two strains that authors have variously identified (Szporluk 1989; Laruelle 2009a; Rogoza 2014). First, there is a nationalism of ethnic Russian purity. By these lights, making the nation and state coterminous could include such actions as purging Russia of non-Russian elements and, perhaps, incorporating ethnic Russians living outside Russia into a single state. Second, there is a Russian nationalism that is explicitly multi-ethnic, defining the 'Russian nation' much more broadly, typically including some or all ethnic groups that have longstanding historic ties to Russian states, empires, culture, history or lands. Taken to its extreme, making the state coterminous with this kind of nation could lead not only to the tolerance of ethnic diversity within Russia, but also to some form of reincorporation of now (broadly) 'Russian' lands that are currently outside of the Russian state. To some degree, these distinct notions of nation are (respectively) captured by two Russian-language terms that are usually both translated as 'Russian' in English, *russkii* and *rossiiskii*. But it is often overlooked by analysts that, in practice, the distinction is not so clear. Sometimes *russkii* can include other ethnic groups, too, and the exact meaning of rossiiskii is even more ambiguous, with the state long doing much actually to promote this ambiguity (Shevel 2011). In any case, while the terms *russkii* and *rossiiskii* do not cleanly demarcate them, one can speak of two broad strains of Russian nationalism that may be called 'ethnic Russian nationalism' and 'imperial Russian nationalism'.

For the sake of clarity, these concepts of nationalism should be distinguished from actions that may be carried out in the name of the nation but that are not actually aimed at increasing congruence between state and nation. For example, making the nation more powerful for its own sake is better captured by a term like 'patriotism'. 'Nationalism' would, however, include strategies aimed at defending the state from threats to the nation's control over the state.

The following subsections assess the degree to which nationalism has played an important role in Putin's gaining and remaining in power as well as in his management of the political machine more generally.

Nationalism and Putin's rise to power and popularity

Putin's rise to power in 1999–2000 resulted directly from his popular support, although nationalism as defined here was only a minor part of this appeal. Given the Kremlin's strength in 2014, it is easy to forget that as late as August 1999, opposition forces were the odds-on favourites to win the presidency in the 2000 election. The popular support for incumbent President Boris Eltsin, after virtual economic collapse and a disastrous war in Chechnya, was abysmally low. When in early August 1999 Eltsin appointed the little-known FSB chief Vladimir Putin his prime minister and declared him his handpicked political heir, many considered this a kiss of political death. Indeed, polls showed Putin with only 2 per cent support in the presidential race, far behind the leaders. The big money, both figuratively and literally, was on former Prime Minister Evgenii Primakov, who had guided Russia through the acute financial crisis of 1998, had stood strongly for Russian interests earlier as foreign minister and generally had impeccable patriotic credentials, including his own ties to intelligence agencies. Primakov, moreover, had recently struck a coalitional deal with the powerful mayor of Moscow to form a large coalition of oligarchs and regional and political machines. Indeed, with Eltsin approaching the end of his constitutionally final term in office and so ill he was reported to be able to work only a few hours a day at times and being frequently absent from the Kremlin, Russia's major networks saw him as a classic lame duck. Looking to wind up on the side of the most likely winner, major oligarchs like Vladimir Gusinskii and regional machines like those in Tatarstan, Moscow and St Petersburg sooner or later abandoned their earlier support for Eltsin and now placed their bets on Primakov (Shvetsova 2003). Primakov came to head what was then dubbed the Fatherland–All Russia bloc, which in turn was harshly critical of the incumbent team and whose leaders sounded many nationalist themes (Hale 2006).

What turned the tide in favour of Putin was a dramatic shift in public opinion that resulted after a major tragedy that befell Russia in September 1999: Terrorist bombs were detonated in two large, ordinary apartment buildings in Moscow, and together with attacks in other cities, some 300 innocents were killed. Putin was quick to blame rebels in Chechnya, launching a massive military operation that effectively levelled the republic's capital city and killed thousands. Putin's ratings in public opinion soared, from just 4 per cent in the presidential race in reliable September polls to over 50 per cent in December. Seeing that Putin would clearly win even a completely free and fair vote for president, most oligarchs and regional political machines now shifted over to Putin, with even some who had been in Fatherland–All Russia now attempting to make amends and get into his good graces. Eltsin capitalised on the situation by resigning early, which resulted in Putin's becoming acting president and forced early elections, in March 2000 (Hale 2006).

Some have interpreted this as Putin's riding a wave of nationalism to power, but the bulk of the evidence suggests it was not mainly nationalism that appealed to people in Putin. For one thing, nationalism does not explain why people would have preferred Putin to Primakov, who had a strong reputation for defending the broadly defined Russian nation from outside threats, or to Primakov's chief ally Iurii Luzhkov, the Moscow mayor who had long been calling for Sevastopol to be returned to Russian hands from Ukraine – something Putin and his Kremlin supporters were not doing at the time (*RFE/RL* 1999a). And once Primakov and Luzhkov bowed out of contention, Putin's main challenger became Communist Party leader Gennadii Ziuganov, widely recognised for his nationalist and revanchist stands (Urban and Solovei 1997; March 2002). Equally importantly, Putin did not frame his actions on Chechnya as being about nationalism as defined here. Instead, they were portrayed as an operation against 'terrorism' and 'bandit formations' (*RFE/RL* 1999b). Chechens *as a nation* were not blamed by Putin, just the specific perpetrators and the corrupt or incompetent leadership in the republic that enabled or supported them, and he was always careful not to exclude Chechens from the Russian nation in his rhetoric (*Polit.ru* 1999).

The evidence is strong that this is largely how ordinary Russians interpreted Putin's actions despite the fact that many held nationalist beliefs themselves. According to surveys conducted shortly after the terrorist bombings in September 1999 by VTsIOM, a highly reputable survey agency whose key figures later created the Levada Centre, only 10–11 per cent of the Russian population equated the terrorists and fighters thought guilty of the apartment bombings with the actual government of Chechnya. Instead, the agency found, a majority mainly wanted to punish the perpetrators rather than punish the Chechen people as a whole (Levada 1999).

At the same time, the polling shows that what Russia's citizenry was most worried about were perceived threats of terrorism and crime coming from such Chechen criminals, and they were in fact willing to be quite pragmatic in how to deal with this threat. To be sure, some of the acceptable responses lumped good Chechens together with the bad indiscriminately, a sacrifice many found worth paying for their own security. Thus, on the one hand, a VTsIOM survey in September 1999 asking about different responses to the apartment bombings found that a shocking 64 per cent would have supported deporting all Chechens from Russia. At the same time, however, an even larger percentage would have accepted granting independence to Chechnya as a solution. In fact, remarkably, 53 per cent would have 'welcomed' Chechnya's secession at that time, with another 14 per cent saying they would not mind such a solution, and yet another 12 per cent saying that they were against it but were prepared to accept it. Only 12 per cent thought Chechen independence should be 'resisted by any means' (Levada 1999). Putin was certainly calling neither for mass deportations nor Chechen independence.

Instead, survey research indicates that what Russians wanted most of all from Putin at that time was not the blood of Chechens or subduing Chechnya to prevent secession, but leadership capable of dealing with the threat of terrorism and crime in *some* way. In fact, we find public opinion on Chechnya largely following what Putin did rather than the other way around, as we would expect if people mainly wanted leadership and as we would not expect if Putin's rise was mainly driven by a surge in nationalist sentiment. In fact, prior to Putin's launching the Russian government assault on Chechnya, VTsIOM found that only 32 per cent of the Russian population definitively agreed that Russia should start military operations there. Another 40 per cent were only willing to back it if there were some 'guarantee' that it would not result in more terrorism in Russia (Levada 1999). But by 26–29 November 1999, after Putin had actually led the military operation and pursued it decisively, support for continuing it (61 per cent) had come to far outweigh support for pursuing peaceful negotiations with Chechen leaders instead (27 per cent). But even this figure was highly contingent on what Putin himself was proposing to do: the same survey also asked whether people would support the negotiations option if Putin proposed it, and it turns out that if Putin had proposed negotiations, public opinion would flip. Putin's endorsement would have generated an outcome in which 48 per cent supported negotiations and 42 per cent opposed them (VTsIOM 1999b).

What the balance of evidence suggests, then, is that the initial surge in support for Putin was mostly about *leadership*, not nationalism – or any other issue, for that matter. Finally, after a decade of decline and turmoil, and a president who often appeared to be drunk or otherwise incapacitated, here was a leader reacting with apparent vigour and strength to address what huge numbers of Russians saw as a major and immediate threat to their lives. Thus when another survey asked in October 1999 what people liked about Putin (with multiple responses possible), the top response (41 per cent) was that he was 'energetic, decisive, and wilful'. Tellingly, this figure is significantly higher than the percentage of people who said they liked him for his stance on Chechnya (24 per cent) even though his leadership had only really been demonstrated *through his Chechnya policy* at that time. Other concentrations of responses included such qualities as his capacity to introduce order and personal characteristics such as his general experience, physical appearance, leadership style, principled nature and honesty (VTsIOM 1999a). Thus while Putin surely held some nationalist views as described elsewhere in this volume, and while one cannot rule out that had he voiced outright anti-nationalist views he would have been rejected by the public, his nationalism was not what distinguished him from other prominent leaders in Russian eyes and was not what drove the initial surge in his public support that finally helped stabilise Russia's political system after the tumult of the 1990s.

Putin's broadening public appeal 2000–9

While Putin's initial rise to the presidency owed primarily to the leadership qualities he showed in responding to the 1999 terrorist acts, he soon developed other bases of support among the Russian public. One of the most important has been economic development. While economic growth started returning to Russia slightly before Putin came to power, he certainly reaped the benefits of the country's material recovery, driven in large part but not entirely by high world prices for Russia's energy-related exports (McAllister and White 2008; Treisman 2011a). Other studies have confirmed several additional consistent bases of public support for Putin. Survey research, for example, has found that he connects with widespread popular views on the general economic policy direction of the country (refining the market economy rather than seeking a return to socialism) and a general slightly right-of-centre political orientation. Also linked to his support has been growing attachment to the United Russia party, a political vehicle he created that absorbed the Fatherland–All Russia coalition (Colton and Hale 2009, 2014).

These same studies, however, have found little evidence that his public appeal has been based strongly on nationalistic ideas, or at least that these views have been what distinguishes him in Russian eyes from other politicians, the vast majority of whom voice views that are at least as strongly nationalistic as Putin's. People who said they cast ballots for him, for example, did not stand out for particularly anti-Western views. In fact, Putin was seen as a relatively *pro-Western* candidate in the Russian context; he was widely interpreted as someone who wanted cooperation with the West, but guardedly and on Russia's own terms. This contrasted with the public positions of Russia's most broadly supported alternative politicians and parties, almost all of which took more radical stands on foreign policy and ethnic politics than did Putin. This includes the Communist Party of the Russian Federation, Vladimir Zhirinovskii's Liberal Democratic Party of Russia and the A Just Russia party, and even some self-avowedly liberal leaders of the street protest movement, such as Aleksei Navalnyi (Colton and Hale 2009, 2014).

Whatever its source, this strong public support helped the Kremlin weather the presidential succession of 2008, when Putin ceded the presidency to his close associate Dmitrii Medvedev and occupied the prime ministership himself. Putin had long said that he would step away from the presidency at the end of his second term rather than attempt to change the constitution so as to allow himself a third one, and, as expected, great tensions arose within the regime during the run-up to the handoff. Different groups vied to influence the succession process, and some evidently to convince Putin himself to stay on (Sakwa 2011a). With Putin enjoying extremely high approval ratings, regularly as high as 60 to 80 per cent, it became clear that whomever he endorsed would have an enormous advantage even in a completely free and fair election. This helped ensure that he survived his lame duck period, as elites saw it as unpromising to cast their lots with someone who would not get this endorsement. Thus when Putin finally announced that Medvedev was his choice, done at nearly the last possible moment before the 2008 presidential campaign process was to start, the system's major networks almost all fell in line behind him and ushered the protégé to a comfortable victory, no runoff necessary (Hale and Colton 2010). This protégé, Dmitrii Medvedev, represented perhaps the least nationalist of the available credible alternatives for Putin, being widely seen as relatively 'pro-Western' (Sakwa 2011a).

This is not to say that nationalism played no role whatsoever during this period, of course. Spikes of nationalist rhetoric could be noticed around the campaign seasons, as with Putin's warnings that anti-Russian 'jackals' were feeding around Western embassies, that forces in the West were aiming to carve up Russia, and that Western election observation activity was nefarious and needed to be curtailed in the run-up to the 2007–8 elections (*Polit.ru* 2007; *RFE/RL* 2007a, 2007b, 2007c; various media news reports observed by the author on 1 December 2007 in Russia). Such rhetoric could be interpreted as essentially defensive from a domestic politics perspective, however, designed to pre-empt political opponents with stronger nationalist reputations from mobilising such issues while simultaneously undercutting any support there may have been for Western criticism of Russian elections and backing for Russia's opposition. Regardless, as noted above, surveys have consistently found that Putin backers tended to stand out not for harder-line stances on such issues, but instead for more moderate stands, although on the whole nationalist issues were not the strongest drivers of citizens' leadership preferences (White and McAllister 2008; Colton and Hale 2009; Hale and Colton 2010; Treisman 2011b; Colton and Hale 2014).

The drop in Putin's support and succesion as regime destabiliser 2009–12

As the 2000s wound to a close, then, nationalism was not much needed politically by Putin and he had generally relied more on other bases of support, especially since his main opponents all had more pronounced stands on nationalist issues than did he. This situation started to change, however, as the global financial crisis of 2008–9 hit Russia. To be sure, Putin's (and Medvedev's) approval levels did not collapse as many had predicted, even during the sharp economic decline that occurred in 2009. This reflects the fact that, contrary to some interpretations, Putin's support has from the beginning been about much more than the economy. These other bases of support, first and foremost popular support for his leadership style and capacities and broad ideational connections with the electorate, prevented a free-fall in his overall approval ratings. But these ratings did start to decline, a deterioration that had become noticeable as the 2011–12 election cycle approached. The Kremlin exacerbated this problem on 23 September 2011, when Putin and Medvedev announced that the former would return to the presidency, that the latter would take Putin's place as prime minister, and that this had been planned long ago. This proved to be a public relations disaster, as people widely felt duped and those who had liked the idea of the younger Medvedev retaining the presidency were deeply disappointed, especially since a recent lengthening of presidential terms meant that Putin could be coming back for another dozen years. Putin was even booed (whistled) at a sporting event on live television. A vigorous new round of anti-American rhetoric dramatically failed to save the day, also strongly suggesting that nationalism was no 'magic bullet' for the regime.[2]

With its ratings dipping dramatically as the December 2011 parliamentary elections approached, the pro-Putin United Russia party panicked. Many of its members evidently resorted to significantly greater efforts to perpetrate fraud than had previously been the case in order to compensate for the low ratings. But these efforts were clumsy, often exposed on the Internet, sometimes by the party's own former supporters. When official vote totals turned out to give that party a significantly greater share of the vote than was credible, protesters poured out into Moscow's streets in far larger numbers than had been seen since the start of the Putin era. A major part of the surprise for the regime was *who* was protesting: No longer primarily the pensioners who had turned out in a large set of demonstrations against market reforms in 2005 and that were periodically mobilised by the Communist Party, but now the capital city's emerging upwardly mobile population that had previously been largely passive when it came to politics, many of whom had previously concentrated mainly on business or other professional activity but envisioned a more 'modern' Russia with a more open political system free of corruption. The protesters were not unified in their political persuasions beyond their detestation of the fraud and machinations of the regime, however. They included not only Western-oriented liberals, but a wide range of patriots and nationalists, some of whom (like Navalnyi) sought to forge a brand of liberal nationalism. With the protesters turning out in such numbers and coming from Russia's rising classes, some predicted that the regime was doomed, bound to fall from power in the next year or two.

The authorities' initial response was to loosen political controls and convince people that they would not resort to such fraud in the 2012 presidential election scheduled for three months later, in March. Many opposition figures who had long since disappeared from state-controlled television except in a negative light now reappeared as commentators or the subject of ordinary reporting, laws restricting party registration were liberalised, a form of direct gubernatorial elections was restored and online-viewable web cameras were installed in nearly all precincts for the presidential contest. The Kremlin's chief political mastermind, Vladislav Surkov, was ushered out of the presidential administration, a move that was also compatible with bringing in a new figure who could shift strategy later on. All this did take some of the steam out of the protest movement, leading many to hope for a political thaw in response to the newfound assertiveness of Russia's growing 'creative class'.

Also part of the Kremlin's response, however, was actively to seek out new bases of popular support. One such move focused on the immediate task of getting Putin elected back to the presidency in March 2012 and put the emphasis back on his personality and leadership style (his most fundamental basis of support) and, now, adding to it the status of 'father of the nation', something that could also turn his older age into a positive. While this was the strategy featured in Putin's formal campaign activity, Kremlin officials and allies were taking the first tentative steps toward a major shift in how it sought to connect with the public.

Having already lost the support of large numbers of Moscow and St Petersburg urbanites, and wanting to isolate their restiveness as much as possible from the rest of the country, the authorities began sounding a set of 'conservative' and nationalist themes that it had previously largely avoided and that would not only appeal to Russia's vast countryside and smaller cities but would drive a wedge between them and the urbanites. The Kremlin had previously tended to avoid such issues because they were divisive, but with so many of the urbanites' support lost anyway, the appeal to conservative and 'new' nationalist values promised to reconnect strongly with the rest of the country, which was in the end the majority.

This 'conservative' turn included a number of steps. One of the first and most visible was the dramatic arrest, trial and media coverage of three young women from the art-punk collective Pussy Riot, whose name alone made it extremely tempting for a Kremlin interested in playing wedge politics. The women had donned their trademark coloured balaclavas and illicitly filmed a raucous protest music video in the Christ the Saviour Cathedral, 'praying' that Putin be taken away. They were stopped mid-film, arrested and ultimately sentenced to two years in prison. Media at the time gave all this extensive coverage, emphasising the moral outrage that they said many Russians felt at seeing one of their holy sanctuaries defiled.[3] Protests in the women's support were covered so as to show that the Muscovite protest leaders were also corrupted and disrespectful of traditional Russian values, attempting to lead Russia down a road to sin and debauchery. Polls indicate the media effort ultimately worked, with majorities tending to think that Pussy Riot deserved punishment (Levada Centre 2012a).

This set the stage for a rapid-fire series of laws (the parliament's printer run amok, by one snarky account) that staked out 'conservative' pro-Kremlin positions on issues that could be used to inflame passions and shore up new support. One barred 'propagandising homosexuality to minors'. Another made it illegal to offend religious beliefs. After the US government imposed sanctions on a list of officials it believed were linked to the prison death of anti-corruption lawyer Sergei Magnitskii, and after a tragic case was reported in which an adopted Russian child died in Texas, Russia's parliament barred Americans from adopting Russian children and then threw in a ban on gays adopting Russian children for good measure. The strategy, reviled by many in the West and upsetting to many liberal Russians who saw their country as integrating into the international community and 'modern' values, largely worked. Polls consistently showed significant support for these laws, and over the course of 2012–13 United Russia's ratings had largely recovered and Putin's support was strong (Levada Centre 2013d. 2014a).

Putin's nationalist turn 2013–14

It was only in 2014, however, that nationalism came to play a truly central role in sustaining support for Putin and thereby stabilising the regime – at least temporarily. The Kremlin had hesitated to invoke nationalism as a primary basis of support prior to this point for three main reasons. First, most of the Kremlin's main opposition parties had long been sounding nationalist themes, as noted above, meaning that nationalism would not necessarily help the Kremlin stand out from them unless it took some truly radical stands. Second, adopting a much stronger nationalist stance would be divisive, potentially alienating a significant segment of the Russian citizenry that had prioritised liberal values, 'modernisation', and integrating Russia into the world economy and considered nationalism unsavoury or dangerous.

A third reason was even more potent: there are multiple forms of nationalism, and in Russia they are often in conflict with one another. This is evident upon reflection. If the chief goal of narrowly ethnic Russian nationalism is an ethnically pure Russian state, the imperial version of nationalism means precisely reintegrating with many peoples who do not fit the narrow ethnic definition of 'Russian'. This tension was evident just below the surface during 2013, especially in the case of riots in the Biriulevo-Zapadnoe district of Moscow. In that incident, an Azerbaijani migrant worker was accused of killing an ethnic Russian, prompting many Russians to go on a rampage, including an attack on a company that employed many migrant workers. Most of these migrants were from areas of the former Soviet Union, such as

Azerbaijan. Indeed, one of the chief demands of ethnic Russian nationalists is to restrict the flow of migrants from countries in the Caucasus and Central Asian regions of the former USSR. In the wake of the riots, therefore, new calls emerged to strengthen the border between Russia and these regions, including imposing new visa requirements on them. This, obviously, directly contradicts the goals of the more inclusive Russian nationalists, who want not only to break down borders but even to make the Caucasian and Central Asian homelands of these migrants fully part of the Russian state itself. We see the tension as well when it comes to the North Caucasus. Recall that in 1999, many Russians would have been happy to let Chechnya become independent, seeing it as not really being part of 'Russia', while others were prepared to fight to keep it part of the unified, more broadly defined 'Russian' state.

Putin's statements indicate fairly consistently that he is more sympathetic to the broader rather than the narrower version of Russian nationalism, as discussed elsewhere in this volume, but the tension between the two sheds light on why he has generally tried to avoid taking a stand too far on either side. He has clearly voiced his support for more integration with territories of the former USSR, but has been especially cautious when it comes to migration policy. In the wake of the Biriulevo riots, for example, he resisted widespread calls from even many of his own supporters to impose a tight visa regime on other former Soviet countries, but at the same time refrained from directly opposing it and countering with a call to break down borders entirely. Nationalism, in short, was seen by the Kremlin throughout the 2000s and the start of the 2010s as a politically dangerous issue, one that could threaten to divide Putin's electorate more than unite it, prompting the Russian leader's strategists to tread carefully and generally avoid politicising it where possible.

Indeed, the May 2013 NEORUSS survey conducted by the Romir polling agency found that Russians were quite divided on the ideal state of Russia's borders. As is illustrated in Figure 8.1, some 37 per cent favoured the status quo, while another 13 per cent actually preferred shrinking Russia, which would increase the country's ethno-religious 'purity'. Most of the other half of

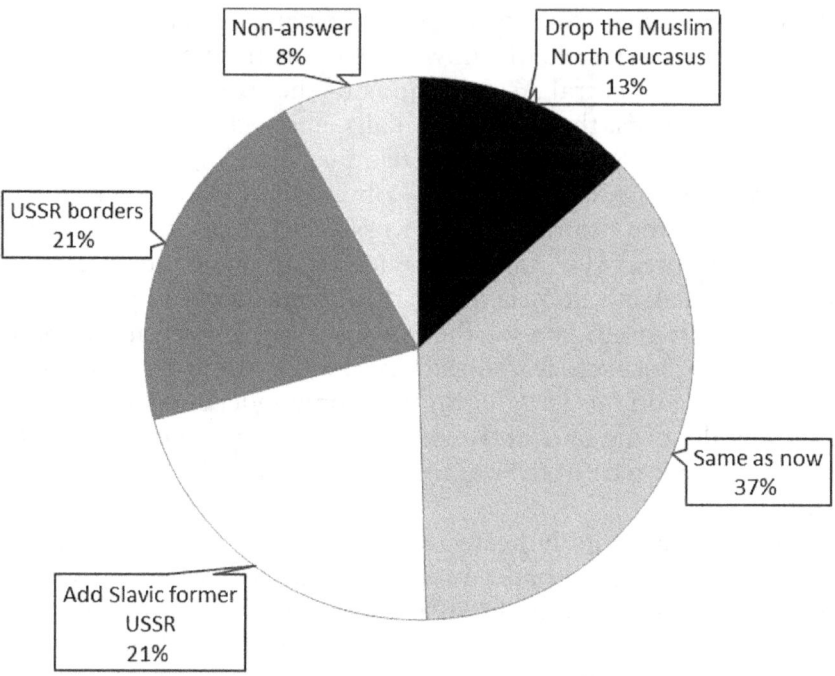

Figure 8.1 Per cent responses to 'What should be the borders of Russia?'

the population favoured augmenting Russian territory, although some would limit expansion only to Slavs while others would prefer wholly restoring the Soviet Union's old borders. Since there is no clear majority opinion, pushing any particular nationalist agenda strongly could threaten to alienate adherents to other forms of nationalism, not to mention the large share happy with the status quo.[4]

So what changed in 2014, when the Kremlin for the first time made nationalism a central part of its strategy for sustaining and gaining public support? To understand this, it is helpful to refer to the three considerations given at the start of this section that had previously made it unpromising for the Kremlin to politicise nationalism. First, in the past, other parties had been more prominent champions of nationalist ideals, making it unclear that the Kremlin would benefit more than these other parties from politicising it. But in 2014, the Kremlin began to lose control of the nationalist issue, starting to make it more risky for the authorities to avoid nationalism than to accentuate it. The key event was the overthrow of the Ukrainian president who had long been supported by Putin as an advocate for closer integration with Russia, Viktor Yanukovych. The Ukrainian leader had been ousted by forces that not only made joining Europe a central part of their agenda, but that also harboured many elements deeply hostile to Russia itself. Not only did these events make Putin look weak as an advocate for post-Soviet reintegration, but they raised the spectre of Russia's losing its Ukrainian base for the militarily vital Black Sea Fleet in Crimea. This meant for Putin that if he did not react strongly, he would likely lose support to those parties that had consistently been calling for a more assertive Russia. Or at least he would be ceding to them a central issue they could use against him later. Better, in that case, to lead the politicisation of nationalism than to be on the defensive if others led it.

Second, if Putin had taken a strongly nationalistic stance in the past, he would have risked alienating large numbers of liberals and modernisers in key cities like Moscow and St Petersburg; while some of these groups supported nationalist ideas, many were strongly opposed to them. But much support from these classes was already lost in late 2011, when they turned out in huge numbers to protest election fraud in the parliamentary elections, as described above. This lowered the political risks involved in politicising nationalism because the groups most likely to be alienated were already alienated. Moreover, the 2011–12 wave of protests had largely died out by the end of 2013, but events in Ukraine threatened to revive it, giving those dissatisfied with Putin new hope that street action could actually succeed in changing a regime. This made it imperative to find a way to consolidate the Kremlin's hold over the support of that part of the population that was still sympathetic. And perhaps even more importantly, the massive 2011–12 protests had involved not just pro-Western liberals and democratic modernisers, but also many nationalists who had been dissatisfied with the Putin regime. In this context, appearing weak as Ukraine was lost could have inspired the nationalists to return to the streets as well, perhaps in numbers even larger than before. The cost–benefit analysis of politicising nationalism had thus changed dramatically with respect to the prospect of renewed street protests. Suddenly, playing the nationalist card seemed more like the safer option.

Third, one particular move in response to Putin's domestic political crisis on Ukraine – the brazen step of annexing Crimea – not only promised to address the first two considerations just discussed, but also held out the nearly unique promise of neatly sidestepping the tension between the two strands of Russian nationalism described above. This is because Crimea's residents consist of an ethnic Russian majority, and the largest minority, Ukrainians, is also Slavic. Crimea, then, effectively hit the 'sweet spot' of Russian nationalism, offering an opportunity to expand Russian territory toward the USSR's frontiers while also bringing in primarily ethnic Russians. Moreover, this territory also possessed several additional traits that made annexation politically appealing. For one thing, Crimea already hosted Russia's Black Sea Fleet, which meant both that annexation could be explained in part as an effort to protect national military interests and also that Russian troops were already available there to assist the annexation effort and to deter a possible Ukrainian military response. Because Crimea is a peninsula, with only a thin reed of land connecting it to the rest of Ukraine, it had naturally defensible borders and could relatively easily be 'snipped off'. Finally, with its historic connection to Russia itself, transferred to the USSR's Ukrainian republic from the Russian one only in 1954 in an act that many Russians considered arbitrary, a majority already believed that Crimea was actually 'Russian (*rossiiskaia*) territory' (*Polit.ru* 2013). While this move clearly risked a powerful negative response abroad, this could also be portrayed at home as challenging an international order that had worked against Russian interests, a challenge that Putin's strategists had long considered making.

The effect of the Crimean annexation, coming shortly after Russia's successful hosting of the Olympic Winter Games in Sochi in February 2014, was a dramatic surge in public support for Putin. Importantly, as the chapter in this volume by Alexseev and Hale shows, there was no lasting concomitant surge in nationalist sentiment in Russia; instead, what took place was a powerful 'rally-around-the-leader' effect that newly connected Putin with Russians who had long held nationalist views of many kinds. Putin thus capped his Crimean move with a dramatic speech in which he cast himself as a defender of the Russian nation. Many nationalists who had previously opposed him now supported him. A classic example was writer Eduard Limonov, leader of the radical (unregistered) National Bolshevik Party that had been a mainstay of opposition protests throughout the Putin era. Limonov declared his support for Crimea's joining Russia and toned down his criticism of the regime more generally. For the first time in years, the Moscow City authorities allowed him to hold his '31st day of the month' rally in the centre of Moscow legally, the 31st symbolically also referring to the clause in the Russian constitution guaranteeing freedom of assembly, which Limonov had previously argued had been denied. A multi-barrelled media campaign supported the Kremlin cause, characterising the move as Russia's generous welcoming back of compatriots who had freely voted to leave Ukraine for Russia after a 'fascist junta' bent on anti-Russian genocide had taken power in Kyiv. By almost all accounts, support for Putin's Crimean gambit was not only broad but deep, even to the point of rupturing close friendships for a few who openly expressed scepticism or disapproval (author's personal observations).

By September 2014, an astonishing 87 per cent of the likely voting public declared their readiness to vote again for Putin were elections to be held at that time – even according to one of Russia's most reputable polling firms, the Levada Centre (Podosenov and Rozanov 2014). To many, Putin now appeared virtually invincible, supported not only by an impressive repressive apparatus and tight media control but also by a genuine majority outpouring of intense public support now seeing him as a man for the ages. He was personally anchoring what came to be called 'the Crimean consensus' (Ivanov et al. 2014). In the short term, at least, Russia's regime had become very stable, founded on the broad public support that patronal presidents need to survive moments of weakness and possible nearing succession.

Conclusion

This chapter has argued that despite the strong role of corruption and machine politics in Russia's patronal presidential system, public support has been consistently important not only in helping keep Putin and his team in power in Russia, but also in facilitating his ability to close the political space and foreclose opposition. While this support has certainly been facilitated by strong control over the most influential mass media (especially television), the experience of the USSR shows that even complete media control does not guarantee a regime the approval of the ruled. Indeed, Putin's public support had its roots well before the regime obtained such media control, and its sources have been Putin's own personal appeal, his connection with the public on important broad policy directions (such as continuing to favour a market-based economy over socialism) and – very importantly – his association with the rapid economic growth experienced by the country over the course of the 2000s and, to a lesser extent, the 2010s. Putin's team heavily emphasised these factors – particularly in contrast with the fecklessness of his predecessors in the economically difficult 1990s – in its vigorous efforts to sustain and augment its public support.

At the same time, this chapter has argued that nationalism had not been a major part of the Kremlin's strategy for sustaining or gaining public support until 2014. Prior to that time, politicising nationalism was considered too risky. This was less because of any widespread public opposition to nationalism – indeed, the Kremlin's main political opponents all championed it. Instead, part of the challenge nationalism posed for Putin was that his own support had consistently tended to come from relative moderates on Russia's spectrum of nationalism. Indeed, his main opponents had much earlier staked out stronger stands at the extremes, so there was also a risk that politicising the issue could benefit them more than him. But even if the Kremlin could hope to completely 'capture' whatever stand on the issue it wanted, there was another problem: There is not just one 'Russian nationalism', but instead there are multiple Russian nationalisms. And these nationalisms tend to contradict one another, meaning that the regime's 'playing the nationalist card' could engender political conflict more than broad support. The calculation leading the Kremlin to keep nationalism to a secondary role in its public appeal changed dramatically with the crisis in Ukraine and the decline in the Kremlin's other bases of support (most notably the economic growth rate) leading up to 2014. By orchestrating a referendum in Crimea for secession from Ukraine and accession to Russia, and by dramatically annexing it for the Russian Federation, the Kremlin hit the sweet spot of Russian nationalism, enhancing Russia's purity from the perspective of narrowly ethnic Russian nationalists while also restoring Moscow's control over more lands of the former USSR.

But while this move produced a dramatic surge in public support for Putin and those associated with him in the short run, it may have sown the seeds for political problems in the long or even medium term. For one thing, while Crimea is a cause around which both narrowly ethnic and broadly expansionist Russian nationalists can agree, other moves are likely to generate tensions even among nationalists. And the remaining areas where ethnic Russians are a majority outside Russia present much greater problems logistically for Russian territorial expansionists, lacking local Russian military bases and having no clear and easily defensible borders. A risk is thus that with their appetites whetted, expansionist nationalists will fault Putin for not moving further when he had the chance if he does not do so. But if he does do so, he is likely to face challenges domestically from those unwilling to pay a high price in terms of blood shed for the sake of these lands, an influx of unwanted migrants, and/or the economic and political instability that such moves may bring. In addition, if Crimea fails to develop smoothly under Russian control, or if securing its electricity or water from parts of Ukraine draws Russia into further conflicts that it finds hard to control, even Crimea could start to prove a liability to Russia's leadership. 'Rallying effects' around leaders after victorious wars, much research concludes (Baker and Oneal 2001), also tend to subside, at which point Putin and his allies could come in for new challenges. Of course, the logic of patronal presidentialism expects that such challenges will be most acute as moments of expected succession approach, and by Russia's constitution Putin would not be required to leave office until 2024. But other moments can arise that crystallise regime collapse, as the 2011 Arab uprisings illustrate. All this suggests that Putin's Crimean gambit has likely not bought him a carefree decade in office, forcing him to search for new ways to shore up his regime's support in the years ahead in order to survive politically.

Notes

1. The author thanks Dylan Royce for research assistance and the Institute of European, Russian and Eurasian Studies (IERES) of George Washington University for funding this assistance.
2. See, for example, the broadcast of the weekly *Voskresnoe vremia* news programme on Channel 1 on 27 November 2011 at 21:00.
3. See, for example, the broadcast of *Vesti nedeli* on the Rossiia on 14 October 2012 at 20:00.
4. This is supported by findings reported in a separate paper by the present author using experiments embedded in the 2013 NEORUSS survey. It finds that politicising the issue of migration would lead to a decline rather than an increase in public support for Putin. See Henry E. Hale, 'The Impact of Anti-Migrant Nationalism on Non-Democratic Regimes: Experimental Evidence from the Russian Case', draft paper.

9

Blurring the boundary between civic and ethnic: The Kremlin's new approach to national identity under Putin's third term

Helge Blakkisrud

Traditionally, the Russian – and later Soviet – state has always relied on an imperial approach to the 'national question': on loyalty to the state and the dynasty/Communist Party rather than to an ethnically defined community. For a long time, the Romanovs tended to treat all instances of Russian ethnonationalism with considerable scepticism; the very idea of casting the nation in ethnic terms appeared antithetical to their dynastic understanding of the state (Kappeler 2001). And despite their purported 'ethnophilia', Soviet nation-builders repeatedly denounced all expressions of 'Great Russian chauvinism' (Slezkine 1994). The breakup of the Soviet Union did not immediately change this. After 1991, the multi-ethnic 'Soviet people' was replaced by an equally complex and multi-faceted 'Russian' (*rossiiskii*) civic identity intended to encompass everyone residing within the borders of the new state (see, for example, Tolz 2004; Rutland 2010; Shevel 2011). However, as the dust settled and the Soviet overlay started to wear off, a re-appraisal gradually began to take place.

This chapter traces the evolution of President Vladimir Putin's approach to the Russian national idea and national identity after his 2012 return to the Kremlin – a period during which, against a backdrop of internal and external challenges, with the mass protests in Moscow and St Petersburg after the 2011 State Duma elections and the evolving crisis in Ukraine, the Kremlin undertook a re-calibrating of its understanding of the national 'self'.

Based on a reading of Putin's programmatic speeches on national identity, I argue that traditional ethno-political correctness, associated with a civic, multi-ethnic and multi-confessional identity, has been increasingly challenged by a shift in focus towards the traditional ethno-cultural core of this identity: its 'Russianness' (*russkost'*). That said, I find that the Kremlin clearly stops short of pursuing clear-cut ethnonationalism. Instead, to maximise its room for manoeuvre, the Kremlin has been deliberately blurring the borders of the Russian ethnic 'self', making it possible to re-interpret this 'self' as something more narrow but also broader than the body of citizens of the Russian Federation. Internally, such an identity holds the potential to encompass most of the population; externally, it can build up under the Kremlin's self-appointed role of speaking – and acting – on behalf of not only the ethnic Russians in the Diaspora, but of a wider 'Russian world' (*russkii mir*) as well.[1]

After a brief backdrop presenting Putin's take on national identity and the 'Russian idea' during his first two terms as Russian president (2000–8), this chapter examines Putin's key addresses on the national question during the first two years of his third term, culminating with the March 2014 speech on the occasion of the official accession of Crimea and Sevastopol to the Federation. Across these speeches, I argue, Putin redefined the national 'self' from a predominantly civic understanding based on citizenship and identification with the state, to a more ethnic one focused on Russian language and culture, one in which the ethnic Russians take centre stage. I then trace how this new understanding of the national 'self' was translated into federal policy through the adoption of a new 'State Strategy on Nationalities Policy for the Period through 2025', and discuss what response this Russian-centred approach has received in the population at large. The chapter concludes with a discussion of whether Putin's new 'ethnic turn' may have better prospects for taking firm root than the civic *rossiiane* identity the Kremlin sought to promote in the 1990s.

Backdrop: Putin the patriot

The search for a Russian national idea is nothing new; in his 2007 address to the Federal Assembly Putin referred to this as an 'old tradition, a favourite pastime' in Russia (Putin 2007a). On the eve of his accession to power, Putin had himself outlined a vision for Russia's future. In what has been referred to as Putin's Millennium Manifesto (Sakwa 2008), he had identified three key pillars for a successful Russian resurgence: an effective economy, a strong state and further consolidation of the national idea (*rossiiskaia ideia*) (Putin 1999). However, during Putin's first two terms at the helm of Russian politics (2000–8), priority appeared to go to the two first of these pillars, with Russian economy making a remarkable recovery and Putin presiding over the comprehensive re-centralisation of a wide range of sectors within Russian politics and society.

As for the third pillar, the national idea, the Kremlin's main strategy for nation-building during these eight years seemed to be to sponsor a revival of civic patriotism (see, for example, Sperling 2010). In his Millennium Manifesto, Putin had singled out such patriotism – together with 'great-powerness' (*derzhavnost'*), 'state-centredness' (*gosudarstvennichestvo*) and 'social solidarity' – as 'primordial, traditional Russian (*rossiiskie*) values' (Putin 1999). At the onset of Putin's first term, state patriotism found itself at a historical low ebb; as pointed out in Pål Kolstø's chapter, during the Eltsin years, the Russian population had struggled to come to terms with the loss of empire and with having to re-align their identity with the new Russian state.[2] Now, after a decade of disintegration and decay, Putin set about instilling a new sense of pride and direction by promoting civic patriotism.

For obvious reasons, the Eltsin administration had had to distance itself from the Soviet past, and focused instead on Russia's pre-1917 history as the current state's historical backdrop. With the change in presidency, however, the Kremlin switched to a more pragmatic approach, selectively rehabilitating those aspects of the Soviet experience that were considered positive and conducive to state patriotism – a process illustrated by the decision to adopt the old Soviet hymn with a new set of lyrics as the new national anthem of the Russian Federation (see Kolstø 2006). The Kremlin thus drew selectively on Soviet as well as imperial Russian history – and by committing to strengthening the economy and the state structures (the first two pillars outlined in the Manifesto), Putin held up the vision of a future in which Russia would again assume its 'rightful place' among the world's great powers.

Putin's approach to the national idea was in other words state-centred rather than ethnic: the 'Russian people' (*rossiiskii narod*) was understood as a multi-ethnic and multi-confessional union of peoples residing within the borders of the current state. According to Putin, 'since ancient times, the idea of a shared community (*obshchii mir*) – shared by people of different nationalities and faiths – has constituted the foundation for the spiritual outlook of the Russian people' (Putin 2007a). Hence, the Kremlin continued to espouse the civic *rossiiane* identity that had been introduced by the Eltsin administration (Tishkov 1995; see also introductory chapter). In essence, the Putin regime tried to bolster a patriotic identity along the same lines as its imperial and Soviet predecessors: a civic (non-ethnic) nation model with significant cultural and political rights to non-Russians, held together by a broad set of common values and traditions (Kappeler 2001; Kolstø and Blakkisrud 2004).

Although Putin had identified the further evolution of the national idea as key for a successful consolidation of Russian society, he nevertheless spoke against forcing this development. In his Millennium Manifesto, he argued that the national idea would have to evolve in an organic process, through a gradual merger of 'universal human values and primordial Russian (*iskonnye rossiiskie*) values that have withstood the test of time' (Putin 1999). Aside from adopting some high-profiled programmes aimed at boosting patriotism among the younger generation in particular (see Sperling 2010), the Kremlin did not adopt an especially proactive nation-building strategy at the time.[3]

In parallel, while officially promoting the concept of civic patriotism, the Kremlin also recognised the potential in tapping Russian ethnonationalist sentiments to feed its vision of a great Russia (the *derzhavnost*-strand of Putin's national idea). As a consequence, for most of the first decade of the new millennium, the distinction between what were considered positive expressions of patriotism and what constituted more clear-cut – and negative – nationalism remained blurred (Laruelle 2010b: 22–33). The Kremlin tolerated, and sometimes even actively encouraged, the activities of more moderate nationalist organisations such as Dmitrii Rogozin's Motherland (*Rodina*) and the pro-Kremlin youth-movement Nashi (Laruelle 2010b). And although the regime took care not to let Russian ethnonationalists develop into an independent political force (Sakwa 2011a), certain more extreme expressions of nationalist sentiment were nevertheless condoned – like the organising of the 'Russian March', an annual event uniting Russian nationalist groups of various stripes, including skinheads and neo-Nazis.

In December 2010, however, this was all to change. When mass riots broke out at the Manezhnaia Square, just a stone's throw from the Kremlin walls, with several thousands of angry protesters gathering to shout nationalistic and anti-Caucasian slogans, the authorities had to reconsider their hitherto complacent approach toward Russian ethnonationalists.[4] To be sure, these were not the first ethnically motivated riots after the turn of the millennium; the first major incident to hit the headlines had been the violent clashes in the small Karelian city of Kondopoga in August 2006. Here, a brawl that left two ethnic Russians dead developed into what Russian media described as a 'pogrom', with an angry mob attacking businesses associated with people hailing from the Caucasus (Shlapentokh 2010). The Manezhnaia riot, however, took the issue to the nation's capital – and to the top of the political agenda.

Realising that Russian nationalists may draw advantage of widespread latent anti-migrant sentiments in the population at large (see, for example, Malakhov 2014), the Kremlin now decided to clamp down on un-sanctioned expressions of Russian ethnonationalism. The following months saw an increase in the number of court cases against alleged nationalists; in April 2011, for example, one of the key gathering points for the Russian nationalists, the Movement against Illegal Immigration, was banned for espousing extremism. In this way, the Kremlin tried to force the genie back in the bottle and push the nationalists to the margins of Russian politics.

In a parallel process, United Russia had already for some time been preoccupied with developing its own 'Russian Project' (*Russkii proekt*), so as – as put by Andrei Isaev, a member of the United Russia General Council – 'to destroy the monopoly of extremists and scoundrels to speak on behalf of the Russian (*russkii*) nation' (quoted in Azar 2007). The ground had therefore already been prepared for a partial reorientation, with the powers-that-be reconsidering its approach to Russian ethnonationalism and trying to appropriate some of the political niche the ethnonationalist had carved out for themselves. Nevertheless, the formulation of a new, comprehensive federal policy on the 'national question' would have to wait until Putin's return to the Kremlin.

A new take for a new presidency: From marginalisation to partial co-optation

When Dmitrii Medvedev and Putin in September 2011 announced their decision to swap positions after the March 2012 presidential elections, the outcome of these elections was a foregone conclusion. During the campaign, Putin – true to tradition – refrained from engaging in public debates with his opponents, preferring to communicate with the electorate through a series of thematic newspaper articles. One of these, published in *Nezavisimaia gazeta* in January 2012, was devoted to 'the national question'. Here Putin took stock of various approaches to how to tackle the multi-ethnic reality of the contemporary state system, lashing out against European-style multi-culturalism, which he claimed had proven to be a failure, as well as against Russian ethnonationalism.[5] The latter he described as 'a bacillus' that, if left unchecked, held the potential to destroy Russia. Ethnonationalism had already contributed to the collapse of the Soviet Union; according to Putin, Russian nationalism may take the Russian Federation down the same path. He therefore continued to argue the case of patriotism, maintaining that Russia had been shaped by a unique process that had resulted in 'a multi-ethnic society, but a united people' (Putin 2012b).

Nonetheless, compared to, for example, the Millennium Manifesto, there was a distinct shift in emphasis: Putin now accorded a much more prominent role to the ethnic Russians, who were held up as 'the state-forming nation (*gosudarstvo-obrazuiushchii narod*)': 'The core and the binding fabric of this unique civilisation is the [ethnic] Russian people, [ethnic] Russian culture' (Putin 2012b). Hence, while retaining a traditional state-centred orientation, Putin now signalled an ethnic turn. While categorically rejecting the idea of 'building a Russian "national", mono-ethnic state', an idea that, Putin held, contradicted Russia's entire thousand-year-old history, he declared Russianness to be the ethno-cultural core of the state-centred identity (ibid.).

This shift must be seen in the context of the mass demonstrations that took place in Moscow and other big cities in the wake of the flawed December 2011 State Duma elections. In addition to being the biggest manifestations of political opposition since the collapse of the Soviet Union, these demonstrations represented a breakthrough for cooperation across ideological divides, with the Western-oriented liberals overcoming some of their traditional distaste for the Russian ethnonationalists (see, for example, Kolstø 2014; Laruelle 2014b). The authorities were clearly taken by surprise by this development as well as the sheer scale of popular mobilisation. In order to regain momentum, Putin's team therefore decided to grant some (minor) concessions to the demonstrators[6] while also co-opting some of their rhetoric. As for the latter, Russian ethnonationalist demands about self-determination and the need for a Russian nation state were reformulated in a way more palatable to the Kremlin: 'Self-determination for [ethnic] Russians – that is a poly-ethnic civilisation held together by a Russian cultural core ... The great mission of the [ethnic] Russians is to unite and cement this civilisation' (Putin 2012b).

The borders of this Russian 'self' were kept vague: there was a clearly defined core – Russianness represented the centre of gravity in this 'poly-ethnic civilisation' – but at the fringes, non-Russians were welcomed and encouraged to re-align with the majority population. This was an understandable approach. The Kremlin could simply not risk alienating the numerous ethnic minorities residing within the borders of the current Russian

Federation by pursuing a narrowly defined, exclusivist version of 'Russianness'. A balance had to be struck between reaching out to the ethnic Russian majority population, without provoking a counter-mobilisation among strong and well-organised minority communities like the Tatars, for example. Putin's solution was to hold up the possibility of cultural incorporation of these minorities into the broader 'Russian civilisation'.

From Valdai to Crimea – Narrowing in and widening up?

In his article in *Nezavisimaia gazeta*, Putin had called for the development of a new federal strategy on how to approach 'the national question'. Once elected, he set about realising this campaign promise, transforming the lofty ideas into practical policy (see below). On the one hand, Putin emphasised that this new policy should be civic and state-centred – 'any person living in our country should not forget about his faith and ethnicity. But he should first of all be a citizen of Russia (*grazhdanin Rossii*) and be proud of it' (Putin 2012b). On the other hand, he continued to highlight the special role of ethnic Russians within the Russian state project. In his first annual address to the Federal Assembly after returning to the Kremlin, for example, Putin once again stressed the 'Russianness' of the Russian people (*rossiiskii narod*). While acknowledging that Russia comprised a 'unique, multi-ethnic nation', he underlined that this nation was held together by 'the [ethnic] Russians (*russkii narod*), a Russian language and a Russian culture native to all of us, uniting us, and preventing us from dissolving in this diverse world' (Putin 2012c).

The current state-formation was built not only on the foundations of the multi-ethnic Soviet predecessor, but on those of Imperial Russia and of Muscovy. In order to revive national consciousness, Putin averred,

> we need to link historical eras together and revert to understanding the simple truth that Russia did not begin in 1917, or even in 1991, but rather, that we have a single, uninterrupted history spanning over one thousand years that we rely on to find inner strength and purpose in our national development. (Putin 2012c)

Putin thus explicitly linked the nation-building project with the history of the ethnic Russians and their statehood. He also used the opportunity to denounce again nationalism and chauvinism 'of various stripes and persuasions' (Putin 2012c): all manifestations of separatism and nationalism should be removed from the political agenda. This time around, however, the main addressees among putative nationalists were not the Russian ethnonationalists, but the *non*-Russians:

> We must not forget that nationalism and chauvinism do direct and enormous damage especially to the people and the ethnic group whose interests the nationalists are supposedly defending ... We must regard attempts to provoke ethnic tensions and religious intolerance as a challenge to the unity of the Russian state and as a threat to all of us. We will not allow the emergence of closed ethnic enclaves in Russia with their informal jurisdiction, existing outside the country's common legal and cultural norms, and disdainfully disregarding the accepted standards, laws and regulations. (Putin 2012c)

In the course of the next year and half, Putin delivered two landmark speeches pertaining to the Russian identity project: in September 2013, a keynote address to the Valdai Club gathering of international Russia specialists; and then in March 2014, a speech to the Federal Assembly and regional heads, outlining the background for welcoming Crimea and Sevastopol as new subjects of the Federation.

The 2013 Valdai Club meeting was devoted to the theme 'Russia's diversity for the modern world'– but, instead of praising diversity, Putin's speech accentuated the fundamental need for developing a *unified* nation in terms of values and outlook:

> In the end, economic growth, prosperity and geopolitical influence all derive from societal conditions; from to what extent citizens of a given country consider themselves a unified nation, to what extent they are anchored in their own history, values and traditions; whether they are united by common goals and responsibilities. In this sense, the question of finding and strengthening national identity really is fundamental for Russia. (Putin 2013a)

In order to consolidate such a national identity, Putin called for a concerted effort involving various strands of society. The first post-independence decade had represented a lost decade: 'After 1991, there existed an illusion about a new national ideology ... that would simply appear all by itself', he declared. However, history had proven that 'a new national idea does not simply appear, nor does it develop according to market rules' (Putin 2013a). Putin thus seemed to have abandoned his former stance (as outlined in the Millennium Manifesto) on how to approach this issue: while reiterating that a national idea cannot simply be imposed from above, he now opened up for much more active state involvement in the process.

Mechanically copying other countries' experiences would be a futile venture, however; the Russian national idea would have to be firmly rooted in history and society. 'Who are we?' and 'Who do we want to be?' These questions the Russians were asking themselves 'louder and louder', Putin declared. The answer, he continued, was to be found in a national identity that was civic in nature, based on 'shared values, a patriotic consciousness, civic responsibility and solidarity, respect for the law, communion with the fate of the Fatherland without losing touch with ethnic or religious roots' (Putin 2013a). But at the same time, no doubt should remain about the (ethnic) Russian core of this state-centred identity. The President repeated the now-customary homage to the Russian people, Russian language and Russian culture: but now he also underscored the importance of the Russian Orthodox Church.

That was in keeping with the new conservative, values-based approach that had increasingly come to colour the world outlook of the new presidency (Byzov 2014; Sharafutdinova 2014; see also Putin 2013b). Putin's 2012 state of the nation address had been peppered with references to the importance of history, tradition and family virtues – values Putin associated with his revamped vision of the national community. In the Valdai speech, Putin lashed out against the 'excessive political correctness' and multi-culturalism that permeated Western societies, which, he said, led to a

> rejection of their roots, including the Christian values that constitute the basis of Western civilisation. [Many Euro-Atlantic states] are

denying moral principles and all traditional identities: national, cultural, religious and even sexual. They are implementing policies that put same-sex partnerships on a par with large families; belief in Satan on a par with the belief in God. (Putin 2013a)

Up against this decadence, decay and moral upheaval, Putin proclaimed Russia as a beacon of traditional virtues and family values, and called for the people to rally in defence of this values-based national identity. The 'ethnic turn' that commenced with Putin's third term was, in other words, part and parcel of a broader conservative, traditionalist reorientation.

In the March 2014 address devoted to the inclusion of Crimea and Sevastopol as subjects of the Russian Federation, Putin went even further in linking the fate of the ethnic Russians and Russian statehood. As noted elsewhere in this volume, Putin put forward historical arguments to justify the revision of the state borders: Crimea had previously been part of the Russian Empire and then of the RSFSR; and the 1954 decision to transfer the peninsula to Ukraine, a grand gesture by First Secretary Nikita Khrushchev on the occasion of the 300th anniversary of the treaty uniting contemporary Eastern Ukraine with Muscovy, was written off as a historical mistake and an unconstitutional act. However, in making his case, Putin consistently used the term *russkii* rather than *rossiiskii*. In his emotional appeal, he insisted that 'in the hearts, in the minds of people, Crimea always was and remains an integral part of Russia . . . Crimea is primordial Russian land (*iskonno russkaia zemlia*) and Sevastopol a Russian city (*russkii gorod*)' (Putin 2014a). In other words, bringing the peninsula back in under Moscow's control was not only legitimised by Crimea historically having been part of the Russian Empire and the RSFSR – the peninsula was also considered *ethnic* Russian lands. Accession to the Federation was presented both as an act of rectifying historical injustice and of ethnic self-determination. With the dissolution of the Soviet Union, the Russian people had 'turned into one of the biggest divided nations in the world, if not the biggest' (Putin 2014a). Now, the ethnic Russians – along the local Ukrainians and Crimean Tatars – and the 'Russian' lands were being welcomed back home to the motherland.

Putin could not, and probably had no desire to, present Russia as a nation state in ethnic terms, but the language had definitely changed. Gone were the references to an overarching, civic *rossiiane* identity – in fact, in the key speeches from Putin's third term examined here not a single time did he apply this term; when he now spoke of the population as a collective, he used the more neutral 'citizens of Russia' (*grazhdane Rossii*). But, as we saw in the Crimea speech, there was also a tendency for *rossiiskii* to be replaced by *russkii*, as when Putin spoke of the *russkii* Black Sea Fleet or of *russkii* Sevastopol (Putin 2014a).

Putin's Crimea speech must be interpreted in the wider context of the Ukrainian crisis. When in February 2014 President Viktor Yanukovych had fled Kyiv head over heels, that represented a serious blow to the Kremlin's image of Moscow as the ultimate power-broker in post-Soviet politics. The subsequent stealth operation paving the way for the 'reunification' of Crimea and Sevastopol with the Russian Federation served to restore confidence and spurred unprecedented outbursts of patriotism. Putin's speech marked the apogee of this.

Still, Putin's readjustment of national identity, gradually shifting the emphasis toward a more Russian-centred, values-based project, served him well also at this crossroads. Thus far, Putin's focus on the Russian core of the national identity project had helped in stealing some of the Russian ethnonationalists' thunder. The Crimea speech demonstrated that an emphasis on ethnocultural Russianness also could yield dividends in Russia's external relations: a civic *rossiiane* identity linked to the Russian state could not so easily be mobilised to legitimise expansionist adventures in Ukraine. When identity now was re-cast in ethnocultural terms, however, the Kremlin could appeal not only to the will of the Crimean population as expressed in the recent referendum,[7] but also to the unacceptable separation of ethnic kin. The incorporation of Crimea and Sevastopol into the Federation thus served to rally both Russian ethnonationalists and the *impertsy*, the adherents of the restoration of a Russian/Soviet Empire (see Emil Pain's chapter), under Putin's banner.[8]

While Putin in the Crimea speech came out with stronger support of Russian ethnonational arguments than in any other major speech discussed here, and this speech has been seen by many as a watershed in Russian identity debate, upping the rhetoric is one thing – practical implementation through adopting policy changes quite another. To what extent was Putin's rhetorical shift reflected in policy changes in the field of nationalities policy and nation-building over this same period?

From words to policy: Formulating a new approach to Russian nationalities policy

During the election campaign, Putin had signalled a need for updating federal nationalities policy. At the time, Russia's approach to nation-building and minority politics was still officially guided by the somewhat dated 'Concept of State Nationalities Policy' (*Kontseptsiia* ... 1996). This concept had been adopted in the spring of 1996 when the Russian Federation found itself in the midst of a process of largely uncontrolled, ad hoc decentralisation, and its territorial integrity was threatened by the ongoing war in Chechnya. The orientation of the Concept clearly reflected this. Now, when the trends had turned and Moscow was once again firmly in control, Putin pointed to the need for revising the federal framework for nationalities policy, so that it could better reflect current challenges and needs.

Once back in charge in the Kremlin, Putin wasted no time. On 7 May 2012 – the same day as he was officially inaugurated – he issued a series of decrees outlining the main priorities for his new term (Zav'ialova 2012). One of these decrees, 'On ensuring interethnic harmony', addressed the issues of nationalities policy and migration. Here Putin instructed his administration to develop, in cooperation with the federal government, a new strategy for a state nationalities policy by December that year, as well as to establish a presidential consultative council tasked with monitoring the development of inter-ethnic relations (Ukaz Prezidenta RF 2012b).[9]

A month later, Putin unveiled the mandate and composition of the new Presidential Council on Interethnic Relations. Its fifty seats were filled by top bureaucrats, leaders of various ethnic minority organisations and prominent scholars. According to the accompanying statutes, the Council was to convene at least once every six months and facilitate cooperation between federal, regional and municipal authorities and public associations, research institutes and other relevant organisations in addressing issues related to the implementation of state policy on inter-ethnic relations.[10] More urgently, in light of Putin's call for a new strategy, the Council was also to 'consider the conceptual basis, goals and objectives' of this policy (*Prezident Rossii* 2012).

In October 2012, the Council presented a first draft of the new strategy. Prior to this, some pundits, such as Boris Makarenko at the Centre for Political Technologies, had expressed concerns that the strategy may further extend the 'bias towards Great Russian chauvinism' detected in Putin's election manifesto (quoted in Gorodetskaia 2012a). When the draft was unveiled, however, such fears proved largely unwarranted. Indeed, a noteworthy difference between this draft and Putin's above-mentioned article was that the ethnic Russians were no longer described as the 'state-forming people'. This formulation had caused a great deal of controversy, not least in several ethnic republics, and had now been edited out (Gorodetskaia 2012b). Instead, the draft briefly acknowledged the 'unifying role' of the ethnic Russians:

> Thanks to the unifying role of the Russian people (*russkii narod*) and centuries of intercultural and interethnic interaction, a unique civilisational community has been formed, the multinational Russian nation (*rossiiskaia natsiia*), the members of which consider Russia their Motherland. (*Proekt* . . . 2012)

This re-formulation, which was actually more in line with the original 1996 Concept,[11] was perceived as a nod to the non-Russian part of the population. However, many Russian nationalists were outraged at this decision to downplay the contribution of ethnic Russians to Russian statehood, interpreting this as a yet another proof of the Putin regime's betrayal of the Russian nation and its right to self-determination. During the hearing process, Vsevolod Chaplin, head of the Orthodox Church's Synodal Department for Church–Society Relations, warned against the consequences of continuing to neglect the interests of the ethnic Russians as well as not taking seriously the spread of 'Russophobia' within Russian society. 'To me it is obvious that today, the Russian people (*russkii narod*) needs systematic support of its culture, language, forms of self-organisation, forms of citizenship [and] community action' (Chaplin 2012). Dmitrii Demushkin, one of the leaders of the Russian nationalist organisation Russkie, simply dismissed the whole strategy as 'empty and toothless' (Natsional'nyi aktsent 2012).

Also representatives of the ethnic minority communities voiced criticism during the public hearing process. Although the state was to guarantee equal rights to all peoples residing in the Russian Federation – the draft had fixed the number of such peoples to 193, and the number of different languages used in the public education system to 89 – and protect the cultural and linguistic diversity these groups represented (*Proekt* . . . 2012), formulations about the need for further consolidating Russia's administrative structure caused considerable concern. In the ethnic autonomies, the latter was interpreted as a thinly veiled attack on their status as independent federal subjects; in terms of population, the autonomies tend to be much smaller than the oblasts and krais, so the leaders of these autonomies feared that the authorities would use the strategy as a pretext for reviving the merger process. After vigorous protests from, *inter alia*, Tatarstan, overt calls for merging ethnic autonomies with other federal subjects were omitted from the final draft (Litoi 2012; Khisamiev and Coalson 2012).

Finally, the draft strategy was also criticised for ignoring the elephant in the room: the definition of what constitutes Russia's 'national idea'. Viacheslav Mikhailov, co-chair of the working group that prepared the draft and former Minister of Nationalities Affairs and Federal Relations (1995–2000), admitted that the authors had been 'criticised for the fact that we formulate the goal of the state nationalities policy without having formulated a national idea', but went on to explain that the strategy should be 'a consensus-oriented document, a form of social contract' (Gorodetskaia 2012b).

On the whole, the draft provoked considerable debate and reaction. According to one of its authors, Valerii Tishkov, former Minister of Nationalities Affairs (1992) and Director of the

Institute of Ethnology and Anthropology, the Council received more than a thousand comments during the hearing process.[12] To avoid inflaming ethnonationalist feelings unnecessarily, the drafters thus sought to have it both ways: to promote both a unifying civic identity as well as individual ethnic affiliation. In the words of Mikhailov, 'We for the first time introduce the concept of a "Russian civic nation" (*rossiiskaia grazhdanskaia natsiia*), but do not desert the ethnic definition' (quoted in BBC 2012). During the election campaign, Putin could woo Russian ethnonationalist sentiments, but for the nationalities strategy to win widespread acceptance, the powers-that-be would have to find a middle way. The result was a watered-down version in which the Russians were merely the first among equals: in the final version of the strategy, they were fobbed off with a reference to historically having played a key role in the unification of the Russian nation (*rossiiskaia natsiia*): 'The Russian state was formed as a union of peoples with the Russian people (*russkii narod*) historically playing the system-forming core (*sistemoobrazuiushchoe iadro*) (*Strategiia* . . . 2012).

On 19 December 2012, Putin signed a decree approving the new 'State Strategy on Nationalities Policy for the Period through 2025' (Ukaz Prezidenta RF 2012c). The media hailed the strategy as the first comprehensive document on nationalities policy in Russia for several decades. With this move, the Kremlin had laid down the general guidelines for political, economic and cultural policies towards Russia's various ethnic groups for the coming two decades.[13] The text represented less than a clear-cut 'ethnic turn', it remained more preoccupied with the civic *rossiiskaia natsiia* than the ethnically defined *russkii narod*, but Putin had given the marching orders, and this was probably in itself more important for providing further direction to the debate on the national identity than the compromise- and consensus-oriented strategy.

Reception among the general population

What about the public reaction? How did the population at large respond to Putin's ethnonationalist overtures? In recent years, many ethnic Russians have unquestionably become more vocal in their claims to proprietorship of Russian statehood, demanding to be recognised as representing the 'state-forming nation'. While ethnic Russians currently constitute a clear majority of the population, their interests have, according to Russian ethnonationalist discourse, repeatedly and consistently been ignored (see, for example, Rogozin 2012).

One frequently used indicator for ethnonationalist sentiments in the Russian population is support for the slogan 'Russia for Russians' (*Rossiia dlia russkikh*). According to the Romir 2013 NEORUSS survey, in spring 2013, almost two-thirds of our respondents (59.3 per cent) supported this slogan, fully or partly.[14] This result may reflect the failure of the Kremlin to take a clear stance against Russian ethnonationalism during much of the first decade of the new millennium, but also that the Soviet overlay has begun to wear thin: while the older generations have been raised on slogans about 'the friendship of the peoples' (*druzhba narodov*) – a slogan that, incidentally, also made it into the new strategy on nationalities policy[15] – research has consistently shown the post-Soviet generation as more prone to espouse xenophobic attitudes (see, for example, Sokolov 2013). In our survey, no single age cohort came out as more supportive of the slogan than those 18 to 24 years old.[16]

When asked who these '*russkie*' in the slogan 'Russia for Russians' were, however, somewhat surprisingly only 39.0 per cent opted for a purely ethnic definition. More than half of the respondents offered a more inclusive interpretation: either that the *russkie* included all citizens (in other words, indicating a full merger between the *rossiiskii* and the *russkii* identity) (24.9 per cent) or 'predominantly ethnic Russians, but not only them' (what can be described as an 'ethnic Russian plus' approach) (30.0 per cent). Interestingly, the age cohort that most frequently chose the 'ethnic Russian plus' option was the post-Soviet generation (18–24 years old). Apparently, a majority of the respondents are ready to support Putin's Russo-centric but non-ethnic interpretation of the national self.

Who are potentially included, and who are defined out of this *russkii* in-group? In the survey, we did not ask explicitly about what other ethnic groups the respondents were willing to subsume under the category *russkii*. Elsewhere, however, Emil Pain has discussed such an expanded self in the context of 'us' versus 'the migrants'. He finds that among internal migrants, representatives of ethnic groups from the North Caucasus stand out as a culturally alien group that the majority population find hard to include in the wider 'self'. According to Pain, 'In Moscow no one calls someone hailing from St Petersburg, Tyumen or Oryol a "migrant", the same goes for Tatars or Bashkirs originating in their respective republics'; in fact, even people hailing from Ukraine and Belarus may escape this epithet (quoted in Filina 2013). Instead, the term 'migrant', a code-word for 'the Other', is reserved mainly for people arriving from the Caucasus and Central Asia. In other words, even though the North Caucasus has been part of the Russian/Soviet state for more than 150 years, the majority population still finds it hard to include ethnic groups hailing from this region in the national 'self'; the cultural and religious characteristics of these ethnic groups are perceived as difficult to align with the *russkii* 'self'.

In his 2012 speech to the Federal Assembly, Putin recalled how a World War II veteran who was not a Russian by ethnicity once had told him: 'As far as the entire world is concerned, we are one people, we are Russian (*russkie*).' Putin added, 'That was true during the war, and it has always been true' (Putin 2012c). Although there exist cultural barriers that most probably will prevent certain ethnic minorities from being absorbed into a greater *russkii* community, the Romir 2013 NEORUSS survey indicates that the ethnic Russian population is ready to accept minorities as part of a national *russkii* self.

Concluding discussion

While Putin has characterised the Russian search for a national idea as 'an old tradition, a favourite pastime', he has also made it clear that national identity is a work in progress (see, for example, Putin 2013a). The current 'ethnic turn' with a 'Russification' of the national idea is probably best understood as a delayed reaction. While the other fourteen former union republics immediately set about engaging in nation-building processes in which they positioned themselves against the old Soviet superstructure, it took time before Moscow began to come to terms with the new realities. The *rossiiane* identity could be seen as a stopgap measure: a slightly modified version of the Soviet civic identity readjusted to a greatly reduced territory. As time went by, however, the new demographic and political circumstances called for a revision of the initial post-Soviet identity project.[17]

The Kremlin's response during Putin's third term has been to deliberately blur the boundaries between the civic *rossiiskii* and the ethnic *russkii* identities. The civic identity has become more explicitly Russian, with the Kremlin holding up the Russian language, culture and traditional values as the core of this identity. At the same time, Putin has distanced himself from more radical expressions of Russian ethnonationalism. Adherence to culture and values is seen as more important than ancestry and genes when it comes to defining who is in and who is out. The boundaries of the *russkii* identity are opened up so as to include members of other ethnic groups that subscribe to the values-based identity now promoted by the Kremlin.

To what extent does this project stand a better chance of winning widespread acceptance among the general population than the *rossiiane* project of the early 1990s? Several factors complicate a more universal acceptance of a *russkii*-centred identity.

First of all, an obvious obstacle is the way the state itself continues to be organised. When the Soviet Union broke apart, the new rulers in the Kremlin opted for preserving the Soviet ethnofederal structure more or less intact. This meant that thirty-two of the altogether eighty-nine constituent entities of the Russian Federation were defined as ethnic autonomies – as ethnic homelands of one or more titular groups. After the turn of the millennium, the Kremlin engaged in a campaign to rationalise the federal structure, singling out some of the scarcely populated autonomous okrugs for abrogation. During Putin's second presidential term, six okrugs were merged with neighbouring oblasts or krais. Due to strong local resistance in some republics, however, that campaign was soon shelved. By the time of the accession of

Crimea and Sevastopol, the Federation thus still consisted of no less than twenty-six autonomies.[18]

The debate on the federal structure is not dead in Russia. As the Crimean euphoria began to subside, and the harsh realities of a faltering economy began to sink in, some actors began to dust off old plans for re-centralisation and de-federalisation. Former Prime Minister Evgenii Primakov, for one, argued that autonomies where ethnic Russians form a majority ought to be abolished and merged with 'regular' subjects (Primakov 2015). Still, even if such plans should come to fruition, no serious politician would at this stage dare to question the future of republics like Tatarstan or Bashkortostan. A switch to a fully unitary state structure is currently not an option. And as long as such republics continue to form constituent parts of the Federation, these ethnic homelands will continue to serve as a constant reminder to their titular populations about their 'non-Russianness'. An ethno-federal state structure may pair well with the old *rossiiane* identity, but is harder to reconcile with a more Russian-centred identity project.

Second, the new identity project is not starting with a clean slate. To the contrary: for seventy years, Soviet citizens were taught that ethnic affiliation mattered. In the 1920s, during *korenizatsiia*, Soviet authorities undertook an unprecedented project of ethnic engineering – of consolidating and indeed also inventing ethnic identities (Slezkine 1994). Not only did the Soviet authorities sponsor minority-language education, media and cultural institutions, they also intervened on the individual level, requiring all citizens to have their ethnic affiliation written into their internal passports, the standard ID document. This affiliation was not based on self-ascription, but on the ethnicity of the bearer's parents. No-one was allowed to escape his or her ethnic roots. At the same time, ethnicity opened doors, with jobs and privileges being accorded in line with ethnic affiliation and quotas: the Soviet Union has been described as an 'affirmative action empire' (Martin 2001). This heritage has left a deep imprint also on post-Soviet generations. Especially when such ethnic identities are combined with – and reinforced by – ethno-federal political and administrative structures, they may be quite well-positioned to withstand assimilatory pressures.

Finally, although the Soviet ethno-political overlay is wearing thinner over time, Soviet discourse and practices continue to have an influence on Russian society. According to the Soviet self-understanding, the 'nationality question' had been resolved. Officially, there were no ethnic conflicts; the multi-national Soviet people lived peacefully together in the spirit of the slogan of 'friendship of the peoples' (*druzhba narodov*). Even though the breakup of the Soviet Union had been fuelled by ethnonationalist mobilisation and the new Russian Federation had subsequently gone through two gruelling wars against Chechen separatists, we have seen that Putin has continued to insist on describing the nation as a 'multi-ethnic' or 'poly-ethnic' civilisation (see, for example, Putin 2012b, 2012c). The reluctance to acknowledge the ethnic Russians as the 'state-forming nation', as well as the fact that the old Soviet slogan about the 'friendship of the peoples' found its way into the final version of the new State Strategy on Nationalities Policy, further testify to the resilience of traditional Soviet political correctness.

On the other hand, there are also several factors that would seem to support such a new identity project. First, despite the official rhetoric about Russia being a multi-ethnic and multi-confessional state, the vast majority of the population considers itself to be *russkii*. In the latest census (2010), no less than 80.9 per cent of the population identified itself as ethnic Russians (Federal'naia sluzhba ... n.d.), a higher share than in several putative 'nation states'. Greater emphasis on the Russian core can therefore be expected to resonate well with the bulk of the population.

Second, while the Russian Federation takes pride in encompassing the traditional homelands of a large number of ethnic groups, and in many cases also seeks to uphold these in the form of autonomies, most of the ethnic minority groups are quite small in numerical terms. While the new State Strategy on Nationalities Policy establishes that Russia is the home to 193 different ethnic groups, as of today, only five minority groups constitute more than 1 per cent of the total population (the Tatars, with 3.9 per cent; Ukrainians, with 1.4; Bashkirs, with 1.1; Chuvash with 1.1; and Chechens, with 1.0) (Federal'naia sluzhba ... n.d.). In terms of absolute figures, there are only seventeen groups that count more than half a million members.[19] Many others find themselves at the brink of extinction. While the Kremlin clearly wishes to avoid spurring counter-mobilisation among the minorities, minority nationalism thus serves only as a soft constraint on the 'ethnic turn'.

Moreover, while Soviet policy served to prevent formal assimilation – even if a person became linguistically or culturally Russified, he or she could not legally change 'passport nationality' – political liberalisation in the 1990s lowered the bar for re-identification. When the Eltsin Administration decided that the state was no longer to interfere in the ethnic self-identification of individual citizens and abolished the Soviet practice of specifying ethnic affiliation in the internal passport, this was conceived as an anti-discriminatory measure (Simonsen 2005). However, the 'passport nationality' had also functioned as a barrier against potential defection: as a constant – and unescapable – reminder about each individual's ethnic origins. Now it became much easier to sever the bonds that still tied linguistically and culturally Russified individuals to their minority origins.[20] This opened up for reinforcing the ethnic core with an influx of Russified minorities – something that, with the onset of the 'ethnic turn', served the Putin administration well.

Finally, one could also question how profoundly different Putin's new identity project is in terms of actual content. While the *rossiiane* identity was certainly more inclusive in that it automatically incorporated all citizens into the national 'self', the cultural core of this civic identity has always been Russian or 'Russian plus'. The Russian language has been the state language. The history taught in state schools is that of the Russian state, from ancient Kievan Rus via Muscovy and Imperial Russia to the present Russian Federation. And Russian culture – with all its multi-ethnic contributors – has provided the civic identity with a cultural depth. Arguably, then, the shift in emphasis from *rossiiskii* to *russkii* did not really challenge the core of the old identity project.[21]

At the same time, the new project's more explicit reference to – and reliance on – the ethnic Russian core may make this a more robust identity than the old *rossiiane* one. Instead of postulating a community based on state borders, the Kremlin now narrows down the national identity to something immediately recognisable for the majority of the population – while also keeping the borders of the in-group sufficiently blurred to be able to welcome much of the rest of the population into an expanded self. When Putin in his election platform spoke of 'Russian Tatars' and 'Russian Germans', using the epithet *russkie* and not *rossiiskie* (Putin 2012b), this indicates the inclusive, even potentially expansionist, nature of the new project. Some non-Russians may be 'ethnic' in form, but can be accepted as 'Russian' in content.

On the whole, as stressed in Mikhail Alexseev's contribution to this volume, Russia's national identity is far more dynamic than its Western counterparts; more than two decades after the breakup of the Soviet Union, it is still very much in the making. And as shown here, the Kremlin is unwilling to define this identity further: it is ethno-culturally Russian at the core, but it is also multi-ethnic and multi-confessional. The ethnic Russians may be held up as the 'state-forming' nation – and yet, Putin categorically refuses to redefine the Russian Federation as a Russian nation state.

This is undoubtedly a deliberate ambiguity and a calculated blurring of borders. According to the Kremlin, the *russkii* identity should not be constrained by state borders; it represents a separate, unique civilisation (*russkii mir*). The new take on national identity thus not only contributes to rallying considerable support for the regime within the Russian Federation, it also opens up for reaching out to the Russian and Russified diaspora in the neighbouring states. The lack of a clear definition has sometimes been seen as a challenge to successful nation-building in Russia (see, for example, Shevel 2011) – but it also has the advantage of leaving the Kremlin with maximum room for manoeuvre.

Notes

1. The *russkii mir* refers to a supranational community bonded by Russian culture, the Russian language and the Orthodox faith, a

community extending far beyond the borders of the present Russian state (see, for example, Saari 2014: 60–1; Laruelle 2015b).
2. The challenges involved in coming up with a new, unifying identity that matched the changed geopolitical realities can be seen in the failure of Eltsin's 1996 competition for a 'new national idea'.
3. In 2001, the government adopted a five-year plan for 'patriotic upbringing'. For the full text of this plan, as well as the subsequent plans for 2006–10 and 2011–15, see <http://rosvoencentr-rf.ru/index.php?option=com_content&view=category&id=51:2008-12-22-12-36-56&Itemid=72&layout=default> (last accessed 27 May 2014).
4. Some observers argue that the shift in the Kremlin's approach pre-dated the Manezhnaia riot. According to Alexander Verkhovsky, for example, the re-evaluation of the usefulness of 'controllable', moderate nationalism took place already in 2009, following a dramatic rise in hate crime: 'Since then the only policy is suppression', Verkhovsky argues (quoted in Grove 2011).
5. Putin's open dismissal of multi-culturalism was in no way unique in a European context; here he was following in the footsteps of several prominent Western leaders. Already in 2010, President Nicholas Sarkozy of France went on record declaring that multi-culturalism was dead. Sarkozy was later echoed by German Chancellor Angela Merkel, who averred that the 'Multikulti' approach had 'failed utterly', and also by British Prime Minister David Cameron (Marquand 2011; see also Koopmans 2013). While these leaders, like Putin, seemed to rally round a national *Leitkultur*, Putin differed in that he dismissed *Western-style* multi-culturalism, while insisting that the Russian state identity was a successful example of the forging of a multi-ethnic and multi-confessional identity.
6. Before stepping down as president, Medvedev agreed to re-introduce gubernatorial elections, to simplify the procedure for registering parties, as well as to lower the threshold for running as an independent candidate in presidential campaigns (Medvedev 2011).
7. On 16 March, in a highly controversial referendum – and in the presence of Russian soldiers – the population of Crimea and Sevastopol had voted overwhelmingly in support of unification with Russia (according to the official results, unification was supported by 96.8 per cent of the voters in Crimea and 95.6 per cent in Sevastopol).
8. However, the protracted conflict in Eastern Ukraine has been extremely counterproductive for winning support for the new identity project beyond Russia's border. Up to now, the border between

Russian and Ukrainian identities has been exceptionally fuzzy (as regards language, for example, expressed through *Surzhyk*, a non-standardised mix of Russian and Ukrainian spoken in large tracts of Ukraine, especially in the East). As a consequence of the war, however, people have increasingly sided with Ukrainian identity and Ukrainian statehood (see, for example, Feifer 2014). The conflict may thus have deprived the Russian identity project of one of its most promising catchment areas.

9. In addition, the decree ordered the introduction of a compulsory exam for foreign workers in Russian language and history as well as the basics of Russian legislation. Only highly qualified specialists were to be exempt from this requirement.
10. For the full list of Council members, see *Prezident Rossii* (2012). The proceedings of the Council's meetings are posted on <http://state.kremlin.ru/council/28/news?page=1> (last accessed 25 May 2014).
11. The 1996 Concept of State Nationalities Policy described the role of ethnic Russians in the state-building project in the following way: 'Thanks to the unifying role of the Russian people (*russkii narod*), a unique unity and diversity, spiritual communality and a union of different peoples have been preserved on the territory of Russia' (*Kontseptsiia* ... 1996).
12. Author's interview, Moscow, 16 June 2014.
13. In August 2013, the Strategy was followed up by the adoption of a federal targeted programme 'On strengthening the unity of the Russian nation (*rossiiskaia natsiia*) and the ethno-cultural development of the peoples of the Russian Federation' for the period 2014–20 (Federal'naia ... 2013). The programme specified how authorities at all levels should work together with civil society, the education system and mass media – through the Internet, social advertising and the staging of mass events – to strengthen an 'all-Russian civil identity' and 'civil patriotism'. The authorities set as a target that by 2020, 65 per cent of the population should assess the state of interethnic relations in the Federation positively (Gorodetskaia 2013).
14. Support for this slogan seems remarkably stable over time. The Levada Centre routinely asks about how their respondents relate to the slogan. In July 2002, 17 per cent fully supported the slogan and an additional 38 per cent held that within reasonable limits, it would be good to realise such a project; in July 2014 the corresponding figures were 18 per cent and 36 per cent (Levada Centre 2014f).

15. According to the State Strategy on Nationalities Policy, the state is responsible for 'ensuring the conservation and enhancement of the spiritual and cultural potential of the multi-ethnic people of the Russian Federation on the basis of the ideas about unity and friendship of the peoples, interethnic consensus and Russian (*rossiiskii*) patriotism' (*Strategiia* . . . 2012).
16. The average score for this cohort was a full ten percentage points higher than that of the oldest cohort, the 60+.
17. As pointed out in several other contributions to this volume, increased labour migration also played an important part. The combination of the need to import workers – Russia is estimated to be second only to the USA in the number of immigrants (United Nations 2013) – and a weakened identification with the sending countries and their cultures accentuated the perceived need for redefining the national 'self'.
18. Despite its overwhelmingly ethnic Russian population and Putin's assertion that Crimea was 'Russian land' (*russkaia zemlia*) (Putin 2014a), Crimea joined the group of ethnic autonomies, being granted the status as a republic within the Federation, whereas Sevastopol became a 'city of federal importance' (the same status as the two 'capitals', Moscow and St Petersburg).
19. Four of these are groups with external homelands: the Ukrainians, Armenians, Kazakhs and Belorussians.
20. This danger of accelerated re-identification was recognised by the leaders of several of Russia's ethnically defined republics, who insisted on maintaining information about ethnic affiliation in the internal passports. In the end, the republics won the right to include an insert containing information about ethnic affiliation in the passports issued on their territory (see, for example, Simonsen 2005).
21. According to Oxana Shevel (2011: 183) it has always been open to interpretation how Russo-centric the *rossiiskii* nation is.

10
Russia as an anti-liberal European civilisation

Marlene Laruelle

In this chapter I agree with Henry Hale's double argument that Putin has generally avoided making nationalism a central element of his popular appeal, and that the majority of the population has not interpreted Putin as a standard-bearer of nationalism – other, competing political groups are more distinctly associated with the nationalism niche. I share the view that in his third presidential term, marked by a sharp decrease in popular support and the anti-regime protests of 2011/12, Putin has been advancing a conservative value agenda in order to reinforce some of the regime's constituencies and to marginalise the liberals – and the nationalists. However, I challenge the view, advanced in several chapters in this volume, that Putin has suddenly brought nationalism into the picture, despite what is widely said about his 'shift' toward ethnonationalism during the Ukrainian crisis.

I interpret Putin's use of the term *russkii* in his 18 March 2014 speech justifying the annexation of Crimea as simply reflecting what had already become the mainstream use of the term. The term *russkii* is employed in a very blurry way to define both what is Russian by *culture* (and culture has always been more important than ethnicity: Russian culture is *russkaia*, not *rossiiskaia*, even if Gogol is of Ukrainian origin and Vasilii Grossman from a Jewish family) and in relation to the state in general. While *rossiiskii* is still used by those who identify with ethnic minorities to dissociate their ethnic from their civic identity, for most of the 80 per cent of those citizens who are both *russkie* and *rossiiane*, *rossiiskii* has a purely official flavour: it is used in speaking about Russia in terms of citizenship, legal system and what pertains to the state as an administration, whereas *russkii* is increasingly associated with 'everything Russian', and therefore also as the Russian state understood in its historical *longue durée*.

Thus, I argue that Putin is merely reproducing the general terminological ambiguity – that of course serves the authorities' line of not taking a definite stance on the national identity of Russia. Further, I hold that if the presidential administration had really shifted toward nationalism, Russia would have been keen to annex Donbas, instead of allowing it to become a secessionist region that has made Putin look like a weak leader incapable of advancing the Russian nationalist cause. Moreover, Putin has continued his strong advocacy for a Eurasian Union with free movement of member-state citizens (and therefore of labour migrants), despite clear expressions of xenophobia in the Russian population. Finally, I maintain that the emphasis on the geopolitical competition with the West over Ukraine – on the status of Sevastopol as the final bulwark of Russian national security on its Western front, and on the need for Russia to react and to stop being humiliated by what it sees as North Atlantic Treaty Organization (NATO) advances – are the critical arguments in Putin's 18 March 2014 speech – far beyond the *russkii* nature of Crimea, which arrived only as a supplementary bonus. The massive support given by Russian public opinion – including ethnic minorities, as Mikhail Alexseev notes in his chapter – to this annexation confirms that the general consensus is founded on geopolitical/civilisational readings of Russia's relations with the West, not on the ethnic, *russkii*, nature of the annexation.

In this chapter, I develop an alternate reading of the Russian state's use of motives pertaining to the repertoire too often identified as that of 'nationalism', and offer some tools that I consider more heuristic. One of them involves examining how the Kremlin promotes Russia as the torchbearer of an anti-liberal Europe. In March 2000, Putin declared to the BBC: 'Russia is part of the European culture. And I cannot imagine my own country in isolation from Europe and what we often call the civilised world. So it is hard for me to visualise NATO as an enemy' (BBC 2000).

Read after the Ukrainian crisis that started in 2014, Putin's declarations would seem to belong to another historical era, one that is now closed. However, the gap is not solely temporal, nor can it be explained only in terms of the circumvolutions of relations between Russia and 'the West'. Other analytical tools are needed to understand how the Russian authorities 'situate' their country. In this chapter I seek to untangle the apparent contradiction between the claim that Russia is a European country and that it has an anti-Western destiny.

Any attempt to delineate the Kremlin's use of ideological tools necessitates certain precautions and theoretical explanations. As used to define the Soviet regime, the term 'ideology' is often equated with Marxist-Leninist doctrine, taught as a profession of strict faith. However, here we must distinguish clearly between ideology and doctrine. By 'doctrine' I understand a body of teachings or positions that are codified into a logical whole, and promulgated to a group of people or to a country's citizens (hence the related term of 'indoctrination'). By 'ideology' I understand a comprehensive vision of the world, a way of interpreting what is normative in a society. Paul James and Manfred Steger (2013: 23) define ideologies as 'patterned clusters of normatively imbued ideas and concepts, including particular representations of power relations. These conceptual maps help people navigate the complexity of their political universe and carry claims to social truth.'

To avoid the catch-all nature of the concept of ideology, especially in the Russian context, I employ three additional concepts. The first is that of 'grammar', which comes from French sociology and is used to describe the overarching frameworks of legitimacy through which individuals, collectivities and states apprehend the world. The second is that of 'ideological posture', which designates an approach or an attitude embedded in broad terms and scattered perceptions, and that offers a certain degree of normativity. The third is political 'declensions', which defines the more precise state-run policies that aim to set the public agenda in terms of values, principles and behavioural standards.

I argue that the Russian state chooses from among three possible *civilisational grammars* and has built an *ideological posture* – 'conservatism' – that has materialised in several *political* '*declensions*', but without resulting in the promulgation of a *doctrine*. In the conclusion, I turn to the topic that is the focus of this edited volume – nationalism – and explain the linkages between my analysis and the broader debate on Russian nationalism.

Russia's triple 'civilisational grammar': Europe, the West, and the rest

Since at least the eighteenth century, Russian intellectuals and official circles have used a civilisational grammar to define Russia's identity and place in the world, debating their country's belonging to several possible 'civilisations'. The terms of the identity debate as they have been formulated historically to date are not binary – Europe versus non-Europe, the West or the rest – but *trinary*. In the Russian view, there is a triple choice of identity: being a European country that follows the Western path of development; being a European country that follows a non-Western path of development; or being a non-European country. Defining Russia as belonging to a 'civilisation' is always made in relation to Europe as the yardstick, never to Asia.

In Russian, as in other languages, the idea of the 'Occident' or the 'West' (*Zapad*) easily overlaps in everyday speech with that of Europe (*Evropa*). In the nineteenth century, Russian intellectuals wrestled with whether their country ought to follow a Western model of civilisation or develop a specific path, variously identified with Slavophile/Pan-Slavic or Byzantine-inspired terminology – the former terms see the people as the core of the nation's legitimacy; the latter emphasises the dynastic power and autocratic structure of the state (Walicki 1989; Engelstein 2009). In this debate, Westerners were defined as *zapadniki*. The call was for Russia to become part of the Occident/*Zapad*, but not Europe. Indeed, all nineteenth-century Russian intellectuals apprehended Russia as being part of Europe as a civilisation, understanding by that term above all their shared Christian roots and faith. Even the anti-*zapadniki*, who contested Russia's need to follow a Western path of development, agreed that Russia was part of European civilisation. According to them, Western Europe represented only one way of understanding European identity, while Russia offered another interpretation of a shared European legacy. This division has been anchored in the history of Christianity: one root, two traditions – Catholic (and later Protestant) and Orthodox; and two empires – the Roman and the Byzantine (Thaden 1990; Billington 2004).

For all Russian intellectuals, *zapadniki* as well as anti-*zapadniki*, Russia had to be understood, since its domination by the Golden Horde, as the outpost of European/Christian civilisation against the Asian/non-Christian world. For the *zapadniki*, this destiny was a drama, a burden that had 'retarded' Russia's progress as compared with its European neighbours; for the anti-*zapadniki*, it was a chance, a blessing that had enabled Russia to maintain a Byzantine interpretation of Europe. Although Russia was defined as being at the borders of Europe, all participants in the debate considered it as being *in* Europe. The rapid extension of the Russian Empire during the nineteenth century did not structurally modify this definition, since all the major European powers were pursuing colonial policies of conquest of other territories. On the contrary, Russia's territorial continuity with its colonies was one more argument for the 'naturalness' of Russia's civilising mission of bringing European enlightenment to Asia (Hauner 1992; Layton 1994; Gorshenina 2014). It was only in the last third of the nineteenth century that certain intellectuals, mainly Orientalists by training and figures from the artistic world who sought non-conformism, began to interpret Russia's geography as shaping its identity (Tolz 2011; Schimmelpenninck van der Oye 2001). For them, and more clearly for their successors in the 1920s and 1930s, the Eurasianists, Russia was part of neither Europe nor Asia: it was a third continent, endowed with its own identity and destiny (Laruelle 1999). These intellectuals were the first to break with the binary tradition of Russia's civilisational grammar.

This brief historical detour helps to explain how the debate is being shaped today, and why it is misleading to represent Putin or other state officials as having an 'inconsistent' narrative about Russia's relationship to the West. Indeed, what is striking is the almost-perfect reproduction of the nineteenth-century debate in today's terms. Among the three civilisational grammars offered to

Russia for understanding its path after the collapse of the Soviet Union, the first one – Russia as a European country that would follow a Western path – was supported by the Kremlin only briefly, from the final years of perestroika – with Mikhail Gorbachev calling for Russia to rejoin the 'common European home' and to become a 'normal' (that is, Western) country – to the early/mid-1990s (Malcolm 1989). With the clash between Boris Eltsin and the Supreme Soviet in October 1993, the amnesty for supporters of the latter and the resignation of Egor Gaidar, father of the 'shock therapy', in 1994, and that of Andrei Kozyrev, promoter of Russian total alignment with Western geopolitical interests, in 1996, the 'path to the West' was partly closed (Shevtsova 1999). It did not disappear from the state language, but became intermittent, visible mostly in economic and financial policies, around ministers Boris Nemtsov or Aleksei Kudrin, among others.

The third grammar is that of a non-European destiny – understood in the sense promoted by the founding fathers of Eurasianism, as seeking Russia's growing identification with Asia and complete rejection of Europe as a civilisation. Eurasianism emerged in the interwar period among Russian émigrés trying to cope with the catharsis of the 1917 Revolution and hoping to construct a structured ideology of Russian uniqueness based on its distinct Euro-Asian territory and the common destiny of its people. It was developed, with similar arguments, by Lev Gumilev in the 1960s–1980s before becoming a main doctrine of all those opposed to the collapse of the Soviet Union and Eltsin's 'turn' to the West (Laruelle 2008).

This Eurasianist choice has not been particularly attractive to the elites in power, and has had success only on the margins. The few who see Russia as having an Asian destiny, such as Mikhail Titarenko, director of the Institute of the Far East in Moscow, and partisans of Russia following the Chinese model, have attracted very few disciples within the Kremlin (Rangsimaporn 2006; Laruelle 2012a). Proponents of Russia's destiny as being 'Eurasian', such as the prolific and vocal geopolitician Aleksandr Dugin, take care not to promote an Asian destiny for the country, and by no means exalt China or Japan, or the Asia-Pacific in general (Laruelle 2008). They also remain ambivalent as to cultural mixing between 'Russians' and other 'Eurasian' people from Central Asia and the South Caucasus: while they celebrate Islam as a geopolitical weapon for opposing Western values, they do not favour mixed marriages, for instance. Indeed, they laud the ability of Russia/Eurasia to conserve its hermetically sealed ethnic identities, with all of them living in peace together but without mixing.[1] This third grammar, the non-European one, seems an identity deadlock, not least given the growing xenophobia towards labour migrants in Russian society (Levada Centre 2013a: 154–9). China can be apprehended as Russia's geopolitical ally against the West (Trenin 2012), but any closer integration with Asian countries or with the southern republics of Central Asia and South Caucasus would be rejected by an overwhelming majority of Russians.

Supporting the first grammar means that one is identified with the political opposition to Putin's regime. This opposition can be embodied by the old generation of liberals, who are totally discredited, or by the new 'Bolotnaia' generation. This name was given to those who protested against Putin in the winter of 2011/12, mostly from the middle and upper classes, and whose liberal claims were in large part based on values like dignity, respect and ethics (Sakwa 2014). This grammar is also promoted by the 'national democrats', who urge Russia to follow a Western path of development but with elements of anti-liberalism in terms of defence of ethnic identities and rejection of diversity (see Kolstø, this volume).

Unlike the first grammar, the third one is not viewed by the regime as a political threat, as it does not challenge Putin's legitimacy. That said, it would be mistaken to believe that the first and the third grammars have hermetically sealed borders and never interact with the regime. For instance, the links between Igor Iurgens' think tank INSOR (see below) and Dmitrii Medvedev during his presidency reveal the presence of influential people with liberal views (in the economic and political senses) among elites, especially in the private sector. The same goes for the third grammar: the Institute of the Far East has gained support from military circles that regard China as a model, and chameleon personalities like Dugin flirt with many Kremlin-sponsored lobbies. Minister of Culture Vladimir Medinskii is close to the

Eurasianists and does not consider Russia as being part of Europe (Lipman 2014). The links between the second and third grammars are also facilitated by a specific terminological fluidity. Both use the concept of 'Eurasia' to describe two diverging projects, an ambiguity present already in the founding Eurasianist ideology (Laruelle 2008).

The gradual elaboration of an ideological state posture

It is from within the second grammar – of a European but anti-Western Russia – that the Kremlin expresses itself. The choice has not been elaborated overnight. More than a decade passed before it took on the shape it has today. This slow process of maturation can be explained by the legacy of the Soviet decades, when everything related to 'ideology' was exclusively assimilated to the official doctrine of Marxism-Leninism. But it is also a product of the perestroika years, when ideological conflicts between liberals and communists led to the division of the country and to the spectre of civil war, symbolised by the bloody conflict over the Supreme Soviet of October 1993. The Kremlin thus slowly got involved in the rebuilding of an ideological posture. In the first phase, it denied any state need for an ideology, claiming instead to be operating in a purely pragmatic manner. In the second phase, the Kremlin recognised that there existed many possible opinions within the presidential party, guided by a vague ideological posture that was rapidly identified as conservatism. In the third phase, this posture became structured into several 'declensions', embodied by more authoritative public policies.

PHASE 1: POLITICAL CENTRISM AS THE NEW STATE POSTURE, 1994–2004

The first phase unfolded during the second half of the 1990s, when the failure of the first option for Russia – following a Western path of development – opened a new space of expression for political figures representing 'patriotic centrism'. The term 'centrism' is crucial here, because it explains how the Kremlin has positioned itself, rejecting what it sees as two dangerous extremes, the 'liberal' and the 'communist', deemed equally incapable of bringing positive solutions to Russia's crisis (Laruelle 2009a: 120–33). As early as in 1994, the Kremlin sought to avoid the allegedly 'liberal' versus 'communist' polarisation that engendered the violence between the Supreme Soviet and the president. The fiftieth anniversary of the end of the Second World War in May 1995 offered an opportunity to reaffirm the importance of national sentiment and to glorify Russia's prestigious past.[2] But as early as in February 1994, the State Duma granted amnesty to the August 1991 putsch-planners and the October 1993 insurgents, thereby enabling figures like Ruslan Khasbulatov and Aleksandr Rutskoi to reintegrate into the political arena.

Once re-elected to a second term in 1996, Boris Eltsin immediately set about promoting Russian national identity and quickly lifted the ideological ban imposed on patriotic themes. He raised the possibility of forming a new national ideal: 'There were different periods in Russia's 20th-century history – monarchy, totalitarianism, perestroika, and the democratic path of development. Each era had its ideology. We do not have one' (quoted in *Nezavisimaia gazeta* 1996). Further: 'The most important thing for Russia is the search for a national idea, a national ideology' (ibid.). From 1994 to 1996, several foreign observers, among them Fiona Hill (1998), noted a massive return to debates about the idea of great power (*derzhavnost'*), particularly in the press. In the second half of the 1990s three key figures embodied this move toward 'patriotic centrism': Moscow Mayor Iurii Luzhkov; former presidential candidate, Governor of Krasnoyarsk Aleksandr Lebed; and Minister of Foreign Affairs and Prime Minister Evgenii Primakov. All three called for Russia to preserve its strategic interests in its 'near abroad' without returning to a Soviet or to an imperial logic; to develop a distinct stance in the international arena without reverting to Cold War patterns of confrontation with the West; and to restructure itself domestically by reaffirming the role of central power without re-creating an ideology-based regime (Laruelle 2009a).

Putin's first mandate was a direct product of this evolution, which occurred in the final years of Eltsin's reign. The new president was able to consolidate vertical power structures, and to rebuild Russia's image abroad. The birth of the pro-presidential party United Russia 'kidnapped' the electoral niche and ideological orientation of the Primakov–Luzhkov bloc, Fatherland–All Russia, which presented itself as the 'party of governors', made up of regional elites, industrial groups and major financial groups, as well as members of the security services, all of whom would later constitute the backbone of Putin's power (Sakwa 2008; Soldatov and Borogan 2011; Dawisha 2014). This first 'patriotic centrism' was largely empty of ideological content, except for calling for Russia's stabilisation and revival. Putin cast himself as a-ideological, claiming to be working solely in line with technocratic objectives (Hanson 2003). In 2003 the authorities discussed the creation of a Council for National Ideology (*Sovet po natsional'noi ideologii*) to be convened by major intellectual and cultural figures, but the project never led to anything concrete, and it aroused little enthusiasm within the state bodies (Prochat v glavy . . . 2003).

PHASE 2: STRUCTURING AN IDEOLOGICAL STATE POSTURE, 2004–12

The second period covers the years of Putin's second term and Medvedev's term (2004–12). This chronological division may seem paradoxical, as Medvedev's term is conventionally described as separate from Putin's terms. However, both are part of the same era during which the Russian state structured an ideological posture, and increased cooperation with some non-state actors that influenced the 'content' of this posture, such as the Moscow Patriarchate.

The a-ideological narrative of the Russian authorities found itself challenged by the 'colour revolutions', especially the 2004 Orange Revolution in Ukraine. While references to liberalism and the Western model have become intermittent in the public arena after the Eltsin-era failures, the return of political contestation in the name of democracy in the 'near abroad' induced the Kremlin to react (Laruelle 2012b). Moreover, on the domestic scene, the authorities also had to face up to the large popular demonstrations of 2005, which took the regime by surprise and showed that social contestation was still possible.[3] Just as unexpected was the dissidence of the Rodina party, led by Dmitrii Rogozin – especially as it had been created with the support of the presidential administration, and the Kremlin therefore had expected it to show total loyalty (Laruelle 2009a: 102–17). United Russia thus understood that a space of political contestation existed, not only in the so-called liberal camp, but also to its left, a space where the focus was on topics of a more nationalist and socialist nature. If the presidential party wanted to leave its stamp on Russian political life for the coming decade, it would no longer be able to limit itself to glorifying the president's person: it would have to formulate a more coherent ideological posture.

However, this strategy was far from unanimously accepted within Putin's inner circle, or within United Russia and the government elites more broadly. In 2006, the publication of a book by Aleksei Chadaev titled *Putin: His Ideology* provoked a stir within the presidential administration (see Chadaev 2006). While some supported the move toward recognising the need for an ideology, other figures did not hide their lack of enthusiasm for the idea itself.

The contentious figure of Vladislav Surkov, Putin's long-time *eminence grise* – a former deputy head of the presidential administration, later deputy prime minister and then assistant to the president on foreign affairs – embodies this paradoxical attitude of the state elites toward ideology. Surkov was the main architect of both the ideologisation and the 'packaging' of the Putin regime: he supplied it with its most refined tools, inspired by marketing and public relations techniques from the private sector. He initiated new concepts such as 'sovereign democracy' (*suverennaia demokratiia*) to define Russia's position on the world stage and the nature of its regime (Okara 2007). He followed the example of Gleb Pavlovskii in launching numerous media platforms, especially online portals and a news agency. Among other things, he organised the pro-presidential youth movement Nashi, and was involved in the creation of A Just Russia (*Spravedlivaia Rossiia*) as a loyalist centre-left social alternative to United Russia. Surkov's vision of Russia's role in the world is one of Russia embracing globalisation by creating a specific Russian 'brand' or 'voice' that would make the country an attractive great power, with an economy on its way to modernisation, strengthened by soft-power tools. Surkov has been highly critical of those who look back to the Soviet experience and those who feel attracted by a Eurasian or Asian destiny for Russia. Instead, he stresses the need for Russian national identity to look forward and to identify as a 'second Europe' (Surkov 2010; see also Sakwa 2011b).

The question of ideology again took centre-stage during the presidential elections of March 2008 and the transfer of power from Putin and Medvedev. During the December 2007 legislative elections, Putin made a point of criticising United Russia for its lack of ideology: 'Has United Russia proven to be an ideal political structure? Quite obviously not. It has no formed ideology, no principles for which the majority of its members would be ready to do battle and to stake its authority' (Putin 2007b). The establishment of a Putin/Medvedev diarchy (*dvoevlastie*) in 2008 expanded the space for greater ideological content inside the presidential party itself.

Party wings had begun to take shape from 2005 on, but they first became institutionalised under Medvedev. The liberal wing, led by Vladimir Pligin and Valerii Fadeev, includes several figures who began their political careers in the Union of Right Forces before rallying behind United Russia. This wing has been close to the magazine *Ekspert*. Its club, the Club of 4 November, wanted the Kremlin to prioritise the monetisation of social benefits, promote private property and private entrepreneurship and reduce the role of the security services in Russia's political and economic life. By contrast, the conservative wing and its think tank, the Centre for Social Conservative Policy, calls for Russia to develop a policy giving priority to the state in the economy, and underscores Russia's Soviet great-power legacy and the need for national pride in 'Russianness' (Laruelle 2009b).

Outside of the presidential party, Medvedev authorised more provocative ideological trends, like that represented by the Institute for Modern Development (INSOR), which advocates Russia's return to a Western path. Led by Igor Iurgens, a prominent lobbyist in the investment and insurance sector, INSOR quickly became Medvedev's spearhead for the narrative of 'modernisation' (Smith 2010). The institute has published several scandal-creating reports, asserting the need for Russia to make far-reaching reforms not only of its economy but also of its political regime, questioning the usefulness of regional bodies like the Collective Security Treaty Organisation (CSTO) for promoting Russia's role in its 'near abroad', and openly debating possible Russian membership in NATO (Iurgens 2011a, 2011b; see also Aragonés 2010). The real value of INSOR was probably not so much connected to developing concrete policy recommendations, as to opening new spaces for discussion, analyse reactions from public opinion and various interests groups, and foster the formation of a 'modernisation' lobby.

PHASE 3: CONSERVATISM AS THE OFFICIAL STATE POSTURE, 2011–

The third phase began with the announcement, in September 2011, that Medvedev and Putin would be swapping roles as president and prime minister. The fact that Medvedev's presidency ended with the first massive anti-Putin protests, which took place in the winter of 2011/12, and the birth of the Bolotnaia movement, which re-introduced liberal voices in the public space (albeit only the opposition one), contributed to closing the space for ideological pluralism that was then flourishing inside the establishment (Robertson 2013; Greene 2013).

In these three discernible phases in the Kremlin's structuring of an ideological posture, the terminology was chosen relatively early: that of conservatism. In the mid-1990s, the authorities did not use this term widely, as they were still framing their position in terms of centrism against the two 'extremes'. From 1999 on, the site of the Unity Party, the direct precursor to United Russia, contained a rubric called 'Our Ideology', which made reference to conservatism. The director of the Centre for Development of Programmatic Documents of the Unity Party, German Moro, a recognised researcher on conservative theories, saw in conservatism the 'only system of ideas capable of saving Russia'. He defined it as a way of thinking that 'is based on eternal social and moral values: respect for one's own tradition, trust in the tradition of one's forefathers, and priority given to the interests of society' (quoted in Popov 2006). In 2000, Putin himself drew an explicit parallel between Russia's need to share common moral values and the Moral Code of the Builder of Communism (*Moral'nyi kodeks stroitelia kommunizma*) – the 'twelve commandments' that had been introduced by the Communist Party in 1961 in hopes of strengthening the morality of citizens – thereby permitting himself a positive reference to the doctrinal strictness of the Soviet regime (Putin 2000).

In 2007, as debates were taking place on the necessity to institutionalise wings inside the presidential party, Boris Gryzlov, then Chairman of the State Duma, intervened in order to clarify United Russia's viewpoint. The party, he declared, has only one ideology: 'social conservatism' (Gryzlov 2007). By this term, Gryzlov meant to define the party's centrism as part of the ideological field (opposing both 'extremisms', that of liberalism and that of communism), its pragmatism in economic matters and its desire to dominate the entirety of the political checkerboard. He lambasted the principle of revolution, charged with having caused Russia heavy damage and with slowing down the modernisation of the country, whether during the 1910s and 1920s or during the 1990s. In his view, Russian modernisation can be realised only by a process of gradual reforms, ones that proceed without inducing devastating social effects, without endangering state stability and without borrowing from foreign ideologies, whether Marxism or liberalism. Furthermore, the ideology of the party was, according to Gryzlov, 'the support provided to the middle class and the actions undertaken in the interest of that class, which has no need of a revolution of any kind whether financial, economic, cultural, political, orange [that is, colour revolutions, *ML*], red [communist], brown [fascist] or blue [homosexual]' (Gryzlov 2004).

With Putin's return to power in 2012, the presidential administration moved forward and made this ideological posture official. It set about commissioning works on conservative ideology from several think tanks, tasked with elaborating a certain set of references. The main think tank, the Institute for Social-Economic and Political Research (*Institut sotsial'no-ekonomicheskikh i politicheskikh issledovanii*) (ISEPI), is headed by Dmitrii Badovskii, a former deputy director of the Department of Domestic Policy of the Presidential Administration. ISEPI is the main umbrella structure engaged in elaborating ideas of conservatism, and provides grants to smaller institutions and movements. In 2014, ISEPI published an almanac titled *Notebooks on Conservatism* (*Tetradi po konservatizmu*), the aim being to systematise the Kremlin's set of references. The texts are mainly proceedings of the Berdiaevian Lectures, which are organised by ISEPI. Nikolai Berdiaev (1874–1948), a champion of the 'Russian idea' and an embodiment of Russian religious philosophy of the early twentieth century, is central in references that the Kremlin and its circle of think tanks choose to cite. However, he is overtaken by the very conservative theoretician Ivan Ilin (1883–1954), a monarchist who died in emigration and whose remains have been repatriated back to Russia, the latter with Putin's personal involvement. A third key figure is Konstantin Leontev (1831–91), one of the main proponents of the Byzantine legacy as Russia's political and historical matrix.

Other less important think tanks are also active in this market of ideological production, among them the Foundation for the Development of Civil Society (*Fond razvitiia grazhdanskogo obshchestva*) headed by Konstantin Kostin, himself also a former deputy director of the Department of Domestic Policy of the Presidential Administration; the Institute for Priority Regional Projects (*Institut prioritetnykh regional'nykh proektov*) run by Nikolai Mironov; the Agency of Political and Economic Communications (*Agenstvo politicheskikh i ekonomicheskikh kommunikatsii*) headed by Dmitrii Orlov; and the Centre for Political Analysis (*Tsentr politicheskogo analiza*) at ITAR-TASS led by Pavel Danilin (see *Insider* 2014).

This ideological outsourcing has nothing Russia-specific about it, and is rather similar to that in place between the US federal administration and think tanks in the Washington area. The outsourcing appears to be supervised by Viacheslav Volodin, first deputy head of the presidential administration, who is in charge of domestic policy and relations with civil society. It is complemented by the actions and declarations of several political/public figures, whose roles include articulating the official stance: Viacheslav Nikonov, former director of the foundation 'Russian

World', now chair of the Duma Committee on Education; Nataliia Narochnitskaia, director of the Paris-based Institute of Democracy and Cooperation, and famed as a promoter of political Orthodoxy; and Elena Mizulina, chair of the Duma Committee on Family, Women, and Children Affairs, and a champion of the Kremlin's morality crusade.

The three political 'declensions' of the state posture

During the third phase, the conservative posture became more elaborated and began to target not only the presidential structure and party, but the broader audience as well. The presidential administration has invested in three categories of political language to give it content: the languages of patriotism, morality and national culture. These 'declensions' are agenda-setters: they result in the implementation of public policies to promote them, accompanied by budget allocations, massive investments in the media and the introduction of new coercive laws to target and sometimes penalise anyone who challenges them.

The first, primordial state language is that of patriotism, defined as 'love of the motherland (*rodina*), devotion to the fatherland (*otechestvo*), and willingness to serve its interests and defend it, up to and including self-sacrifice (*samopozhertvovanie*)' (Gosudarstvennaia programma... 2001). By sponsoring patriotism, the Russian authorities hope to 'give a renewed impetus to the spiritual rebirth of the people of Russia..., to maintain social stability, to restore the national economy, and to strengthen the defensive capability of the country... and to weaken ideological opposition to the state' (ibid.). Criticising the state would put Russia at risk: the citizens are invited to work at dealing with the problems of their country without participating in anti-state activities or criticising the functioning of the state structure. This patriotism was the first object of the state policy of 'revival', with its early stages under Eltsin's second term (1996–2000), and the programmes for 'patriotic education of the Russian citizens', launched by Putin in 2001. This Kremlin-backed patriotism is embodied by the state's investment in theatrical historical commemorations; the re-introduction of patriotic activities at schools and in extra-curricular activities for children and teenagers; the propaganda to revalorise the military services and the army, granting greater rights to Cossacks, who can form vigilante militia groups to patrol the streets of certain Russian towns; and so on (Nemtsova 2014). However, despite high visibility, this does not necessarily impact on the everyday social practices of the population.[4]

On the foundation of patriotism another ideological content has been erected: that of moral values (*tsennosti*). By morality, the Kremlin understands the respect for 'traditional' values: the heterosexual family (non-recognition of LGBT rights); an emphasis on having children as a basis for individual life but also for the country's demographic health; maintaining a healthy lifestyle (the fight against alcoholism); respect for the elderly and the hierarchy and so forth. This has been concretised in a series of new laws, or draft laws, since 2012: the law against so-called gay propaganda, the anti-blasphemy law in response to the Pussy Riot trial, the Internet restriction bill in the name of child protection, the ban on obscene language in the cinema, books and music, and others. In addition have come new state policies on financial benefits for families with two or more children, new draft laws to limit abortion and many public relations actions to promote healthier lifestyles – all with very limited impact.

According to the analyses of Gulnaz Sharafutdinova (2014), the frequency of the term 'morality' (*nravstvennost'*) and of the adjective 'spiritual' (*dukhovnyi*) in Putin's speeches has increased in recent years, especially since 2012. She claims that the Kremlin's attempt to appear as a provider of morality able to fill the ethical void of Russian society is above all a response tactic to the Bolotnaia movement, often qualified as 'ethical protests', as the theme of ethics in politics was central to it. However, the concept of a deficit in spiritual values has been a common narrative in Russia ever since the collapse of the Soviet Union, and had entered the state language before Bolotnaia. Above all, it is to be found in the Russian Orthodox Church, which has elaborated the pantheon of these moral values and progressively introduced them into the language of the state, in particular through the state programmes for patriotic education (see Knox 2003; Mitrokhin 2005; Mozgovoi 2005; Fagan 2014).

The third state language is that of celebrating Russia's 'culture', a way to create a cultural consensus in the country and smooth over political tensions. Three major directions of public policy and discourse can be discerned here. The first is that of re-writing history, attempting to promote a single reading of the pivotal events of Russian history. As part of this, Russia's Historical Society, led by Sergei Naryshkin, Chairman of the State Duma, listed twenty 'difficult questions', going from the birth of the first Russian state to the reign of Putin (Rodin 2013). The history re-writing initiative has had some successes with the preparation of a single history textbook for the twentieth century, which ventures to celebrate Stalin and Soviet exploits and reduces the dark chapters concerning the regime,[5] as well as with the attacks on Memorial, which was threatened with closure at the end of 2014 (*Moscow Times* 2014).

The second direction is the progressive officialisation of the role of the Russian Orthodox Church, which is increasingly present at state ceremonies at all levels, and in ever-closer interaction with the structures of the state. Patriarch Kirill has gone so far as to speak of Putin as being a 'miracle of God' (Bryanski 2012), and the World Russian People's Council, which is close to the Church, gave its first award to the Russian president for the preservation of Russia's 'great power statehood' (*Russia beyond the Headlines* 2013). The Church has succeeded in entering the prisons and the army, and has tried, although with greater difficulty, to gain access to the school system.

The third direction is Putin's re-establishment of high-profiled meetings with representatives of the arts and culture (*Ekho Moskvy* 2011), and with descendants of all the great names of Russian literature: Tolstoy, Dostoevskii, Sholokhov, Pasternak and Solzhenitsyn (Loginov, M. 2013). Putin is echoed in this by his Minister of Culture, Vladimir Medinskii, whose public policies follow this self-glorification of an a-temporal and Russian culture superior to that of Western Europe (Lipman 2014).

Structuring the 'anti-Western European civilisation' narrative

Conservatism as the official state posture is intrinsically linked to Russia's location among the three 'civilisational grammars' discussed above. Indeed, with 'the West' becoming increasingly assimilated to liberalism (political, economic and moral), conservatism is seen as another way of formulating Russia's status as the *other* Europe, the one that does *not* follow the Western path of development. Once again, today's official narratives echo intellectual debates of the nineteenth century – a time when Western Europe was decried for its liberalism, materialism and consumerism, whereas Russia was celebrated for representing authentic European values. Among the traditional umbrella-terms used to define this civilisational path in recent years, the Kremlin did not select the Slavophile narrative, which would be challenging to elaborate on the international arena (no foreign policy could be based on 'Slavic solidarity'), or for domestic consumption (it would promote a too overly ethnocentric definition of the Russian nation). Instead, another set of references was selected and celebrated: that of the Byzantine legacy. In official discourse, multiple parallels were made to Byzantium as an empire; as an autocracy where temporal and secular powers interacted closely; and as a bulwark against the 'West', around the theological notion of '*katechon*' (fortress).[6]

In the statements of Russian officials we can see a clear-cut separation between criticisms of the West and claims about Russia's Europeanness. On several occasions Russian officials have unequivocally supported the thesis of Russia's Europeanness. Speaking in Washington, DC in 2011, Minister of Foreign Affairs Sergei Lavrov defined Europe, the United States and the Russian Federation as 'the three pillars and three branches of European civilization' (Lavrov 2011). Several official texts have stressed the common values that Russia shares with Europe: 'Russia's opting for Europe is not a fashion or a result of political circumstance. It is the natural result of several centuries of state and societal development' (*Agitator* . . . 2006: 35).

In the early 2010s, with the polarisation of European public opinion over the issue of LGBT rights, and the Kremlin's use of the morality language, a broad path opened up for Russia to officialise its status as an 'alternative Europe' by adopting a posture as the saviour of Christian values. This was exemplified by Putin's speech at the Valdai Discussion Club on 20 September 2013, in which he stated:

> Today we need new strategies to preserve our identity in a rapidly changing world, a world that has become more open, transparent, and interdependent . . . For us, questions about who we are and who we want to be are increasingly prominent in our society . . . It is evident that it is impossible to move forward without spiritual, cultural, and national self-determination . . . We can see how many of the Euro-Atlantic countries are actually rejecting their roots, including the Christian values that constitute the basis of Western civilisation. They are denying moral principles and all traditional identities: national, cultural, religious, and even sexual. (Putin 2013a)

In nineteenth-century thought, Russia's self-proclaimed mission was to tell Europe, which it deemed to be losing its identity, who it really was. Today, the same vision has been updated – with the Kremlin no longer willing to be a recipient of lessons, but instead intending to be a teacher of the West. The Kremlin has elaborated an ideological language that makes it possible to give meaning to Russia's foreign policy (support to established regimes against street revolutions; attempts to modify UN and European legislation in the name of traditional values and respect for national contexts), to its domestic policy (narrowing of public freedoms in the name of the three 'declensions' of power: patriotism, morality and national culture) and presenting Russia as the antiliberal force of Europe. In fostering this conservative posture, the Kremlin hopes to cement its power at home while also establishing Russia abroad, by procuring for itself new fellow travellers around Europe and in the United States – in the former, among the circles of populist right-wing parties; and in the latter, among the religious right (Orenstein 2014).

Conclusions

Among the three 'civilisational grammars' available for positioning Russia in relation to Europe, the Kremlin chose the second one – of being a European country that follows a non-Western path of development – already in the second half of the 1990s. Since then, it has been gradually constructing an ideological posture, cemented around the concept of conservatism. This posture has been progressively refined into the three 'declensions', manifest in concrete public policies and new coercive legislation. The conservative posture, and in particular the language of morality, are seen as the way to rehabilitate Russia as the *other* Europe, making it possible to reject Western liberalism while claiming to be the authentic Europe. Within this ideological posture, plurality is maintained, and even the institutionalisation of the three 'declensions' still offers some sort of room for manoeuvre, including many internal disagreements. This limited plurality has prevented the constitution of a doctrine, properly speaking, on such key matters as the relation between Church and state, the definition of a core Russian identity, the relation to the imperial past and current migration policy.

How does the analysis presented in this chapter relate to the broader debate about Russian nationalism? Scholarly debates have tended to overestimate the ideological contents advanced by Russian intellectuals and politicians and underestimate the personal trajectory or the institutional location of these *entrepreneurs* of nationalism. As a result, nationalism becomes a confusing notion employed to define several groups of people or agencies, with different tools for disseminating their ideas, speaking to different constituencies, and with highly diverging agendas (for more on this, see Laruelle 2014a). State representatives, politicians rallying around the regime or in opposition, the clergy, academic or quasi-academic figures, skinhead groups – all these may be encompassed as bearers of 'Russian nationalism', something that does not help in building a relevant interpretative framework.

Taking the state narrative as my focal point, I have sought to encapsulate what is often interpreted as nationalism and show that it can be construed through different hermeneutical prisms, as with 'ideological grammars'. These grammars address the issue of Russia's identity and place in the world scene. Their political 'declensions' instrumentalise classic topics of 'nationalism', such as glorifying national culture and traditions. However, even if the terminologies used may be the same, these must not be conflated with the 'nationalism' of skinhead groups, or the sophisticated ideological constructions of some intellectuals. Analysing these elements as 'state grammars' enables us to capture better the underlying political dynamics, their actors and their aims, than by using the normative notion of 'nationalism'.

The Kremlin sees this ideological posture as a *function*, so it must be operationalised. It needs to offer a consensus-based vision of Russia's role and destiny, a set of precepts fluid enough to allow flux and reinterpretations, depending on the circumstances, domestically and internationally. Deciding on a specific doctrinal content would reduce the plasticity of this posture, in turn generating new challenges from within the state structure and the elite itself, and requiring a more elaborate coercive apparatus. The Putin regime's ability to maintain social consensus as the country's economic prospects become bleaker will be a crucial test for the Kremlin's ideological posture. It will force a decision on whether to 'freeze' the posture as a flexible and operational tool, or to transform it into a rigid doctrine – with everything that would imply in terms of coercive policies.

Notes

1. Dugin has criticised the old expression 'Scratch a Russian and you will find a Tatar' as a 'pseudo-historical Russophobic myth', which he claims is easy to disprove, as genetic analyses have shown 'little trace of Mongol or Tatar genes among Russians and a dominance of the Slavo-Aryan genetic type' (Dugin 2013: 45).
2. On the cult of the Second World War in Russia, see Tumarkin (1994); Wood (2011: 172–200).
3. The largest social mobilisation the country has known was that of January 2005: the state had decided to replace the benefits in kind (mainly free public transport and medications) traditionally granted to the poorest classes with financial compensation. This monetisation

of social benefits triggered large spontaneous demonstrations from several tens of thousands of persons around the country and forced the Kremlin to reverse its decision.
4. See the special cluster 'Patriotism from Below in Russia' in *Europe–Asia Studies*, 67, 1.
5. There also seems to be an obvious financial interest in offering a unified history textbook to Russian schools (see Becker and Myers 2014).
6. See, for instance, the Byzantine portal Katekhon, <http://www.katehon> (last accessed 12 March 2015), and the anti-liberal think-tank Izborskii Klub, <http://www.dynacon.ru> (last accessed 12 March 2015).

11

Ethnicity and nationhood on Russian state-aligned television: Contextualising geopolitical crisis

Stephen Hutchings and Vera Tolz

This chapter explores Russian state-aligned television's approaches to representing ethnicity and nationhood in its news broadcasts, considering the medium's effectiveness as a tool for forging a sense of belonging among the citizens of the Russian Federation. The material on which it is based largely precedes the 2014 political crisis around Ukraine. But that material, and our reading of it, is framed by the crisis and by Russian federal television's role in fanning the flames that continue to engulf the actors at its heart. The pertinence and purpose of the points we make are not restricted to the Ukraine context. Their significance relates also to our understanding both of Russian nation-building and of the responsibilities of the media in complex multi-cultural societies more generally. However, central to our argument is the conviction that neither the conflict with the West that Russia's actions in Ukraine precipitated, nor the rationale for those actions promoted in news broadcasts on state-aligned channels, can be understood without reference to tensions within the Putin regime's nation-building project that had long been evident in television news broadcasts, and that we focus on below. While our analysis is primarily historical with respect to the Ukraine crisis, it identifies several factors with a direct bearing on those later events. These have to do with contradictions between different versions of Russian nationalism; concerns regarding a disconnection between official policy on national cohesion and popular sentiment; and ambiguities surrounding the Kremlin's relationship with broadcasters. We summarise their bearing on the Ukraine crisis in our conclusion.

Historically, the media have been central to every nation-building project, as they disseminate particular imaginings of the community, of its shared values and its constitutive 'others' (Postill 2006). By selecting certain issues for coverage and by framing news reports in one way or another, the media contribute to building community consensus around particular perceptions (McCombs 1997). Since the 1960s, television has remained the main news source for most Europeans. Moreover, precisely because of the spread of the 'narrow casting' modes favoured by newer technologies, television's unique capacity to 'broadcast' to an entire 'imagined community' paradoxically acquires still greater value (Morozov 2011).

Contemporary Russia is a new state, struggling to unify a plurality of identities in flux following the disintegration of the multi-ethnic Soviet state, and to formulate policies capable of dealing with that event's combustible aftermath. That it is doing so at the time when many European states face doubts about the efficacy of multi-culturalist policies in ameliorating the consequences of the demise of their own empires, only adds to the complexity of the situation. Russia, one of the world's most ethno-culturally diverse countries, provides a distinctive angle on how globalisation is causing a radical rethinking of approaches to national cohesion. Russia's authoritarian, centripetal state, weak civil society and high vulnerability to extreme ideologies lends it particular importance in this context, since it tests to the limits the ability of the state, and of community-building led by public broadcasters, to withstand the pressures that they face across the European continent.

Official Russian discourse of national unity and identity is neither coherent nor univocal. A particularly strong contradiction pits the official rhetoric of a civic pan-Russian nation (*grazhdanskaia rossiiskaia natsiia*) that embraces members of all nationalities as equal citizens, against the representation of Russia as the homeland of ethnic Russians (Laruelle 2009a; Shevel 2011). In fact, this disjunction between civic and ethnic conceptions of nationhood is acknowledged by Russia's leaders who, as our analysis suggests, collaborate with state-aligned media in cultivating the ambiguity that the disjunction creates in order to render Kremlin-sponsored discourse simultaneously appealing to different societal groups and to different television audiences. The balance between the two sides of the disjunction is, however, highly unstable and liable to tilt heavily in favour of one or the other, depending on circumstances (we witnessed just such a tilt when the crisis in Ukraine exploded).

A potentially more complex fault-line, particularly as it remains un-reflected upon by broadcasters and politicians, is that that exists between the new rhetoric of Russian national unity and community cohesion on the one hand, and two reinvented narratives from the past, on the other. The first of these is the highly hierarchical account of cultural diversity in Russia and globally that has been reshaped in turn by imperial, Soviet and European New Right legacies (Hutchings and Tolz 2012). For, despite the vision of the *grazhdanskaia* multi-ethnic Russian nationhood promoted by the official discourse in the past decade, the rigidity of the hierarchies and of the boundaries between communities defined by ethno-cultural markers has paradoxically increased in comparison with Soviet times and the 1990s. The second, related, narrative, rooted in Soviet ethnic 'federalism', is that of the non-Russian nationalities as belonging solely in their own sub-state administrative autonomies. This narrative limits the propensity of ethnic minorities to identify and be identified with the Russian Federation as a whole.

How Russian national television mediates the shifts and contradictions of the Kremlin's approaches to achieving community cohesion and managing ethno-cultural diversity in Russia, as well as the currents of populist xenophobia and nationalist extremism that infiltrate public discourse from below, is the main concern of this chapter, which concludes with an evaluation of how those issues played out in the context of conflict in Ukraine. Television's mediatory role is central to our analysis. For even Russia's highly regulated media system – even when in full 'propaganda' mode, as throughout 2014 – must accommodate a circulation of meanings emanating from official, sub-official and unofficial sources. Despite the fact that Putin's leadership from the start has striven to align the main television channels closely to the Kremlin (Burrett 2011), the Russian media environment is different from its Soviet predecessor. Although the television news agenda is shaped actively by the Kremlin,[1] the media are nevertheless open to infiltration by ideas and forms formerly deemed 'alien' and there is a greater requirement to respond to grassroots voices external to approved discourse; indeed, as we shall suggest, the trajectory that culminated in the extreme univocalism characterising federal television news broadcasts in 2014 has its roots partially in the earlier perceived need to accommodate voices 'from below'. Most importantly, the very speed with which the trajectory was covered is but one indication of the fact that, in the absence of the single ideological framework that prevailed in the Soviet period, the current relationship between state and broadcaster is, and will remain, uncertain.

Sources and methods

We focus on Russia's two main television channels, Channel 1 and Rossiia, which are still viewed by the majority of its citizens as the most 'trustworthy' information sources.[2] Technically only part-owned by the state, Channel 1 follows the Kremlin's line closely.[3] Rossiia is the main fully state-owned channel. Curiously, the financial constraints it operates under mean that it plays second string to Channel 1 as regards its information management function. It is therefore accorded less attention from its political overseers, often leading to a wider range of voices than may be expected. Rossiia has been assigned the task of integrating local interests with the national perspective. Therefore, it is expected to play a particularly important role in promoting national cohesion.

Television news is located at the intersection of the official policy positions of the state and the beliefs and concerns of citizens. With its unique mediatory capacity, the news bulletin is our source material in this article. We base our analysis on two years of recordings of the flagship news programmes: *Vremia* (Channel 1) and *Vesti* (Rossiia) for the period from 1 September 2010 to 31 May 2012. The sheer volume of material to be processed ruled out the possibility of a continuous analysis covering the whole two years. Instead, we recorded the material in equally spaced blocks. Three months of recording were followed by a three-month break in recording, producing four recording periods containing a total of 9,352 items viewed, of which 654 were coded. To guard against omissions and arbitrariness in our analysis, we continued monitoring ethnicity-related news in between our recording blocks, relying on the two channels' comprehensive web-archives. While we cannot trace the peaks and troughs in coverage in a continuous line, our blocks nevertheless reveal broad changes in emphasis over the entire period. Following the end of the recording period, we continued to closely monitor *Vremia* and *Vesti* via their archives up to the summer of 2014. We are, therefore, able to trace shifts in reporting that have been taking place during Putin's third presidency, including the new environment that ensued after regime change in Ukraine.

The period to which the recordings belong encompassed important changes in Russia's political landscape. The winter of 2011–12 saw the first major street protests that Russia had experienced for nearly two decades, following the December 2011 parliamentary election (the election was mired in suspicions of falsification). Despite the scale of the protests, Putin returned to the presidency in May 2012. Putin's perceived manipulation of the constitution to permit him to run for a third term led to further mass demonstrations on the streets of Russia's cities. The period prior to Putin's re-election witnessed the Pussy Riot scandal and deteriorating inter-ethnic relations throughout Russia. (It was also immediately preceded by major, Islamist-inspired, suicide bombings in Moscow's metro system in March 2010 and at Moscow's Domodedovo International Airport in January 2011, when the separatist insurgency in Russia's North Caucasian periphery dealt devastating blows to the (post-)imperial heartland.) The state-aligned broadcast media bore responsibility for some of that deterioration, yet frequently resorted to suppressing the controversial topics associated with it in order not to fuel the conflict. Our news recordings captured some of the major milestones in this contradictory process, notably the media's confused reaction to the racially motivated riots in Moscow's Manezhnaia Square in December 2010. The period following Putin's re-election was marked by the intensification of riots similar to Manezhnaia and also witnessed increased attention by state-aligned broadcasters to migration-related issues.

In depicting the interpretative framework that news broadcasters applied to events ascribed, whether implicitly or explicitly, an ethnic dimension, we developed a coding system, applying both deductive and inductive approaches. As a first step, we selected the two primary categories dominating contemporary discourse on ethnicity-related topics throughout the world: 'migration' (stories centring on issues raised by population movements within and beyond the Russian Federation) and 'inter-ethnic conflict' (stories detailing clashes between individuals and groups, to which ethnic motivations are attributed by broadcasters and/or the public). We supplemented these with two categories based on our prior knowledge of the specific situation in Russia: 'ethnic [or community] cohesion' (that covers optimistic reports dictated by the Kremlin's agenda of creating a sense of common belonging among Russia's citizens) and 'separatist violence' (coverage of assaults on Russian interests launched by armed opponents of Russia's rule in the autonomous republics of the North Caucasus). We then watched selected news programmes for a month and, following an inductive processing of that material, identified three further categories: 'the Russian Orthodox Church' (the sheer weight of whose presence in the news agenda, and whose intimate connections to ethnicity in the Russian context, projected it to the centre of our analysis); 'other religions' (that incorporated the emerging emphasis on Islam's importance to inter-ethnic relations in Russia); and 'other/miscellaneous' (to which we assigned few news items and that, because those items revealed no clear patterns, we do not include in the interpretation of our data).

We generally worked on the principle of thematic preponderance; thus, an item that dealt with issues other than ethnicity would only be coded if the invocation (implicit or explicit) of ethnicity outweighed that of other factors. This approach was not always applied to reports in the category 'separatist violence in the North Caucasus'. In their coverage of this topic, state-aligned broadcasters often denied religion- or ethnicity-related factors, using the alleged efficiency of the Special Forces as the most common frame. Our decision to incorporate such reports into our dataset is a response to the widespread tendency among the public to ethnicise developments in the North Caucasus. Furthermore, ethnic and religious factors were at times visually underscored in the news coverage, even if they were not verbally acknowledged. Reports about violence in the North Caucasus illustrate how state-aligned television confronts interpretations that are undesirable from the leadership's point of view, yet widespread in society and promoted by those media outlets that the government cannot control (for example, the Internet).

Finally, items that dealt with more than one of our chosen categories would be assigned to the one that predominated, ensuring that no item was coded more than once. We catalogued every news item in every news bulletin, noting, for each item, whether ethnicity-related or not, the length of time allotted to it within the bulletin, and its position in the running order. This enabled us to gauge both the frequency (number of items) and the intensity (amount of time allotted) of the coverage, and to gain a sense of the topic's saliency (aggregate running order position) within the Russian news agenda.

Our categories included items in foreign countries. These fulfil a vital function for news broadcasters in providing points of contrast with, and similarity to, domestic events. The categories are shaped both by our own understanding of the terms we selected to name them, and by what the broadcasters themselves believe those terms to mean. Thus, in a Russian context, international (*mezhnatsional'nyi*) often encompasses what we would define as 'inter-ethnic'; the latter term (*mezhetnicheskii*) is at times used by the Russian broadcasters interchangeably with what we may interpret as 'inter-racial'.

The very definition of 'ethnicity' is elusive and, as Rogers Brubaker argues, radically contingent (Brubaker 2002). Therefore some events without an obvious ethnic dimension, but ethnicised by our broadcasters, were included in the typology. We further agree with Brubaker's argument that ethnicity, race and nationhood should not be treated as separate sub-fields of enquiry, as they are closely interconnected (Brubaker 1996). This is particularly relevant to the Russian case, where the word 'nation' (*natsiia*) is utilised not only to define the entire Russian Federation as the imagined community of all its citizens, but in line with the Soviet approach, continues to be used interchangeably with the term 'ethnos'. In the latter usage both 'nation' and 'ethnos' describe another type of imagined community – a sub-state community of people who claim common ancestry, specific cultural traditions and even common behavioural characteristics. Race in the rigidly biological sense is utilised by marginal activists (Umland 2008). In Kremlin-sponsored discourse, race is not explicitly evoked, yet it is implicitly present.

Our statistical data relates primarily to coverage of 'ethnicity' and 'migration' in the sense that these terms are deployed in the Russian media. We do so because we are interested in building an inclusive picture of the variety of ethnicity-related meanings, legitimate and illegitimate, accorded these terms by Russian television news.

In presenting our content analysis, we begin by assessing the overall presence of ethnicity- and nationhood-related news on Channel 1 and Rossiia. We then look at coverage within each coding category, beginning with those relating to the positive promotion of the nation-building agenda ('ethnic cohesion', 'Russian Orthodox Church', 'other religions'). We next focus on the reporting of migration issues as we begin to discuss how news events liable to provoke national discontent are handled within the nation-building framework. Finally, we discuss items assigned to the categories dealing with events in which discontent explodes into interpersonal and inter-group strife ('inter-ethnic conflict' and 'separatist violence').

Analysis of the corpus

The overriding impression produced by our data is that the stated importance of inter-ethnic relations to the government's agenda is not reflected in the patterns of news coverage. Stories coded as relevant made up only a small portion of the total news coverage, from 6 to 8 per cent respectively, both in terms of frequency (number) and intensity (time) (see Figure 11.1).[4]

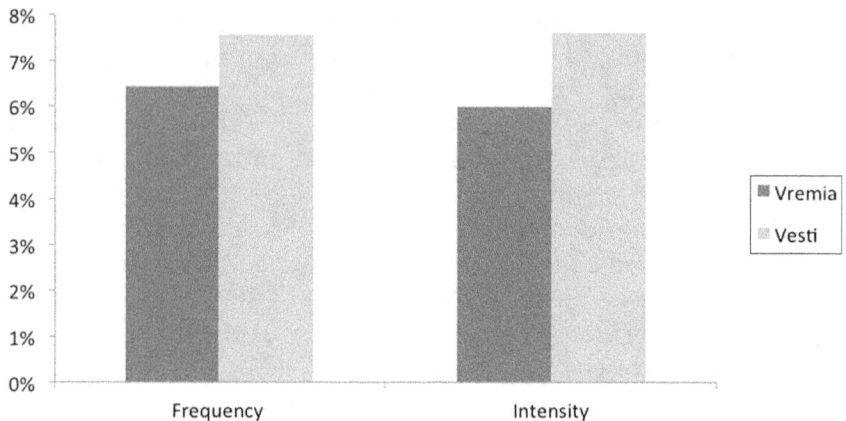

Figure 11.1 Frequency and intensity of ethnicity-related news as a percentage of the overall news content

Of all inter-ethnic stories, a significant portion is accounted for by coverage of issues that relate to other countries (particularly migration and violent conflict) and that alleviate any impression that Russia is unusually plagued by inter-ethnic tensions (Figures 11.2 and 11.3).

In the context of the barrage of conflicting messages that national television was compelled to disseminate in reaction to unanticipated crises such as the Manezhnaia riots (Hutchings and Tolz 2012), the paltry airtime domestic inter-ethnic relations normally receives indicates the extent to which the Kremlin had been struggling with its own nation-building policy. Within this overall picture, however, the topic of separatist violence in the North Caucasus demonstrated a relatively high degree of salience, at least on *Vremia*, which follows the Kremlin's line more closely than *Vesti*, and that aimed to reaffirm it in relation to a particularly sensitive problem. As we see from Figure 11.4, more than North-Caucasus-related stories featured among the first three items within the running order of *Vremia* bulletins during the recording period, with all other categories on both channels attracting fewer than twenty-five items in the top three.

To explore the tensions further, on the one hand, the Kremlin was consistent throughout most of our recording period in

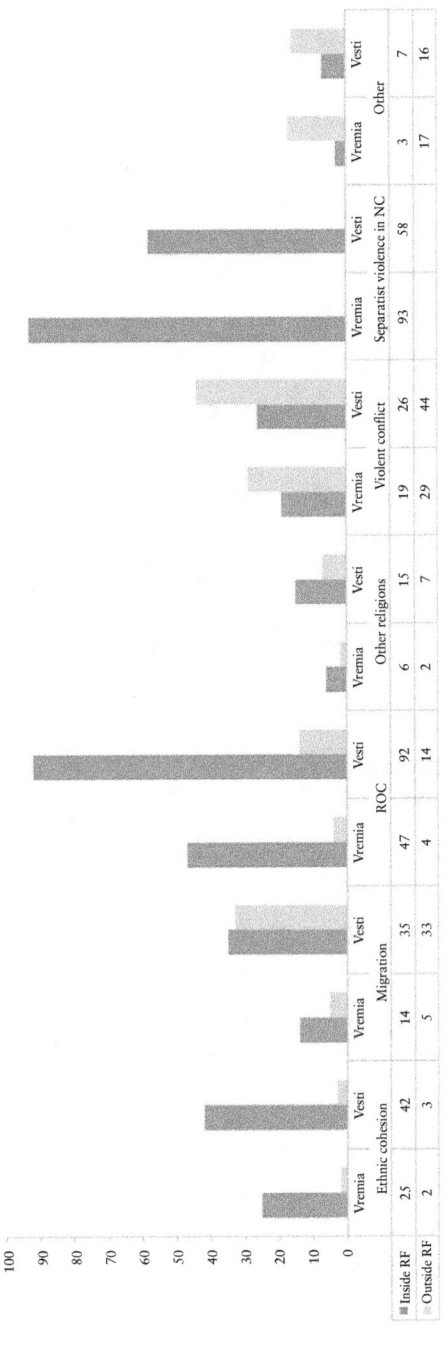

Figure 11.2 Frequency of ethnicity-related news inside and outside the Russian Federation, *Vremia* and *Vesti*

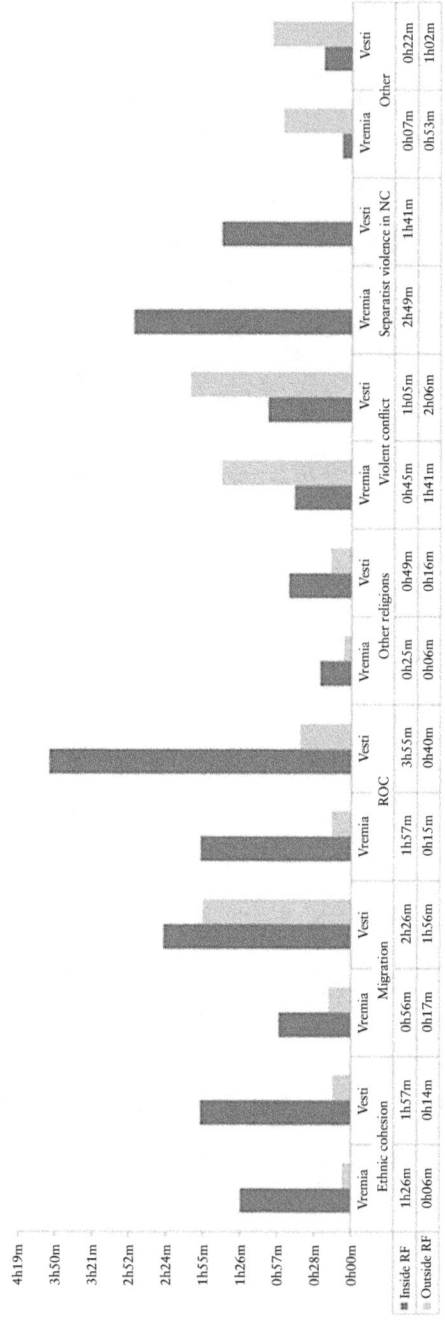

Figure 11.3 Intensity of ethnicity-related news inside and outside the Russian Federation, *Vremia* and *Vesti*

ETHNICITY & NATIONHOOD ON RUSSIAN STATE-ALIGNED TV

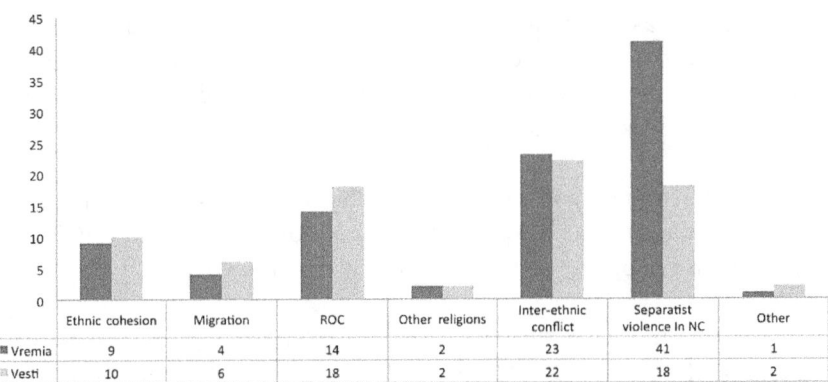

Figure 11.4 Salience of ethnicity-related news, *Vremia* and *Vesti*

promoting an image of multi-ethnic harmony, underscoring ethnic diversity as the country's strength. These assertions were, not unsurprisingly, highlighted in news bulletins. On the other hand, the confidence these claims exude is not borne out by the fact that the level of news coverage of inter-ethnic relations actually drops at politically sensitive moments. At the lowest point it accounted for only 4.2 per cent in May 2012, the time of Putin's inauguration as president. Already prior to this, during the entire presidential election campaign, the media largely refrained from reporting on related topics. According to our Channel 1 and Rossiia interviewees, reporters receive instructions during certain periods not to report on issues of a potentially inflammatory nature, including, specifically, inter-ethnic relations.[5]

The under-reporting of ethnic issues is partly connected to unresolved tensions deriving from the Russian Federation's status as a multi-ethnic, multi-faith state. Russian nationalists traditionally see ethnic Russians as marginalised by the state, and other nationalities as favoured, but our word frequency analysis of the term 'Russian' (*russkii*) indicates that the state-aligned media are far from neglecting things Russian.[6] In fact, as the context of the usage of the terms *russkii* and *rossiiskii* confirms, the Russian language, Russian culture and Russian Orthodoxy are seen as the key binding force in the Federation, and the role of the state as a key factor in creating a pan-Russian (*rossiiskii*) national community has remained without challenge throughout the Putin period. In his interview with us, the Channel 1 presenter, Maksim Shevchenko, acknowledged his own responsibility to contribute to resolving the tension:

> Our task is to figure out how to . . . establish a united political nation and at the same time preserve the diversity of ethnicities in Russia and give them the opportunity to develop within the country.[7]

We begin our more detailed analysis by focusing on the coding category designed to capture those reports most actively and deliberately deployed in support of the ambitious mission that Shevchenko describes 'ethnic cohesion' or national unity.

Ethnic cohesion

In terms of both intensity and frequency, and as we see from Figures 11.2 and 11.3, 'ethnic cohesion' amounted to a modest portion of all ethnicity-coded news. In percentage terms, this category accounted for approximately 12 per cent of the intensity of news coverage relating to our topic area for both *Vremia* and *Vesti* (see Figures 11.5 and 11.6).

This is lower than the mean across all seven categories, but still high when one considers the difficulties that stories in this category normally raise in terms of their newsworthiness (in the post-Soviet, semi-commercialised news environment, Russia's state-aligned broadcasters cannot afford entirely to ignore such factors). For all of the events we included in the category during the recording period amounted to regularised state-initiated activities like national holidays and anniversaries, none of which offered spontaneous narrative content. Other reports related to traditional regional and local festivities. These stories highlighted thriving minority cultures and harmonious ethnic relations. The arch, folk-cultural approach characterising them was reminiscent of the Soviet celebration of inter-ethnic harmony. While this may resonate nostalgically with older viewers, the younger audience demographic that Channel 1 in particular has periodically hankered after would be less impressed.

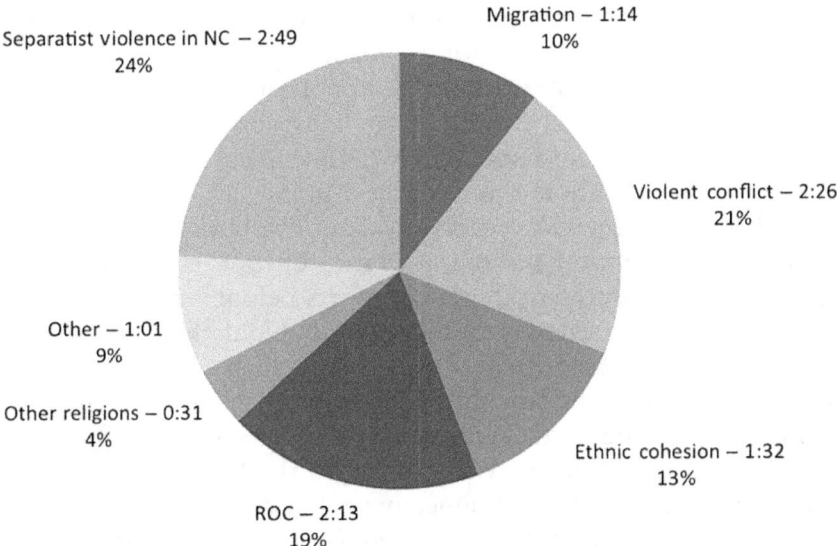

Figure 11.5 Intensity of each category as a percentage of all ethnicity-related news, *Vremia*

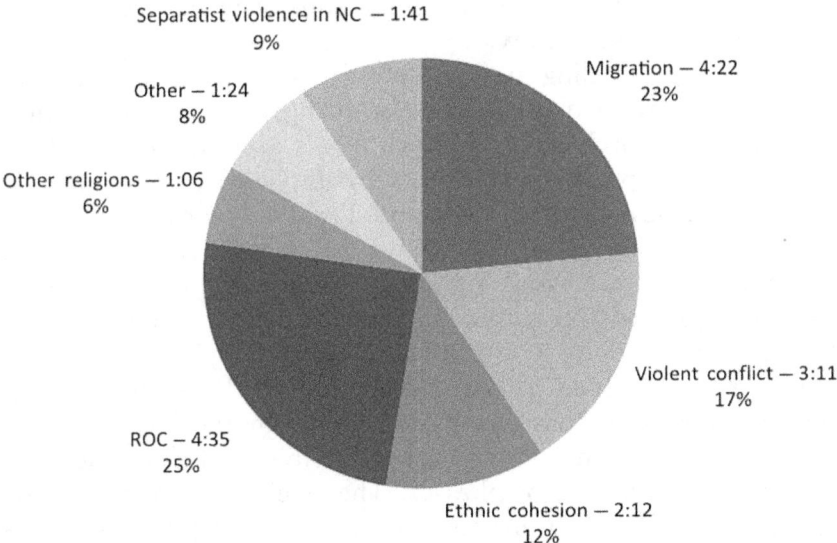

Figure 11.6 Intensity of each category as a percentage of all ethnicity-related news, *Vesti*

The only negative news item in the 'ethnic cohesion' category covered a meeting in 2011 of the Federation Council in which President Medvedev stated that the 'inflation of inter-ethnic conflict and religious dissension during the upcoming election campaign [would] be punishable by law'.[8] This measure had received consistent legitimation from earlier points in our recording period, through regular reports on deteriorating ethnic relations in the West. Their key message – that in Europe, ethnic cohesion is doomed – was present in many reports belonging to other categories. Within all categories, these stories highlighted the *lack* of ethnic cohesion. Among them was a report on Angela Merkel's speech of 2010 on the 'absolute failure' of multi-culturalism, presented as a 'failing battle' against an influx of migrants who have failed to integrate.[9] Such events provided the Russian authorities with cover not only for announcements like Medvedev's, but also for the anti-migration and anti-Islamic rhetoric that took hold during Putin's third presidency. During the recording period, the channels systematically contrasted genuine Russian 'friendship of the peoples' with the 'cold', artificial and ineffective Western concept of 'tolerance'.[10] Such comparisons recur in several of the categories discussed below.

After our recording period, 'ethnic cohesion' and national unity frames were used intensively during Russia's annexation of Crimea in March 2014. Western media accusations of aggressive Russian imperialism were thereby implicitly challenged. The annexation, described by *Vesti* and *Vremia* as Crimea's 'homecoming' (*vozvrashchenie domoi*), was often compared in terms of its importance for Russia's national cohesion and unity to Soviet victory over Nazi Germany. The date 16 March (the day of the Crimean referendum) was dubbed 'Victory Day' (*den' pobedy*) with direct reference to the 9 May holiday.[11] In their highly scripted representations of a nation united by the events around Crimea, both channels towed the Kremlin's line, using identical terminology and turn of phrases. The celebration of the ethnic Russian core of the nation was foreground. *Vesti* quoted a prominent Moscow political analyst as saying that the Crimean referendum 'discovered for us Russians (*russkie*), those Russians who are much more Russian in spirit than we [Russia's citizens] are'.[12]

Yet the notion of ethnic diversity as Russia's strength was also highlighted and contrasted with Ukraine's reported aim of imposing a monoethnic straightjacket on its heterogeneous population. In a highly manipulative gesture, Crimean Tatars, among whom, according to the Western media, only a minority supported Crimea's unification with Russia, were represented as a symbol of multi-ethnic support for the results of the referendum. *Vesti* quoted a Crimean Tatar as saying 'Ukraine does not need us. We are treated as bastards (*nezakonnorozhdennye*) [there]. Our place is in Russia.'[13] This was contrasted with the situation in Russia, which was proud of its ethnic diversity.[14] Sanctions imposed by the West could only further strengthen the Russian nation, whose values were distinct, the channels insisted.[15]

RUSSIAN ORTHODOX CHURCH

The contrast between Russian and Western values was also reinforced in coverage of the Russian Orthodox Church. It became particularly sharp towards the end of our recording period during the presidential election campaign and the unfolding case against Pussy Riot. In that period, leading journalists transformed Orthodox Christianity from an important national value into the very foundation of Russian statehood, which had historically protected the nation from harmful foreign influences.[16] The Church's centrality to the state-sponsored nation-building project was reflected in the number of *Vesti* reports on Orthodox Christianity – more, in fact, than on any other of our categories (see Figure 11.2) on Rossiia. Furthermore, the de facto superior status of the Church compared to other 'traditional' Russian religions was confirmed by the fact that both *Vremia* and *Vesti*'s coverage of Orthodoxy was four times longer than that devoted to all other religions combined (see Figure 11.3).

Points when the coverage of Orthodoxy peaked during our recording period further attest to the special relationship the Church, and Patriarch Kirill personally, enjoy with the state. There were two peak months in terms of both frequency and intensity of the relevant coverage: November 2011 and April 2012 (see Figures 11.7 and 11.8).

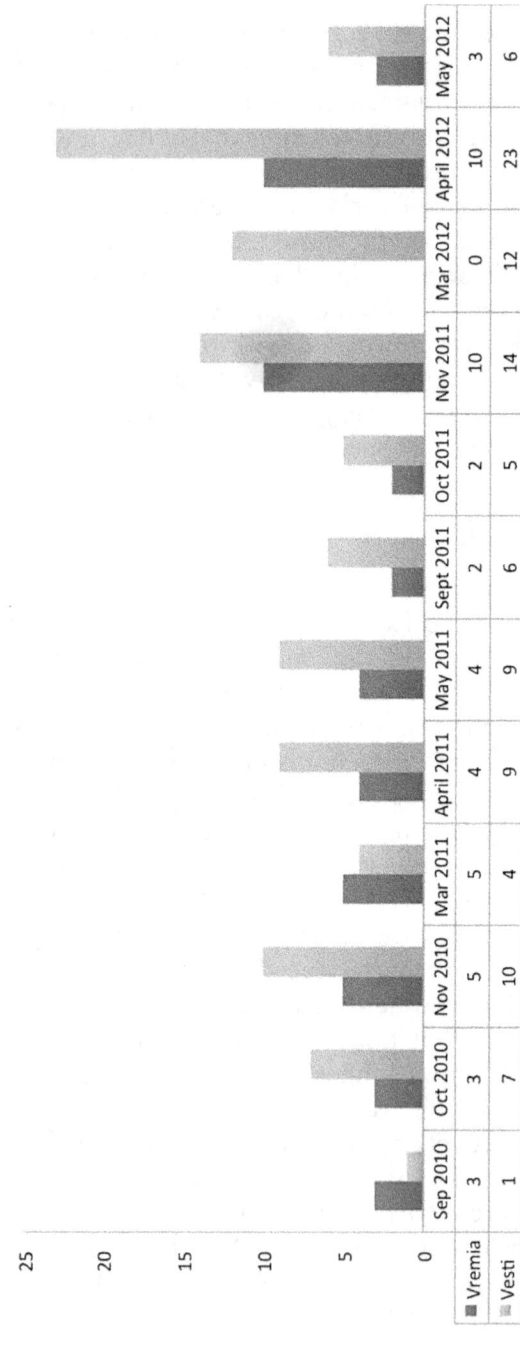

Figure 11.7 Frequency of Russian Orthodox Church-coded stories over the total recording period, *Vremia* and *Vesti*

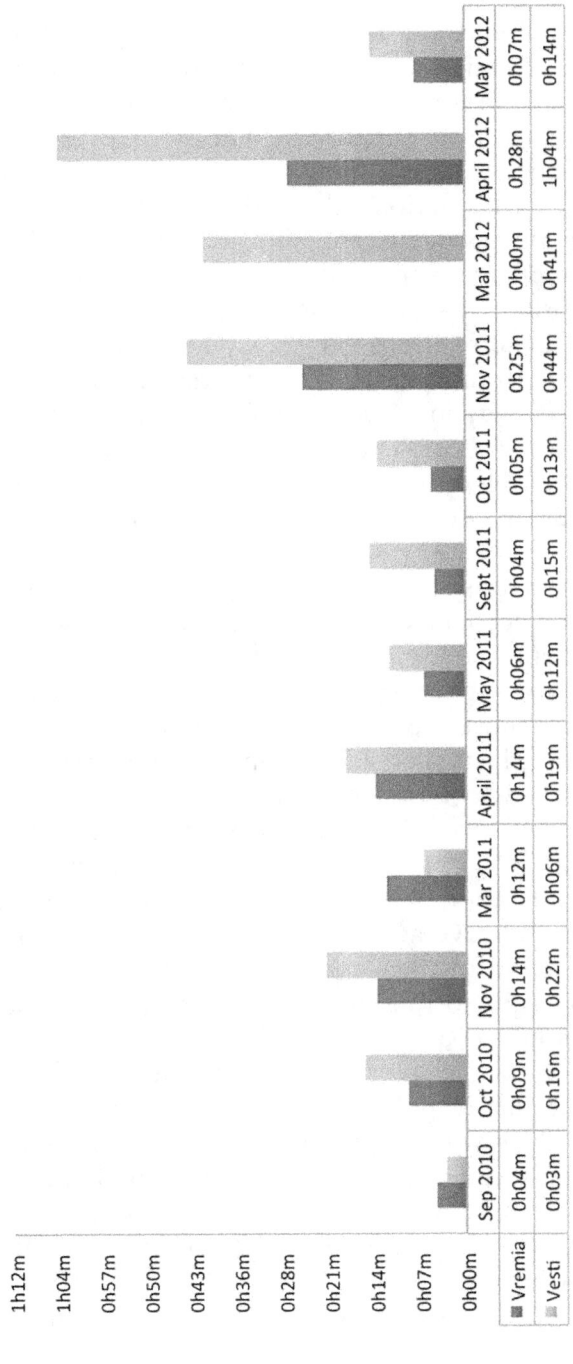

Figure 11.8 Intensity of Russian Orthodox Church-coded stories over the total recording period, *Vremia* and *Vesti*

Both peaks occur when the alliance between the Church and the state was becoming even stronger, following the announcement of Putin's decision to run for a third presidential term in September 2011. The Church's overt support for Putin provoked criticism from the opposition and the alternative media, which began featuring damaging revelations about the lavish lifestyle of the Patriarch and examples of questionable activities through which the Church attempted to increase its material wealth. In response, and assisted by state-aligned television, the Church mounted a well-organised public relations campaign. The first step was the bringing to Russia from Mount Athos of a revered relic – 'Virgin Mary's belt'. Its display in Moscow and a number of other cities attracted numerous visitors. The journey of the relic across Russia was systematically televised, and relevant reports accounted for the November 2011 rise in the coverage of Orthodoxy-related issues.[17]

The second peak was still more striking, as in April 2012 the Orthodox Church accounted for more than half of all our coded *Vesti* reports. There were three reasons for this increase. One was the particularly heavy coverage on both channels of the celebration of Easter – the most important holiday in the Orthodox tradition. Whereas in 2011 this extended only to the Easter weekend, in 2012 it stretched to most of Passion Week. The expansion provided an indication of the further elevation of the status of the Church in the context of Putin's re-election. Second, Pussy Riot's alleged desecration of an Orthodox cathedral triggered an intensification in the coverage of Church activities, with reports featuring the reaction of the clergy and ordinary believers. But, whereas *Vesti* began reporting the case in March, *Vremia* delayed its first report on Pussy Riot to 19 April.[18]

The final reason for the rise in coverage of the Church in April 2012 was another major public relations initiative organised by Patriarch Kirill. This was the so-called prayer vigil 'in defence of faith, profaned shrines, the Church and her good name', held in Moscow and across the country on 22 April. With the state's help, thousands of people from around Russia were brought to Moscow to pray with the Patriarch for the end of what he dramatically described as a 'war' against Orthodox Christianity, triggered by the Pussy Riot performance. *Vesti* and *Vremia* covered the event at length,[19] promoting an image of Russia as primarily the homeland of ethnic Russians, completely marginalising the alternative state-sponsored vision of a multi-confessional and multi-ethnic society. The marginalisation recurred throughout our recording period, as the minimal attention accorded to other religions attests (see below). Subsequent Kremlin support for Russian separatists in Eastern Ukraine was to fit the narrative all too easily, but this was far less true of the proposition that, with its generous accommodation of the Muslim Tatar minority, post-annexation Crimea represented a microcosm of the multi-ethnic, multi-faith Russian Federation.

OTHER RELIGIONS

Under the category of 'other religions' we expected above all to see stories about Islam, Buddhism and Judaism, which, like Orthodoxy, enjoy an official status as Russia's 'traditional religions'. Yet Buddhism had no presence at all on the federal news, and Judaism had virtually none; the only relevant report related to New Year celebrations in Israel in September 2011.[20]

Islam was less peripheral to the news agenda. In official discourse, Russia's multi-cultural nature is often described with reference to the centuries of peaceful co-existence between Orthodoxy and Islam. During the recording period, this line was strongly endorsed in coverage of the celebrations of Muslim religious holidays in Moscow. Reporting on one such celebration in September 2011, *Vesti* gave a brief history of the life of 'the Muslim community' in Moscow, stressing its beginnings in the fourteenth century, and noting that approximately twenty million Muslims live in Russia today.[21]

Nonetheless, in 2010 and 2011 overall coverage of Islam was limited, particularly on *Vremia* (six stories). On *Vesti* there were twenty-one stories, many of which were about the celebrations of religious holidays in Russia's predominantly Muslim regions of Tatarstan and the North Caucasus. As with Orthodox Christianity, the display of relics was a familiar theme.[22] These parallels helped to project an image of the harmonious co-existence of Orthodoxy and Islam. The message of harmony, in accordance with the official Eurasianist outlook, was further reinforced by the repeated characterisation of the form of Islam that was said to be 'historically traditional' to Russia as 'moderate and peaceful'.[23]

With the exception of major terrorist events in the Russian heartlands, Islam was rarely evoked in the reporting of violence in the North Caucasus. Inter-confessional disharmony was stressed mainly in relation to Western Europe, usually in the context of stories we categorised as 'migration'. These pointed to growing societal Islamophobia in response to the policies of Western governments on multi-culturalism, which were invariably described as a failure.[24]

However, the period from spring 2012 to autumn 2013 witnessed dramatic changes. Alarmist representations of Islam as a violent religion, which had been common on Russian state-controlled television in the early years of the new millennium, but less from 2006 onwards, reappeared (Hutchings and Rulyova 2009: 86). A media campaign, in which the criticism of 'radical Islam' (*radikal'nyi islam*) at times turned into the vilification of Islam in general, was facilitated by a public controversy in October 2012 over the wearing of hijabs in the Stavropol region by local schoolgirls. Parents who insisted on dressing their daughters in hijabs were represented by *Vesti* and *Vremia* as violent Muslim fanatics.[25] According to Dmitrii Kiselev, the moderator of the Sunday *Vesti* edition (*Vesti nedeli*), which played a key role in the articulation of a new narrative about (radical) Islam, the hijab incident prompted him personally to 'discover' a whole range of Islam-related problems in Russia and beyond.[26]

New television representations of Islam deployed ideological frames used in the construction of official discourse during the electoral period. In late 2012 and 2013 both channels systematically blamed 'the liberal West' for the spread of 'radical Islam', arguing that, by pursuing their own short-term foreign policy goals around the world without concern for the plight of local people and the long-term stability in the regions, Western governments triggered the spread of 'radical Islam'.[27] It was further suggested that 'the West' deliberately supported the spread of radical Islamist literature in Russia and encouraged the corruption of the religious traditions indigenous to Russia's Muslim communities in order to destabilise the country.[28]

As elsewhere, television in Russia tends to represent Islamism as a force that is 'disconnected from real people, places and histories' (Yemelianova 2010: 1; see also Hafez 2000; Jackson 2007). No analysis of the political, social and economic context in which radical Islamism may appeal to some Russian citizens was offered and the different forms militant Islamism took in different parts of the country remained unacknowledged. Although in parts of the North Caucasus the emergence of Islamism dates to the late 1980s (Yemelianova 2010), most news reports represented it as a new phenomenon. Likewise, when expressions of Tatar outrage at Russian actions in Crimea were linked to what were claimed to be extremist Islamist elements in the Council of Representatives of the Crimean Tatar People, no context was provided. This rendered subsequent portrayals of Crimean Tatars as 'Russia's new Muslims' unconvincing. Such twists in the Russian television representation of Islam impacted on the coverage of migration, the issue that broadcasters world-wide tend to link to the notions of identity, ethnicity and race.

MIGRATION

In academic literature definitions of migration are complex and contradictory. As Bridget Anderson and Scott Blinder note, there is no consensus on a single definition of 'migrants', who can be defined by foreign birth and citizenship as well as by their temporary or long-term geographical mobility across and within national boundaries (Anderson and Blinder 2013). The confusion increases in media representations and in the discourses of politicians, who regularly politicise migration-related issues. Media outlets in many European countries have been criticised for their discriminatory treatment of migrants, for using criminalising terminology and for engaging in a systematic process of 'othering'. When covering migration, journalists everywhere tend to ethnicise the social and economic issues at the roots of migration trends (King and Wood 2001).

In the absence of reporting guidelines dealing with sensitive issues, the danger that journalists will use discriminatory language further increases.²⁹ Particularly controversial is the application of the terms 'migrant' or even 'illegal migrant' to Russian citizens. Even the Kremlin-sponsored discourse lacks consistency on this issue. Putin has sometimes argued that no citizen of Russia could be called a migrant.³⁰ But he has also used the term 'migration' to describe the residency of North Caucasians in cities of Central Russia (Putin 2012b). Such contradictory pronouncements are reported without reflection. Likewise, Russian television news often covers stories about Russia's *tsygane* (Gypsies) as part of the discussion of the impact of migration flows on Europe, even though Russia's Roma communities date back centuries and their members are Russian citizens.³¹ Such terminological laxity inevitably has social and political implications.

Migration stories exhibited several striking features. From 2010 onwards, opinion polls have indicated rising resentment towards non-Slavic nationalities (Levada Centre 2012b). While the print media and television channels like NTV were already featuring alarmist reports on the effects of migration on Russia, in 2010 and 2011 *Vesti* and *Vremia* were avoiding opportunistic exploitation of these widespread perceptions, following the Kremlin's general view of migration as essential to the Russian economy.

As Figure 11.2 demonstrates, in frequency terms, migration was *Vremia*'s second least covered topic, and on *Vesti* it generated less coverage even than 'ethnic cohesion'. During our first recordings from September to November 2010, migration-coded stories were absent from *Vremia*, at a time when the controversial deportations of East European Roma from France were being criticised by the EU (*Vesti*, however, used the opportunity to claim better conditions for Russian Roma). Overall, *Vremia*'s coverage of migration remained minimal (see Figure 11.9). The amount of coverage on *Vesti* was greater (see Figure 11.10) and, unlike *Vremia*, it featured occasional reports on clashes between labour migrants and locals, particularly in Moscow. Thus, with migration, differences between the two channels became particularly noticeable.

As Figures 11.9 and 11.10 indicate, both channels highlight migration-related issues outside Russia. During our recording period, the situation in Russia was contrasted to developments in Europe, where migration, it was argued, had fostered societal

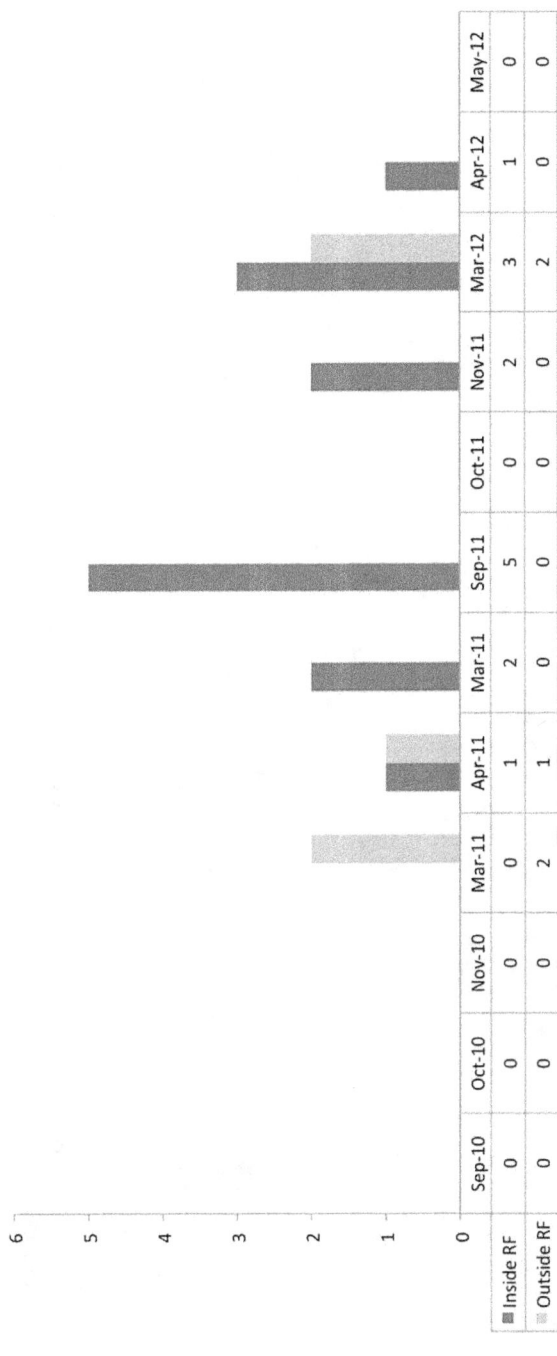

Figure 11.9 Frequency of migration-coded stories inside and outside the Russian Federation over the total recording period, *Vremia*

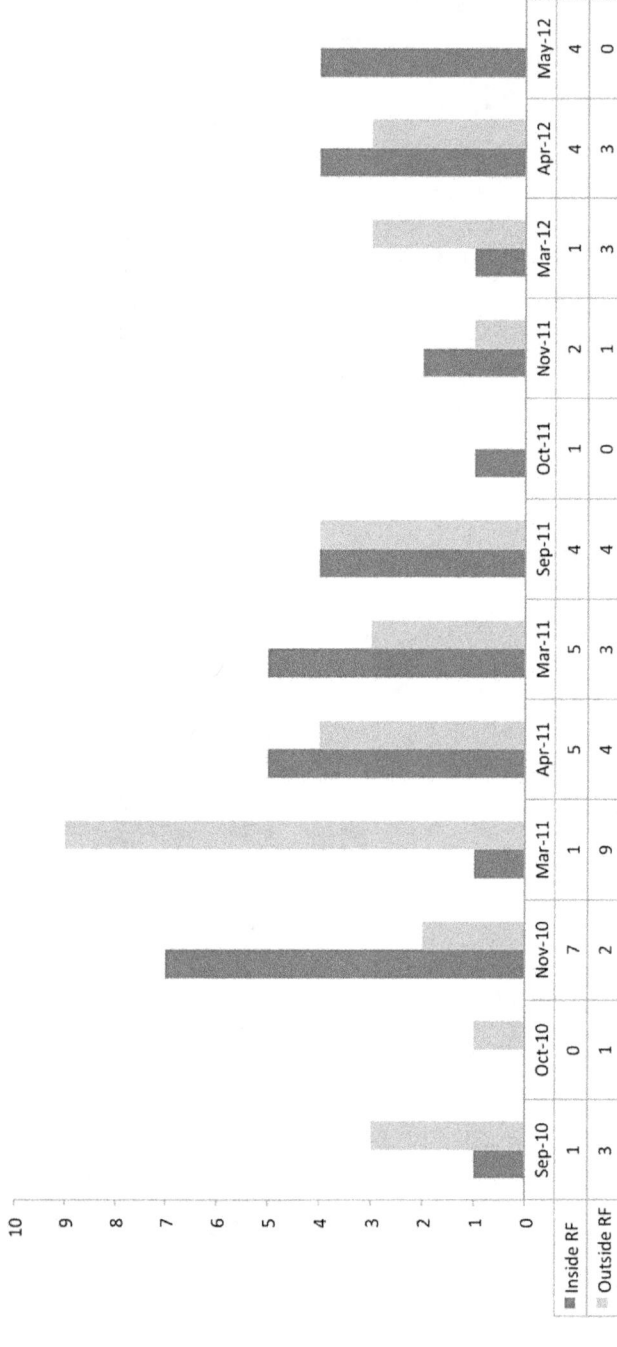

Figure 11.10 Frequency of migration-coded stories inside and outside the Russian Federation over the total recording period, *Vesti*

problems. Both channels linked the difficulties to Europe's crisis of multi-culturalism. The broadcasters also claimed that the inevitable consequence of Europe's migration policies was a rise in radical right-wing popular support and electoral success. The message was that Russia should not mimic Western diversity management policies.[32]

After the 2012 presidential election, several factors combined to create a context in which broadcasters drastically changed their treatment of migration. These included the legitimation of Putin's regime through the intensified identification of 'foreign' and 'internal enemies' supposedly keen to exploit the country's problems; increased concern in the Kremlin about Russian ethnonationalism; and the effect on reporting practices of journalists' prejudices unchecked by codified reporting guidelines. Soon after Putin's inauguration the two channels began an anti-immigration campaign that lasted until the autumn of the following year when a series of ethnically motivated riots across Russia prompted a return to more restrained reporting. Rather than being depicted as 'compatriots' (*sootechestvenniki*), Central Asian migrants began to be represented as a major threat to Russian identity, and direct parallels were drawn between migrants in Russia and in the West.[33] North Caucasian citizens of the Russian Federation residing in Moscow were systematically described as migrants and 'parasites' (*glisty*). Unlike in earlier coverage, the reported inability of migrants in Western Europe to integrate was linked to what was now depicted as the incompatibility of Muslim and Christian values.[34] Previously, migration reports rarely, if ever, evoked Islam (Tolz and Harding 2015). Dominated by anti-Western (and anti-Ukrainian) sentiment, the late 2013–early 2014 saw a significant lull in the anti-migrant campaign, but, as Paul Goble suggests, an article claiming extensive Central Asian migrant involvement in extremist activities posted on the *Svobodnaia pressa* portal in July 2014 indicated that its dormancy may be but temporary (Goble 2014).

Inter-ethnic conflict

The overrepresentation of negative examples related to Western Europe was also noticeable in the coverage of 'inter-ethnic conflict'. More than half the items in this category concerned developments outside the Russian Federation. Most reports were of physical violence, often misrepresented as being motivated by ethnic or religious hostility. Conflicts in Europe were linked to wider social and political issues. *Vremia* reported at length on the serial killer shootings in Toulouse and Montauban, which targeted French North-African soldiers and Jewish civilians in early 2012, describing the event as a 'jihad at the heart of Europe' demonstrating 'the complete ineffectiveness of the modern West European state'.[35] The trial of the far-right Norwegian terrorist, Anders Breivik, was similarly linked to the failure of European immigration policies and the resulting spread of far-right extremism.[36] Those states of the former Soviet Union with which Russia had troubled relationships, like Ukraine, were also negatively represented. The Ukrainian police were particularly criticised for their allegedly lenient treatment of 'Ukrainian Nazis',[37] an allegation that the Russian media exploited intensively during the 2014 stand-off between Russia and the West over Ukraine.

In contrast to their treatment of ethnic conflict abroad, in 2010 and 2011 the two channels downplayed the ethnic and/or racist aspects of violence in Russia and devoted little attention to them. Extreme Russian nationalism is a sensitive issue for the Kremlin and, following the Manezhnaia riots, it began to take more stringent measures against their activities. Previously, liberal critics of the regime had accused the Kremlin of collaborating with Russian nationalists and of using radical nationalist groups to do the government's bidding (Kichanova and Buribaev 2013). The nationalists themselves regularly criticise the Kremlin for being too harsh towards ethnic Russian activists, while displaying leniency towards manifestations of extreme nationalism among minorities.[38] The issue represents a major challenge for broadcasters.

State-aligned television coverage of 'ethnic conflict' includes examples of responsible reporting. Our interviewees demonstrated a clear understanding that media reporting can inflame an already problematic situation.³⁹ So in addition to paying little attention to the activities of extreme Russian nationalists, the broadcasters also followed the Kremlin's position that certain conflicts, particularly those involving Russians and Caucasians, had social origins and were unrelated to ethnicity, even if the public thought otherwise. Yet today broadcasters must take popular perceptions into account and engage with ethnicised interpretations of cases that attract heated debates on the Internet and other media.

Such a conundrum emerged in coverage of an incident involving a well-known Sambo master, Rasul Mirzaev, who in August 2011 got into a fight with a youth in Moscow, as a result of which Mirzaev's opponent died. The incident attracted attention not only because of Mirzaev's celebrity status, but also because he was a Dagestani and his opponent a Russian. In the public discussion that followed, the case became ethnicised. The light sentence Mirzaev received provoked outrage among Russian nationalists, who argued that this was another example of the state failing to defend the *russkie* from systematic abuse. While an inter-ethnic dimension was superimposed on the incident in certain talk-show discussions, news bulletins represented the confrontation as a private dispute that had nothing to do with their ethnic backgrounds.⁴⁰ Yet when Mirzaev was released from detention at the end of the trial, *Vesti* became less cautious. A strong objection to the verdict from Russian nationalist activists was aired and the reporter demonstrated open sympathy for the victim's angry father who questioned the court's impartiality.⁴¹ *Vesti*'s treatment of the case seems to have reflected the critical view of the outcome of the trial taken by the news production team, as our interview with the moderator of *Vesti nedeli* suggests.⁴² Here we see how perceptions prevailing in society at large influence the frames through which events are interpreted in the media.

During Putin's third presidency, the number of instances of violence, including not just individuals, but large groups, to which the public attributed an ethnic dimension increased, particularly in 2013, when in July alone three large-scale riots took place in different Russian cities (Pain 2013). The two biggest incidents occurred in Pugachev in central Russia and in Moscow's Biriulevo-Zapadnoe district where 'everyday' fights between ethnic Russians and Caucasians ended with the death of the former, leading to mass attacks on Caucasians by local residents. Alarmed by the eruption of public disorder, yet unable to satisfy the rioters' unconstitutional demand for the expulsion of the Caucasians, the authorities were keen to calm the situation quickly. Under these circumstances, the broadcasters became cautious in their reporting, insisting that the locals misunderstood the situation by introducing an ethnic factor into an everyday alcohol-induced tragedy.[43]

Separatist violence in the North Caucasus

There tends to be no apparent continuity between the treatment of inter-ethnic violence in the Russian heartlands and coverage of the separatist insurgency in the North Caucasus, although the situation changed somewhat in the second half of, and beyond, our two-year recording period. While the 'international terrorism' theme continued to surface sporadically, the violent incidents in the North Caucasus were generally reported as acts of crime, sabotage and banditry, summarily dealt with by the law-enforcement agencies, rather than as examples of terrorism. Direct references to ethnicity and religion were rare, and accounts of the anti-imperial rhetoric and separatist ambitions of the perpetrators rarer still; the term 'separatist' in all of its contexts – Russian and international – occurred a total of only twenty-eight times throughout the entire corpus. This is an irony in light of Russia's later support for Russian-speaking separatists fighting the post-Yanukovych Kyiv regime, although Russian media sources used the positive term *opolchentsy* – volunteer fighters – with its historical connotations of popular uprisings against illegitimate rulers. When causality and motives were broached at all, economic and social factors were at the forefront, rather than the Islamist or political dimensions. If the link between Islam and separatist violence was acknowledged, the term 'Wahhabist' (*Vakhkhabit*), with its foreign origins (eleven occurrences), was preferred to 'Islamist' (zero occurrences). References linking insurgents to al Qaeda and the broader 'war on terror' were occasional and perfunctory.

The lack of background analysis extended beyond the taboo on exploring the stated goals of the culprits. Heavy with the lexicon of military operations, munitions and impersonal casualty numbers, these reports were conveniently context-free. 'Militants' (*boeviki*), 'criminals' and 'terrorists' were routinely 'eliminated', 'destroyed', 'liquidated' or arrested by the Special Forces. The perpetual threat of indeterminate origin that the *boeviki* represented was cancelled out by the equally constant decisiveness of the regime as it dealt with each situation. The events described occurred in a disjointed temporality of self-contained incidents with minimal connection. The approach adopted is not unique to Russian broadcasters. In news reporting around the world war reporting tends to provide scant analysis of the circumstances under which conflicts erupt, or of the motives of the participants (Jackson 2005). In discourse on international terrorism in particular, the threat posed is indeterminate and without motive, yet never so great that it cannot be contained.

The most significant event in the 'separatist violence' category was an explosion in the North Ossetian city of Vladikavkaz in September 2010 that claimed nearly twenty lives and injured more than a hundred people. Both channels avoided referring to the ethnicity of the suicide bomber, or speculating about his motives. Instead, they provided detailed accounts of what had occurred and the efficient work of the authorities.[44] In many reports belonging to this category, visual footage clearly (if inadvertently) revealed ethnic and religious content. A long story on *Vesti* recounting a special operation in Ingushetia in March 2011 claimed that Russian forces had captured terrorists involved in the organisation of the Domodedovo bombing in January 2011 in which nearly forty people were killed.[45] However, the reporter's narrative was complimented by imagery of the Quran and footage of men whose long beards and Islamic attire connoted the fanaticism of al Qaeda, rendering the broadcaster's refusal to acknowledge the terrorists' demands all the more contradictory. The tensions were compounded when, not long after, *Vremia* run a feature on Ingushetia presenting a picture of a republic whose calm stability was 'the result of constant and successful special operations'.[46]

At about the time of the shocking assault on Domodedovo International Airport in early 2011, we begin to witness a gradual shift in emphasis. Following the comprehensive international coverage the event generated, it became more difficult entirely to suppress the threat posed by radical Islamism. Reporting on the Domodedovo assault itself was littered with references to, and ominous images of, the Chechen 'black widow' (*chernaia vdova* or *shakhidka*) fanatic who was implicated in the attack. At this point, although the state media re-invoked the strategy of inscribing Russia into the global 'war on terror' that has been deployed at intervals since the 9/11 attacks of 2001, it co-existed in tension with the reverse strategy of occluding the role of jihadist ideology and portraying a region undergoing a protracted process of normalisation (Flood et al. 2012: 120–2, 185–9). But the balance of references to Islamist extremism in the North Caucasus slowly increased. This preceded a deluge of scaremongering stories broadcast on Rossiia in 2012 and 2013, and linking the problem of 'illegal migrants' in Moscow and St Petersburg to jihadist groupings planning terrorist acts in Russian cities.[47]

Conclusions: From domestic contradiction to international conflict

Our analysis reveals that Russia's nation-building policy has, until recently, been replete with contradictions. On the one hand, television news reports presented ethnic and cultural diversity as one of Russia's uniquely positive qualities. On the other hand, with multi-ethnicity and migration proving to be a powder keg within the population at large, and with xenophobia growing, state broadcasters were caught between (a) attempting to preserve ethnic cohesion by under-reporting inflammatory topics and (b) acceding to popular sentiments by echoing the prejudicial fears to which those topics gave rise. Throughout, we noted certain discrepancies between the two channels. Rossiia, although state-owned, tended to be more provocative and swifter in responding to the public mood. With its more international audience, Channel 1 tacked closer to the Kremlin's line and was more cautious about ethnicising news.

Channel 1 and Rossiia are well aware of their responsibility to support state diversity management policy. This was particularly visible in relation to migration issues, where in 2010 and 2011 they differentiated themselves from other media outlets by exercising restraint. A crude anti-migration campaign that the broadcasters, particularly Rossiia, waged following Putin's re-election as president proved short-lived, as a wave of anti-Caucasian riots across Russia in the summer and autumn of 2013 prompted a return to more careful reporting.

Notwithstanding the constitutional commitment to multi-confessionality, both channels consistently promoted Orthodoxy as an unchallenged pillar of Russianness transcending national and religious identities. Benefiting from the Eurasianist thinking underpinning elements within official rhetoric, Islam received more attention than other 'traditional religions', although nothing to rival that accorded to Orthodoxy. The hysteria about 'radical Islam' prominent since our recording period finished was foreshadowed in reactions to the terrorist attacks on the Moscow metro and at Domodedovo International Airport in 2010 and 2011 respectively. Major incidents such as the Vladikavkaz bombing were rarely reported in terms of ethnic or religious conflict, despite the popular importance attributed to such factors.

One of several paradoxes that we noted was the dual function played by the emphasis placed on Western Europe's failure to handle migration flows and ethnic tensions, and the perceived crisis within European multi-culturalism. For while Russia's diversity management approach could be presented in a more positive light, the deadlock in Europe also provides an alibi for the strong measures that Russia itself has been forced to take with respect to its own problems in the area of inter-ethnic relations.

The contradictions we have identified and the unpredictable terrain we have mapped are cast into sharp relief when juxtaposed with television news coverage of inter-ethnic relations in present-day Western Europe, and also that of the preceding Soviet period. In each case we can speak of similarities and differences. Thus, while the baton of Soviet state television's obligations as an instrument of Kremlin policy has been passed to its post-Soviet successor, the relationship between policy and broadcast output is now more complex and less 'transitive' than in Soviet times. Until the events of 2014 there has been greater heterogeneity, more editorial autonomy and journalistic room for manoeuvre, more inconsistency in response to changing circumstances and a stronger sense of the need to account for popular opinion than in Soviet times, than many Western observers have acknowledged.

As for the comparison with West European public service broadcasters, we must acknowledge that the latter are often grappling with similar issues to their Russian counterparts. They, too, fulfil a powerful nation-building function within their respective establishment. But the post-Enlightenment principles and language of tolerance are more deeply entrenched within their collective psyches than in that of their Eastern neighbour. Moreover, their public service ethos, sheltered by mature democratic systems within which they represent the outer limit of a powerful 'fourth estate', is lacking in Russia. For that reason, they exhibit more consistency in their approach to diversity management issues, and their adherence to a relatively narrow band of opinion on the subject is, ironically, stronger than that of either Channel 1 or Rossiia.

We move finally, then, to the significance of our research for the geopolitical crisis of 2014, and the role of Russian television in mediating it. That significance is twofold, relating to how our findings contextualise first Russia's actions in Ukraine, and the rationale it provided for them and, second, federal television's part in creating the conditions in which that rationale may take root within Russian popular consciousness.

The pretext for Russia's behaviour focused on the protection of its 'compatriots' (*sootechestvenniki*), a term whose arbitrary conflation with 'ethnic Russians' (*etnicheskie russkie*) and 'Russian speakers' (*russkoiazychnye*) was replicated by many Western commentators, who also failed to distinguish the latter terms from the distinct notion of 'Russian citizens' (*rossiiskie grazhdane*). There can be no more graphic illustration of the consequences of the confused ethnicisation of national identity that we have traced.

Nor would the bemused alienation expressed in Western outlets at the jubilant crowds welcoming Putin's Crimean annexation have surprised readers of a chapter that has charted the progressive subjugation of Russian broadcasters less to the Kremlin, than to a Kremlin-endorsed ideology of Russian national pride that has threatened to breach the control of its instigators. The fact that it is an empty, short-circuited ideology whose lack of viable content means that it has nothing other to fill its hollow shell than an intensified version of itself, makes it no less dangerous. The core ideological concepts with which broadcasters frame their news programmes are in permanent flux, including such disparate ideas as unity in diversity; Orthodox Christianity as the primary pillar of Russian nationhood; and the 'Muslim migrant' as a threat to Russian identity. Against this backdrop, two currents dating to the 1990s have been constantly present in the public discourse – Russia as a protector of its 'compatriots' abroad and the West as Russia's perennial foe. Since 2012, the likes of Kiselev have ensured that such ideological frames have been deployed in a particularly confrontational manner.

Kiselev was at the centre of the anti-Western rhetoric that gripped Russia following the imposition of punitive sanctions. Kiselev used the platform of his *Vesti nedeli* programme to point out that Russia alone among nations has the capacity to turn the USA into 'radioactive dust'.[48] He was echoed by right-wing commentator, Aleksandr Prokhanov, who announced that his long dream of a return to the Cold War had been fulfilled (Barry 2014). The two commentators, both close to Putin's inner circle, demonstrated the dependency of Russian national pride in its distortive, Putinesque manifestation on the 'treacherous, conspiratorial West' that is Russia's nemesis.

The third element of the familiar triad, Russia's internal ethnic other, was supplied by the Crimean Tatars, news coverage of whose predicament contained its contradictions. The *Vesti nedeli* bulletin of 2 March 2014, for example, acknowledged Tatar unease about the possibility of a Russian takeover. The 9 March broadcast developed this theme and included an open admission that many Crimean Tatars were not pro-Russian. Other reports, however, echoed Putin's triumphal annexation speech that insisted (against the evidence) that most Crimean Tatars supported reunification with Russia (Putin 2014a). Here, the Tatars were used as a symbol of Crimea's and Russia's unity in diversity.[49] This recognition and simultaneous denial of the 'Crimean Tatar problem' exposes the tension between Putin's neo-imperialist/Eurasianist variant on Russian patriotism (that like its nineteenth- and twentieth-century predecessors, aspires to square the need for inclusivity and inter-ethnic harmony with the imperative to maintain the dominant ethnic group's power), and the isolationist nationalism of media figures like Kiselev, for whom 'Muslim minorities' constitute a problem.

But neo-imperialist pretensions towards Ukrainian territory (Eastern Ukraine was frequently characterised by official sources from Putin downwards as Novorossiia), Eurasianist indignation at Kyiv's tilt towards the EU and isolationist privileging of ethnic Russian interests, converge in Russian support for the separatist fighters. In short, rather than the actions of a geopolitical empire builder aspiring to re-establish the former Soviet bloc, Russia's illegitimate venture in Ukraine represents a deeply insecure regime projecting an inner struggle to articulate a coherent national identity on to its external environment.

Likewise, the anti-Western bile that saturated the Russian media as the Ukraine crisis reached its peak cannot be seen outside the context of the more generalised 'othering' process we observed in relation to the coverage of migration issues. An illustration of the line of continuity came with *Vesti*'s tarring of the Crimean Tatar leader, Mustafa Dzhemilev, with the brush of Islamist extremism, and its portrayal of his efforts to mobilise opposition to Russia's annexation of Crimea as the consequence of his prominence within a Euromaidan movement coordinated by hostile Western forces and determined to provoke sedition among the Tatars.[50] In this paranoid cocktail, Islam, Tatar ethnicity, Western conspirators and Ukrainian dupes take turns in occupying the slot of a hostile Other whose precise identity mutates according to circumstance.

When contextualising the descent of federal television discourse into crude state propaganda designed to solidify public support for Putin's controversial Ukraine policy, we must recognise that, as our analysis showed, prominent media personae like Kiselev, rather than passively implementing Kremlin edicts, are also active players in shaping the Kremlin's media strategy. But the very ideological space accorded to the likes of Kiselev, and the speed of the trajectory from the (precariously) managed pluralism of the pre-2012 period to the rigid conformity of 2014, confirms rather than negates the fluidity and uncertainty that consistently characterises the Russian media environment. Whether the current level of uniformity and anti-Western hysteria will prevail once the Ukraine crisis subsides is unclear. What is beyond doubt are the symbiotic ties binding the struggle to construct a coherent approach to nation-building within Russia, and the unpalatable postures that Russia adopts on the international stage. The final outcome of the geopolitical stand-off and the long-term future of the West's relations with Russia depend on a willingness among Western policymakers to appreciate the strength of those ties.

Notes

1. This was confirmed by television journalists whom we interviewed in late 2012–early 2013.
2. According to Levada Centre polling of March 2013, federal television is still considered by more than 57 per cent of the Russian population as the most trustworthy source of information (Levada Centre 2013b).
3. Interview with a Channel 1 journalist, 29 January 2013.
4. All the graphs cover the period from September 2010 to May 2012.
5. Interviews with a Rossiia journalist, 29 March 2013; and with a Channel 1 journalist, 29 January 2013.
6. The word 'Russian' as an ethnic denominator (*russkii*) appeared 1,483 times in our transcripts. The civic classification of Russian (*rossiiskii*) appeared slightly less often (1,035 times) and predominantly in official contexts.
7. Interview, 3 April 2013.
8. *Vesti*, 17 October 2011. We do not provide links to the *Vesti* web-archive, because, unlike in the *Vremia* archive, *Vesti* links change frequently.
9. *Vesti*, 18 October 2010.
10. This contrast was emphasised by the Rossiia Deputy Director Kiselev, whom we interviewed on 27 March 2013.
11. See also the same comparison in a *Vremia* report of 18 March, available at <www.1tv.ru/news/social/254436> (last accessed 1 August 2014).

12. *Vesti*, 17 March 2014.
13. *Vesti*, 17 March 2014; *Vremia*, 18 March 2014, available at <www.1tv.ru/news/social/254436> (last accessed 1 August 2014).
14. *Vremia*, 28 July 2014, available at <http://www.1tv.ru/news/social/264062> (last accessed 1 August 2014).
15. *Vesti*, 17 March 2014.
16. *Vesti nedeli*, 22 April 2012; *Vremia*, 22 April 2012, available at <http://www.1tv.ru/news/social/205068> (last accessed 1 November 2012).
17. *Vesti*, 2 November 2011 and 7 January 2012.
18. *Vremia*, 19 April 2012, available at <http://www.1tv.ru/news/social/204898> (last accessed 11 November 2013).
19. *Vremia*, 22 April 2012, available at <http://www.1tv.ru/news/social/205068> (last accessed 1 November 2012) and *Vesti*, 22 April 2012.
20. *Vesti*, 29 September 2011.
21. *Vesti nedeli*, 4 September 2011.
22. *Vesti nedeli*, 25 September 2011.
23. *Vesti nedeli*, 20 November 2011.
24. *Vesti*, 2 August 2011 and 21 April 2011.
25. *Vesti nedeli*, 21 October 2012; *Vremia*, 21 October 2012, available at <http://www.1tv.ru/news/social/218107>; and *Vremia*, 23 October 2012 <http://www.1tv.ru/news/leontiev/218271> (both last accessed 1 November 2012).
26. Interview with Kiselev.
27. *Vesti nedeli*, 26 May 2013. See also Mikhail Leontev, 'Odnako', 16 January 2013, available at <www.1tv.ru/news/leontiev/224101> (last accessed 20 January 2013).
28. *Vesti nedeli*, 9 December 2012.
29. Interviews with a Channel 1 journalist, 29 March 2012; and with a RIA Novosti journalist, 15 February 2013.
30. *Vesti nedeli*, 29 January 2012.
31. *Vesti nedeli*, 26 September 2010.
32. *Vesti*, 30 March 2011; *Vremia*, 31 March 2011, available at <http://www.1tv.ru/news/world/173811> (last accessed 19 October 2012).
33. *Vesti*, 20 April 2013 and 30 May 2013.
34. *Vesti nedeli*, 2 December 2012 and 27 January 2013; *Vremia*, 26 May 2013, available at <http://www.1tv.ru/news/social/233810> (last accessed 28 April 2014).
35. *Vremia*, 25 March 2012, available at <http://www.1tv.ru/news/world/202466> (last accessed 19 October 2012).

36. *Vesti*, 21 April 2012 and *Vesti nedeli*, 22 April 2012.
37. See, for instance, *Vesti*, 9 May 2011.
38. For example, <http://sputnikipogrom.com/politics/4126/pogroms_are_coming>, <http://krylov.livejournal.com/2319664.html> and <www.km.ru/v-rossii/2012/11/27/delo-rasula-mirzaeva/698206-natsionalisty-nameknuli-na-novuyu-manezhku-iz-za-osv> (all last accessed 18 November 2013).
39. Interview with a Rossiia journalist, 29 March 2013.
40. Already in its first report, *Vremia* stressed that the conflict was of an 'everyday' character, see *Vremia*, 19 August 2011, available at <http://www.1tv.ru/news/social/183116> (last accessed 1 September 2011). *Vesti* re-affirmed this, for example, on 31 August 2011.
41. *Vesti*, 27 November 2012.
42. Interview with Kiselev.
43. See *Vremia*, 10 July 2013, available at <http://www.1tv.ru/news/crime/237117> and <http://www.1tv.ru/news/crime/237099> (both last accessed 1 September 2013); *Vesti*, 9 and 10 July 2013; *Vremia*, 13 October 2013, available at <http://www.1tv.ru/news/crime/243976>; and *Vremia*, 15 October 2013, available at <http://www.1tv.ru/news/crime/243862> (both last accessed 30 October 2013).
44. *Vremia*, 13 September 2010, available at <http://www.1tv.ru/news/other/161046> (last accessed 19 October 2012).
45. *Vesti*, 30 March 2011.
46. *Vremia*, 10 April 2011, available at <http://www.1tv.ru/news/crime/174419> (last accessed 19 October 2012).
47. *Vesti*, 4 March, 2013; *Vesti nedeli*, 2 December 2012.
48. *Vesti nedeli*, 16 March 2014.
49. *Vesti*, 17 March 2014.
50. *Vesti*, 23 April 2014.

12

The place of economics in Russian national identity debates

Peter Rutland

'We are a rich country of poor people. And this is an intolerable situation'.

(Vladimir Putin, 28 February 2000)

This chapter traces the role of economics in intellectual debates over Russian national identity. On one side are the modernisers who believe that the only way to restore Russia's prosperity and standing in the world is to embrace Western market institutions. On the other side are nationalists who believe that economic integration will erode the political institutions and cultural norms that are central to Russian identity. They argue that erecting barriers to Western economic influence, and creating an alternate trading bloc, are necessary to prevent the exploitation of the Russian economy and even the possible destruction of the Russian state. The chapter traces these debates from the chaotic reforms of the 1990s through what appeared to be a winning Putin model in the 2000s, and then the uncertain waters after the 2008 financial crash, culminating with the Western sanctions (and Russian counter-sanctions) imposed after the annexation of Crimea in 2014.

It is possible to imagine a middle position, a third way between the modernisers and the nationalists: a distinctively Russian economic model that combines elements of trade openness with measures to ensure Russia's long-term development. However, Russia has by and large failed to come up with its own third way model, and has instead remained trapped between the polarities of integration and autarky.

Vladimir Putin was trying to build a third-way model of state corporatism plus international integration in the period 2000–8, but the model showed its limitations in the stagnation following the 2008 financial crash. He then shifted to an alternative approach in the form of the Eurasian Economic Union: a regional trading bloc that would be under Russia's control and would be to a degree insulated from the global economic institutions dominated by the US and its allies. However, that approach also proved wanting. The change of government in Ukraine that occurred in February 2014 signalled that Ukraine was pulling away from economic integration with Russia, and the subsequent military confrontation seems to have pushed Russia in the direction of autarky – or into the arms of China, which poses risks to national identity of a new type (*Ekonomicheskie izvestiia* 2014).

It has been a difficult challenge for Kremlin ideologists to package these complex and somewhat contradictory economic policies as part of a coherent strategy to restore Russian pride and identity. As Ted Hopf (2013) has shown, at the level of Russia's national leaders the rhetoric of Western-oriented modernisation has prevailed; while in the broader political society, as represented in the mass media, tropes of hostility towards global integration are still prevalent.

Most of the discussion about Russian nationalism concentrates on intellectual history and geopolitical strategy, and rarely turns to economics. Outsiders tend to see nationalism as something emotional, irrational and distinctively Russian – in contrast to economics, which is portrayed as rational, bloodless and based on universal principles that are not confined to Russian shores.

At the same time, most of the Western analysis of the economic transition in Russia has overlooked questions of nationalism and national identity.[1] Neoliberals – and even some of their social democratic critics – tend to assume that the world is 'flat', and that globalisation is making the nation state increasingly redundant as a locus of economic policy and a focus of political identity (Cerny 2010).

In reality, of course, nationalism and economics closely intersect.

As Liah Greenfeld (1993) has shown, nationalism and capitalism evolved in tandem in early modern Europe: not by coincidence did Adam Smith title his famous work defining the essence of capitalism *The Wealth of Nations*. It was published the same year – 1776 – that saw the birth of political nationalism, with the signing of the US Declaration of Independence.

This chapter seeks to close the gap between economic and political analysis by examining the ways in which economic considerations have shaped the national identity discourse in Russia since the breakup of the Soviet Union. The period falls fairly neatly into two phases – the 1990s under Boris Eltsin, characterised by institutional turmoil and economic decline; and the 2000s under Vladimir Putin, characterised by institutional stability and steady growth. We are now entering a third phase whose contours are still unclear. Since the 2008 crash, Russia's economy has struggled to regain the equilibrium of the 2000–8 period, and the crisis over Ukraine and Western sanctions may be tipping the Putin model into a new autarkic paradigm, with unknown consequences for the stability of Putin's political regime.

At the level of mass politics, economics impacts national identity in a variety of ways – from the embrace or rejection of Western consumer products, to the impact on living standards of the sanctions introduced after the annexation of Crimea. The most important single vector for the impact of economics on public opinion is the presence of immigrants and migrant workers from the former Soviet Union, which has stimulated a xenophobic reaction from sections of the Russian population. However, this chapter will focus on the debates among policy elites about the place of economics in Russian national identity. The political impact of migration is covered extensively by other authors in this volume.

The role of the nation state in the era of globalisation

Globalisation – understood as the intensification of cross-border flows of goods, people, money and ideas – took off in the 1990s. Increased international trade and investment brings a country faster growth, greater prosperity and more international respect. At the same time, it leads to social disruption and increased inequality. The nation is increasingly exposed to the volatility of the global economy, while control over economic decision-making slips out of the grasp of national policymakers and into the hands of international corporations and financial institutions, mostly dominated by the US and European Union.

The desire to boost trade and attract investment pushes national governments to embrace the package of policies known as the 'Washington Consensus', or more colloquially 'neoliberalism' (Åslund 2003; Rutland 2013a). These policies may be formally set as conditions for the release of loans from the International Monetary Fund (IMF) or World Bank, or they may be independently adopted by a nation's leaders with a view to convincing international corporations or banks that their country is a safe place to invest.

Ideological critics of neoliberalism usually assume that under conditions of globalisation the state is forced to retreat to a minimal, 'nightwatchman' role while the market works its magic. That laissez-faire vision is also propagated by some of the advocates of neoliberalism, who invoke the legacy of Milton Friedman and Friedrich von Hayek. However, the reality is that while the neoliberal state has a different set of functions from its welfare-state predecessor, it is not necessarily more disengaged from the social and economic life of the country (Rodrik 2013). It becomes, in Philip Cerny's words, a 'competition state' (Cerny 1997), whose role is to promote the international competitiveness of the national economy through investments in infrastructure and human capital; regulating banks and firms to promote competition; and restructuring the welfare state to cope with those who fall through the cracks in an increasingly volatile and unequal economy.

Turning to Russia, we find that the economic debate has been polarised between those who embrace the logic of globalisation and those who reject it outright. This pattern can also be found elsewhere in the rest of the world, but the division seems more acute in Russia. Russian political thinking is notoriously prone to binary categories, something that Mikhail Epstein traces back to the sacred versus profane worldview of Russian Orthodoxy (Epstein 2013). Since the nineteenth century, one of the most prominent dichotomies in Russian thought has been the division in debates over national identity between Westernisers and Slavophiles (Engelstein 2009; Katasonov 2014). This divide has obstinately resurfaced in successive phases of Russian history – from the Trotskyist opposition to Stalin's 'Socialism in One Country' in the 1920s; to the market reformers versus their nationalist and communist critics in the 1990s. It continues to haunt the discussion of national economic strategy into the twenty-first century.

The modernisation hypothesis

Modernisers recognise the inevitability of global integration and the prevailing logic of modernity as exemplified by the leading capitalist countries. For any country to survive and prosper it must embrace the rules of the game of contemporary capitalism – while hopefully taking countervailing measures to preserve national identity and culture, in the spirit of Bertrand Badie's 'conservative modernisation' (Badie 1992). One advantage of this approach is that it is relatively straightforward to administer – the country side-steps the problem of inadequate domestic policy capacity by importing policies off the shelf from other countries. A catching-up moderniser can benefit from the experience of more advanced countries, learning what works and what does not work. The state is the leading actor in the drive to catch up with other countries, and gets recognition and support from the international community in this project. This serves to legitimise and strengthen the current rulers of the country.

The disadvantage of the modernisation strategy is that the imported institutions and practices may cut against the grain of the already existing ways of doing business, and the policies may fail. If money was borrowed on the assumption that the policies would succeed, a cycle of debt crises and currency collapses may result. There may be a political backlash against the international elites that are forcing the pace of change – and those perceived as their local agents, in the form of the incumbent national leadership.

Pursuit of market reform in order to catch up with the West was the prevalent spirit during the Eltsin years, when the reformist government led by Finance Minister (and later Prime Minister) Egor Gaidar strove to introduce polices of liberalisation, privatisation and stabilisation more or less in accordance with the precepts of the 'Washington Consensus' (Rutland 2013a). Gaidar was adamant that the Soviet Union's failure to adapt to the changing world economy had doomed that system to collapse, and the Russian Federation would suffer the same fate if it did not embrace the institutions of modern capitalism (Gaidar 2006). However, during the 1990s Russia experienced a precipitous fall in GDP and living standards, culminating in the August 1998 crisis, which saw Russia default on international debts, the collapse of many banks and a 75 per cent devaluation of the ruble. These troubles were blamed – fairly or unfairly – on the neoliberal reform policies, which were widely seen as part of a Western conspiracy to undermine Russia.

Russia's leaders have faced a unique challenge in trying to modernise their country's economy. Russia suffers from a triple challenge. First, as the world's largest producer of oil and gas it is burdened by the 'oil curse' – a well-documented combination of pathologies that dog the development of countries heavily dependent on oil export revenues: an overvalued currency, volatile exchange rates, corruption, concentration of wealth and power and so forth. Second, the country suffers from what one may call the 'Russian curse': a centuries-old tradition of a strong, centralised state, deemed necessary to preserve internal stability and external security of what became the largest country in the world. Third, it suffers from the 'Soviet curse': seventy years of socialist central planning that reinforced the statist tradition of Tsarist Russia and adding new distortions such as a bloated military industry complex, disdain for entrepreneurship, dependency on state handouts and networks of trust that inhibit competition.

The autarkic impulse

Opponents of globalisation and neoliberalism argued that Russia has to protect itself against foreign exploitation. The global economy is rigged to favour the core at the expense of the periphery, so late arrivals such as Russia should use the powers of the sovereign state to limit the impact of global capital. More broadly, international capitalism is seen as a conspiracy against national cultures, a force that puts the profit-seeking of a 'rootless' cosmopolitan class ahead of the preservation of national values and communities. Global trends such as the deindustrialisation of the West – that was encouraged by the environmental movement – are seen as part of a deliberate neoliberal strategy to insulate capitalism from the democratic challenges that it faced from the 1970s onwards (Fursov 2013).

In the 1990s these views were prevalent in the parliament (but not in the executive branch), and despite Eltsin's 'super-presidential' regime the Russian legislature was still able to impose a number of limits on the free rein of international capital. For example, during the privatisation campaigns of the 1990s foreign buyers were excluded from the most important programmes – they were barred from the 1992 mass voucher programme that processed the majority of firms into private ownership; and they were not allowed to participate in the 1995 'loans for shares' auctions through which the choice oil and mineral companies were sold off. This was in sharp contrast to countries like Hungary and the Czech Republic, where foreign companies acquired many choice assets during the privatisation process. The 1995 law on production sharing agreements (PSA) set such stringent limits on foreign participation that no new PSAs were launched after its passage, while the new land code finally introduced in 2002 barred foreigners from owning agricultural land.

THE SEARCH FOR A SPECIAL PATH

Many countries have sought a third way, and have created special institutional structures that constitute neither a full embrace nor a complete rejection of the Western model. In the nineteenth century, Wilhelmine Germany came up with a special path (*Sonderweg*) that embraced competitive economic institutions but rejected Western liberal democracy (Grimmer-Solem 2015).

After the Second World War the Japanese and Koreans successfully created distinctive corporate structures – the zaibatsu and chaebols – that allowed the national government to steer industrial development, creating national champions that were able to compete on international markets while protecting large swathes of the domestic economy from international competition. Closer to home, in the 1990s and 2000s the social market economy in Germany was renewed to remain competitive (by holding down wages), while in the UK Tony Blair's New Labour adopted many of the policies of their Thatcherite nemesis (austerity budgets, public–private partnerships and so forth) while increasing state spending on health and education to forge a new social market consensus in Britain.

In the 1990s Russia had neither the leadership nor the capacity to come up with such an innovative solution to the dilemma of modernisation. The political system was polarised between the two extremes – Westernisers versus Communist restorationists – and parties that tried to appeal to a social democratic middle ground never took root.

The accession of Putin to the presidency in 2000, and his subsequent consolidation of power, created the political conditions in which the Russian state could possibly pursue its own 'special path'. In his first address to the Federal Assembly in July 2000 Putin was harshly critical of the policies of the 1990s, which led to a situation where 'the growing gap between the leading countries and Russia is pushing us towards the Third World' (Putin 2000). He argued, 'We have had to choose: operate on alien aid, advice and credits or rely on our own resources.' Only in the 2000s, with the creation of state corporations in defence technology (Rostekh, Rosatom and Rosnano) and national champions in the energy sector (Gazprom, Rosneft and Lukoil), have we seen the emergence of something like a distinctive Russian model of state corporatism.

But it was recognised that these faltering steps towards a new model of state capitalism would require some support from outside Russia. Only if Russia was able to change the way the rules were made at international level would it be able to escape from stringencies of the neoliberal paradigm. Moscow pursued two tracks towards a more favourable international environment, neither of which has enjoyed any significant success.

First, it pursued regional integration, in a bid to emulate the success of the European Union and Association of South-East Asian Nations (ASEAN) trading blocs. The Commonwealth of Independent States, created during the breakup of the Soviet Union, proved too unwieldy and disparate a grouping to facilitate economic cooperation. Putin instead concentrated his efforts on creating a narrower association capable of creating a real customs union and free trade zone. Belarus and Kazakhstan were cajoled into joining the Eurasian Customs Union that was launched in 2010, which expanded into the Common Economic Space in 2012 and the Eurasian Economic Union in 2015. In 2014 Kyrgyzstan and Armenia were arm-twisted into agreeing to join the latter body, but Ukraine has stayed aloof, so this project has failed to reach a critical mass capable of representing a serious alternative to trade with the European Union. The Euromaidan revolution in Ukraine, which overthrew the government of President Viktor Yanukovych in February 2014 after he refused to sign an Association Agreement with the EU at the November 2013 Vilnius summit, was arguably a fatal blow to Putin's effort to create a significant regional trading bloc in the post-Soviet space.

Second, Putin embraced the concept of the BRICS, a term casually invented by Goldman Sachs economist Jim O'Neill in 2001 to describe the rising economies of Brazil, Russia, India and China (joined later by South Africa). The idea was that this quartet of countries, with a rapidly rising share of the global economy (20 per cent by 2014), would be able to overturn US hegemony and draw up new rules of the game. A series of diplomatic summits were held, starting with one in Ekaterinburg, Russia in 2009. However, the timing was unfortunate: the 2008 financial crash merely served to underline the central role of the US dollar and financial institutions. In any event, the disparate interests of the BRICS members (energy exporters versus importers, democracies versus autocracies) made it hard for them to come up with a common agenda. In practice, striking bilateral economic development deals with China would turn out to be more important for

Russia's economic development than conjuring up any multilateral initiatives through the BRICS framework.

Russian nationalists mostly preferred to adopt a position of unequivocal hostility to efforts to integrate the Russian economy with the outside world. They had at best ambivalent responses to Putin's efforts to develop an international third way. The nationalist camp was divided between the ethnonationalists who wanted to build a nation state around ethnic Russians and Russian culture, and the imperialists who favoured a multi-ethnic, expansive polity along the lines of the former Soviet Union. Ethnonationalists were mostly sceptical of the Eurasian Union, seeing it as a Soviet-style project that carried the risk of Russia's wealth being used to buy political support from Minsk, Astana, Yerevan and Bishkek (Makarkin 2012). They accused Putin of being a statist, advancing the interests of the state bureaucracy (and the oligarchic class attached to them) at the expense of the Russian people. A key political problem for advocates of the Eurasian Union is its reliance on open borders and increased dependence on migrant labour – since anti-migrant xenophobia is one of the most powerful currents in contemporary Russian opinion. So most nationalist thinkers favoured pursuing the option of autarky, and used hostility to foreign economic ties (whether with the 'far abroad' or the 'near abroad') as a central plank in their political programme.

The politics of the 1990s transition

Western proponents of market reforms believe that their policies are self-evidently in the long-term interests of the majority of society, so forming a winning coalition should be within the grasp of any competent political leader who can appeal to the enlightened, long-term self-interest of the electorate. To the extent that nationalism factors into their analysis at all, it is seen as a threat to progress from reactionaries who fail to understand the logic of economics and who want to turn back the tide of history.

However, it can be argued that there may be a positive relationship between market economics and nationalist politics, since the latter's political goals 'may sometimes be best served by liberal or neoliberal policies' (Kangas 2013: 574; Ehl 2013).

One can argue that the key factor in explaining the success of market reform in Eastern Europe and its failure in Russia was the contrasting trajectory of nationalist politics in the two regions. Political leaders in the new democracies of Eastern Europe had to worry about getting themselves re-elected at the same time as they were embarking on wrenching market reforms that they knew would impose severe short-term costs on their population. In an influential book published in 1991, Adam Przeworski argued – mainly extrapolating from Latin American experience – that workers would never vote for capitalism, since this would mean the concentration of wealth and power in the hands of the few (Przeworski 1991). Events in Eastern Europe quickly turned Przeworski's logic on its head, however, since it was the country with the most active labour movement – Poland – that became the first and most ardent advocate of shock therapy (Orenstein 2001).

Workers voted for capitalism partly because their daily experiences with communism had been so negative, but also because national identity trumped class identity. For Czechs, Hungarians and Poles, their national identity was vested in breaking with Soviet control and tying their national fate to Western Europe – which happened to be democratic and capitalist. In Russia, nationalism initially worked in Eltsin's favour – when he was standing up for the Russian Federation and the other republics against the Soviet government headed by Mikhail Gorbachev (Dunlop 1993). It was Russian nationalism that enabled Eltsin to prevail against the August 1991 putsch, by appealing to the patriotic feelings of the (predominantly Russian) officers and men of the security forces. However, Eltsin's nationalist legitimacy eroded as the economic turmoil deepened – and the reforms he was enacting came to be seen as Western impositions. Some of Eltsin's closest lieutenants broke with him over the market reforms and went over to the nationalists – men such as vice president Aleksandr Rutskoi and the speaker of the Supreme Soviet, Ruslan Khasbulatov.

Given Russia's history as a great power that defined itself in opposition to the West, it was hard for the Gaidar government to package the market reforms as a re-assertion of Russian identity. Efforts by individual politicians to carve out a 'liberal nationalist' position fell on stony ground. For example, the liberal statist Boris Fedorov, who served as finance minister 1993–4, formed a party in 1995 called Forward Russia!, but it failed to clear the minimum 5 per cent threshold in the December 1995 State Duma elections (Sakwa 2008: 223). The 1990s privatisation tsar Anatolii Chubais, who was kept on by Putin after 2000 as head of the electricity monopoly RAO EES, floated the idea of a 'liberal empire' in 2003. He proposed using Russian energy exports to project Russian influence into the former Soviet space (Chubais 2003). While Gazprom and RAO EES made some progress buying up infrastructure in small countries like Armenia, Georgia and Kyrgyzstan, the big players such as Kazakhstan and Uzbekistan were wary of increasing their economic dependency on Russia and instead opened the door to Western investors – and to China. (Kazakhstan pursued a balanced policy, deepening ties to Russia while also bringing in new partners.) Chubais' project never gained any traction in the Russian political sphere – not least because Chubais himself was widely disliked because of his role as the architect of the 1990s privatisation.

Putin's record

As discussed above, Putin did not pursue absolute autarky for Russia, but instead endeavoured to follow a 'special path' that would enable Russia to protect its autonomy while benefiting from the international division of labour.

The 1990s had left the task of building a market economy half-finished – but it had also left the Russian public deeply sceptical about the goals and results of market reforms. According to a Friedrich Ebert Foundation survey in 2000, 70 per cent of Russians favoured more state planning, and 63 per cent approved of confiscating the property acquired by the 'New Russians' (*Izvestiia* 2002). One could easily imagine a 'Fortress Russia' scenario in which Putin could have tried to reintroduce central planning, raise tariff barriers and use energy revenues to re-equip Russian manufacturing industry. However, this did not happen. Rather, the modernisation logic was still accepted by the incoming Putin Administration in 2000, which recognised the advantages that could be gained from participation in the international division of labour – access to cheap capital, superior management skills and the latest technology (Putin 1999).[2]

The promise of economic growth enabled Putin to renew the unwritten 'social contract' of the Soviet era, in which citizens offered political loyalty – or at least acquiescence – in return for rising living standards and upwards social mobility (Makarkin and Oppenheimer 2011). Although Daniel Treisman (2011b) argues that economics has been the main factor driving Putin's extraordinary popularity, his relationship with the Russian electorate is more complex than merely pocketbook factors – it also involves his pledge to protect them from Chechen/Islamist terrorism, and an appeal to their pride in Russia as a great power.

Whether or not Putin genuinely believed that international economic integration was best for Russia, it was certainly extremely beneficial for Putin's inner circle, and Russia's oligarchic elite, who made vast fortunes from continued engagement with the global economy – while using the state to protect themselves from competition inside Russia (Dawisha 2014). Only in certain areas did Putin adopt what could be seen as autarkic-nationalist policies. The arrest of Mikhail Khodorkovskii in 2003 and the subsequent acquisition of his company Yukos – Russia's largest oil producer – by state-owned Rosneft showed that Putin wanted to bring most of the oil sector back under state control. (Among the factors that influenced Putin's decision were reports that Khodorkovskii was preparing to sell Yukos to Exxon.) State-owned Gazprom then acquired the second-largest oil company, Roman Abramovich's Sibneft. In 2013 the last remaining oil company where a foreign firm owned a controlling stake, the joint venture TNK-BP, was bought by Rosneft. Moreover, the limits on foreign ownership of what were deemed as strategic companies were tightened in 2008, applying to the oil, gas and minerals sectors. Foreign Investment Law no. 57 limits foreigners to 25 per cent ownership of any strategic asset, and law no. 58 sets very low limits for a mineral deposit to be deemed strategic (Locatelli and Rossiaud 2011).

In his first state of the nation address on 8 July 2000 Putin reaffirmed his commitment to the market (Putin 2000). He admitted that he used to favour protectionist tariffs but now saw such a policy as ineffective and as a recipe for corruption. Putin offered some protection to the dwindling band of liberal economic managers in his government, ensuring that they kept in control of the ministries of finance and economic development, and the Central Bank. However, personnel from the security forces (the *siloviki*) formed a powerful bloc in the Putin Administration, and in the course of the 2000s they managed to tighten their control over the military industry and energy sectors of the economy. The *siloviki* often wrapped their economic agenda in patriotic clothing, sometimes appealing to Russian Orthodoxy. An early example is Vladimir Iakunin, a founding member of Putin's Ozero dacha collective who went on to become head of the powerful Russian Railroads (Russia's largest employer) and a sponsor of religious charities (Dawisha 2014: 99). A later entrant is the forty-year old investment banker and billionaire Konstantin Malofeev, a monarchist and Orthodox patriot who came to prominence providing support for Ukrainian separatists in 2014 (Weaver 2014).

Putin's first presidential term saw the passage of some important new reform legislation, such as cutting personal income tax to a flat rate of 13 per cent, a new tax code, a land code, a new labour code and bank deposit insurance. Measures that aroused public anxiety, such as pension reform and the privatisation of the electricity monopoly, went ahead, but at a cautious pace. Unlike in China, where the yuan exchange rate was held down as a tool to promote export-led growth, the Russian ruble was freely convertible. Limits on capital flows in and out of the country were progressively lifted, and Russia achieved near-full capital account convertibility by 2007 (Sutela 2012: 154).

In the early years of his presidency Putin acted quickly and decisively to restore the 'power vertical', reining in the autonomy that Russia's regions and especially ethnic republics had seized in the 1990s. To preserve national unity, the federal government took steps to redistribute resources from richer to poorer provinces and sought to develop lagging regions such as the North Caucasus and Russian Far East. In 2003 Putin appointed Dmitrii Medvedev deputy prime minister in charge of a new programme of 'national projects', signalling the federal government's concern with nationwide development goals. In 2005 four projects were launched to promote the modernisation of farming, health care, education and housing. This sort of active state leadership role is perfectly compatible with the state interventions envisioned under neoliberalism, intended to create the conditions for a successful market economy. Some 10 billion USD a year was spent on these programmes, leading to a rise in the wages of those working in education and health care, but no breakthroughs in performance. In the face of indifferent results and the accelerating global financial crisis, the cabinet department responsible for administering the projects was disbanded in March 2009 (Medetsky 2009).

The modernisation school reached its apogee during the presidency of Medvedev from 2008 to 2012, when Russia was ruled by the uneasy 'tandem' of President Medvedev and Prime Minister Putin. Medvedev described himself as a 'conservative' and not a liberal (Medvedev 2004), but he made 'modernisation' the watchword of his presidency, reportedly on the advice of his first deputy chief of staff Vladislav Surkov (Glikin and Kostenko 2010). The year 2008 saw the launch of 'Strategy 2020', a bold road map of the steps needed to turn Russia into a more competitive, productive economy. Policies introduced by President Medvedev ranged from introducing more open electronic government to a series of expensive infrastructure projects, such as the East Siberia–Pacific Ocean (ESPO) oil export pipeline and the Skolkovo innovation park. However, in reality Medvedev's modernisation rhetoric, while appealing to Western observers, ran ahead of his ability to implement policies on the ground (Trenin 2010; Pynnöniemi 2014).

There were some signs of policy dissonance between Medvedev and Putin. For example, at the G20 summit in Washington, DC in November 2008, Medvedev and the other participants agreed not to erect protectionist trade barriers against one another. Then, just a few days later, Putin announced the introduction of higher customs duties on the import of used cars in order to protect the domestic auto industry.

The Strategy 2020 reform programme was derailed by the 2008 economic crisis, which caused Russia's GDP to shrink by 8 per cent in 2009. The state was forced to step in, spending down its reserves to delay the depreciation of the ruble, and bailing out banks unable to meet their foreign loan payments (Robinson

2013). At least the government did not resort to outright protectionism after the crisis (Bykov et al. 2011). Although growth resumed a year later, it was at a sluggish pace. The core of the problem was that companies were not investing enough, due to a combination of slack demand in Europe, uncertainty over Russia's political future and Putin's willingness to ease the state's overbearing role in the economy (Mau 2014).[3]

Despite the economic turbulence of 2008–9, real wages and pensions continued to rise, and – in sharp contrast to the 1998 crash – the crisis did not significantly weaken the political authority of the Putin–Medvedev tandem leadership. However, in September 2011 Putin revealed that he would be returning to the presidency in 2012, triggering mass discontent and a slump in his popularity. The Kremlin was frightened by the sight of tens of thousands of protestors who took to the streets of Moscow to challenge the results of the December 2011 State Duma elections. In response to this political challenge, on his return to the presidency in May 2012 Putin encouraged a series of legislative measures to appeal to traditional values (such as a ban on foreign adoptions and LGBT 'propaganda') and cracked down on civil society groups receiving foreign money. He also targeted the Pussy Riot group after their performance in the Cathedral of Christ the Saviour as a symbol of the gulf between Russian and Western values (Sharafutdinova 2014).

At the same time, Putin laid out a programme of state spending to improve Russia's long-term growth prospects while also boosting living standards and the quality of public services (Putin 2012a; Rutland 2013b). Putin's decree no. 596 'On the state's long run economic policy' of 17 May 2012 set a dozen ambitious long-term goals, including: twenty-five million new job places by 2020; investment to reach 25 per cent of GDP by 2018; a 30 per cent increase in high-tech products; a 50 per cent increase in labour productivity; and to boost Russia's World Bank 'ease of doing business' rating from 120th place to 50th by 2015 (and 20th by 2018) (Ukaz Prezidenta RF 2012a). Over the course of the next year Putin pressured ministry officials to follow through on the new programme (Kolesnikov 2013). These programmes were given a high degree of visibility by the Kremlin-controlled mass media, and provided a vehicle for Putin to display his active concern for the nation's socio-economic progress. However, at the conclusion of the programme's first year, in May 2013, Deputy Prime Minister Vladislav Surkov, co-chair of the commission for implementing the presidential decrees, was forced to resign because of failures in implementing the decrees (Koshcheev and Afanas'ev 2013).

Throughout the Putin era, there was unresolved tension between the liberal and statist wings of his administration. The standard-bearer for the liberal wing is former minister of finance and personal friend of Putin Aleksei Kudrin (see, for example, Kudrin 2013; Pis'mennaia 2013). The intellectual differences between these two groups were overlaid by clashing interests of various oligarchs and state officials. Some of them stood to gain from the preservation of a relatively open economy, while others would benefit from a return to protectionism. Anders Åslund dubbed this a clash between crony capitalists (Putin's inner circle) and state capitalists (Åslund 2013), while Andrei Piontkovskii framed it as a struggle between global kleptocrats and national kleptocrats (Piontkovskii 2014).

In January 2010 President Medvedev adopted a decree introducing a 'Food security doctrine' for Russia, and in 2012 a Eurasian Centre for Food Security was opened in Moscow (World Bank 2012). Since the 1990s the Communist Party and their nationalist allies had been pushing the idea of 'food security': the need to protect Russia's agricultural producers from cheaper, subsidised food imports (Spoor et al. 2013; Azarieva 2014). The campaign also involves the idea of protecting Russian consumers from unhealthy and potentially dangerous foreign foods. 'Securitising' the issue made it easier for the state to adopt guarding the nation's food supply as one of its core functions. Over the years the Russian food safety agency Rospotrebnadzor imposed import bans on a wide variety of foodstuffs, from Georgian wine to US pork. In many case these bans seemed to be punishment for political actions by the targeted state, rather than part of a systematic protectionist strategy (Cenusa et al. 2014).[4]

At the same time, Russia was finally accepted as a member of the World Trade Organization (WTO), something that they had been seeking since 1993. Liberals saw WTO membership as vital to promoting competitiveness and breaking up the cosy monopolies that had come to dominate the Russian economy. WTO entry was also of symbolic importance: China had been allowed to join back in 2001, and Russia remained the only major economy outside the preeminent global trade body. Entry was opposed by some producers – such as farmers and the auto industry – that feared foreign competition. Svetlana Barsukova and Caroline Dufy found that patriotic rhetoric was quite commonly adopted by regional businesses lobbying in defence of their interests (Barsukova and Dufi 2013). Putin persisted through years of difficult negotiations, finally securing entry in 2012. By then, Russia had already removed most non-tariff barriers in preparation for WTO entry, and had lowered its average tariffs to a level (10.7 per cent) acceptable to the WTO, so the impact on the competitiveness of the Russian domestic market was likely to be modest. However, Russian exporters of steel and chemicals could expect to benefit from lower tariff barriers and access to WTO procedures for fighting anti-dumping measures.[5] Putin refused to breakup Gazprom or to liberalise Russia's domestic energy market as a condition for WTO entry, as the European Union initially tried to insist (Rutland 2012b).

A top priority for Putin has been turning the Eurasian Economic Union into a fully integrated economic entity, building on the Common Economic Space introduced between Russia, Belarus and Kazakhstan in January 2012 (following the Customs Union that the three countries formed in 2009). However, there are only modest efficiency gains for Russia from integrating with those two much smaller economies, and the 2014 crisis in Ukraine put paid to the prospects for that country joining the project anytime soon.

The nationalist alternative

Russian nationalists have an ambiguous relationship to Putin. On the one hand, the statists admire Putin for having resurrected a strong state, willing to act decisively against Russia's enemies – domestic and foreign, real and imagined. On the other hand, despite the fact that Putin has repeatedly invoked the history, culture and values of the Russian people (*russkii narod*), Russian ethnonationalists accuse him of putting the interests of the state before those of the Russian people. They suspect Putin of being too 'Soviet' in his thinking – as exemplified by his plans for a Eurasian Economic Union, which ethnonationalists fear would be a vehicle for Russia to subsidise its poorer neighbours. Although Putin has stressed the importance of the Russian Orthodox Church for Russian identity, and praised the Tsarist legacy, he has tended to describe Russia as a multi-ethnic project rather than a state only for ethnic Russians. Nationalists rejoiced when Putin acted decisively to annex Crimea in March 2014, but were disillusioned by his refusal to openly support the separatists in eastern Ukraine, instead limiting himself to (thinly disguised) covert military assistance to prevent them from being overrun by Ukraine government forces.

This ambivalence also extends to Putin's economic policies. The nationalists resent the spread of capitalism to Russia, and the dominant role played by the cohort of 100 billionaire oligarchs – whose number has increased tenfold during Putin's rule. They are angry that pro-market economists continue to set policy at the Finance Ministry and Central Bank – institutions that they see as agents of Western capitalist thinking. They complain that the Central Bank has pursued a tight monetary policy, and as a result the ruble had become over-valued (prior to the 2014 depreciation), with the money supply (M2) only 50 per cent of the size of Russian GDP, below the level of other developed economies (Koptiubenko et al. 2014). Mikhail Leontev, a veteran attack journalist who was appointed Rosneft's vice president for communications in January 2014, has made the Central Bank a central target of his invective. He condemned Russia's economic course as 'A colonial arrangement, a raw materials appendage, where rents are spent on foreign imports and the destruction of domestic industry' (Kuzichev 2014).

Nationalist economists such as Mikhail Iurev argue that the economic openness promoted by neoliberals is a recipe for the deindustrialisation of Russia and its conversion into a source of raw materials for the West – and for China (Iur'ev 2013). Such thinking is shared by many mainstream Russian economists such as Viktor Polterovich and Vladimir Popov, who argue that protectionism has been successful for many countries in the past, enabling them to develop high-value-added industries and not see their economies shrink to low-value sectors in which they have a global comparative advantage, such as resource extraction or agriculture (Polterovich and Popov 2005). In fact, critics of neoliberalism dominate the pages of the leading academic economics journal in Russia, *Voprosy ekonomiki*, the publication of the Institute of Economics of the Academy of Sciences.

Russia's anaemic party structure consists of a dominant ruling party and a handful of officially tolerated 'opposition' parties. As Leonid Poliakov noted, 'There are no nationalist parties, if one does not take the LDPR as a nationalist party' (quoted in K. Loginov 2013). This is not because of a lack of support among voters, but because of divisions within the nationalist camp – and because of the Kremlin's determination to prevent such a party emerging.

The Kremlin's own nationalism built on state patriotism and anti-Western rhetoric. This was clear in Surkov's concept of 'sovereign democracy', reaffirmed in his 2006 article 'Nationalising the future', in which he looked for a community of sovereign democracies standing up against the 'global dictator' and critiqued liberal 'intellectuals for whom the sun rises in the West' (Surkov 2006). Surkov argued that Russia faced the challenge 'to preserve sovereignty without harming democracy, and to be open without losing one's identity'. However, 'the main guarantor of sovereignty is not only military but also all-round competitiveness'. He called therefore for a 'nationally oriented open economy' (Surkov 2006). He had no time for ethnic Russian nationalists – he mockingly asked if they would want 'a Russian Republic within the borders of early Muscovy, an ethnic preserve with a "do not disturb" sign on the fence'. Surkov's approach was purely instrumental, seeking to use nationalism to bolster Putin's political authority. Andrei Okara characterised his approach as based on 'clever marketing, studying the demands of the target audience and a calculated pursuit of the fashion for "genuineness"' (Okara 2007). The Kremlin was able to wrest the nationalism agenda out of the hands of the communists, in part because although a majority of the Russian public share the left-wing critique of globalisation, they have no enthusiasm for a return to Soviet-type central planning as a solution (Mikhailin 2013).

One of the most outspoken and prolific nationalist critics of neoliberalism in Russia is Mikhail Deliagin, a former member of Eltsin's liberal economic team (1990–8) who then worked for Evgenii Primakov and became one of the leaders of the nationalist Rodina party (2004–6).[6] From his position as head of the Institute for Problems of Globalisation he has penned a stream of articles and books calling for an autarkic development strategy based on infrastructural investment and industrial protectionism (see, for example, Deliagin 2009). He has been a consistent critic of the liberalisation policies pursued by Putin-Medvedev: in 2007 he was digitally erased from a TV talk show because of comments critical of Putin (Levy 2008).

The leading standard bearer for nationalist economics is nevertheless Sergei Glazev. Like Deliagin, Glazev was part of the early 1990s Eltsin reform team, serving as Minister for External Economic Relations in 1992–3. He was a member of the State Duma 1993–5 and 1997–2007, first on the ticket of the Democratic Party of Russia and then the Communist Party. In 2003 he was one of the founders of the nationalist Rodina Party, which made higher taxes on natural resource rents a plank in its programme in the December 2003 State Duma elections. Rodina won an impressive 9 per cent of the vote: fearful of its success, in 2006 the Kremlin shut it down, forcing it to merge into the new A Just Russia party.

Glazev has developed a coherent and consistent analysis of the challenges facing the Russian economy – the intensification of globalisation that leads to the deindustrialisation of mature economies, and the deepening financialisation that exposes countries to speculative bubbles while strengthening the power of the US (Glaz'ev 2011). He believes that recycling the petro-wealth through a state-led investment campaign in infrastructure and manufacturing, behind protectionist barriers, can preserve Russia's industrial base. However, he overlooks the fact that countries like China and Brazil have shown that the way to catch up is to form partnerships with Western firms, learn their technologies through joint ventures and licensing and then develop indigenous production facilities.

In July 2012 Glazev was appointed an advisor to Putin for the Customs Union with Belarus and Kazakhstan – a significant step, bringing this outspoken critic into the presidential administration. However, in May of that year Putin had promoted his economic advisor, the liberal Arkadii Dvorkovich, to deputy prime minister in charge of economic policy, replacing Dvorkovich with another liberal, Elvira Nabiullina (Sycheva 2012). In 2013, despite vigorous lobbying, Glazev failed to be nominated head of the Central Bank, losing out to the liberal Nabiullina.

In a ceremony in the Cathedral of Christ the Saviour on 27 November 2013, Sergei Glazev was awarded a prize as one of the 'Men of the Year 2013' for his work in bringing Ukraine into the Common Economic Space with Russia – one week after Ukrainian President Yanukovych had refused to sign the Association Agreement with the EU.[7] The celebrations were premature: protests in Kyiv would topple the Ukrainian government in February 2014, and on 27 June the new government signed the agreement with the EU, putting paid to any chance of Ukraine joining the Eurasian Economic Union.

Impact of the Ukraine crisis

Putin's annexation of Crimea in March 2014 triggered a swift Western response to signal the West's shock at Russia's use of force to change international borders, in violation of the 1994 Budapest Memorandum that Russia had signed recognising Ukraine's sovereignty and territorial integrity. The first round of 'smart' sanctions targeted named individuals and corporations involved in the Crimean annexation. (The WTO allows any country to break their free trade rules if it invokes a national security exemption.) Covert Russian support for separatist rebels in eastern Ukraine led to a second wave of broader sectoral sanctions in July that hit corporations in the banking and energy sectors. Remarkably, Putin responded to the Western sanctions by imposing counter-sanctions: banning the import of foodstuffs from countries that had applied the sanctions.

Even more remarkably, Putin's tough posture proved popular with the Russian public. His personal approval rating hit 88 per cent in October 2014 (Volkov 2014), and some observers argue that Russian society has settled into a new 'post Crimea' social contract, in which the people accept economic hardship in return for Russia's restoration to the ranks of the great powers. However, it is not clear how much economic pain ordinary people are willing to endure in the long term for the sake of Putin's great power adventurism. Nor is it clear that Putin will be able to maintain political control in this situation, given that Russian nationalists continue to push for yet more aggressive action in eastern Ukraine (Morozov 2015). Perhaps this is what led Putin to defensively declare, in response to a question at the Valdai Club in October 2014, that 'I am the biggest nationalist in Russia' (Putin 2014b).

The sectoral sanctions made it difficult for Russian firms to refinance their debts, and their impact was multiplied by a slump in global oil prices, which fell from 100 USD at the start of 2014 to 60 USD by year's end. The ruble lost half its value, inflation surged and the Russian economy plunged into a recession with a projected 5 per cent drop in GDP in 2015 (Rutland 2014; Secreriu and Cziek-Karpowicz 2015). The liberal former finance minister Aleksei Kudrin (2014) warned, 'Business is very concerned by what it is hearing on the radio and TV', and he feared cutting ties with the West 'that will hold back modernisation is all directions'. He continued, 'There are forces in the country who have long wanted . . . isolation, maybe a certain self-sufficiency. Today this has all fallen on fertile ground.'

The Ukraine crisis saw a prominent political role for Glazev who emerged as a key Putin advisor on the issue. The sanctions provided Glazev with a perfect opportunity to advance his alternative economic agenda (Glaz'ev 2014). He argued for the creation of a separate international payments system with the BRICS countries to insulate themselves against Western sanctions; more investment in research and development (R&D) to prevent bans on technology transfer from disrupting key industries; and the introduction of capital controls to stop capital flight (Koptiubenko et al. 2014). Nationalist critics outside the government such as Deliagin blamed Nabiullina's Central Bank for failing to head off the impact of the sanctions by imposing capital controls, leaving Russia exposed to rapid ruble depreciation and inflation (Deliagin 2015). Likewise, nationalist intellectual Andrei Fursov called for the 'nationalisation' of the Central Bank to wrest control of the Russian economy back from the '20 families that control the world economy' (Fursov 2014).

While nationalist economists are on the offensive, liberals are in despair. Billionaire and former presidential candidate Mikhail Prokhorov penned an unconvincing article in which he argued that the crisis may force the government to embrace long-overdue reforms and unleash a 'market mobilisation' (Prokhorov 2014).

Putin aligned himself unequivocally with the nationalist side of the debate. He told a meeting of the Security Council on 22 July 2014 that the sanctions were part of a systematic policy by the Western powers to deny sovereignty to other nations, a policy that includes the fomenting of 'colour revolutions' of the sort that brought down President Yanukovych (*Kremlin.ru* 2014). The main task of economic policy should be to develop regions such as the Far East while keeping inter-regional differences in check. 'We must think of additional steps to reduce the dependence of our economy and financial system on negative external factors.' In his 2014 address to the Federal Assembly Putin stated, 'We should wipe the critical dependence on foreign technologies and industrial production. The main thing we need to understand is that our development depends on ourselves first and foremost' (Putin 2014c).

For fifteen years, Putin's economic policy had been pulled between the conflicting logics of liberalism and statism. The Crimean crisis served as an external shock that seems to have pushed Putin into a full embrace of anti-Western, protectionist policies, in support of his determination to hold on to his political and territorial gains in Ukraine.

Conclusion

There are many puzzles facing the analyst trying to understand the trajectory of Russian politics. Why did democracy fail in the 1990s? How was a small, corrupt elite able to seize control of the commanding heights of the economy, becoming fabulously wealthy in the process? Among the puzzles is also the failure of Russian nationalists to capitalise on the public's deep dissatisfaction with the performance of the Russian economy in the 1990s. Then, after the accession to power of Vladimir Putin in 2000, the new, patriotic leader confounded the nationalists by sticking with many of the policies of the liberal market reformers: eschewing protectionism and trying to maintain and deepen Russia's integration into the global economy.

Putin concluded that Russia's viability as a great power required him to accelerate economic modernisation and deepen global integration. Other leaders of developing countries, such as the populist President Luiz Inacio Lula da Silva in Brazil and the nationalist Prime Minister Narendra Modi in India, came to a similar conclusion, and tried to adopt select elements of the neoliberal policy package without alienating their domestic constituencies. These international comparisons are an important reminder that Russia's dilemma of embracing the global economy while preserving national identity is not unique.

Notes

1. Exceptions include Abdelal (2001), Appel (2004) and Helleiner and Pickel (2005).
2. Russia did manage to reach Portugal's 2000 GDP per capita in 2012, although its GDP still lagged 22 per cent behind the 2012 Portugal level (Gilman 2012).
3. The Strategy 2020 plan would be re-launched in 2012 under the leadership of two liberal economists, Vladimir Mau, Rector of the Academy of National Economy, and Iaroslav Kuzminov, Rector of the Higher School of Economics (Mau and Kuzminov 2012).
4. One case study of the ban on Norwegian fish concludes that the motivation was not so much protectionism but a reflex desire to maintain state control (Elvestad and Nilssen 2010).

5. Predictions of a 2–3 per cent boost to annual GDP growth were based on heroic assumptions about the possible impact of liberalisation on Russia's domestic financial markets.
6. Deliagin's publications can be found on his website <http://delyagin.ru> (last accessed 1 March 2015).
7. See <www.glazev.ru/about/343/> (last accessed 1 March 2015).

Bibliography

Abdelal, R. (2001), *National Purpose in the World Economy: Post-Soviet States in Comparative Perspective*, Ithaca: Cornell University Press.
Agitator Edinoi Rossii [Agitator of United Russia] (2006), Moscow: Evropa.
Agurskii, M. (2003), *Ideologiia natsional-bol'shevizma* [The Ideology of National-Bolshevism], Moscow: Algoritm.
Aleksandrova, M. (2014), 'Net liubvi bez pravdy' [There is no love without truth], *Ofitsial'nyi sait Moskovskogo patriarkhata*, 30 September, <http://www.patriarchia.ru/db/text/3769807.html> (last accessed 25 January 2015).
Alexseev, M. A. (2010), 'Fear has wide eyes: why do Russians see some migrant minorities as more numerous than others?', in M. Laruelle, ed., *Russian Nationalism and the National Reassertion of Russia*, London: Routledge, pp. 167–84.
Alksnis, V. (2007), 'Proshchai, Imperiia (nakanune russkoi Rossii)' [Farewell, Empire (at the dawn of a Russian Russia)], *Strategicheskii zhurnal*, 3: 29–46.
Al'perovich, V. (2014), 'Ideologicheskie batalii russkikh natsionalistov na ukrainskikh frontakh' [The ideological battles of Russian nationalists on the Ukrainian fronts], in A. Verkhovskii, ed., *Rossiia – ne Ukraina: sovremennye aktsenty natsionalizma* [Russia is not Ukraine: Contemporary Accents of Nationalism], Moscow: SOVA Center for Information and Analysis, pp. 292–305.
Al'perovich, V. and N. Yudina (2013), 'The ultra-right on the streets with a pro-democracy poster in their hands or a knife in their pocket: xenophobia and radical nationalism in Russia, and efforts to counter-

act them in 2012', in *Xenophobia, Freedom of Conscience and Anti-Extremism in Russia in 2012*, Moscow: SOVA Center for Information and Analysis, pp. 5–60.

Al'perovich, V. and N. Yudina (2014a), 'The ultra-right shrugged: xenophobia and radical nationalism in Russia, and efforts to counteract them in 2013', in *Xenophobia, Freedom of Conscience and Anti-Extremism in Russia in 2013*, Moscow: SOVA Center for Information and Analysis, pp. 5–55.

Al'perovich, V. and N. Yudina (2014b), 'Ukraine upsets the nationalist apple-cart: xenophobia, radical nationalism and efforts to counteract them in Russia during the first half of 2014', *SOVA Center for Information and Analysis*, 6 August, <http://www.sova-center.ru/en/xenophobia/reports-analyses/2014/08/d30003> (last accessed 1 March 2015).

Anderson, B. (2006), *Imagined Communities: Reflections on the Origin and Spread of Nationalism*, London: Verso.

Anderson, B. and S. Blinder (2013), 'Who counts as a migrant? Definitions and their consequences', *Migration Observatory Briefing*, Oxford: The Migration Observatory.

Anderson, J. (2012), 'Dreaming of Christian nations in the USA and Russia: the importance of history', *Journal of Transatlantic Studies*, 10, 3: 201–21.

Appel, H. (2004), *Building a New Capitalist Order*, Pittsburgh: University of Pittsburgh Press.

Aragonés, G. (2010), 'Igor' Iurgens: "Ia ne iskliuchaiu integratsii Rossii v NATO"' [Igor Iurgens: 'I do not exclude the possibility of Russia's integration with NATO'], *InoSMI*, 18 November, <http://inosmi.ru/europe/20101118/164327795.html> (last accessed 10 March 2015).

Aridici, N. (2014), 'How Vladimir Putin has changed the meaning of "Russian"', *The Conversation*, 9 April, <http://theconversation.com/how-vladimir-putin-has-changed-the-meaning-of-russian-24928> (last accessed 11 July 2014).

Aron, L. (2008), *Putinism*, Washington, DC: American Enterprise Institute.

Arutiunian, Iu., L. Drobizheva and A. Susokolov (1999), *Etnosotsiologiia* [Ethnosociology], Moscow: Nauka.

Åslund, A. (2003), *Building Capitalism: The Transformation of the Former Soviet Bloc*, Cambridge: Cambridge University Press.

Åslund, A. (2013), 'Sergei Glazyev and the revival of Soviet economics', *Post-Soviet Affairs*, 29, 5: 375–86.

Azar, I. (2007), 'Russkii gosudarstvennyi trep' [Russian state babble],

Gazeta.ru, 7 February, <http://www.gazeta.ru/2007/02/07/oa_230 946.shtml> (last accessed 20 December 2014).

Azarieva, J. (2014), 'Food independence – populist tool and policy guidelines in Russia', paper presented at the Central European University (CEU)–Association for the Study of Nationalities (ASN) conference, Budapest, 12–14 June.

Baberina, K. (2010), 'Nadelenie polnomochiiami glav sub"ektov RF: modeli, tendentsii, vektory' [Empowerment of the heads of the federal subjects of the Russian Federation: models, trends, vectors], *Ars administrandi*, 4: 56–60, <http://www.ars-administrandi.comarticleBaberina_2010_4.pdf> (last accessed 3 May 2015).

Badie, B. (1992), *The Imported State: The Westernization of the Political Order*, Palo Alto: Stanford University Press.

Baker, W. and J. Oneal (2001), 'Patriotism or opinion leadership? The nature and origins of the "rally 'round the flag" effect', *Journal of Conflict Resolution*, 45, 4: 661–87.

Balzer, H. (2014), 'The Ukraine invasion and public opinion', *Georgetown Journal of International Affairs*, 15, 2, <http://journal.georgetown.edu/spotlight-on-16-1-inequality-the-ukraine-invasion-and-public-opinion> (last accessed 13 May 2015).

Barghoorn, F. (1956), *Soviet Russian Nationalism*, Westport: Greenwood Press.

Barghoorn, F. (1980), 'Four faces of Soviet Russian ethnocentrism', in E. Allworth, ed., *Ethnic Russia in the USSR*, New York: Pergamon Press, pp. 55–66.

Barkashov, A. (1993), 'Natsionalizm ili patriotizm? O neizbezhnosti natsional'noi revoliutsii' [Nationalism or patriotism? On the inevitability of a national revolution], *Russkii poriadok*, 2: 1–2.

Barry, E. (2014), 'Foes of America in Russia crave rupture in ties', *The New York Times*, 15 March, <http://www.nytimes.com/2014/03/16/world/europe/foes-of-america-in-russia-crave-rupture-in-ties.html?smid=tw-share&_r=0> (last accessed 19 March 2014).

Barsukova, S. and K. Diufi [C. Duffy] (2013), 'Vospriiatie rynka i patriotizm v sovremennom rossiiskom biznese' [The understanding of the market and patriotism in Russian business today], *Russkii mir*, 22, 4: 40–60, <http://ecsocman.hse.ru/mags/mirros/2013-22-4/96383880.html> (last accessed 7 March 2015).

BBC (2000), 'Interview to "BBC breakfast with Frost"', 5 March, <http://en.kremlin.ru/events/president/transcripts/24194> (last accessed 30 April 2015).

BBC (2012), 'V Rossii poiavitsia "rossiiskaia grazhdanskaia natsiia"' [A

'Russian civic nation' is appearing in Russia], 15 November, <http://www.bbc.co.uk/russian/russia/2012/11/121115_russia_ethnic_strategy> (last accessed 10 February 2015).

Becker, J. and S. L. Myers (2014), 'Putin's friend profits in purge of schoolbooks', *The New York Times*, 1 November, <http://www.nytimes.com/2014/11/02/world/europe/putins-friend-profits-in-purge-of-schoolbooks.html> (last accessed 30 April 2015).

Beglov, A. (2014), 'Eschatological expectations in post-Soviet Russia: historical context and modes of interpretation', in K. Tolstaya, ed., *Orthodox Paradoxes: Heterogeneities and Complexities in Contemporary Russian Orthodoxy*, Leiden: Brill, pp. 106–33.

Beissinger, M. (2005), 'Pereosmyslenie imperii posle raspada Sovetskogo soiuza' [Rethinking empire in the wake of the collapse of the Soviet Union], *Ab Imperio*, 3: 35–88.

Belov, A. (2005), 'Rossiia nikogda ne byla pravoslavnoi stranoi. Interv'iu s Vladimirom Avdeevym' [Russia has never been an Orthodox country: an interview with Vladimir Avdeev], *Portal-Credo.ru*, 11 January, <http://portal-credo.ru/site/?act=news&id=29897&topic=310> (last accessed 25 January 2015).

Bergesen, A. and M. Herman (1998), 'Immigration, race, and riot: the 1992 Los Angeles uprising', *American Sociological Review*, 63, 1: 39–54.

Beskov, A. (2014), 'Paradoksy russkogo neoiazychestva' [Paradoxes of Russian neopaganism], *Colloquium Heptaplomeres*, 1: 11–24.

Bessudnov, A. (2014), 'Skol'ko gastarbaiterov v Rossii?' [How many labour migrants are there in Russia?], *Slon*, <http://slon.ru/russia/skolko_gastarbayterov_v_rossii-870263.xhtml> (last accessed 31 July 2014).

Bevelander, P. and J. Otterbeck (2010), 'Young people's attitudes towards Muslims in Sweden', *Ethnic and Racial Studies*, 33, 3: 404–25.

Biktimirova, N. (2014), 'Tatarstantsam ustroili Krym na Volge' [Tatarstan residents set up Crimea on the Volga River], *Moskovskii Komsomolets Kazan'*, 7 April, <http://kazan.mk.ru/article/2014/04/07/1009967-tatarstantsam-ustroili-kryim-na-volge.html> (last accessed 13 May 2015).

Billig, M. (1995), *Banal Nationalism*, London: SAGE.

Billington, J. (2004), *Russia in Search of Itself*, Washington, DC: Woodrow Wilson Center Press.

Bilodeau, A. and N. Fadol (2011), 'The roots of contemporary attitudes toward immigration in Australia: contextual and individual-level influences', *Ethnic and Racial Studies*, 34, 6: 1,088–1,109.

Blumer, H. (1958), 'Race prejudice as a sense of group position', *Pacific Sociological Review*, 1, 1: 3–7.

Bobo, L. and V. L. Hutchings (1996), 'Perceptions of racial group competition: extending Blumer's theory of group position to a multiracial social context', *American Sociological Review*, 61, 6: 951–72.

Bodin, P.-A. (2009), *Language, Canonization and Holy Foolishness: Studies in Post-Soviet Russian Culture and the Orthodox Tradition*, Stockholm: Stockholm University.

Böltken, F. (2003), 'Social distance and physical proximity: day-to-day attitudes and experiences of foreigners and Germans living in the same residential areas', in R. Alba, P. Schmidt and M. Wasmer, eds, *Germans or Foreigners? Attitudes toward Ethnic Minorities in Post-Reunification Germany*, New York: Palgrave Macmillan, pp. 233–54.

Brandenberger, D. (2002), *National Bolshevism: Stalinist Mass Culture and the Formation of Modern Russian National Identity 1931–1956*, Cambridge: Harvard University Press.

Breslauer, G. and C. Dale (1997), 'Boris Yeltsin and the invention of a Russian nation-state', *Post-Soviet Affairs*, 13, 4: 303–32.

Breuilly, J. (1993), *Nationalism and the State*, Manchester: Manchester University Press.

Brubaker, R. (1996), *Nationalism Reframed: Nationhood and the National Question in the New Europe*, Cambridge: Cambridge University Press.

Brubaker, R. (1998), *Citizenship and Nationhood in France and Germany*, Cambridge: Harvard University Press.

Brubaker, R. (2002), 'Ethnicity without groups', *Archives Européennes de Sociologie*, 43, 2: 163–89.

Brubaker, R., M. Feischmidt, J. Fox and L. Grancea (2006), *Nationalist Politics and Everyday Ethnicity in a Transylvanian Town*, Princeton: Princeton University Press.

Brudny, Y. M. (2000), *Reinventing Russia: Russian Nationalism and the Soviet State 1953–1991*, Cambridge: Harvard University Press.

Bryanski, G. (2012), 'Russian patriarch calls Putin era "miracle of God"', *Reuters*, 8 February, <http://uk.reuters.com/article/2012/02/08/uk-russia-putin-religion-idUKTRE81722Y20120208> (last accessed 24 April 2015).

Burrett, T. (2011), *Television and Presidential Power in Putin's Russia*, London: Routledge.

Bykov, P., T. Gurova and Iu. Polunin (2011), 'V shage ot ekonomicheskogo natsionalizma' [One step from economic nationalism], *Ekspert*, 2

May, <http://expert.ru/expert/2011/17/v-shage-ot-ekonomicheskogo-natsionalizma> (last accessed 25 April 2015).
Byzov, L. (2014), 'Novoe konservativnoe bol'shinstvo kak sotsial'no-politicheskii fenomen' [The new conservative majority as a social-political phenomenon], *Mir Rossii*, 23, 4: 6–34.
Careja, R. and H. J. Andres (2013), 'Needed but not liked – the impact of labor market policies on natives' opinions about immigration', *International Migration Review*, 47, 2: 374–413.
Carrère d'Encausse, H. (1993), *The End of the Soviet Empire: The Triumph of the Nations*, New York: Basic Books.
Carter, S. (1990), *Russian Nationalism: Yesterday, Today, Tomorrow*, New York: St Martin's Press.
Cenusa, D., M. Emerson, T. Kovziridse and V. Movchan (2014), 'Russia's punitive trade policy measures towards Ukraine, Moldova and Georgia', *CEPS Working Document*, 400, <http://www.ceps.eu/publications/russia's-punitive-trade-policy-measures-towards-ukraine-moldova-and-georgia> (last accessed 25 April 2015).
Cerny, P. G. (1997), 'Paradoxes of the competition state: the dynamics of political globalisation', *Government and Opposition*, 32, 2: 251–74.
Cerny, P. G. (2010), *Rethinking World Politics: A Theory of Transnational Pluralism*, Oxford: Oxford University Press.
Chadaev, A. (2006), *Putin. Ego ideologiia* [Putin: His Ideology], Moscow: Evropa.
Chaplin, V. (2012), 'Russkii narod nuzhdaetsia v sistemnoi podderzhke' [The Russian people is in need of a support system], *Vsemirnyi Narodnyi Russkii Sobor*, 13 November, <http://www.vrns.ru/news/721/#.VNn53BqDtBF> (last accessed 5 February 2015).
Chelnokov, A. (2011), '150 dnei do zakhvata Kremlia' [150 days before the Kremlin is taken], *Sovershenno sekretno*, 2 March, <http://www.sovsekretno.ru/magazines/article/2725> (last accessed 25 January 2015).
Chubais, A. (2003), 'Missiia Rossii v XXIom veke' [Russia's mission in the 21st century], *Nezavisimaia gazeta*, 1 October, <http://www.ng.ru/ideas/2003-10-01/1_mission.html> (last accessed 7 March 2015).
Coalson, R. (2014), 'Putin pledges to protect all ethnic Russians anywhere. So, where are they?', *Radio Free Europe/Radio Liberty*, 10 April, <http://www.rferl.org/content/russia-ethnic-russification-baltics-kazakhstan-soviet/25328281.html> (last accessed 14 July 2014).

Colton, T. and H. E. Hale (2009), 'The Putin vote: presidential electorates in a hybrid regime', *Slavic Review*, 68, 3: 473–503.
Colton, T. and H. E. Hale (2014), 'Putin's uneasy return and hybrid regime stability: the 2012 Russian Election Studies survey', *Problems of Post-Communism*, 61, 2: 3–22.
Cooley, A. (2005), *Logics of Hierarchy: The Organization of Empires, States, and Military Occupations*, Ithaca: Cornell University Press.
Cottiero, C., K. Kucharski, E. Olimpieva and R. W. Orttung (2015), 'War of words: the impact of Russian state television on the Russian internet', *Nationalities Papers*, <http://www.tandfonline.com/doi/abs/10.1080/00905992.2015.1013527#.VTO1DpNna8g> (last accessed 18 April 2015).
Curanovic, A. (2012), *The Religious Factor in Russia's Foreign Policy*, London: Routledge.
Dawisha, K. (2014), *Putin's Kleptocracy: Who Owns Russia?*, New York: Simon & Schuster.
Deliagin, M. (2009), *Rossiia dlia rossiian* [Russia for Russian Citizens], Moscow: Eksmo.
Deliagin, M. (2015), 'Rossii nuzhna politika razvitiia' [Russia needs a development policy], 21 January, <http://delyagin.ru/articles/84134-rossii-nuzhna-politika-razvitiya.html> (last accessed 7 March 2015).
Demintseva, E., ed. (2013), *Rasizm, ksenofobiia, diskriminatsiia. Kakimi my ikh uvideli . . .* [Racism, Xenophobia, Discrimination: How We Have Seen Them . . .], Moscow: Novoe literaturnoe obozrenie.
Den' (1992), 'Obrashchenie k grazhdanam Rossii orgkomiteta fronta natsional'nogo spaseniia' [An appeal to the citizens of Russia from the organisational committee of the National Salvation Front], 11–17 October, 1.
Deutsch, K. (1966), *Nationalism and Social Communication: An Inquiry into the Foundations of Nationalism*, Cambridge: MIT Press.
Divov, O. (2000), *Vybrakovka* [Culling], Moscow: Eksmo.
Dobroslav [Dobrovolskii, A.] (2010), 'Materialy interv'iu' [Interview materials], in R. Shizhenskii, ed., *'Rus' iazycheskaia': etnicheskaia religioznost' v Rossii i Ukraine XX–XXI vv.* ['Pagan Rus': Ethnic Religiosity in Russia and Ukraine in the 20th–21st Centuries], Nizhnii Novgorod: NGPU, pp. 77–8.
DPNI (2009), 'Programma DPNI' [Programme of the DPNI], <http://www.dpni.org/articles/dokumenti/13255> (last accessed 7 March 2015).
DPNI (2010), 'Deklaratsiia russkikh natsional'nykh organizatsii' [Declaration of Russian nationalist organisations], 16 December,

<http://www.dpni.org/articles/novosti_dp/18928> (last accessed 1 March 2015).
Dubin, B. (2003a), 'Zapad dlia vnutrennego potrebleniia' [The West for domestic consumption], *Kosmopolis*, 1: 137–53.
Dubin, B. (2003b), 'Stalin i drugie: figury vysshei vlasti v obshchestvennom mnenii sovremennoi Rossii' [Stalin and others: figures of supreme power in contemporary Russian public opinion], *Polit.ru*, 26 February, <http://polit.ru/article/2003/02/26/585074> (last accessed 20 April 2015).
Dubin, B. (2014), 'Natsionalizm v Rossii: obshchestvennye nastroeniia i gosudarstvennaia politika' [Nationalism in Russia: public mood and state policies], *Pro et Contra*, 18, 1–2: 6–18.
Dugin, A. (1997), *Osnovy geopolitiki. Geopoliticheskoe budushchee Rossii* [The Fundamentals of Geopolitics: The Geopolitical Future of Russia], Moscow: Arktogeia.
Dugin, A. (1999), *Nash put'. Strategicheskie perspektivy razvitiia Rossii v XXI veke* [Our path: strategic perspectives on the development of Russia in the 21st century], Moscow: Arktogeia.
Dugin, A. (2013), 'Tretii put' i tret'ia sila. O geopolitike evraziiskoi integratsii' [The third way and third power: on the geopolitics of Eurasian integration], *Izborskii klub*, 29 May, <http://www.dynacon.ru/content/articles/1300/> (last accessed 20 April 2015).
Duncan, P. J. S. (2000), *Russian Messianism: Third Rome, Revolution, Communism and After*, London: Routledge.
Dunlop, J. B. (1983), *The Faces of Contemporary Russian Nationalism*, Princeton: Princeton University Press.
Dunlop, J. B. (1985), *The New Russian Nationalism*, New York: Praeger.
Dunlop, J. B. (1993), *The Rise of Russia and the Fall of the Soviet Empire*, Princeton: Princeton University Press.
Dushenov, K. (2006), 'Vystuplenie na otkrytom sobranii Severo-zapadnogo otdeleniia Soiuza Russkogo Naroda 25 marta 2006 goda' [Speech at an open meeting of the North-Western section of the Union of the Russian People on 25 March 2006], in *Poka my russkie* [While We Are Russians], film, directed by K. Dushenov, Russia: Pole Kulikovo.
Ehl, M. (2013), 'The nationalist paradox', *Transitions Online*, 5 March, <http://www.tol.org/client/article/23637-central-europe-economy-jobs-nationalism.html> (last accessed 13 May 2015).
Ekho Moskvy (2011), 'Vstrecha Vladimira Putina s literatorami' [Vladimir Putin meets with men of letters], 28 September, <http://

echo.msk.ru/blog/echomsk/816060-echo> (last accessed 25 April 2015).
Ekonomicheskie izvestiia (2014), 'Kak Putin sdal Rossiiu kitaitsam' [How Putin handed over Russia to the Chinese], 15 October, <http://news.eizvestia.com/news_abroad/full/723-kak-putin-sdal-rossiyu-kitajcam-inosmi> (last accessed 7 March 2015).
El'tsin, B. (1994), 'Poslanie Prezidenta Rossii Borisa El'tsina Federal'nomu Sobraniiu RF: "Ob ukreplenii Rossiiskogo Gosudarstva"' [Russian President Boris Eltsin's address to the Federal Assembly: 'On the consolidation of the Russian state'], *Intelros.ru*, 24 February, <http://www.intelros.ru/2007/02/04/poslanija_prezidenta_rossii_borisa_elcina_federalnomu_sobraniju_rf_1994_god.html> (last accessed 7 March 2015).
Elvestad, C. and F. Nilssen (2010), 'Restricting imports to the Russian food market: simply an act of protectionism?', *Post-Communist Economies*, 22, 3: 267–82.
Engelstein, L. (2009), *Slavophile Empire: Imperial Russia's Illiberal Path*, Ithaca: Cornell University Press.
Epstein, M. (2013), *Religiia posle ateizma* [Religion after Atheism], Moscow: AST Press.
Escandell, X. and A. M. Ceobanu (2009), 'When contact with immigrants matters: threat, interethnic attitudes and foreign exclusionism in Spain's *comunidades autónomas*', *Ethnic and Racial Studies*, 32, 1: 44–69.
Fagan, G. (2014), 'Russia: religion, schools and the right to choose', *Forum 18 News Service*, 20 January, <http://www.forum18.org/archive.php?article_id=1917&pdf=Y> (last accessed 30 April 2015).
Falomir-Pichastor, J. M. and N. S. Frederic (2013), 'The dark side of heterogeneous ingroup identities: national identification, perceived threat, and prejudice against immigrants', *Journal of Experimental Social Psychology*, 49, 1: 72–9.
Federal'naia sluzhba gosudarstvennoi statistiki (n.d.), *Ob itogakh Vserossiiskoi perepisi 2010* [On the results of the all-Russian census of 2010], <http://www.gks.ru/free_doc/new_site/perepis2010/croc/perepis_itogi1612.htm> (last accessed 16 January 2015).
Federal'naia tselevaia programma (2013), 'Ukreplenie edinstva rossiiskoi natsii i etnokul'turnoe razvitie narodov Rossii (2014–2020 gg)' [Strengthening of the unity of the Russian nation and the ethno-cultural development of the peoples of Russia (2014–2020)], *Government.ru*, 20 August, <http://government.ru/media/files/41d4862001ad2a4e5359.pdf> (last accessed 10 February 2015).

Federal'nyi zakon (1999), 'O gosudarstvennoi politike Rossiiskoi Federatsii v otnoshenii sootechestvennikov za rubezhom' [On the state policy of the Russian Federation towards compatriots abroad], N 99-FZ, 24 May, <http://base.consultant.ru/cons/cgi/online.cgi?req=doc;base=LAW;n=150465> (last accessed 18 April 2015).

Feifer, G. (2014), 'Ukraine's conflict is shaping a new national identity', *Global Post*, 25 September, <http://www.globalpost.com/dispatch/news/regions/europe/140925/ukraine-kyiv-russia-new-national-identity> (last accessed 12 February 2015).

Fetzer, J. S. (2000), *Public Attitudes toward Immigration in the United States, France and Germany*, Cambridge: Cambridge University Press.

Filina, O. (2013), 'U nas obshchestvo dograzhdanskoi kul'tury' [We have a society of pre-civic culture], *Kommersant*, 19 August, <http://www.kommersant.ru/doc/2244366> (last accessed 8 May 2014).

Flood, C., S. Hutchings, G. Miazhevich and H. Nickels (2012), *Islam, Security and Television*, Basingstoke: Palgrave.

FOM (2014), 'Rossiiskoe obshchestvennoe mnenie o Kryme' [Russian public opinion about Crimea], Fond obshchestvennoe mnenie, 17 March, <http://fom.ru/Mir/11401> (last accessed 2 May 2015).

Fursov, A. (2013), 'The current world crisis', *The International Schiller Institute*, 13 April, <http://newparadigm.schillerinstitute.com/media/andrey-fursov-the-current-world-crisis-its-social-nature-and-challenge-to-social-science> (last accessed 7 March 2015).

Fursov, A. (2014), 'Chtoby seichas natsionalizirovat' Tsentrobank – eto nuzhno byt' samoubiitsei' [To nationalize the Central Bank now – one has to be suicidal], *Andrei Fursov*, 18 December, <http://andreyfursov.ru/news/chtoby_sejchas_nacionalizirovat_centrobank_ehto_nuzhno_byt_samoubijcej/2014-12-19-389> (last accessed 7 March 2015).

Gaidar, E. (2006), *Gibel' imperii: uroki dlia sovremennoi Rossii* [Collapse of an Empire: Lessons for Modern Russia], Moscow: ROSSPEN.

Galkina, E. (2012), 'Russkii natsionalizm nachala XXI veka i sovetskoe nasledie' [Russian nationalism in the early 21st century and the Soviet legacy], in I. Glushchenko, B. Kagarlitskii and V. Kurennoi, eds, *SSSR: Zhizn' posle smerti* [The USSR: Life after Death], Moscow: Izdatel'skii dom Vysshei shkoly ekonomiki, pp. 80–8.

Gavrov, S. (2004), *Modernizatsiia vo imia imperii. Sotsiokul'turnye aspekty modernizatsionnykh protsessov v Rossii* [Modernisation in the Name of Empire: Socio-cultural Aspects of the Modernising Processes in Russia], Moscow: URSS.

Gellner, E. (1983), *Nations and Nationalism*, Oxford: Blackwell.

Gershtein, E. (1941), 'Lermontov i "kruzhok shestnadtsati"' [Lermontov and the 'circle of sixteen'], in N. Brodskii, V. Kirpotin, E. Mikhailov and A. Tolstoi, eds, *Zhizn' i tvorchestvo M. Iu. Lermontova* [The Life and Work of M. Iu. Lermontov], Moscow: OGIZ, pp. 77–124.

Gessen, M. (2013), *The Man without a Face: The Unlikely Rise of Vladimir Putin*, New York: Riverhead Trade.

Gevorkian, E. (2000), *Vremena negodiaev* [Age of Scoundrels], Moscow: AST.

Gilman, M. (2012), 'Russia overtakes Portugal – and Spain is next', *Moscow Times*, 9 October, <http://www.themoscowtimes.com/opinion/article/russia-overtakes-portugal--and-spain-is-next/469517.html> (last accessed 18 April 2015).

Glaz'ev, S. (2011), 'O strategii modernizatsii i razvitiia ekonomiki Rossii v usloviiakh global'noi depressii' [On the strategy for modernizing and developing Russia during the global depression], *Sergei Glaz'ev*, 17 May, <http://www.glazev.ru/econom_polit/269/> (last accessed 7 March 2015).

Glaz'ev, S. (2014), 'Nuzhno opirat'sia na sobstvennye sily' [We must rely on our own strength], *Profil'*, 12 May, <http://www.glazev.ru/econom_polit/359/> (last accessed 7 March 2015).

Glikin, M. and N. Kostenko (2010), 'Chudo vozmozhno' [A miracle can happen], *Vedomosti*, 15 February, <http://www.vedomosti.ru/newspaper/articles/2010/02/15/vladislav-surkov-zovet-chitatelej-vedomostej-proektirovat-kremnievuyu-dolinu> (last accessed 14 May 2015).

Goble, P. (2014), 'The "immigrant threat" returns to Russian media', *The Interpreter*, 14 July, <http://www.interpretermag.com/the-immigrant-threat-theme-returns-to-russian-media> (last accessed 14 August 2014).

Gorodetskaia, N. (2012a), 'Natsional'noi politike dali Sovet' [The nationalities policy was granted a Council], *Kommersant*, 8 June, <http://www.kommersant.ru/doc/1953659> (last accessed 22 May 2014).

Gorodetskaia, N. (2012b), 'Russkii narod probuetsia na ob"ediniaiushchuiu rol"' [The Russian nation is auditioning for a unifying role], *Kommersant*, 18 October, <http://www.kommersant.ru/doc/2047014> (last accessed 22 May 2014).

Gorodetskaia, N. (2013), 'Litsa rossiiskoi natsional'nosti' [Faces of Russian nationality], *Kommersant*, 26 August, <http://kommersant.ru/doc/2263724> (last accessed 22 May 2014).

Gorshenina, S. (2014), *L'invention de l'Asie centrale* [The Invention of Central Asia], Geneva: Droz.

Gosudarstvennaia programma 'Patrioticheskoe vospitanie grazhdan RF na 2001–2005 gody' [State programme on 'Patriotic upbringing of the citizens of the Russian Federation for 2001–2005] (2001), *Rossiiskaia gazeta*, 10 February, <http://www.rg.ru/oficial/doc/postan_rf/122_1.Shtm> (last accessed 13 May 2015).

Greene, S. A. (2013), 'Beyond Bolotnaya: bridging old and new in Russia's election protest movement', *Problems of Post-Communism*, 60, 2: 40–52.

Greenfeld, L. (1992), *Nationalism: Five Roads to Modernity*, Cambridge: Harvard University Press.

Grigor'eva, K., I. Kuznetsov, V. Mukomel' and A. Rocheva (2010), 'Sotsial'naia sreda rossiiskikh gorodov v vospriiatii "gastarbaiterov" i mestnogo naseleniia' [The Social Environment of Russian Towns in the Perceptions of 'Guest Workers' and the Local Population], Moscow: Institut sotsiologii RAN.

Grimmer-Solem, E. (2015), 'The mature limited access order at the doorstep: imperial Germany and contemporary China in transition', *Constitutional Political Economy*, 26, 1: 103–20.

Grove, T. (2011), 'Insight: in Russia, nationalists turn on Putin', *Reuters*, 1 December, <http://www.reuters.com/article/2011/12/01/us-russia-nationalism-idUSTRE7B013220111201> (last accessed 27 May 2014).

Gryzlov, B. (2004), 'U Edinoi Rossii kryl'ev ne budet' [United Russia will not have wings], *Russkaia liniia*, 23 April, <http://www.rusk.ru/st.php?idar=150593> (last accessed 30 April 2015).

Gryzlov, B. (2007), 'Sovremennyi rossiiskii konservatizm' [Contemporary Russian conservatism], *Tsentr sotsial'no-konservativnoi politiki*, 15 December, <http://wayback.archive.org/web/20090123083528/http://www.cscp-pfo.ru/index.php?option=com_content&task=view&id=187&Itemid=34> (last accessed 11 May 2015).

Gudkov, L. (2002), 'Russkii neotraditsionalizm i soprotivlenie peremenam' [Russian neo-traditionalism and resistance to changes], in V. Malakhov and V. Tishkov, eds, *Mul'tikul'turalism i transformatsiia postsovetskikh obshchestv* [Multiculturalism and the Transformation of Post-Soviet Societies], Moscow: Nauka, pp. 124–47.

Gulyga, A. (1995), *Russkaia ideia i ee tvortsy* [The Russian Idea and Its Creators], Moscow: Soratnik.

Hafez, K., ed. (2000), *Islam and the West in the Mass Media: Fragmented Images in a Globalizing World*, Cresskill: Hampton Press.

Hale, H. E. (2006), *Why Not Parties in Russia: Democracy, Federalism, and the State*, New York: Cambridge University Press.

Hale, H. E. (2008), *The Foundations of Ethnic Politics: Separatism of States and Nations in Eurasia and the World*, New York: Cambridge University Press.

Hale, H. E. (2014), 'The impact of anti-migrant nationalism on non-democratic regimes: experimental evidence from the Russian case', paper presented at the Association for Slavic, East European, and Eurasian Studies (ASEEES) Convention, San Antonio, 20–23 November.

Hale, H. E. (2015), *Patronal Politics: Eurasian Regime Dynamics in Comparative Perspective*, New York: Cambridge University Press.

Hale, H. E. and T. Colton (2010), 'Russians and the Putin–Medvedev "tandemocracy": a survey-based portrait of the 2007–08 election season', *Problems of Post-Communism*, 57, 2: 3–20.

Hanson, S. (2003), 'Instrumental democracy: the end of ideology and the decline of Russian political parties', in V. Hesli and W. Reisinger, eds, *Elections, Parties, and the Future of Russia*, Cambridge: Cambridge University Press, pp. 163–85.

Hauner, M. (1992), *What is Asia for Us: Russia's Asian Heartland Yesterday and Today*, London: Routledge.

Hayes, B. C. and L. Dowds (2006), 'Social contact, cultural marginality or economic self-interest? Attitudes towards migrants in Northern Ireland', *Journal of Ethnic and Migration Studies*, 32, 3: 455–76.

Hechter, M. (1995), 'Explaining nationalist violence', *Nations and Nationalism*, 1, 1: 53–68.

Hechter, M. (2000), *Containing Nationalism*, Oxford: Oxford University Press.

Helleiner, E. and A. Pickel, eds (2005), *Economic Nationalism in a Globalizing World*, Ithaca: Cornell University Press.

Hill, F. (1998), *In Search of Great Russia: Elites, Ideas, Power, the State, and the Pre-Revolutionary Past in the New Russia, 1991–1996*, doctoral dissertation, Cambridge: Harvard University.

Hodnett, G. (1979), *Leadership in the Soviet National Republics*, Oakville: Mosaic Press.

Hopf, T. (2013), 'Common-sense constructivism and hegemony in world politics', *International Organization*, 67, 2: 317–54.

Horowitz, D. (1985), *Ethnic Groups in Conflict*. Berkeley: University of California Press.

Horvath, R. (2014), 'Russkii Obraz and the politics of "managed nationalism"', *Nationalities Papers*, 42, 3: 469–88.

Hosking, G. (1998), 'Empire and nation-building in late Imperial

Russia', in G. Hosking and R. Service, eds, *Russian Nationalism, Past and Present*, London: Macmillan, pp. 19–33.

Hugick, L. and M. Engle (2003), 'Rally events and presidential approval: an update', paper presented at the annual meeting of the American Association for Public Opinion Research, Nashville, 16 August, <http://www.allacademic.com/meta/p116394_index.html> (last accessed 12 March 2015).

Huntington, S. (2003), *Tret'ia volna. Demokratizatsiia v kontse XX veka* [The Third Wave: Democratisation in the Late Twentieth Century], Moscow: ROSSPEN.

Hutchings, S. and N. Rulyova (2009), *Television and Culture in Putin's Russia: Remote Control*, London: Routledge.

Hutchings, S. and V. Tolz (2012), 'Fault lines in Russia's discourse of nation: television coverage of the December 2010 Moscow riots', *Slavic Review*, 71, 4: 873–99.

Ichino, N. and N. L. Nathan (2013), 'Crossing the line: local ethnic geography and voting in Ghana', *American Political Science Review*, 107, 2: 344–61.

Ingram, A. (1999), '"A nation split into fragments": the Congress of Russian Communities and Russian nationalist ideology', *Europe–Asia Studies*, 51, 4: 687–704.

Insider (2014), 'Konservatory na autsorsinge. Kto formiruet kremlevskuiu ideologiiu' [Conservatives on outsourcing: who forms the Kremlin's ideology], *The Insider*, 9 October, <http://theins.ru/politika/1797> (last accessed 30 April 2015).

Istarkhov, V. (1999), *Udar russkikh bogov* [The Strike of the Russian Gods], Kaluga: Oblizdat.

Itskovich, S. (2002), 'Kem formiruetsia gosudarstvennaia ideologiia Rossii' [Who forms the state ideology of Russia], *Vestnik*, 17 January, <http://www.vestnik.com/issues/2002/0117/win/itskovich.htm> (last accessed 27 April 2015).

Iur'ev, M. (2013), 'Novyi ekonomicheskii natsionalizm' [The new economic nationalism], *Evraziiskoe obozrenie*, 6, <http://evrazia.info/article/377> (last accessed 24 April 2015).

Iurgens, I., ed. (2011a), *Obretenie budushchego. Strategiia 2012* [Finding the Future: The Strategy for 2012], Moscow: INSOR, <http://www.insor-russia.ru/files/Finding_of_the_Future%20.FULL_.pdf> (last accessed 30 April 2015).

Iurgens, I., ed. (2011b), *ODKB: otvetstvennaia bezopasnost'* [CSTO: Responsible Security], Moscow: INSOR, <http://www.insor-russia.ru/files/ODKB.pdf> (last accessed 30 April 2015).

Ivanov, M., N. Korchenkova and S. Goriashko (2014), 'Odin v bol'shinstve' [One in majority], *Kommersant*, 26 December, <http://www.kommersant.ru/doc/2641017> (last accessed 30 April 2015).
Izvestiia (2002), 'Anatomiia russkoi dushi' [Anatomy of the Russian soul], 15 April, <http://izvestia.ru/news/260866> (last accessed 1 May 2015).
Jackson, R. (2005), *Writing the War on Terrorism: Language, Politics and Counter-Terrorism*, Manchester: Manchester University Press.
Jackson, R. (2007), 'Constructing enemies: "Islamic terrorism" in political and academic discourse', *Government and Opposition*, 42, 3: 394–426.
James, P. and M. Steger (2013), 'Levels of subjective globalization: ideologies, imaginaries, ontologies', *Perspectives on Global Development and Technology*, 12, 1–2: 17–40.
Kam, C. D. and J. M. Ramos (2008), 'Joining and leaving the rally: understanding the surge and decline in presidential approval following 9/11', *Public Opinion Quarterly*, 72, 4: 619–50.
Kangas, A. (2013), 'Market civilisation meets economic nationalism: the discourse of nation in Russia's modernisation', *Nations and Nationalism*, 19, 3: 572–91.
Kappeler, A. (1993), *Russland als Vielvölkerreich: Entstehung, Geschichte, Zerfall*, Munich: C. H. Beck.
Kappeler, A. (2001), *The Russian Empire: A Multi-Ethnic History*, Harlow: Longman.
Kara-Murza, A. (1999), *Kak vozmozhna Rossiia?* [How is Russia possible?], Moscow: Sovetskii sport.
Karavaev, A. (2008), 'Russkaia rech' i kul'tura v stranakh SNG (na primere Azerbaidzhana): issledovanie fonda "Nasledie Evrazii"' [Russian language and culture in the CIS countries, the case of Azerbaijan: a study by the Eurasian Heritage Foundation], *Fond 'Nasledie Evrazii'*, <http://www.fundeh.org/about/articles/40> (last accessed 18 July 2014).
Karpenko, O. (2002), 'Kak eksperty proizvodiat "etnofobiu"' [How experts produce 'ethnophobia'], in V. Voronkov, O. Karpenko and A. Osipov, eds, *Rasizm v iazyke sotsial'nykh nauk* [Racism in the Language of Social Sciences], St Petersburg: Aleteiia, pp. 23–31.
Katasonov, V. (2014), *Ekonomicheskaia teoriia slavianofilov i sovremennaia Rossiia* [The Economic Theory of Slavophiles and Contemporary Russia], Moscow: Institut russkoi tsivilizatsii.
Kaufman, S. J. (2001), *Modern Hatreds: The Symbolic Politics of Ethnic War*, Ithaca: Cornell University Press.

Khisamiev, N. and R. Coalson (2012), 'Rumblings in the republics: new Russian nationalities policy sparks outcry', *Radio Free Europe/Radio Liberty*, 1 December, <http://www.rferl.org/content/new-russian-nationalities-policy-sparks-outcry/24786140.html> (last accessed 8 June 2014).

Kholmogorov, E. (2008), 'Anatomiia raskola' [The anatomy of schism], *Anti-raskol*, 17 June, <http://www.anti-raskol.ru/pages/891> (last accessed 25 January 2015).

Khramov, A. (2013), 'Mozhet li natsionalist byt' liberalom?' [Can a nationalist be a liberal?], *Voprosy natsionalizma*, 13: 222–30.

Kichanova, V. and A. Buribaev (2013), 'Neupravliaemyi natsionalizm Surkova' [Surkov's uncontrolled nationalism], *Slon.ru*, 16 May, <http://slon.ru/russia/goryachev_ivanov_surkov_povyazannye_obrazom-941946.xhtml> (last accessed 18 November 2013).

King, R. and N. Wood, eds (2001), *Media and Migration: Construction of Mobility and Difference*, London: Routledge.

Knox, Z. (2003), 'The symphonic ideal: the Moscow Patriarchate's post-Soviet leadership', *Europe–Asia Studies*, 55, 4: 575–96.

Knox, Z. and A. Mitrofanova (2014), 'The Russian Orthodox Church', in L. Leustean, ed., *Eastern Christianity and Politics in the Twenty-First Century*, London: Routledge, pp. 38–66.

Kohn, H. (1971), *Nationalism, its Meaning and History*, New York: D. Van Nostrand.

Kolesnikov, A. (2013), 'Rukovodiashchie prikazaniia' [Marching orders], *Kommersant*, 8 May, <http://www.kommersant.ru/doc/2185440> (last accessed 30 April 2015).

Kolstø, P. (1995), *Russians in the Former Soviet Republics*, London: Hurst.

Kolstø, P. (1999), 'Territorializing diasporas: the case of Russians in the former Soviet republics', *Millennium*, 28, 3: 607–31.

Kolstø, P. (2000), *Political Construction Sites: Nation-building in Russia and the Post-Soviet States*, Boulder: Westview Press.

Kolstø, P. (2006), 'National symbols as signs of unity and division', *Ethnic and Racial Studies*, 29, 4: 676–701.

Kolstø, P. (2009), 'Sources of Russian anti-Semitism in the late nineteenth century: a socio-economic explanation', *Scando-Slavica*, 55, 1: 43–64.

Kolstø, P. (2011), 'Beyond Russia, becoming local: trajectories of adaption to the fall of the Soviet Union among ethnic Russians in the former Soviet republics', *Journal of Eurasian Studies*, 2, 2: 153–63.

Kolstø, P. (2014), 'Russia's nationalists flirt with democracy', *Journal of Democracy*, 25, 3: 120–34.

Kolstø, P. and H. Blakkisrud, eds (2004), *Nation-building and Common Values in Russia*, Lanham: Rowman & Littlefield.

Kontseptsiia gosudarstvennoi natsional'noi politiki Rossiiskoi Federatsii [The concept of state nationalities policy of the Russian Federation] (1996), <http://www.russia.edu.ru/information/legal/law/up/909/2051.php/?year=2014&today=1&month=7> (last accessed 1 June 2014).

Koopmans, R. (2013), 'Multiculturalism and immigration: a contested field in cross-national comparison', *Annual Review of Sociology*, 39: 147–69.

Koptiubenko, D., R. Badanin and M. Rubin (2014), 'Sergei Glaz'ev: Amerikantsy khotiat zapretit' dollar dlia Rossii' [Sergei Glazev: Americans want to ban the dollar for Russia], *RBK*, 14 May, <http://top.rbc.ru/economics/11/05/2014/922968.shtml> (last accessed 7 March 2015).

Koshcheev, S. and S. Afanas'ev (2013), 'Siloviki "s"eli" troianskogo konia "Medvedevskikh"' [The siloviki 'swallowed' Medvedev's Trojan horse], *Biznes online*, 8 May, <http://www.business-gazeta.ru/article/79859> (last accessed 13 May 2015).

Kozhevnikova, G. (2009), 'Radical nationalism in Russia in 2008, and efforts to counteract it', in *Xenophobia, Freedom of Conscience and Anti-Extremism in Russia in 2008*, Moscow: SOVA Center for Information and Analysis, pp. 5–42.

Kozhevnikova, G. (2010), 'Ul'trapravye tendentsii v prokremlevskikh molodezhnykh organizatsiiakh' [Ultra-right tendencies in pro-Kremlin youth organisations], in *Russkii natsionalizm mezhdu vlast'iu i oppozitsiei* [Russian Nationalism between the Authorities and the Opposition], Moscow: Panorama Centre, pp. 4–17.

Kozhevnikova, G. and A. Shekhovtsov (2009), *Radikal'nyi russkii natsionalizm: struktury, idei, litsa* [Radical Russian Nationalism: Structures, Ideas, Individuals], Moscow: SOVA Center for Information and Analysis.

Kozlov, V. and G. Tumanov (2014), 'Vskrytie BORNa' [A dissection of BORN], *Lenta.ru*, 17 February, <http://lenta.ru/articles/2014/02/17/born> (last accessed 1 March 2015).

Kremlin.ru (2014), 'Zasedanie Soveta Bezopasnosti' [Meeting of the Security Council], 22 July, <http://kremlin.ru/news/46305> (last accessed 14 May 2015).

Krusanov, P. (2000), *Ukus angela* [The Angel's Bite], St Petersburg: Amfora.

Krylov, K. (2011), 'Umeret' ili pomuchit'sia? K sporam o liberalizme, imperstve, i russkom natsionalizme' [To die or to suffer on? To the disputes on liberalism, imperialism and Russian nationalism], *Voprosy natsionalizma*, 6: 3–9.

Krylov, K. (2012), 'Erefiia kak politicheskaia realnost'' [RF-iia as a political reality], in *Russkie vopreki Putinu* [Russians in Opposition to Putin], Moscow: Algoritm, pp. 4–12.

Kudrin, A. (2013), 'Vliianie dokhodov ot eksporta neftegazovykh resursov na denezhno-kreditnuiu politiku Rossii' [The influence of oil and gas export revenues on Russia's monetary policy], *Voprosy ekonomiki*, 3: 4–19.

Kudrin, A. (2014), 'My snova stali protivnikami zapada' [We once again became enemies of the West], *Itar-Tass*, 22 July, <http://itar-tass.com/opinions/interviews/2223> (last accessed 7 March 2015).

Kuzichev, A. (2014), 'Istoriia s sanktsiiami dolgo zhit' ne budet' [The sanctions story will not last long], *Kommersant FM*, 25 July, <http://www.kommersant.ru/doc/2531867> (last accessed 7 March 2015).

Kuzmin, A. (2011), *Russkii radikal'nyi natsionalizm v sovremennoi Rossii: traditsii i evoliutsiia* [Russian Radical Nationalism in Contemporary Russia: Traditions and Evolution], Syktyvkar: SGU.

Laitin, D. D. (1991), 'The national uprisings in the Soviet Union', *World Politics*, 44, 1: 139–77.

Laitin, D. D. (1998), *Identity in Formation: The Russian-Speaking Populations in the Near Abroad*, Ithaca: Cornell University Press.

Laqueur, W. (1993), *Black Hundred: The Rise of the Extreme Right in Russia*, New York: Harper/Collins.

Laruelle, M. (1999), *L'idéologie eurasiste russe, ou comment penser l'empire* [Russian Eurasianism, or How to Think Imperial], Paris: L'Harmattan.

Laruelle, M. (2008), *Russian Eurasianism: An Ideology of Empire*, Washington, DC: Woodrow Wilson Press/Johns Hopkins University Press.

Laruelle, M. (2009a), *In the Name of the Nation: Nationalism and Politics in Contemporary Russia*, Basingstoke: Palgrave Macmillan.

Laruelle, M. (2009b), 'Inside and around the Kremlin's black box: the new nationalist think tanks in Russia', *Stockholm Papers*, <http://www.isdp.eu/images/stories/isdp-main-pdf/2009_laruelle_inside-and-around-the-kremlins-black-box.pdf> (last accessed 12 May 2015).

Laruelle, M. (2010a), 'Introduction', in M. Laruelle, ed., *Russian*

Nationalism and the National Reassertion of Russia, London: Routledge, pp. 1–10.
Laruelle, M. (2010b), 'Rethinking Russian nationalism: historical continuity, political diversity, and doctrinal fragmentation', in M. Laruelle, ed., *Russian Nationalism and the National Reassertion of Russia*, London: Routledge, pp. 13–48.
Laruelle, M. (2012a), 'Moscow's China dilemma: evolving perceptions of Russian security in Eurasia and Asia', in R. E. Bedetski and N. Swanström, eds, *Eurasia's Ascent in Energy and Geopolitics: Rivalry or Partnership for China, Russia, and Central Asia?*, London: Routledge, pp. 76–91.
Laruelle, M., ed. (2012b), *Russian Nationalism, Foreign Policy and Identity Debates in Putin's Russia: New Ideological Patterns after the Orange Revolution*, Stuttgart: ibidem-Verlag.
Laruelle, M. (2014a), 'Russkii natsionalizm kak oblast' nauchnykh issledovanii' [Russian nationalism as an object of research], *Pro et Contra*, 62, 1–2: 54–72.
Laruelle, M. (2014b), 'Alexei Navalny and the challenges in reconciling "nationalism" and "liberalism"', *Post-Soviet Affairs*, 30, 4: 276–97.
Laruelle, M. (2014c), 'Is anyone in charge of Russian nationalists fighting in Ukraine?', *Washington Post*, 26 June, <http://www.washingtonpost.com/blogs/monkey-cage/wp/2014/06/26/is-anyone-in-charge-of-russian-nationalists-fighting-in-ukraine> (last accessed 13 May 2015).
Laruelle, M. (2015a), 'The three colors of Novorossiya, or the Russian nationalist mythmaking of the Ukrainian crisis', *Post-Soviet Affairs*, doi: 10.1080/1060586X.2015.1023004.
Laruelle, M. (2015b), *The 'Russian World': Russia's Soft Power and Geopolitical Imagination*, Washington, DC: Center on Global Interests.
Lavrov, S. (2011), 'Russia in a multipolar world: implications for Russia-EU-US', speech at the Centre for Strategic and International Studies, Washington, DC, 16 July, <http://www.rusembassy.ca/ru/node/589> (last accessed 1 May 2015).
Layton, S. (1994), *Russian Literature and Empire: Conquest of the Caucasus from Pushkin to Tolstoy*, Cambridge: Cambridge University Press.
Lazarenko, I. (2013), 'Diskussiia' [Discussion], 10th Starovoitova Lecture, Higher School of Economics, Moscow, 22 November, <http://www.liberal.ru/articles/6364> (last accessed 3 May 2015).
Lebedev, S. (2007), *Russkie idei i russkoe delo. Natsional'no-*

patrioticheskoe dvizhenie v Rossii v proshlom i nastoiashchem [Russian Ideas and Russian Action: The National-Patriotic Movement in Russia in the Past and Present], St Petersburg: Aleteiia.

Lebedeva, N. and A. Tatarko (2007), 'Sotsial'no-psikhologicheskie ustanovki moskovskoi molodezhi po otnosheniiu k migrantam' [The socio-psychological attitudes of Moscow youth towards migrants], in M. Martynova and N. Lebedeva, eds, *Molodezh' Moskvy: adaptatsiia k mnogokul'turnosti* [Moscow Youth: Adaptation to Multiculturalism], Moscow: RUDN, pp. 230–73.

Leonova, A. (2004), 'Nepriiazn' k migrantam kak forma samozashchity' [Hostility towards migrants as a form of self-protection], *Otechestvennye zapiski*, 4, 2004, <http://www.strana-oz.ru/2004/4/nepriyazn-k-migrantam-kak-forma-samozashchity> (last accessed 30 April 2015).

Levada Centre (2012a), 'Rossiiane o Pussy Riot i tserkvi' [Russians on Pussy Riot and the church], 31 July, <http://www.levada.ru/31-07-2012/rossiyane-o-dele-pussy-riot> (last accessed 28 December 2014).

Levada Centre (2012b), 'Natsional'naia politika i otnoshenie k migrantam' [Nationality policy and the attitude towards migrants], 28 November, <http://www.levada.ru/28-11-2012/natsionalnaya-politika-i-otnoshenie-k-migrantam> (last accessed 16 May 2015).

Levada Centre (2013a), *Russian Public Opinion 2012–2013*, Moscow: Levada Centre.

Levada Centre (2013b), 'Otkuda rossiiane uznaiut novosti' [From where do the Russians get their news], 8 July, <http://www.levada.ru/08-07-2013/otkuda-rossiyane-uznayut-novosti> (last accessed 16 May 2015).

Levada Centre (2013c), 'Rossiiane o migrantsii i mezhnatsional'noi napriazhennosti' [Russians on migrants and inter-ethnic tension], 5 November, <http://www.levada.ru/05-11-2013/rossiyane-o-migratsii-i-mezhnatsionalnoi-napryazhennosti> (last accessed 1 March 2015).

Levada Centre (2013d), 'Rossiiane o repressivnykh zakonakh' [Russians on the repressive laws], 25 November, <http://www.levada.ru/25-11-2013/rossiyane-o-repressivnykh-zakonakh> (last accessed 28 December 2014).

Levada Centre (2014a), 'Grazhdane poverili vo vred inostrannogo usynovleniia' [Citizens have come to believe in the harm of foreign adoption], 3 February, <http://www.levada.ru/03-02-2014/grazhdane-poverili-vo-vred-inostrannogo-usynovleniya> (last accessed 28 December 2014).

Levada Centre (2014b), 'Proiskhodiashchee v Ukraine, Krymu i reaktsiia Rossii' [Developments in Ukraine, Crimea, and public responses in Russia], 26 March, <http://www.levada.ru/26-03-2014/proiskhodyashchee-v-ukraine-krymu-i-reaktsiya-rossii> (last accessed 2 May 2015).

Levada Centre (2014c), 'Pochemu rossiiane odobriaiut politiku Putina?' [Why do Russians approve of Putin's politics?], 17 July, <http://www.levada.ru/15-07-2014/pochemu-rossiyane-odobryayut-politiku-putina> (last accessed 1 March 2015).

Levada Centre (2014d), 'Otnoshenie rossiian k drugim stranam' [Russian attitudes to other countries], 6 August, <http://www.levada.ru/06-08-2014/otnoshenie-rossiyan-k-drugim-stranam> (last accessed 4 May 2015).

Levada Centre (2014e), 'Ukrainskii krizis: deistviia rukovodstva Ukrainy i Rossii' [The Ukrainian crisis: the actions of the leadership of Ukraine and Russia], 12 August, <http://www.levada.ru/12-08-2014/ukrainskii-krizis-deistviya-rukovodstva-ukrainy-i-rossii> (last accessed 4 May 2015).

Levada Centre (2014f), 'Natsionalizm, ksenofobiia i migratsiia' [Nationalism, xenophobia and migration], 26 August, <http://www.levada.ru/26-08-2014/natsionalizm-ksenofobiya-i-migratsiya> (last accessed 28 January 2015).

Levada, Iu. (1999), 'Obshchestvenno-politicheskaia situatsiia v Rossii v sentiabre 1999' [The socio-political situation in Russia in September 1999], *Polit.ru*, 12 October, <http://polit.ru/article/1999/10/12/477126> (last accessed 30 April 2015).

Levine, R. A. and D. T. Campbell (1972), *Ethnocentrism: Theories of Conflict, Ethnic Attitudes, and Group Behavior*, New York: Wiley.

Levy, C. (2008), 'It isn't magic: Putin's opponents vanish from TV', *The New York Times*, 3 June, <http://www.nytimes.com/2008/06/03/world/europe/03russia.html?pagewanted=all&_r=0> (last accessed 13 May 2015).

Levy, J. S. (1989), 'The diversionary theory of war: a critique', in M. I. Midlarsky, ed., *Handbook of War Studies*, London: Allen & Unwin, pp. 258–88.

Lichbach, M. I. (1995), *The Rebel's Dilemma*, Ann Arbor: University of Michigan Press.

Lichbach, M. I. and C. Weerasinghe (2007), 'Mobilizing for peace: majority credibility, minority power, and ethnic politics', paper presented at the 48th Annual Convention of the International Studies

Association, Chicago, 28 February, <http://citation.allacademic.com/meta/p179846_index.html> (last accessed 9 August 2014).

Lieven, D. (2005), Imperiia, istoriia i sovremennyi mirovoi poriadok [Empire, history and the contemporary world order], *Ab Imperio*, 1: 75–116.

Lipman, M. (2014), 'Meet the second-rate academic who is Vladimir Putin's culture cop', *New Republic*, 23 May, <http://www.newrepublic.com/article/117896/vladimir-medinsky-russias-culture-minister-putin-toady> (last accessed 30 April 2015).

Litoi, A. (2012), 'Ukrupnenie regionov priznano nestrategicheskim' [Enlargement of regions is considered as non-strategic], *RBK*, 28 November, <http://www.rbcdaily.ru/society/562949985220194> (last accessed 10 February 2015).

Locatelli, C. and S. Rossiaud (2011), 'Russia's oil and gas policy', *IAEE Energy Forum*, 1, <http://www.iaee.org/en/publications/fullnewsletter.aspx?id=17> (last accessed 28 April 2015).

Loginov, K. (2013), 'Kazhdomu sverchku – po shestku' [Every cricket has its own furnace], *Ekspert*, 3 December, <http://expert.ru/2013/12/3/kazhdomu-sverchku---po-shestku> (last accessed 7 March 2015).

Loginov, M. (2013), 'Teni velikikh predkov' [Shadows of the great ancestors], *Profil'*, 23 November, <http://www.profile.ru/obshchestvo/item/78064-teni-velikikh-predkov-78064> (last accessed 30 April 2015).

McAllister, I. and S. White (2008), '"It's the economy, comrade!" Parties and voters in the 2007 Russian Duma election', *Europe–Asia Studies*, 60, 6: 931–57.

McCombs, M. (1997), 'Building consensus: the news media's agenda-setting roles', *Political Communication*, 14, 4: 433–43.

McLaren, L. (2003), 'Anti-immigrant prejudice in Europe: contact, threat perception, and preferences for the exclusion of migrants', *Social Forces*, 81, 3: 909–36.

Makarkin, A. (2012), 'Russkie natsionalisty mezhdu vlast'iu i oppozitsiei' [Russian nationalists between the authorities and the opposition], *Politcom.ru*, 25 January, <http://www.politcom.ru/print.php?id=13203> (last accessed 7 March 2015).

Makarkin, A. and P. Oppenheimer (2011), 'The Russian social contract and regime legitimacy', *International Affairs*, 87, 6: 1,459–74.

Malakhov, V. (2004), 'Etnizatsiia fenomena migratsii v publichnom diskurse i institutakh: sluchai Rossii i Germanii' [The ethnicisation of the phenomenon of migration in public discourse and institutions: the cases of Russia and Germany], in T. Baraulina and O. Karpenko, eds, *Migratsiia i natsional'noe gosudarstvo* [Migration and the Nation-State], St Petersburg: Centre for Independent Social Research, pp. 85–103.

Malakhov, V. (2007), *Ponaekhali tut. . . Ocherki o natsionalizme, rasizme i kul'turnom pliuralizme* [They Are Overflowing Us. . . Notes on Nationalism, Racism and Cultural Pluralism], Moscow: Novoe literaturnoe obozrenie.

Malakhov, V. (2011), 'Vystuplenie na seminare "Vyzovy gorodskogo raznoobraziia i poisk otveta na nikh v epokhu masshtabnykh migratsii"' [Presentation at the seminar 'Challenges of urban diversity and the search for answers to them in an era of mass migration'], *Gorbachev Foundation*, 19 September, <http://www.gorby.ru/userfiles/file/malahov%281%29.pdf> (last accessed 30 April 2015).

Malakhov, V. S. (2014), 'Russia as a new immigration country: policy response and public debate', *Europe–Asia Studies*, 66, 7: 1,062–79.

Malcolm, N. (1989), 'The "Common European Home" and Soviet European policy', *International Affairs*, 65, 4: 659–76.

March, L. (2002), *The Communist Party in Post-Soviet Russia*, Manchester: Manchester University Press.

Marquand, R. (2011), 'Why Europe is turning away from multiculturalism', *Christian Science Monitor*, 4 March, <http://www.minnpost.com/christian-science-monitor/2011/03/why-europe-turning-away-multiculturalism> (last accessed 28 January 2015).

Marten, K. (2014), 'Vladimir Putin: ethnic Russian nationalist', *Washington Post*, 19 March 2014, <http://www.washingtonpost.com/blogs/monkey-cage/wp/2014/03/19/vladimir-putin-ethnic-russian-nationalist> (last accessed 10 July 2014).

Martin, T. (2001), *The Affirmative Action Empire: Nations and Nationalism in the Soviet Union, 1923–1939*, Ithaca: Cornell University Press.

Martinović, B. (2013), 'The inter-ethnic contacts of immigrants and natives in the Netherlands: a two-sided perspective', *Journal of Ethnic and Migration Studies*, 39, 1: 69–85.

Matsuzato, K. (2009), 'Inter-Orthodox relations and transborder nationalities in and around unrecognised Abkhazia and Transnistria', *Religion, State and Society*, 37, 3: 239–62.

Matsuzato, K. (2010), 'South Ossetia and the Orthodox world: official churches, the Greek Old Calendarist Movement, and the so-called Alan Diocese', *Journal of Church and State*, 52, 2: 271–97.

Mau, V. (2014), 'V ozhidanii novoi modeli rosta: sotsial'no-ekonomicheskoe razvitie Rossii v 2013 godu' (In anticipation of a new growth model: Russia's socio-economic development in 2013), *Voprosy ekonomiki*, 2: 3–42.

Mau, V. and Ia. Kuzminov, eds (2012), *Strategiia-2020: Novaia model' rosta – novaia sotsial'naia politika* [Strategy 2020: A New Growth Model, a New Social Policy], Moscow: Izdatel'skii dom 'Delo' RANKhiGS.

Medetsky, A. (2009), 'National projects moved to back seat', *Moscow Times*, 10 March, <http://www.themoscowtimes.com/article.php?id=375139> (last accessed 13 May 2015).

Medvedev, D. (2004), 'Russia will not stray from the path of reform', *Financial Times*, 20 January, p. 15.

Medvedev, D. (2008), 'Poslanie Federal'nomu Sobraniiu Rossiiskoi Federatsii' [Address to the Federal Assembly of the Russian Federation], *Kremlin.ru*, 5 November, <http://www.kremlin.ru/transcripts/1968> (last accessed 7 March 2015).

Medvedev, D. (2009), 'Poslanie Federal'nomu Sobraniiu Rossiiskoi Federatsii' [Address to the Federal Assembly of the Russian Federation], *Kremlin.ru*, 12 November, <http://www.kremlin.ru/transcripts/5979> (last accessed 7 March 2015).

Medvedev, D. (2011), 'Poslanie Prezidenta Federal'nomy Sobraniiu' [The President's Address to the Federal Assembly], *Kremlin.ru*, 22 December, <http://kremlin.ru/news/14088> (last accessed 13 August 2012).

Melvin, N. (1995), *Russians beyond Russia's Borders: The Politics of National Identity*, London: Royal Institute of International Affairs.

Mikhailin, V. (2013), 'Levye zashli v tupik' [The leftists have hit a dead-end], *Ekspert*, 8 November, <http://expert.ru/2013/11/8/levyie-idut-napravo/> (last accessed 30 April 2015).

Miller, A. (2012), 'Istoriia poniatiia "natsiia" v Rossii' [The history of the 'nation' concept in Russia], *Otechestvennye zapiski*, 1, <http://magazines.russ.ru/oz/2012/1/m22.html> (last accessed 25 April 2015).

Milov, V. (2010), 'Liberal-natsionalizm protiv fashizma' [Liberal-nationalism against fascism], *Gazeta.ru*, 20 December, <http://www.gazeta.ru/column/milov/3470929.shtml> (last accessed 4 May 2015).

Mirsky, G. I. (1997), *On Ruins of Empire: Ethnicity and Nationalism in the Former Soviet Union*, Westport: Greenwood Press.

Mitrofanova, A. (2004), *Politizatsiia 'pravoslavnogo mira'* [The Politicisation of the 'Orthodox World'], Moscow: Nauka.

Mitrofanova, A. (2005), *The Politicization of Russian Orthodoxy: Actors and Ideas*. Stuttgart: ibidem-Verlag.

Mitrofanova, A. (2012), 'Le nouveau nationalisme en Russie' [The new nationalism in Russia], *Hérodote: Revue de géographie et de géopolitique*, 144: 141–53.

Mitrokhin, N. (2003), *Russkaia partiia: dvizhenie russkikh natsionalistov v SSSR. 1953–1985* [The Russian Party: the Russian Nationalist Movement in the USSR, 1953–1985], Moscow: Novoe literaturnoe obozrenie.

Mitrokhin, N. (2005), 'Liubov' bez udovletvoreniia: Russkaia pravoslavnaia tserkov' i rossiiskaia armiia' [Love without satisfaction: the Russian Orthodox Church and the Russian army], *Journal of Power Institutions in Post-Soviet Societies*, 3, <http://www.pipss.org/document401.html> (last accessed 13 May 2015).

Morozov, A. (2015), 'Post-krymskii konsensus' [Post-Crimea consensus], *Russkii zhurnal*, 20 January, <http://russ.ru/Mirovaya-povestka/Postkrymskij-konsensus> (last accessed 7 March 2015).

Morozov, E. (2011), *The Net Delusion: The Dark Side of Internet Freedom*, New York: Public Affairs.

Moscow Times (2014), 'Supreme Court delays hearing on closure of Russian NGO Memorial', 13 November, <http://www.themoscowtimes.com/news/article/supreme-court-delays-hearing-on-closure-of-russian-ngo-memorial/511085.html> (last accessed 25 April 2015).

Motyl, A. (1990), *Sovietology, Rationality, Nationality: Coming to Grips with Nationalism in the USSR*, New York: Columbia University Press.

Motyl, A. (2004), *Puti imperii: upadok, krakh i vozrozhdenie imperskikh gosudarstv* [Imperial Ends: The Decay, Collapse and Revival of Empires], Moscow: Moskovskaia shkola politicheskikh issledovanii.

Mozgovoi, S. (2005), 'Vzaimootnosheniia armii i tserkvi v Rossiiskoi Federatsii' [The mutual relationship of army and church in the Russian Federation], *Journal of Power Institutions in Post-Soviet Societies*, 3, <http://www.pipss.org/document390.html> (last accessed 25 April 2015).

Mukomel', V. (2013), 'Rol' gosudarstva i obshchestva v produtsirovanii diskriminatsii' [The role of state and society in producing discrimination], in E. Demintseva, ed., *Rasizm, ksenofobiia, diskriminatsiia. Kakimi my ikh uvideli...* [Racism, Xenophobia, Discrimination: How We Have Seen Them...], Moscow: Novoe literaturnoe obozrenie, pp. 195–211.

Mukomel', V. and E. Pain, eds (2005), *Tolerantnost' protiv ksenofobii (zarubezhnyi i rossiiskii opyt)* [Tolerance Against Xenophobia (International and Russian Experience)], Moscow: Academia.

Natsional'nyi aktsent (2012), 'Iz Strategii natsional'noi politiki ubrali slova o gosudarstvoobrazuiushchei roli russkogo naroda' [The formulation about the state-forming role of the Russian people was removed from the Strategy on nationalities policy], 20 December, <http://nazaccent.ru/content/6293-iz-strategii-nacpolitiki-ubrali-slova-o.html> (last accessed 6 February 2015).

Nazdem.info (2010), 'Konstantin Krylov: "Luchshie demokraty poluchaiutsia iz byvshikh fashistov..."' [Konstantin Krylov: 'Former fascists make the best democrats...'], 10 May <http://nazdem.info/texts/110> (last accessed 25 April 2015).

Nechkina, M. (1982), *Dekabristy* [The Decembrists], Moscow: Nauka.

Nemenskii, O. (2012), 'Nasledie i vybor' [Heritage and choice], *Voprosy natsionalizma*, 9: 17–21.

Nemtsova, A. (2014), 'Russia's new vigilantes: how anti-immigrant passions are shaping Russia's political scene', *Foreign Policy*, 3 March, <http://foreignpolicy.com/2013/03/04/russias-new-vigilantes> (last accessed 10 March 2015).

Nepogodin, V. (2014), 'Geroi nashego vremeni' [A hero of our time], *Svobodnaia pressa*, 1 August, <http://svpressa.ru/t/94172> (last accessed 4 May 2015).

Newsland.com (2011), 'Pochemu polkovnik Kvachkov sidit v tiur'me?' [Why is Colonel Kvachkov in prison?], 30 March, <http://newsland.com/news/detail/id/666212> (last accessed 25 January 2015).

Nezavisimaia gazeta (1996), 'El'tsin o 'natsional'noi idee' [Eltsin on the 'national idea'], 13 July, p. 1.

Nikulin, P. (2014), 'Delo pravoe. Za kogo voiuiut rossiiskie neonatsisty na Donbasse' [A just cause: for whom are the Russian neo-Nazis fighting in Donbass], *Snob*, 29 August, <http://snob.ru/selected/entry/80241> (last accessed 1 March 2015).

Novaia gazeta (2014), '"Pravyi sektor" Rossii' [Russia's 'right sector'], 22 April, <http://www.novayagazeta.ru/inquests/63313.html> (last accessed 1 March 2015).

Novorossiia (2010), 'Otkrytoe obrashchenie ieroskhimonakha Rafaila 17 iiunia 2010' [Open letter from the schema-priest-monk Rafail 17 June 2010], 17 June, <http://www.novorossia.org/religia/880-otkrytoe-obrashhenie.html> (last accessed 13 May 2015).

Novorossiia (2011), 'Natsional-patrioty pod patronazhem LDPR sozdadut "Russkii Natsional'nyi Front"' [National patriots under the patronage of the LDPR create the 'Russian National Front'], 26 May, <http://www.novorossia.org/obshestvo/1502-nacional-patrioty-pod-patronazhem-ldpr-sozdadut.html> (last accessed 30 April 2015).

Ofitsial'nyi sait Moskovskogo patriarkhata (2009), 'Vystuplenie Sviateishego Patriarkha Kirilla na torzhestvennom otkrytii III Assamblei Russkogo mira' [Speech of His Holiness Patriarch Kirill at the ceremonial opening of the Third Assembly of the Russian World], 3 November, <http://www.patriarchia.ru/db/text/928446.html> (last accessed 25 January 2015).

Ofitsial'nyi sait Moskovskogo patriarkhata (2013), 'Vystuplenie Sviateishego Patriarkha Kirilla na otkrytii XVII Vsemirnogo russkogo narodnogo sobora' [Speech of His Holiness Patriarch Kirill at the opening of the Seventeenth World Russian People's Council], 31 October, <http://www.patriarchia.ru/db/text/3334783> (last accessed 25 January 2015).

Okara, A. (2007), 'Sovereign democracy: a new Russian idea or a PR project?', *Russia in Global Affairs*, 5, 3: 8–20, <http://eng.globalaffairs.ru/number/n_9123> (last accessed 7 March 2015).

Olzak, S. (1992), *The Dynamics of Ethnic Competition and Conflict*, Palo Alto: Stanford University Press.

Ommundsen, R., K. v. d. Veer, O. Yakushko and P. Ulleberg (2013), 'Exploring the relationships between fear-related xenophobia, perceptions of out-group entitativity, and social contact in Norway', *Psychological Reports: Sociocultural Issues in Psychology*, 112, 1: 109–24.

Opalev, S. (2014), 'Ukrainskie sobytiia umen'shili populiarnost' lozunga "Rossiia dlia russkikh"' [The Ukrainian events have reduced the popularity of the slogan 'Russia for Russians'], *RBK*, 23 June, <http://top.rbc.ru/society/23/06/2014/932116.shtml> (last accessed 18 April 2015).

Opredelenie rodnoi very na II rodovom veche [Definition of native belief at the 2nd Ancestral Assembly] (2012), <www.rodnovery.ru/ru.php?id=189> (last accessed 14 May 2015).

Orenstein, M. (2001), *Out of the Red: Building Capitalism and Democracy in Post-Communist Europe*, Ann Arbor: University of Michigan Press.

Orenstein, M. (2014), 'Putin's Western allies: why Europe's far right is on the Kremlin's side', *Foreign Affairs*, 25 March, <http://www.foreignaffairs.com/articles/141067/mitchell-a-orenstein/putins-western-allies> (last accessed 30 April 2015).

OSCE (n.d.), 'Elections in Ukraine', <http://www.osce.org/odihr/elections/ukraine> (last accessed 26 May 2015).

'O simvole griadushchei Rossii' [On the symbol of the coming Russia] (1993), *Russkii poriadok*, 2: 2.

Osipov, A. (2013), 'Interpretatsii sotsial'nykh neravenstv v rasovykh i etnicheskikh terminakh: v chem skhodstvo zapadnykh stran i Rossii?' [The interpretation of social inequality in racial and ethnic terms: what are the similarities between Western countries and Russia?], in E. Demintseva, ed., *Rasizm, ksenofobiia, diskriminatsiia. Kakimi my ikh uvideli...* [Racism, Xenophobia, Discrimination: How We Have Seen Them...], Moscow: Novoe literaturnoe obozrenie, pp. 139–59.

Pain, E. (2001), '"Back to the USSR?" New trends in Russian regional policy', *Demokratizatsiya*, 9, 2: 182–92.

Pain, E. (2004), *Mezhdu imperiei i natsiei* [Between Empire and Nation], Moscow: Novoe izdatel'stvo.

Pain, E. (2007), 'Rossiia mezhdu imperiei i natsiei: kontseptsii natsional'no-gosudarstvennogo ustroistva v usloviiakh krizisa grazhdanskoi identichnosti' [Russia between empire and nation: conceptions of nation-state arrangements in conditions of a crisis in civil identity], *Pro et Contra*, 3: 42–59.

Pain, E. (2008), 'Nationalism and the imperial idea in Russia: confrontation and synthesis', in M. Korinman and J. Laughland, eds, *Russia: A New Cold War?*, Portland: Valentine Mitchell, pp. 143–53.

Pain, E. (2012), 'Ot federalizma k tsivilizatsionnomu natsionalizmu: dreif etnopoliticheskoi problematiki' [From federalism to civilizational nationalism: the drift of the ethnopolitical agenda], *Kazanskii federalist*, 2: 29–42.

Pain, E. (2013), 'From protests to pogroms', *openDemocracy*, 27 August, <http://www.opendemocracy.net/od-russia/emil-pain/from-protests-to-pogroms> (last accessed 2 April 2015).

Pain, E. (2014), 'Ksenofobiia i natsionalizm v epokhu rossiiskogo bezvremen'ia' [Xenophobia and nationalism in the epoch of Russian stagnation], *Pro et Contra*, 1–2: 34–53.

Pain, E., S. Mokhov, E. Poliakov, S. Prostakov and S. Fediunin (2013), 'Etnologicheskie protsessy v zerkale Runeta' [Ethnological processes in the mirror of Runet], *Politicheskaia nauka*, 1: 133–60.

Pain, E. and S. Prostakov (2014), 'Mnogolikii russkii natsionalizm. Ideino-politicheskie raznovidnosti (2001–2014 gg)' [The many faces of Russian nationalism: ideological-political varieties (2001–2014)], *Polis*, 4: 96–113.

Papkova, I. (2011), *The Orthodox Church and Russian Politics*, New York: Oxford University Press.

Piontkovskii, A. (2014), 'Iiulskie "Buki"' ['Buks' of July], *Radio Liberty*, 19 July, <http://www.svoboda.org/content/article/25461423.html> (last accessed 7 March 2015).

Pis'mennaia, E. (2013), *Sistema Kudrina: Istoriia kliuchevogo ekonomista Putinskoi Rossii* [Kudrin's System: The Story of the Key Economist of Putin's Russia], Moscow: Mann, Ivanov, Ferber.

'Podlinnaia istoriia proekta "NS–WP"' [The true story of the 'NS–WP' project] (n.d.) <http://vk.com/note83387374_10101618> reposted on *VKontakte* 10 September 2010 (last accessed 30 April 2015).

Podosenov, S. and D. Rozanov (2014), 'Rossiiane protiv politiki' [Russians against politics], *Gazeta.ru*, 11 September, <http://www.gazeta.ru/politics/2014/10/02_a_6245977.shtml> (last accessed 13 May 2015).

Polit.ru (1999), 'Po slovam Putina, Rossiia gotova dogovarivat'sia v Chechne s kem ugodno, pri uslovii vydachi terroristov, Maskhadov "formal'no neligitimen", a tsel'iu rossiiskikh voisk i vlastei iavliaetsia likvidatsiia terrorizma i uslovii dlia ego vozrozhdeniia' [According to Putin, in Chechnya Russia is ready to negotiate with anyone, provided the extradiction of terrorists; Maskhadov is 'formally illegitimate', and the goal of Russian troops and the authorities is the liquidation of terrorism and the conditions for its revival], 21 October, <http://polit.ru/news/1999/10/21/538630> (last accessed 13 May 2015).

Polit.ru (2007), 'Putin: nekotorye tverdiat do sikh por o neobkhodimosti razdela nashei strany' [Putin: certain people still assert that it is necessary to divide our country], 4 November, <http://polit.ru/news/2007/11/04/putin> (last accessed 13 May 2015).

Polit.ru (2013), 'Tol'ko 7% rossiian schitaiut chechentsev russkimi' [Only 7% of Russians consider Chechens Russian], 10 September, <http://polit.ru/news/2013/09/10/russkie> (last accessed 13 May 2015).

Polit.ru (2014), 'Ukrainskii krizis povysil tolerantnost' rossiian k migrantam' [The Ukrainian crisis has raised the tolerance of Russians towards migrants], 27 August, <http://polit.ru/news/2014/08/27/tolerance> (last accessed 13 May 2015).

Polterovich, V. and V. Popov (2005), 'Appropriate economic policies at different stages of development', *MPRA Paper*, 2006, <http://mpra.ub.uni-muenchen.de/20066/1/MPRA_paper_20066.pdf> (last accessed 13 May 2015).

Popescu, N. (2012), 'The strange alliance of democrats and nationalists', *Journal of Democracy*, 23, 3: 46–54.

Popov, E. (2006), 'Priamye i krivye kremlevskoi ideologii' [Straight lines and curves in the Kremlin's ideology], *Novaia politika*, 20 July, <http://www.novopol.ru/text10384.html> (last accessed 13 May 2015).

Portal-Credo.ru (2005), 'Smysl russkoi voiny' [The meaning of the Russian war], 31 October, <http://portal-credo.ru/site/?act=monitor&id=7127> (last accessed 13 May 2015).

Postill, J. (2006), *Media and Nation Building: How the Iban Became Malaysian*, New York: Berghahn.

Postmes, T. and N. R. Branscombe, eds (2010), *Rediscovering Social Identity*, New York: Psychology Press.

Pozharskii, M. (2013), 'V otvete' [In charge], *Nazdem.info*, 23 April, <http://nazdem.info/texts/369> (last accessed 25 January 2015).

Prezident Rossii (2012), 'Obrazovan Sovet po mezhnatsional'nym otnosheniiam' [A Council on inter-ethnic relations is established], Kremlin.ru, 7 June, <http://kremlin.ru/events/president/news/15577> (last accessed 9 September 2015).

Pribylovskii, V. (2002), 'Neoiazycheskoe krylo v russkom natsionalizme' [The neopagan wing of Russian nationalism], *Religare*, 31 October, <http://www.religare.ru/2_490.html> (last accessed 25 January 2015).

Primakov, E. (2015), 'Ne prosto rabotat', a znat' vo imia chego' [Not only to work, but to know for what], *Rossiiskaia gazeta*, 13 January, <http://www.rg.ru/2015/01/13/primakov-site.html> (last accessed 15 January 2015).

'Prochat v glavy soveta po natsional'noi ideologii' [Tipped to head the council for national ideology] (2003), *Delovaia pressa*, 8 December, <http://www.businesspress.ru/newspaper/article_mId_33_aId_286900.html> (last accessed 25 April 2015).

Proekt: Strategiia gosudarstvennoi natsional'noi politiki Rossiiskoi Federatsii na period do 2025 goda [Project: Strategy on state nationalities policy of the Russian Federation for the period until 2025] (2012), <http://rodnaya-istoriya.ru/index.php/mejnacionalnie-otnosheniya/mejnacionalnie-otnosheniya/strategiya-gosudarstvennoie-nacionalnoie-politiki-rossiieskoie-federacii.html> (last accessed 1 February 2015).

Prokhorov, M. (2014), 'NEP 2.0' [NEP 2.0], *Kommersant*, 17 April, <http://www.kommersant.ru/doc/2453979> (last accessed 7 March 2015).

Prosvirnin, E. (2012), 'Molitva russkogo' [Russian prayer], *Sputnik i Pogrom*, 11 August, <http://sputnikipogrom.com/russia/1011/russianpraying> (last accessed 4 May 2015).

Prosvirnin, E. (2014a), 'Fokusy lzhetsa i evnukha' [The magic tricks of a liar and a eunuch], *Sputnik i Pogrom*, 17 January, <http://sputnikipogrom.com/history/8307/liberaljuggler> (last accessed 4 May 2015).

Prosvirnin, E. (2014b), 'Zachem "Sputnik i Pogrom" prodalsia Kremliu?' [Why did 'Sputnik i Pogrom' sell out to the Kremlin?], *Sputnik i*

Pogrom, 28 February, <http://sputnikipogrom.com/russia/9581/lets-work-for-our-supreme-leader-putin> (last accessed 30 April 2015).

Prosvirnin, E. (n.d.), 'Tsennosti "Sputnika i Pogroma"' [The values of 'Sputnik i Pogrom'], *Sputnik i Pogrom*, <http://sputnikipogrom.com/mustread/12442/sp-values> (last accessed 4 May 2015).

Przeworski, A. (1991), *Democracy and the Market: Political and Economic Reforms in Eastern Europe and Latin America*, New York: Cambridge University Press.

Putin, V. (1999), 'Rossiia na rubezhe tysiacheletii' [Russia on the eve of the millennium], *Nezavisimaia gazeta*, 30 December, <http://www.ng.ru/politics/1999-12-30/4_millenium.html> (last accessed 22 May 2014).

Putin, V. (2000), 'Poslanie Federal'nomu Sobraniiu Rossiiskoi Federatsii' [Address to the Federal Assembly of the Russian Federation], *Kremlin.ru*, 8 July, <http://archive.kremlin.ru/appears/2000/07/08/0000_type63372type63374type82634_28782.shtml> (last accessed 14 May 2015).

Putin, V. (2003), 'Poslanie Federal'nomu Sobraniiu Rossiiskoi Federatsii' [Address to the Federal Assembly of the Russian Federation], *Kremlin.ru*, 16 May, <http://archive.kremlin.ru/text/appears/2003/05/44623.shtml> (last accessed 13 May 2015).

Putin, V. (2005), 'Poslanie Federal'nomu Sobraniiu Rossiiskoi Federatsii' [Address to the Federal Assembly of the Russian Federation], *Kremlin.ru*, 25 April, <http://archive.kremlin.ru/text/appears/2005/04/87049.shtml> (last accessed 30 April 2015).

Putin, V. (2007a), 'Poslanie Federal'nomu Sobraniiu Rossiiskoi Federatsii' [Address to the Federal Assembly of the Russian Federation], *Kremlin.ru*, 26 April, <http://archive.kremlin.ru/appears/2007/04/26/1156_type63372type63374type82634_125339.shtml> (last accessed 22 May 2014).

Putin, V. (2007b), 'Zachem ia vozglavil spisok Edinoi Rossii' [Why I headed the United Russia party list], *Kreml.org*, 13 November, <http://www.kreml.org/media/165463628> (last accessed 30 April 2015).

Putin, V. (2012a), 'Nam nuzhna novaia ekonomika' [We need a new economy], *Vedomosti*, 30 January, <http://www.vedomosti.ru/politics/articles/2012/01/30/o_nashih_ekonomicheskih_zadacha> (last accessed 30 April 2015).

Putin, V. (2012b), 'Rossiia: natsional'nyi vopros' [Russia: the national question], *Nezavisimaia gazeta*, 23 January, <http://www.ng.ru/politics/2012-01-23/1_national.html> (last accessed 7 March 2015).

Putin, V. (2012c), 'Poslanie Prezidenta Federal'nomu Sobraniiu' [The President's Address to the Federal Assembly], *Kremlin.ru*, 12 December, <http://kremlin.ru/transcripts/17118> (last accessed 7 June 2014).

Putin, V. (2013a), 'Zasedanie mezhdunarodnogo diskussionogo kluba "Valdai"' [Meeting of the international discussion club 'Valdai'], *Kremlin.ru*, <http://kremlin.ru/transcripts/19243> (last accessed 25 May 2014).

Putin, V. (2013b), 'Poslanie Prezidenta Federal'nomu Sobraniiu' [The President's Address to the Federal Assembly], *Kremlin.ru*, 12 December, <http://kremlin.ru/transcripts/19825> (last accessed 2 February 2015).

Putin, V. (2014a), 'Obrashchenie Prezidenta Rossiiskoi Federatsii' [Message of the President of the Russian Federation], *Kremlin.ru*, 18 March, <http://www.kremlin.ru/news/20603> (last accessed 25 May 2014).

Putin, V. (2014b), 'Remarks to the meeting of the Valdai International Club', *Kremlin.ru*, 24 October, <http://eng.kremlin.ru/news/23137> (last accessed 7 March 2015).

Putin, V. (2014c), 'Poslanie Prezidenta Federal'nomu Sobraniiu' [The President's Address to the Federal Assembly), *Kremlin.ru*, 4 December, <http://kremlin.ru/news/47173> (last accessed 7 March 2015).

Pynnöniemi, K. (2014), 'Science fiction: President Medvedev's campaign for Russia's "technological modernisation"', *Demokratizatsiya*, 22, 4: 605–25.

RAC 14 (2008), 'Zaiavlenie Natsional-sotsialisticheskoi partii Rusi' [Declaration by the National Socialist Party of Rus], <http://www.liveinternet.ru/users/r_a_c_14/post67633105> (last accessed 1 March 2015).

Radio Free Europe/Radio Liberty (1999a), 'Newsline', 14 July.

Radio Free Europe/Radio Liberty (1999b), 'Newsline', 6 October.

Radio Free Europe/Radio Liberty (2007a), 'Newsline', 30 October, <http://www.rferl.org/content/article/1143983.html> (last accessed 14 May 2015).

Radio Free Europe/Radio Liberty (2007b), 'Newsline', 21 November, <http://www.rferl.org/content/article/1143999.html> (last accessed 14 May 2015).

Radio Free Europe/Radio Liberty (2007c), 'Newsline', 29 November, <http://www.rferl.org/content/article/1144003.html> (last accessed 14 May 2015).

Rafail [Berestov, R.] (2008), 'Obrashchenie v podderzhku vladyki

Diomida' [A statement in support of Vladyka Diomid], *Dukh khristianina*, <http://www.christian-spirit.ru/v51/51.%283%29.htm> (last accessed 9 September 2015).

Rangsimaporn, P. (2006), 'Interpretations of Eurasianism: justifying Russia's role in East Asia', *Europe–Asia Studies*, 58, 3: 371–89.

Regame, A. [Regamey, A.] (2010), 'Obraz migrantov i migratsionnaia politika v Rossii' [The image of migrants and migration politics in Russia], *Antropologicheskii forum*, 13: 389–406.

Regame, A. [Regamey, A.] (2013), 'Iumor, rasizm i otkaz v priznanii: tadzhiki i peredacha "Nasha Russia"' [Humour, racism and denial in acknowledgement: Tajiks and the programme 'Our Russia'], in E. Demintseva, ed., *Rasizm, ksenofobiia, diskriminatsiia. Kakimi my ikh uvideli...* [Racism, Xenophobia, Discrimination: How We Have Seen Them...], Moscow: Novoe literaturnoe obozrenie, pp. 357–76.

Riabykh, G. (2008), 'Russkaia Pravoslavnaia Tserkov' v sisteme sovremennykh mezhdunarodnykh otnoshenii' [The Russian Orthodox Church in the system of contemporary international relations], *Polis*, 2: 23–37.

Ria Novosti (2011), 'Rossiiskaia natsiia dolzhna sostoiat' iz samobytnykh narodov – Medvedev' [The Russian nation ought to consist of distinctive nations – Medvedev], <http://ria.ru/politics/20110211/333366199.html> (last accessed 7 March 2015).

Riasanovsky, N. V. (1959), *Nicholas I and Official Nationality in Russia, 1825–1855*, Berkeley: University of California Press.

Robertson, G. (2013), 'Protesting Putinism: the election protests of 2011–2012 in broader perspective', *Problems of Post-Communism*, 60, 2: 11–23.

Robinson, N. (2013), 'Russia's response to crisis: the paradox of success', *Europe–Asia Studies*, 65, 3: 450–72.

Rodin, I. (2013), 'Vyiavleny trudnye voprosy istorii Rossii' [The difficult questions of Russian history revealed], *Nezavisimaia gazeta*, 11 June, <http://www.ng.ru/politics/2013-06-11/1_history.html> (last accessed 30 April 2015).

Rodrik, D. (2013), 'Who needs the nation-state?', *Economic Geography*, 89, 1: 1–19.

Rogoza, J. (2014), 'Russian nationalism: between imperialism and xenophobia', *European View*, 13, 1: 79–87.

Rogozin, D. (2012), 'Russkii otvet Vladimiru Putinu' [The Russian answer to Vladimir Putin], *Izvestiia*, 31 January, <http://izvestia.ru/news/513702> (last accessed 9 June 2014).

Romanov, M. and V. Stepanov (2014), *Natsional'nyi vopros v Rossii v kontekste ukrainskogo krizisa* [The National Question in Russia in the Context of the Ukrainian Crisis], Moscow: Obshchestvennaia palata RF, <http://www.sova-center.ru/files/xeno/politeh-june14.pdf> (last accessed 14 May 2015).

Rowley, D. G. (2000), 'Imperial versus national discourse: the case of Russia', *Nations and Nationalism*, 6, 1: 23–42.

Russia beyond the Headlines (2013), 'World Russian People's Council bestows award on Putin', 4 November, <http://rbth.com/news/2013/11/04/world_russian_peoples_council_bestows_award_on_putin_31436.html> (last accessed 30 April 2015).

Russia Today (2010), 'Police arrest 1300 in wake of ethnic clashes in Moscow', 17 December, <http://rt.com/news/ethnic-moscow-live-pictures> (last accessed 7 March 2015).

'Russkii natsionalizm: Teoriia i praktika' [Russian nationalism: theory and practice] (2010), *Voprosy natsionalizma*, 2: 3–15.

Russkii svet (n.d.), 'O natsional-liberalizme, o tom, chto rodnit i chto raz"ediniaet liberalov i natsionalistov, i o pol'ze dialoga mezhdu nimi' [On national-liberalism; on what unites and divides liberals and nationalists; and on the advantages of dialogue between them], <http://russkiysvet.narod.ru/rus-pravda/arhiv/nacional-liberal.htm> (last accessed 4 May 2015).

Rustamova, F. (2014), '"Russkaia vesna" rassorila natsionalistov: chast' ul'trapravykh simpatiziruet Maidanu' ['Russian Spring' splits the nationalists: some of the ultra-right are sympathetic to Maidan], *RBK*, <http://top.rbc.ru/politics/09/07/2014/935472.shtml?utm_source=newsmail&utm_medium=news&utm_campaign=news_mail1> (last accessed 20 July 2014).

Rustenbach, E. (2010), 'Sources of negative attitudes toward immigrants in Europe: a multi-level analysis', *International Migration Review*, 44, 1: 53–77.

Rutland, P. (2010), 'The presence of absence: ethnicity policy in Russia', in J. Newton and W. Tompson, eds, *Institutions, Ideas and Leadership in Post-Soviet Russia*, Houndmills: Palgrave Macmillan, pp. 116–36.

Rutland, P. (2012a), 'Putin's nationality dilemma', *Moscow Times*, 30 January, <http://www.themoscowtimes.com/opinion/article/putins-nationality-dilemma/451918.html> (last accessed 7 March 2015).

Rutland, P. (2012b), 'Journey's end: Russia joins the WTO', *Russian Analytical Digest*, 111: 2–5.

Rutland, P. (2013a), 'Neoliberalism in Russia', *Review of International Political Economy*, 20, 2: 332–62.

Rutland, P. (2013b), 'The political economy of Putin 3.0', *Russian Analytical Digest*, 133: 2–5.
Rutland, P. (2014), 'The impact of sanctions on Russia', *Russian Analytical Digest*, 157: 2–7.
Saari, S. (2014), 'Russia's post-orange revolution strategies to increase its influence in former Soviet republics: public diplomacy *po russkii*', *Europe–Asia Studies*, 66, 1: 50–66.
Sabitova, A. (2012), 'Valerii Fedorov: "Rossiane ne ponimaiut, chego khotiat belolentochnye smut'iany"' [Valerii Fedorov: Russians do not understand what the white-ribbon troublemakers want], *Ekspert*, 28 December, <http://expert.ru/2012/12/28/valerij-fedorov-rossiyane-ne-ponimayut-chto-hotyat-belolentochnyie-smutyanyi> (last accessed 18 April 2015).
Sakwa, R. (2008), *Putin: Russia's Choice*, London: Routledge.
Sakwa, R. (2011a), *The Crisis of Russian Democracy: The Dual State, Factionalism, and the Medvedev Succession*, New York: Cambridge University Press.
Sakwa, R. (2011b), 'Surkov: dark prince of the Kremlin', *openDemocracy*, 7 April, <www.opendemocracy.net/od-russia/richard-sakwa/surkov-dark-prince-of-kremlin> (last accessed 18 April 2015).
Sakwa, R. (2014), *Whatever Happened to the Russian Opposition?*, London: Chatham House, <http://www.chathamhouse.org/sites/files/chathamhouse/field/field_document/20140523SakwaFinal.pdf> (last accessed 14 May 2015).
Sambanis, N. and M. Shayo (2013), 'Social identification and ethnic conflict', *American Political Science Review*, 107, 2: 294–325.
Schimmelpenninck van der Oye, D. (2001), *Toward the Rising Sun: Russian Ideologies of Empire and the Path to War with Japan*, Dekalb: Northern Illinois University Press.
Secrieru, S. and J. Cziek-Karpowicz, eds (2015), *Sanctions and Russia*, Warsaw: Polish Institute of International Relations, <http://www.pism.pl/files/?id_plik=19045> (last accessed 14 May 2015).
Semyonov, M., A. Gorodzeisky and R. Raijman (2006), 'The rise of anti-foreigner sentiments in European societies, 1988–2000', *American Sociological Review*, 71, 3: 426–49.
Sergeev, S. (2010), *Prishestvie natsii?* [The Coming of the Nation?], Moscow: Skimen'.
Seton-Watson, H. (1986), 'Russian nationalism in historical perspective', in R. Conquest, ed., *The Last Empire: Nationality and the Soviet Future*, Stanford: Hoover Institution Press, pp. 14–29.
Seul, J. R. (1999), '"Ours is the way of God": religion, iden-

tity, and intergroup conflict', *Journal of Peace Research*, 36, 5: 553–69.
Sevast'ianov, A. (2010), 'Natsional-demokratiia – ne natsional-sotsializm' [National-democracy is not National-Socialism], *Voprosy natsionalizma*, 2: 119–40.
Sevast'ianov, A. (2013), 'Razbalansirovka diskursa: Natsional-demokratiia ili natsional-liberalizm?' [The imbalance of the discourse: national-democracy or national-liberalism?], *Voprosy natsionalizma*, 13: 201–21.
Shakina, M. (1992), 'Natsiia – to zhe plemia, no tol'ko s armiei' [A nation is the same as a tribe, only with an army], *Novoe Vremia*, 35: 9–12.
Sharafutdinova, G. (2014), 'The Pussy Riot affair and Putin's démarche from sovereign democracy to sovereign morality', *Nationalities Papers*, 42, 4: 615–21.
Shayo, M. (2009), 'A model of social identity with an application to political economy: nation, class, and redistribution', *American Political Science Review*, 103, 2: 147–74.
Shenfield, S. D. (2001), *Russian Fascism: Traditions, Tendencies, Movements*, Armonk: M. E. Sharpe.
Shevel, O. (2011), 'Russian nation-building from Yel'tsin to Medvedev: ethnic, civic or purposefully ambiguous?', *Europe–Asia Studies*, 63, 2: 179–202.
Shevtsova, L. (1999), *Yeltsin's Russia: Myths and Reality*, Moscow: Carnegie Endowment for International Peace.
Shevtsova, L. (2007), *Russia: Lost in Transition: The Yeltsin and Putin Legacies*, Washington, DC: Carnegie Endowment for International Peace.
Shiropaev, A. (2011), 'Vlasov' [Vlasov], 1 March, <http://shiropaev.livejournal.com/61289.html> (last accessed 4 May 2015).
Shiropaev, A. (2014), 'Ob Ukraine i istoricheskikh sviaziakh' [On Ukraine and historical ties], *Russkaia Fabula*, 31 January, <http://rufabula.com/articles/2014/01/31/about-ukraine-and-historical-ties> (last accessed 27 April 2015).
Shizhenskii, R. (2010), 'Problema genezisa sovremennogo russkogo iazychestva v rabotakh rossiiskikh issledovatelei' [The problem of genesis of contemporary Russian paganism in the works of Russian scholars], in R. Shizhenskii, ed., *'Rus' iazycheskaia': etnicheskaia religioznost' v Rossii i Ukraine XX–XXI vv.* ['Pagan Rus': Ethnic Religiosity in Russia and Ukraine in the 20th–21st Centuries], Nizhnii Novgorod: NGPU, pp. 18–41.

Shlapentokh, D. (2010), '"Kondopoga" – ethnic/social tension in Putin's Russia', *European Review*, 18, 2: 177–206.
Shnirel'man, V. (2008), 'Lukavye tsifry i obmanchivye teorii: o nekotorykh sovremennykh podkhodakh k izucheniiu migrantov' [False figures and misleading theories: on some contemporary approaches to the study of migrants], *Vestnik Evrazii*, 2, 125–50.
Shnirel'man, V. (2012), *Russkoe rodnoverie. Neoiazychestvo i natsionalizm v sovremennoi Rossii* [Russian Native Belief: Neopaganism and Nationalism in Contemporary Russia], Moscow: BBI.
Shvetsova, O. (2003), 'Resolving the problem of pre-election coordination: the 1999 parliamentary election as elite presidential "primary"', in V. Hesli and W. Reisinger, eds, *Elections, Parties, and the Future of Russia*, Cambridge: Cambridge University Press, pp. 213–31.
Simon, G. (1991), *Nationalism and Policy toward the Nationalities in the Soviet Union: from Totalitarian Dictatorship to post-Stalinist Society*, Boulder: Westview Press.
Simonsen, S. G. (1996), 'Raising the Russian question: ethnicity and statehood, *russkie* and *Rossiya*', *Nationalism and Ethnic Politics*, 2, 1: 91–110.
Simonsen, S. G. (2005), 'Between minority rights and civil liberties: Russia's discourse over "nationality" registration and the internal passport', *Nationalities Papers*, 33, 2: 211–29.
Slezkine, Y. (1994), 'The USSR as a communal apartment, or how a socialist state promoted ethnic particularism', *Slavic Review*, 53, 2: 414–52.
'Slovo k narodu' [A word to the people] (1992), *Den'*, 29: 1.
Smith, M. A. (2010), 'Medvedev and the modernisation dilemma', *Russian Series*, Shrivenham: Defence Academy of the United Kingdom.
Sokolov, A. (2010), 'Etot mir priduman ne nami. Russkii mir: real'nost' ili fantaziia politikov?' [This world is not invented by us. The Russian world: reality or politicians' fantasy?], *Pravoslavnyi zhurnal 'Foma'*, 5 February, <http://foma.ru/etot-mir-priduman-ne-nami.html> (last accessed 18 April 2015).
Sokolov, M. (2013), 'Lev Gudkov: "Rossiia dlia russkikh"? Uzhe ne stydno' [Lev Gudkov: 'Russia for Russians'? It is already not shameful], *Radio Svoboda*, 19 November, <http://www.svoboda.org/content/transcript/25172654.html> (last accessed 10 February 2015).
Soldatov, A. and I. Borogan (2011), *The New Nobility: The Restoration of Russia's Security State and the Enduring Legacy of the KGB*, New York: PublicAffairs.

Solovei, T. and V. Solovei (2009), *Nesostoiavshaiasia revoliutsiia* [The Revolution that Didn't Happen], Moscow: Feoriia.

Solov'ev, V. (1901), 'Natsional'nyi vopros v Rossii' [The national question in Russia], in V. Solov'ev, *Sobranie Sochinenii, 1883–1888*, St Petersburg: Obshchestvennaia pol'za, pp. 1–137.

Solzhenitsyn, A. (1980), 'Letter to the Soviet Leaders', in A. Solzhenitsyn, *East and West*, New York: Harper & Row, pp. 75–142.

Sorokin, V. (2006), *Den' oprichnika* [The Day of the Oprichnik], Moscow: Zakharov.

SOVA Center for Information and Analysis (2012), 'V Mosgorsude nachalsia protsess po delu 'Avtonomnoi boevoi terroristicheskoi organizatsii'' [In Moscow city court the trial against the 'Autonomous military terrorist organisation' began], 11 January 2012, <http://www.sova-center.ru/racism-xenophobia/news/counteraction/2012/01/d23400> (last accessed 14 May 2015).

SOVA Center for Information and Analysis (2013a), 'Samara: vynesen prigovor po delu o rasistskom ubiistve vykhodtsa iz Tadzhikistana' [Samara: sentence on charges of racist murder of native of Tajikistan], 10 April 2013, <http://www.sova-center.ru/racism-xenophobia/news/counteraction/2013/04/d26869> (last accessed 13 May 2015).

SOVA Center for Information and Analysis (2013b), 'Natsionalisticheskie besporiadki v Arzamase' [Nationalist disturbances in Arzamas], 10 December 2013, <http://www.sova-center.ru/racism-xenophobia/news/racism-nationalism/2013/12/d28586> (last accessed 1 March 2015).

Sperling, V. (2010), 'Making the public patriotic: militarism and antimilitarism in Russia', in M. Laruelle, ed., *Russian Nationalism and the National Reassertion of Russia*, London: Routledge, pp. 218–71.

Spoor, M., N. Mamanova, O. Visser and A. Nikulin (2013), 'Food security in a sovereign state and "quiet food sovereignty" of an insecure population: the case of post-Soviet Russia', *Program in Agrarian Studies*, 14 September, <http://www.yale.edu/agrarianstudies/foodsovereignty/pprs/28_Spoor_2013.pdf> (last accessed 7 March 2015).

Stepanov, S. (1992), *Chernaia sotnia v Rossii (1905–1914 gody)* [The Black Hundreds in Russia (1905–1914)], Moscow: Izdatel'stvo VZPI.

Strategiia gosudarstvennoi natsional'noi politiki Rossiiskoi Federatsii na period do 2025 goda (2012), [Strategy on state nationalities policy of the Russian Federation for the period until 2025], <http://base.garant.ru/70284810> (last accessed 14 May 2015).

Strukova, M. (2013a), 'Strukova... kak pravoslavnyi myslitel'' [Strukova... as Orthodox thinker], *Chertopolokh*, 7 May, <http://

strukova-mv.livejournal.com/244461.html> (last accessed 14 May 2015).
Strukova, M. (2013b), 'Uroki ivrita ot russkogo natsionalista' [Hebrew lessons from a Russian Nationalist], *Zavtra*, 13 June, <http://zavtra.ru/content/view/uroki-ivrita> (last accessed 9 September 2015).
Strukova, E. (2014), 'Dym otechestva: siuzhety rossiiskoi istorii v tekstakh i vyskazyvaniiakh sovremmenykh russkikh natsionalistov' [The smoke of the fatherland: scenes from Russian history in the texts and statements of contemporary Russian nationalists], in *Rossiia – ne Ukraina: sovremmenye aktsenty natsionalizma* [Russia is not Ukraine: Contemporary Accents of Nationalism], Moscow: SOVA Center for Information and Analysis, pp. 168–71.
Struve, P. (1997), 'Dva natsionalizma' [Two nationalisms], in P. Struve, *Patriotika: politika, kul'tura, religiia, sotsializm* [Patriotica: Politics, Culture, Religion, Socialism], Moscow: Respublika, pp. 164–72.
Suleimanov, R. (2012), 'Russkikh v Tatarstane zhdet sud'ba russkikh Severnogo Kavkaza' [Russians in Tatarstan await the fate of Russians in the North Caucasus], *APN*, 12 April, <http://www.apn.ru/publications/article26361.htm> (last accessed 30 April 2015).
Suny, R. G. (1993), *Revenge of the Past: Nationalism, Revolution, and the Collapse of the Soviet Union*, Palo Alto: Stanford University Press.
Surkov, V. (2006), 'Natsionalizatsiia budushchego' [Nationalisation of the future], *Ekspert*, 30 July, <http://expert.ru/forum/expert-articles/1066/?page=7> (last accessed 7 March 2015).
Surkov, V. (2010), *Texts 1997–2010*, Moscow: Publishing House 'Europe'.
Sutela, P. (2012), *The Political Economy of Putin's Russia*, London: Routledge.
Sviatenkov, P. (2010), 'Vozmozhna li rossiiskaia identichnost'?' [Is a rossiiskii identity possible?], *Voprosy natsionalizma*, 3: 3–6.
Sycheva, V. (2012), 'Gost' iz budushchego' [A guest from the future], *Itogi*, 11 June, pp. 20–3.
Szporluk, R. (1989), 'Dilemmas of Russian nationalism', *Problems of Communism*, 38, 4: 15–35.
Tajfel, H. (1970), 'Experiments in intergroup discrimination', *Scientific American*, 223, 5: 96–102.
Tajfel, H. and J. C. Turner (1986), 'The social identity theory of intergroup behavior', in S. Worchel and L. W. Austin, eds, *Psychology of Intergroup Relations*, Chicago: Nelson-Hall, pp. 7–24.
Tarasov, A. (2010), 'Subkul'tura futbol'nykh fanatov v Rossii i pravyi radikalizm' [Football fan subculture in Russia and right radicalism], in *Russkii natsionalizm mezhdu vlast'iu i oppozitsiei* [Russian national-

ism between the authorities and the opposition], Moscow: Panorama Centre, pp. 18–50.

Tatarko, A. (2009), 'Rol' vosprinimaemoi ugrozy v otnoshenii moskvichei k migrantam' [The role of perceived threat in the attitudes of Muscovites to migrants], in N. Lebedeva and A. Tatarko, eds, *Strategii mezhkul'turnogo vzaimodeistviia migrantov i naseleniia Rossii* [Strategies for Intercultural Cooperation Between Migrants and the Population of Russia], Moscow: RUDN, pp. 141–65.

Thaden, E. C. (1990), *Interpreting History: Collective Essays on Russia's Relations with Europe*, New York: Columbia University Press.

Theiler, T. (2003), 'Societal security and social psychology', *Review of International Studies*, 29, 2: 249–68.

Tikhonov, N. (2011), 'O "Tret'ei pozitsii", problemakh "pravogo" dvizheniia i anarkhizme' [On the 'Third position', problems of the 'right' movement and anarchism], 6 September, <http://e-hasis.livejournal.com/6106.html> (last accessed 1 March 2015).

Tishkov, V. (1995), 'What is Russia? Prospects for Nation-Building', *Security Dialogue*, 26, 1: 41–54.

Tishkov, V. (1997), *Ethnicity, Nationalism and Conflict in and after the Soviet Union: The Mind Aflame*, London: SAGE.

Tishkov, V. (2010), *Rossiiskii narod. Kniga dlia uchitelia* [The Rossiiskii People: Teacher's Guide], Moscow: Prosveshchenie.

Tishkov, V., ed. (2011), *Rossiiskaia natsiia. Stanovlenie i etnokul'turnoe mnogoobrazie* [The Rossiiskii Nation: Its Formation and Ethnocultural Diversity], Moscow: Nauka.

Tishkov, V. (2013), *Rossiiskii narod. Istoriia i smysl natsional'nogo samosoznaniia* [The Rossiiskii People: The History and Meaning of National Self-Consciousness], Moscow: Nauka.

Tiuriukanova, E. (2009), 'Trudovye migranti v Moskve: "vtoroe" obshchestvo' [Labour migrants in Moscow: a 'second' society], in Zh. Zaionchkovskaia, ed., *Immigranty v Moskve* [Immigrants in Moscow], Moscow: Tri kvadrata, pp. 148–75.

Tolz, V. (1998), 'Conflicting "homeland myths" and nation-state building in postcommunist Russia', *Slavic Review*, 57, 2: 267–94.

Tolz, V. (2001), *Russia: Inventing the Nation*, London: Edward Arnold.

Tolz, V. (2004), 'The search for national identity in Russia of Yeltsin and Putin', in Y. Brudny, J. Frankel and S. Hoffman, eds, *Restructuring Post-Communist Russia*, Cambridge: Cambridge University Press, 160–78.

Tolz, V. (2011), *Russia's Own Orient: The Politics of Identity and Oriental Studies in the Late Imperial and Early Soviet Periods*, Oxford: Oxford University Press.

Tolz, V. and S.-A. Harding (2015), 'From "compatriots" to "aliens": the changing coverage of migration on Russian television', *Russian Review* 74, 3: 452–77.

Tor, V. (2013), 'Pokhval'noe slovo Maidanu' [Panegyric to Maidan], *Russkii obozrevatel'*, 13 December, <http://www.rus-obr.ru/blog/28354> (last accessed 25 April 2015).

Torkunov, A. (1999), *Sovremennye mezhdunarodnye otnosheniia* [Contemporary International Relations], Moscow: ROSSPEN.

Treisman, D. (2011a), *The Return: Russia's Journey from Gorbachev to Medvedev*, New York: Free Press.

Treisman, D. (2011b), 'Presidential popularity in a hybrid regime: Russia under Yeltsin and Putin', *American Journal of Political Science*, 55, 3: 590–609.

Trenin, D. (2010), 'Russia's conservative modernisation: a mission impossible?', *SAIS Review*, 30, 1: 27–37.

Trenin, D. (2012), *True Partners? How Russia and China See Each Other*, London: Centre for European Reform.

Trenin, D. (2014), 'Russia's breakout from the post-cold war system: The drivers of Putin's course', *Carnegie Working Papers*, Washington, DC: Carnegie Endowment for International Peace.

Tsimbaev, N. (1986), *Slavianofil'stvo. Iz istorii russkoi obshchestvenno-politicheskoi mysli XIX veka* [Slavophilism: From the History of Russian Socio-political Thought of the 19th Century], Moscow: Izdatel'stvo MGU.

Tsygankov, A. (2014), *The Strong State in Russia: Development and Crisis*, Oxford: Oxford University Press.

Tumanov, G. (2014), 'Ukrainskii krizis snizil uroven' ksenofobii' [The Ukrainian crisis has lowered the level of xenophobia], *Kommersant*, 24 June, <http://kommersant.ru/doc/2492161> (last accessed 18 August 2014).

Tumarkin, N. (1994), *The Living and the Dead: The Rise and Fall of the Cult of World War II in Russia*, New York: Basic Books.

Tuminez, A. S. (2000), *Russian Nationalism since 1856: Ideology and the Making of Foreign Policy*, Lanham: Rowman & Littlefield.

Tunon, M. and N. Baruah (2012), 'Public attitudes towards migrant workers in Asia', *Migration and Development*, 1, 1: 149–62.

Ukaz Prezidenta RF (2012a), 'O dolgosrochnoi gosudarstvennoi ekonomicheskoi politike' [On long-term economic policy], no. 596, adopted 7 May, <http://graph.document.kremlin.ru/page.aspx?1610833> (last accessed 1 May 2015).

Ukaz Prezidenta RF (2012b), 'Ob obespechenii mezhnatsional'nogo soglasiia' [On ensuring interethnic harmony], no. 602, adopted 7 May, <www.rg.ru/2012/05/09/nacio-dok.html> (last accessed 5 February 2015).

Ukaz Prezidenta RF (2012c), 'O Strategii gosudarstvennoi natsional'noi politiki Rossiiskoi Federatsii na period do 2025 goda' [On the strategy for state nationalities policy of the Russian Federation for the period until 2025], no. 1666, *Kremlin.ru*, adopted 12 December, <http://kremlin.ru/news/17165> (last accessed 22 May 2014).

Umland, A., ed. (2008), *Theorizing Post-Soviet Extreme Right: Comparative Political, Historical and Sociological Approaches*, Armonk: M. E. Sharpe.

United Nations (2013), *International Migration 2013*, New York: UN Department of Economic and Social Affairs, September 2013, <http://www.un.org/en/development/desa/population/migration/publications/wallchart/docs/wallchart2013.pdf> (last accessed 1 February 2015).

Urban, J. and V. Solovei (1997), *Russia's Communists at the Crossroads*, Boulder: Westview Press.

Valkovich, M. (2014), 'Iazychestvo i natsional-demokratiia' [Paganism and national democracy], *Voprosy natsionalizma*, 1, 17: 105–6.

van Zaichik, Kh. (2000), *Delo zhadnogo varvara* [The Case of the Greedy Barbarian], St Petersburg: Azbuka.

Verkhovsky, A. (2005a), 'Pravoslavnye natsionalisty: strategii deistviia v Tserkvi i v politike' [Orthodox nationalists: strategies of action in the Church and in politics], in A. Verkhovsky, ed., *Tsena nenavisti. Natsionalizm v Rossii i protivodeistvie rasistskim prestupleniiam* [The Price of Hate: Nationalism in Russia and Reaction to Racist Crimes], Moscow: SOVA Center for Information and Analysis, pp. 175–95.

Verkhovsky, A. (2005b), 'Rossiiskoe politicheskoe pravoslavie: poniatie i puti razvitiia' [Russian political Orthodoxy: concepts and paths of development], in A. Verkhovsky, ed., *Putiami nesvobody* [By Paths of Unfreedom], Moscow: SOVA Center for Information and Analysisfor Information and Analysis, pp. 48–80.

Verkhovsky, A. (2007a), 'Ideinaia evoliutsiia russkogo natsionalizma: 1990-e i 2000-e gody' [The ideological evolution of Russian nationalism: the 1990s and 2000s], in A. Verkhovsky, ed., *Verkhi i nizy russkogo natsionalizma* [The Upper and Lower Echelons of Russian Nationalism], Moscow: SOVA Center for Information and Analysis, pp. 6–32.

Verkhovsky, A. (2007b), 'Tserkovnyi proekt rossiiskoi identichnosti' [The Church project for Russian identity], in M. Laruelle, ed., *Sovremennye interpretatsii russkogo natsionalizma* [Contemporary

Interpretations of Russian Nationalism], Stuttgart: Ibidem-Verlag, pp. 171–88.

Verkhovsky, A. (2010), 'Future prospects of contemporary Russian nationalism', in M. Laruelle, ed., *Russian Nationalism and the National Reassertion of Russia*, London: Routledge, pp. 89–103.

Verkhovsky, A. (2013), 'Natsionalizm: konkurentsiia na "ksenofobskoe bol'shninstvo"' [Nationalism: competition for the 'xenophobic majority'], *Vedomosti*, 14 August, <http://www.vedomosti.ru/newspaper/articles/2013/08/14/konkurenciya-za-ksenofobskoe-bolshinstvo> (last accessed 14 May 2015).

Verkhovsky, A. (2014a), 'Etnopolitika federal'noi vlasti i aktivizatsiia russkogo natsionalizma' [The ethnopolitics of the federal authorities and the activation of Russian nationalism], *Pro et Contra*, 1–2: 19–33.

Verkhovsky, A. (2014b), 'Dinamika nasiliia v russkom natsionalizme' [The dynamic of violence in Russian nationalism], in *Rossiia – ne Ukraina: sovremennye aktsenty natsionalizma* [Russia is not Ukraine: Contemporary Accents of Nationalism], Moscow: SOVA Center for Information and Analysis, pp. 32–61.

Verkhovsky, A. (2014c), '"Kirill's Doctrine" and the potential transformation of Russian Orthodox Christianity', in K. Tolstaya, ed., *Orthodox Paradoxes: Heterogeneities and Complexities in Contemporary Russian Orthodoxy*, Leiden: Brill, pp. 71–84.

Verkhovsky, A. and G. Kozhevnikova, eds (2009), *Radikal'nyi russkii natsionalizm. Struktury, idei, litsa. Spravochnik* [Radical Russian Nationalism: Structures, Ideas, Individuals: A Handbook], Moscow: SOVA Center for Information and Analysis.

Verkhovsky, A. and E. Strukova (2014), 'Partiinoe stroitel'stvo na krainem pravom flange rossiiskogo politicheskogo spektra' [Party-building on the far right of Russia's political spectrum], *Politicheskie issledovaniia*, 4: 131–51.

Visloguzov, V. (2011), 'Migratsionnaia sluzhba dovol'na gastarbaiterami' [The migration service is pleased with the labour migrants], *Kommersant*, 30 June, <http://www.kommersant.ru/doc/1669866> (last accessed 13 May 2015).

Volkov, D. (2014), 'Putin's ratings: anomaly or trend?', *Institute of Modern Russia*, 23 December, <http://imrussia.org/en/analysis/nation/2135-putins-ratings-anomaly-or-trend> (last accessed 7 March 2015).

Vortman, R. (1999), '"Ofitsial'naia narodnost'" i natsional'nyi mif rossiskoi monarkhii XIX veka' ['Official nationality' and the national myth of the Russian monarchy in the 19th century], in *Kul'turnye praktiki i ideologicheskie perspektivy: Rossiia, XVIII – nachalo XX veka* [Cultural Practices and Ideological Perspectives: Russia, 18th – early 20th centuries], Moscow: OGI, pp. 233–44.

VTsIOM (1999a), 'Deiatel'nost' Vladimira Putina' [The activity of Vladimir Putin], *Polit.ru*, 22 October, <http://polit.ru/article/1999/10/22/477129> (last accessed 14 May 2015).

VTsIOM (1999b), 'Nastuplenie v Chechne i parlamentskie vybory' [The offensive in Chechnya and the parliamentary elections], *Polit.ru*, 3 December, <http://polit.ru/article/1999/12/03/477150> (last accessed 14 May 2015).

VTsIOM (2002), *Obshestvennoe mnenie – 2002* [Public Opinion – 2002], Moscow: VTsIOM.

VTsIOM (2014a), 'Krym i Rossiia: Porozn' ili vmeste?' [Crimea and Russia: apart or together?], *Press vypusk*, 17 March, <http://wciom.ru/index.php?id=236&uid=114746> (last accessed 2 May 2015).

VTsIOM (2014b), '"Russkii mir", Ukraina i politika Rossii' [The 'Russian world', Ukraine and Russian politics], *Press vypusk*, 22 July, <http://wciom.ru/index.php?id=236&uid=114905> (last accessed 4 May 2015).

Waever, O., B. Buzan, M. Kelstrup and P. Lemaitre (1993), *Identity, Migration, and the New Security Agenda in Europe*, London: Pinter.

Waldinger, R. (2010), 'Unacceptable realities: public opinion and the challenge of immigration in a Franco–American comparison', in C. Audebert and M. K. Doraï, eds, *Migration in a Globalized World: New Research Issues and Prospects*, Amsterdam: Amsterdam University Press, pp. 41–61.

Walicki, A. (1989), *The Slavophile Controversy: History of a Conservative Utopia in Nineteenth-Century Russian Thought*, Notre Dame: University of Notre Dame Press.

Weaver, C. (2014), 'Malofeev: the Russian billionaire linking Moscow to the rebels', *Financial Times*, 24 July, <http://www.ft.com/cms/s/0/84481538-1103-11e4-94f3-00144feabdc0.html#axzz3a64Wke1g> (last accessed 14 May 2015).

White, S. and I. McAllister (2008), 'The Putin phenomenon', *Journal of Communist Studies and Transition Politics*, 24, 4: 604–28.

Wimmer, A. (2002), *Nationalist Exclusion and Ethnic Conflict: Shadows of Modernity*, Cambridge: Cambridge University Press.

Wintrobe, R. (1995), 'Some economics of ethnic capital formation and conflict', in A. Breton, G. Galeotti, P. Salmon and R. Wintrobe, eds, *Nationalism and Rationality*, Cambridge: Cambridge University Press, pp. 43–71.

Wood, E. (2011), 'Performing memory: Vladimir Putin and the celebration of WWII in Russia', *Soviet and Post-Soviet Review*, 38, 2: 172–200.
World Bank (2012), 'Russia: the Eurasian Food Security Center is launched', 17 March, <http://www.worldbank.org/en/news/feature/2012/03/26/eurasian-center-for-food-security-launched-in-russia> (last accessed 14 May 2015).
Yanov, A. (1978), *The Russian New Right: Right-Wing Ideologies in the Contemporary USSR*, Berkeley: Institute of International Studies.
Yemelianova, G., ed. (2010), *Radical Islam in the Former Soviet Union*, London: Routledge.
Zamiatin, D. and N. Zamiatina (2000), 'Prostranstvo rossiiskogo federalizma' [The landscape of Russian federalism], *Polis*, 5: 98–110.
Zav'ialova, K. (2012), 'Vladimir Putin sdelal pervye rasporiazheniia na postu prezidenta' [Vladimir Putin gave his first orders as president], *Kommersant*, 7 May, <http://www.kommersant.ru/doc/1930174> (last accessed 29 May 2014).
Zemtsov, N. (2012), 'Interv'iu, vziatoe u sviashchennika Romana Zelenskogo posle prochteniia knigi M. A. Babkina "Sviashchenstvo i Tsarstvo"' [Interview with Father Roman Zelenskii after reading M. A. Babkin's book 'Priesthood and Tsardom'], *Petr Velikii*, <http://zargradet.ru/?page_id=1356> (last accessed 25 January 2015).
Zevelev, I. (2001), *Russia and its New Diasporas*, Washington, DC: United States Institute of Peace Press.
Zevelev, I. (2014), 'Granitsy russkogo mira: transformatsiia natsional'noi identichnosti i novaia vneshnepoliticheskaia doktrina Rossii' [The borders of the Russian world: transformation of the national identity and Russia's new foreign policy doctrine], *Rossiia v Global'noi Politike*, 27 April, <http://www.globalaffairs.ru/number/Granitcy-russkogo-mira--16582> (last accessed 7 March 2015).
Zhuchkovskii, I. (2014), '"Pervaia piatiletka" Patriarkha Kirilla. Problemy i vyzovy Russkoi Pravoslavnoi Tserkvi' ['The first five-year plan' of Patriarch Kirill: problems and challenges for the Russian Orthodox Church], *Voprosy natsionalizma*, 1, 17: 33–43.
Ziuganov, G. (1994), *Drama vlasti* [The Drama of Power], Moscow: Paleia.

Index

Note: A page reference in *italics* indicates a figure and tables are shown in **bold**.

Agency of Political and Economic Communications, 289
Aleksandr I, 48
Aleksandr III, 61, 69
Alksnis, Viktor, 36
Anderson, Benedict, 223
Anderson, Bridget, 319
Anderson, John, 105
Andropov, Iurii, 65
anti-fascist (antifa) fighters, 77–8
anti-migrant campaign (2013), 81–2, 87, 88, 94, 95, 323
anti-utopia genre (literature), 67–8
Åslund, Anders, 352
authorities *see* Kremlin
Avdeev, Vladimir, 121, 123

Badie, Bertrand, 340
Badovskii, Dmitrii, 288–9
Barghoorn, Frederick, 25
Barkashov, Aleksandr, 31
Barsukova, Svetlana, 353
Beissinger, Mark, 59
Belov-Potkin, Aleksandr, 34
Benediktov, Kirill, 36
Berdiaev, Nikolai, 289
Berestov, Rafail, 117, 119–20
Beskov, Andrei, 122–3
Bevelander, Pieter, 141

Biriulevo-Zapadnoe riots, 86, 94–5, 240–1, 325–6
Black Hundreds, 24, 30, 98, 105
Blinder, Scott, 319
Blumer, Herbert, 165
Bolotnaia movement, 281, 287, 291
Bondarik, Nikolai, 88, 94, 96
Brezhnev, Leonid, 25
BRICS (Brazil, Russia, India, China and South Africa), 344–5
Brubaker, Rogers, 136n, 304
Bush, George W. H., 169

Caucasus
  labour migration to Russia, 1–2, 40
  migrants from, 1–2, 151, 266
  see also North Caucasus
Central Asia
  labour migration to Russia, 1–2, 40
  migrants from, 1–2, 151, 266
  relinquishment of, Solzhenitsyn, 20, 26
Centre for Political Analysis, 289
Centre for Social Conservative Policy, 286
Channel 1, 301, 305, 328–9
  see also television, state-aligned; *Vremia* (Channel 1)
Chaplin, Vsevolod, 262–3

Chechnya
  Domodedovo assault, 302, 327–8, 329
  public opinion on Chechen terrorists, 232–3
  Putin's response to terrorist attacks, 231–2, 233–4
  support for annexation of Crimea, 162
Chubais, Anatolii, 347
civic nation-state model
  disjunction with ethnic-based nationhood, 299–300
  ethnonationalist opposition to, 36–7, 40
  lack of popular appeal, 43
  Medvedev's support for, 38
  nation, interpretation of, 48–50
  National Democratic Alliance and, 55
  Putin's strategy for, 251–2, 256–7, 258
  Russian civic nation, 264, 299–300
  in state rhetoric, 38
  theoretical underpinning of, 32–3
civilisational grammars
  Byzantine legacy, 293
  concept of, 277–8
  Europeanness, 293–4
  nineteenth century debate over, 278–9
  Russia as a European country following Western development, 278, 280, 281
  Russia as European country following non-Western path, 278, 282, 293–4, 295
  Russia as non-European country, 278, 280–1
civilization, Russian
  Europeanness of Russia, 293–5
  historical identification as part of European civilization, 278–9
  preordained differences with the West, 50–1, 60–2, 340
  russkii mir (Russian world), 72, 83, 110–11, 113, 271
  within triple choice of identity, 278
  universality of, 111–13

collapse of the Soviet Union
  lack of public desire for reunification of, 63
  non-ethnic loyalty to Russian Federation, 26–7
  psychological legacy of, 62
  and revival in imperialism, 60–1
  rise in ethnic nationalism, 26, 35
  tough statists and reinstatement of, 63
Combat Organisation of Russian Nationalists (*Boevaia organizatsiia russkikh natsionalistov*) (BORN), 77, 83
Commonwealth of Independent States, 64, 166, 344
communism, 25, 288
Concept of State Nationalities Policy, 261
Congress of Russian Communities (KRO), 30, 63
conservatism
  conservative policies, 275, 288–90, 293–5
  as ideological state posture, 287–90
  Kremlin policies, 239–40, 258–9
corruption
  and immigration, 153–4
  as source of Russian/Ukrainian division, 212
Crimea, annexation of
  as ethnic consolidation, 188, 202–3, 259–61
  ethnic Russians (*russkie*), Putin's reference to, 18, 160, 206, 259
  ethnonationalist support for, 6, 260–1, 354
  future expansionism and, 247
  historical justification for, 259
  impact of Russian perceptions of Ukrainians, 206, 207–9
  imperial nationalist support for, 6, 70, 260
  increased public support for political unity, 82–3
  media coverage and term 'ethnic cohesion', 312–13
  media coverage of, 192, 201–2, 330–3

INDEX

national democratic nationalist stance on, 56–7, 70
national unity and, 82–3
popular support for, 162
and Putin's approval rating, 6, 72, 162, 198–9, *199*, 244–5, 247–8, 358
Putin's Crimea speech (2014), 18, 160, 206, 259–60, 331–2
and Putin's references to nationalism, 6, 17, 18, 44, 160, 206, 222
radical nationalist divisions and, 82, 97–8
and Russian domestic economy, 215–16, 218, 357–9
Russian dynamic state identity and, 187–8
as step towards Slavic Union, 188
as step towards USSR 2.0, 188–9
and theories of nationalism, 192–3
Western sanctions and, 357–9
see also Ukraine
Crimean Tatars, 163, *164*, 179, 189, 313, 319, 331–2
culturalists (*vozrozhdentsy*), 26, 28–9

Day of Russian Wrath, 94
Decembrist revolutionaries, 48, 51–2, 61, 72
Declaration of the Rights of Man and of the Citizen, 48
declensions, political
  concept of, 277
  language of patriotism, 290–1
  morality, 291–2, 294
  national culture, 292
Deliagin, Mikhail, 356, 359
Demushkin, Dmitrii, 83, 263
Deutsch, Karl, 21
diaspora communities
  as force for irredentism, 63–4
  in the 'near abroad', 30, 32, 37
  of the Orthodox Church, 111
Diomid (Dziuban), Bishop of Anadyr and Chukotka, 117, 120
diversionary theories of war, 217

Domodedovo International Airport, 302, 327–8, 329
Donbas militias, 71
Donbas separatists, 73
Dubin, Boris, 40
Dufy, Caroline, 353
Dugin, Aleksandr, 30, 68n, 68–9, 280, 281
Dunlop, John, 20, 26, 28
Dushenov, Konstantin, 108, 113, 114, 118, 120, 129
Dzhemilev, Mustafa, 332

economy
  alternative to Western capitalist model, 342–3
  debate over globalisation, 339–40
  downturn in and declining migrant worker numbers, 16–17
  economic strength and stability, NEORUSS survey, 214–16, 218
  energy sector, 348–9
  ethnonationalist stance on, 353–7
  market reforms/modernisation of, 340–1, 345–6, 347–50
  model of state capitalism, 343–5
  nationalism and, 16, 337, 345–6
  neoliberal state and, 339
  post-annexation of Crimea, 215–16, 218, 357–9
  privatisation campaigns (1990s), 342
  Putin's strategies for, 336–8, 347–53
  sanctions, post-annexation of Crimea, 357–9
  Strategy 2020 reform programme, 350
  2008 financial crisis, impacts of, 237, 350–1
Ekishev, Iurii, 108, 116–17
Eltsin, Boris
  lame duck syndrome and, 230–1
  power struggle with Gorbachev, 31–2
  red-brown opposition to, 29
  selection of Putin as successor, 230–1
  use of term *rossiiane*, 3–4, 160, 252

Eltsin administration
　economic modernisation strategies, 341–2, 346
　ethnic self-identification, 270
　nation-building project, 27, 31–3, 251, 283
　non-ethnic *rossiiskii* model, 6, 18
　relationship with Europe, 280
　rossiiane, concept, 3, 160, 252
　state-focused nationalism, 20, 251
empire, branding, 69
empire-saving nationalism, 22–3, 27–8, 35–6
　see also supremacist nationalism
energy sector, 348–9
ethnic criminality, 84, 86, 94, 95, 133, 140
ethnic irredentism, 37
ethnic minorities
　criticism of new nationalities policy, 263
　demographics, 161, 269–70
　group threat approach and support for ethnic majority nationalism, 163–6, 182
　as marriage partners, 207–10, *208*, 211
　minority coalitions, 166–7
　within multi-ethnic Russian state, 229
　political non-participation, 179–80
　preferences for Russia's state identity, 184–5, *184*
　pride in Russian citizenship, 178, 186–7
　prospective group status in Russian state identity scenarios, 184–6, *185*
　reduced exclusionist sentiments and territorial expansion, 187
　responsiveness to Putin's message on ethnic diversity, 180–1, **181**
　social identity approach and Russian expansion, 167–8, 182
　social identity in relation to state identity, 182–4
　support for Putin, 179–80, 187
　support for Russian expansionism, 166–7, 169–70, 174–8, *177*, 181–2, 186, 189
　see also migrants; migrants, perceptions of; NEORUSS surveys
ethnic nationalism
　anti-migrant stance, 240
　ethnically homogenous state of Russian people, 107, 229
　evolution of, 105–7
　indicators of, NEORUSS surveys, 203
　political demarcation from patriots, 106–7
　post-annexation of Crimea, 201–2
　religious demarcation, 107
　see also Orthodox nationalism; paganism; secularism
ethnic Russians
　and annexation of Crimea, 18, 160, 206, 259
　as core of Russian state (state-forming), 13, 34, 38–9, 161, 167, 255, 256–7, 262, 265
　demographic dominance of, 4–5, 35
　essentialist opposition with the West, 50–1
　nationalism, post-revolution, 24–5
　nationalism and the Russian Federation, 26–7, 35, 42–3
　in the 'near abroad', 30, 32, 37, 165–8
　NEORUSS survey, 170–4
　political domination of (historical), 51
　population identifying as, 269
　preferences for Russia's state identity, 184–5, *184*
　pride in Russian citizenship, 178, 187
　privileged social position, public support for, 202–3
　prospective group status in Russian state identity scenarios, 184–6, *185*
　and Putin's nation-building project, 256–7
　responsiveness to Putin's message on ethnic diversity, 180–1, **181**

self-identification as, Crimea, 188
Soviet identity and, 55–6
support for Putin, 179–80, 187
support for Russian expansionism, 174–8, *177*, 181–2, 212–13
and the term *russkie*, 168, 205–6
unifying role (nationalities policy), 262
ethnicity
  defined, 304
  ethnicity-related news, 303–4, 305–6, *307–9*, 310, *311*
  importance of, post-Soviet Union, 3–4, 26–7, 300
  of migrant workers, 4
  passport nationality, 268, 270
  rising importance to nationalist debate, 1
ethnonationalism
  among dissidents, post-1917, 26
  and the annexation of Crimea, 6, 260–1, 354
  common anti-Putin stance with pro-Western democrats, 3, 35
  concept of *russkii*, 36
  disillusionment with Putin's economic strategies, 354
  distinction from imperialist nationalism, 22, 35–6
  emergence of, 1, 19–20, 34
  ethnic irredentism of, 37
  Eurasianist opposition to, 30, 35–6
  within neopaganism, 122–4
  opposition to civic nation-state model, 36–7, 40
  popular support and, 40–1, 43–4
  Putin's stance on, 38–9, 252–3, 254, 354
  scepticism of Eurasian Union, 345, 354
  stance on ethnic Russians in the 'near abroad', 37
  in state rhetoric, 37–9, 43–4, 206
  and statism, 1, 19, 21–2
Eurasian Economic Union, 44, 166, 276, 337, 344, 345, 353, 354, 357
Eurasianism
  geography as destiny rhetoric, 62
  integrationist stance, 41
  neo-Eurasianism, 30
  opposition to ethnonationalism, 30, 35–6
  post-1917, 25–6
  and state rhetoric, 44
  support for, 23, 280–2
Euromaidan revolution
  implications for Eurasian Economic Union, 344
  Kremlin's response to, 6, 17, 201–2, 206, 208
  national democratic nationalist support for, 56
  Russian nationalism and, 17, 216
Europe
  lack of ethnic cohesion, 312
  migration, coverage of by Russian state-aligned television, 320–3, 324
  multiculturalism as failed strategy, 254, 258, 299, 312, 318, 323, 329
  negative attitudes towards migrants, 138
  see also civilisational grammars; the West
expansionism
  ethnic minority levels of support for, 166–8, 169–70, 174–8, *177*, 181–2, 186, 189
  ethnic Russian levels of support for, 174–8, *177*, 181–2, 212–13
  group threat approach and ethnic minority support, 165–6, 182
  and Muslim republics, 213
  post-annexation of Crimea, 247
  preferences for Russia's state identity, 184–5, *184*
  preferences for territorial boundaries, 213, *214*
  prospective group status in Russian state identity scenarios, 184–6, *185*
  and reduction of exclusionist sentiments, 187
  social identity approach and ethnic minority support, 167–8, 182
  see also Crimea, annexation of

fascist movements, 31, 34–5
Fatherland–All Russia, 231, 235, 284
Fedorov, Boris, 347
Fedorov, Valerii, 58
football hooligans, 81, 85
Foundation for the Development of Civil Society, 289
France, 139, 140, 141, 320
French Revolution, 48, 49
friendship of the peoples (*druzhba narodov*), 265, 269
Fursov, Andrei, 359

Gaidar, Egor, 47, 59, 280, 341, 346–7
Galkina, Elena, 54
Gellner, Ernest, 21, 223, 229
Gevorkian, Eduard, 68
Glazev, Sergei, 356–7, 358–9
globalisation, 285, 299, 337, 338–9
Gorbachev, Mikhail, 28, 29, 31, 57, 280, 346
Great Russia (*Velikaia Rossiia*), 79, 94
Greenfeld, Liah, 338
group threat approach, 163–6, 182
Gryzlov, Boris, 288
Gulyga, Arsenii, 61

Hechter, Michael, 223
Hill, Fiona, 283
Hopf, Ted, 337
Hosking, Geoffrey, 24
Huntington, Samuel, 111, 112
hybrid regimes, 225

Iakunin, Vladimir, 349
ideological state posture
  concept of, 277–8
  conservatism, 287–90
  political centrism, 282–4
  role of think tanks, 288–90
  and social contestation, 284–5
  structuring of, 284–7
Ilin, Ivan, 62, 289
imagined communities, 223
immigration *see* migrants; migrants, perceptions of; migration

imperial nationalism
  and the annexation of Crimea, 6, 70, 260
  anti-imperialism of national democratic nationalists, 52–3, 56
  forms of, 1, 21
  impertsy, term, 1, 35
  irredentism and, 63–4
  militia leaders, 71
  and multi-ethnic Russian nationalism, 229–30, 240
  and official nationality doctrine, 72–3
  political prospects of, 69–70
  redirection of by authorities, 71–2
  rossiiane, concept and, 252
  state strength, importance of, 1, 5
  tensions with ethnonationalism, 21–2, 35–6
  term, 46, 47
  as traditional state strategy, 249
imperial syndrome
  antidote to separatism, 62
  and civilizational differences with the West, 60–2
  imperial body, 60, 62
  imperial consciousness, 60–3
  imperial legacy and, 58–9
  imperial order, 59–60
  increased Soviet consciousness, 64–7
  rehabilitation of empire, 67–9
Ingram, Alan, 30
Institute for Modern Development (INSOR), 286–7
Institute for Priority Regional Projects, 289
Institute for Social-Economic and Political Research (ISEPI), 288–9
Institute of the Far East, 280, 281
intergroup relations
  group homogeneity (entitativity), 182
  group threat approach, 163–7, 182
  importance of ethnic identity and, 182
  intergroup defection, 165–6, 182

INDEX

intermarriage with migrants, 207–10, *208*, 211
prospective group status, 184–6, *184*, *185*
significance of state identity, 182–3
social identity approach, 163, 167–9
intermovements, 28
irredentism, 37, 63–4, 178
Isaev, Andrei, 254
Islam
anti-Islamic orientation of secular nationalists, 127–8
radical Islam news coverage, 318–19, 326
television news coverage, 317–19
as threat to social stability, 41, 213–14
views on, NEORUSS survey, 213–14
Islamic extremists, North Caucasus, 302, 319, 327–8, 329
Istarkhov, Vladimir, 121, 122
Iurev, Mikhail, 354–5
Iurgens, Igor, 281, 286–7

James, Paul, 277
Jews
anti-Semitism, 127
intermarriage with, public perceptions of, 209–10
presence on the federal news, 317
xenophobia against, 5

Kadyrov, Ramzan, 224
Kara-Murza, Aleksei, 57, 63
Khodorkovskii, Mikhail, 223, 348
Kholmogorov, Egor, 117
Khramov, Aleksandr, 36, 54
Kiselev, Dmitrii, 318, 331, 332–3
Kolegov, Aleksei, 116, 126
Kondopoga riots, 84–5, 253
Konstantinov, Ilia, 36
Kovalev, Igor, 124–5
Kozyrev, Andrei, 280
Kremlin
conservative policies, 239–40, 258–9

Great Patriotic War (WWII) tropes, 210
media-control and, 246
nationalism as strategy for, 6, 17, 240–2, 246–7
negativity over accession to EU by former Soviet states, 197
pro-Kremlin youth groups, 2–3, 78, 80–1, 88, 253, 285
response to 2011 protest movement, 238, 351
response to Euromaidan revolution, 6, 17, 201–2, 206, 207–8
response to Manezhnaia riots, 2, 81, 253–4, 324
stance on Ukrainian Western-backed government, 196, 201–2, 206, 211, 217, 245
suppression of radical nationalists, 80–1, 253–4
2012 campaign strategy, 238–40
see also Eltsin, Boris; Eltsin administration; Medvedev, Dmitrii; Putin, Vladimir; state, the
Krill I, Patriarch of Moscow and all Rus, 111–12, 292, 313, 316–17
Krylov, Konstantin, 20, 35–6, 37, 52–3, 54, 79
Kuchma, Leonid, 226
Kudrin, Aleksei, 280, 352, 358
Kvachkov, Vladimir, 75, 116–17

large-scale surveys, 134
Laruelle, Marlene, 21–2, 26, 29, 55, 197
Lavrov, Sergei, 293
Lazarenko, Ilia, 55
Lebed, Aleksandr, 283
Lebedev, Sergei, 106, 107, 127
Lenin, Vladimir, 67
Leontev, Konstantin, 289
Lieven, Dominic, 47, 59
Limonov, Eduard, 245
Luzhkov, Iurii, 224, 232, 283
Lysenko, Nikolai, 31, 125, 127

Makarenko, Boris, 262
Malofeev, Konstantin, 349
Manezhnaia riots
  Kremlin's response to, 2, 9, 81, 253–4, 324
  media reaction to, 302–3
  radical nationalism and, 81, 85, 96
manifest xenophobia, 157
Martsinkevich, Maksim (Tesak), 81, 88
media
  annexation of Crimea coverage, 192, 201–2, 216–17, 330–3
  influence on public discourse on Ukraine, 312, 324
  Kremlin control of, 246
  migrants, coverage, 41, 194–6, 319–20
  nation-building function, 95, 299, 306–10, 328–9
  and patriotism-inflated popularity ratings, 169
  reaction to Manezhnaia riots, 302–3, 306
  space for 'voices from below', 300–1
  term 'ethnic cohesion', 312–13
  use of term *rossiiskii*, 309–10
  use of term *russkie*, 309–10
  see also Channel 1; Rossiia; television, state-aligned
Medinskii, Vladimir, 281–2, 292
Medvedev, Dmitrii
  appointment as deputy prime minister, 349
  civic nation-state model, 38
  food security doctrine, 352
  links with INSOR think tank, 281
  modernisation programme, 16, 286–7, 350
  within Putin's personal network, 224
  selection as Putin's successor, 226, 235–6, 237, 254, 287
Merkel, Angela, 312
migrantophobia, 2, 41, 43–4, 133, 137, 241
  see also xenophobia

migrants
  anti-migrant campaign (2013), 9, 81–2, 87, 88, 94, 95, 323
  from Central Asia and Caucasus, 1–2
  deportation of, public support for, 203
  illegal worker status, 2
  impact of economic downturn, 16–17
  inclusion of, public support for, 203
  labour and demand for, 4, 41
  lack of Russian cultural knowledge, 2
  media coverage of, 41, 319–20
  numbers of, 4, 41, 138, 138n
  racist violence against, 77, 80, 87
  raids against by radical nationalists, 87–8
  Russian Orthodox Church's work with, 110
  and social change, 156–7
migrants, perceptions of
  Caucasus/Central Asia distinction, 151
  within the community, 148–51
  contact theory and, 145–6
  contextual factors, 142, 152–6
  corruption/migration nexus, 153–4
  defended neighbourhood theory, 154–5
  as economic competition, 139–40, 142–3
  ethnic criminality, 140
  ethno-cultural factors, 141, 151
  gender factors, 145, 156
  impact of socio-political concerns on, 152–6
  intermarriage with ethnic Russians, 207–10, *208*, 211
  migrantophobia, 2, 41, 43–4, 133, 137, 241
  Muslim immigrants, 5, 141
  need for in host counties, 139
  numbers of, perceived, 155–6
  parallels between Russian and Western attitudes, 136–42

personal contact experiences and, 146–7, 151
public's ethnocentric views and, 40–1
Russia contrasted with Europe, 138–9
social status of migrants, 151
socio-demographic indicators and, 142–5
Ukraine question and, 138n
see also Movement against Illegal Immigration (DPNI); xenophobia
migration
 migration cycles, 138
 politicisation of attitudes towards, 137–8
 research on, 132–6
 television news coverage of, 319–23, *321–2*
Mikhailov, Viacheslav, 263, 264
Mikhalkov, Nikita, 66, 69
militia leaders, 71
Miller, Aleksei, 48–9
Mirsky, Georgiy, 26–7
Mirzaev, Rasul, 325
Mitrokhin, Nikolai, 19, 20
modernisation
 criticism of, 354–5, 356–7
 economic, 340–1, 345–6, 347–50
 of the Eltsin Administration, 341–2, 346
 as gradual process, 288
 and imperial legacy, 58–9
 Medvedev's modernisation programme, 16, 286–7, 350
 Strategy 2020 reform programme, 350
 Westernising reforms, 64–5
Moro, German, 287
Motyl, Alexander, 20, 21, 47, 58
Movement against Illegal Immigration (DPNI)
 coalition with Russian Image, 91
 as largest nationalist organisation, 2, 34, 41
 political coalitions, 91–2
 political strategies, 90
 semi-legal violence, 87–8

suppression of by the Kremlin, 80, 253–4
 violent activities of, 78–9
multiculturalism, 254, 258, 299, 312, 318, 323, 329

Nabiullina, Elvira, 357, 359
narodnost, 48, 49
Nashi, 2–3, 253, 285
nation
 civic interpretation of, 48–50, 52
 ethnic interpretation of, 50–1
 understanding of, Tsarist Russia, 48–50
National Bolshevik Party, 25, 42, 97, 245
National Democratic Alliance, 55, 56, 57, 128
national democratic nationalism
 on annexation of Crimea, 56–7, 70
 anti-imperialism of, 52–3, 56
 as anti-regime (*nesistemnyi*) nationalism, 55
 anti-Soviet stance of, 54
 coalition with radical nationalists, 79, 91, 92–3
 opposition to statism, 53–4
 overview of, 35
 political prospects of, 70–1
 2011 protest movement and, 92–3, 237–8
 support for Euromaidan revolution, 56
 Western orientation of, 55, 281
National Democratic Party, 54, 56
National Great Power Party of Russia, 125
national identity
 civic-/ethnic-based nationhood disjunction, 299–300
 as dynamic, 187–8, 271, 299
 and the economy, 337
 non-ethnic, post-Soviet, 3–4
 Putin's strategy for, 255–7, 265–6
 Russianness of, 255–6
 russkii-centred identity, 266–71
national patriots, 106–7
National Republican Party, 125

National Salvation Front, 28–9, 36, 106
National Socialist Society (*Natsional-sotsialisticheskoe obshchestvo*) (NSO), 78, 83
nationalism
  definitions of, 21, 223, 229
  and the economy, 16, 337, 345–6
  evolution of the concept of, 48–52
  ideological grammars and, 296
  as non-patronalistic, 223
  typology of, 22–4
  Western scholarship on, 20–4
nationalities policy
  Concept of State Nationalities Policy, 261
  criticism of, 262–3
  draft strategy, 261–4
National-Republican Party of Russia (NRPR), 30–1
National-socialist Initiative (*Natsional-sotsialisticheskaia initsiativa*) (NSI), 83, 92, 97
nation-building
  Eltsin Administration, 18, 27, 31–3, 283
  ethnic Russians within Putin's strategy, 256–7
  Kremlin (2000-8), 251
  role of Russian Orthodox Church, 258
  role of state-aligned media and, 299, 306–10, 328–9
NATO (North Atlantic Treaty Organization), 276, 287
natsionalnost, 42, 49–50
Navalnyi, Aleksei, 3, 79, 93, 94, 235, 238
'near abroad'
  migrant workers from, 4
  Russian diaspora in, 30, 32, 37
  state influence in, 44
  strategic interests in, 283
Nemenskii, Oleg, 39
neo-Eurasianism, 30
neoliberalism, 337, 339, 341–2, 345, 350, 354–5, 356

neo-Nazis, 2, 77–8, 80, 81, 84, 88, 98, 99, 253
neopaganism *see* paganism
NEORUSS surveys
  competition for work, 143–4
  economic strength and stability, 214–16, 218
  economic valuation, 172–4, *175*
  ethnic and civic ingroup pride, 172, *175*
  on ethnic diversity, 141, 204–5, *205*
  ethnic minorities as marriage partners, 207–10, *208*, 211
  on EU/Eurasian Union membership for Ukraine, 196
  indicators of ethnic nationalism, 203
  intermarriage with migrants, 207–10, *208*, 211
  Islam, views on, 213–14
  methodology, 134–5, 170
  migrants as a threat, 139–40
  Novorossiia concept, public understanding of, 197, **198**
  overview of, 6–7
  perspectives on EU accession of former Soviet countries, 197
  preferences for Russia's state identity, 184–5, *184*
  preferences for territorial boundaries, 171–2, *175*, 213, 214, 241–2, *242*
  pride in ethnic identity, 201–2
  pride in the Russian state, 204
  Putin's competency on nationalist issues, 200–1
  ratings of the political system, 200
  responsiveness to Putin, 174
  Russia for Russians, support for, 265–6
  russkie, understanding of the term, 205–6
  socio-demographic indicators and, 144–5
  socio-political concerns, 152–6
  on territorial expansion, 174–5, 212–13
  Ukraine territorial legitimacy and borders, 196

Ukrainian conflict as domestic not international, 196
Ukrainian leadership, 195–6, *195*
uniting/dividing factors between Russians and Ukrainians, 210–12, *211*
voting preferences, 172
New Force, 54, 71
Nikolai I, 48, 61, 72–3
Nikolai II, 114–15
North Caucasus
  coverage, state-aligned media, 303–4, 326–8
  Islamic extremists, 302, 319, 327–8, 329
  Muslim republics and territorial expansion, 171–2, 176, *177*, 213, 214, *214*
  New Force party in, 71
  separatist violence, 303–4, 306
  see also Caucasus
Novorossiia concept, 197, **198**, 332

official nationality doctrine, 24, 49, 50, 60, 61, 72–3
Okara, Andrei, 355
oligarchic elite, 223–4, 231, 345, 348, 354, 360
Orthodox nationalism
  affiliations with alternative churches, 116–17
  ethnic diversity of, 110–11
  within ethnic nationalism, 107–8
  overview of, 113–15
  and participation in the Orthodox Church, 108, 113, 115, 118–20
  rejection of secular authorities, 115
  and the Russian Orthodox Church Abroad (ROCA), 116
  Russians as a chosen people, 114
  as tsar-worshippers (*tsarebozhniki*), 114, 119
Osipov, Vladimir, 28–9
Otterbeck, Jonas, 141

paganism
  lack of founding traditions, 121–2
  nationalists in, 122–4
  overview of, 121
  rituals and dress, 123
  use of Slavic terminology, 121, 123
Pain, Emil, 20, 22, 112, 266
Pamiat movement, 30, 71–2, 92, 105–6
Panarin, Aleksandr, 30
Paratrooper Day (2 August), 85
patriotic centrism, 282–3
patriotism
  civic, 251–2
  Kremlin's rhetoric of, 355–6
  language of, 290–1
  term, 230
  use of Great Patriotic War (WWII) tropes, 210
patriotism-inflated popularity, 169, 193
patronal politics
  networks of political actors, 223–5, 284
  oligarchic elite, 223–4, 231, 345, 348, 354, 360
  Putin's personal networks, 224, 348
  regional political machines, 224
patronal presidentialism
  defined, 221–2
  and hybrid regimes, 225
  lame-duck syndrome and, 225–6
  overview of, 224–5
  popular support and, 227–8
  power networks and elections, 226–8
patronalism, 222–3
People's Militia of Minin and Pozharskii, 116–17
People's Will (*Narodovoltsy*), 84
perestroika
  ethnification under, 7
  nationalism under, 28, 30–1, 105
  relationship with Europe, 280
Perin, Roman, 124, 127
Peskov, Dmitrii, 160
Piontkovskii, Andrei, 352
Poliakov, Leonid, 355
Polterovich, Viktor, 355
Popov, Vladimir, 355
Presidential Council on Interethnic Relations, 38, 261–2

presidential elections (2000), 230–2, 233–4
Primakov, Evgenii, 230–2, 268, 283, 356
Prokhanov, Aleksandr, 29, 69, 331
Prokhorov, Mikhail, 359
pro-Kremlin youth groups, 2–3, 78, 80–1, 88, 253, 285
pro-regime (*sistemnyi*) nationalism, 55
Prostakov, Sergei, 22
Prosvirnin, Egor, 54–5, 56, 128
pro-Western, liberal opposition
  common anti-Putin stance with ethnonationalists, 3, 35
  state reaction to, 2
Przeworski, Adam, 346
public opinion
  changing views on socialism, 65–6
  declining support for radical nationalism, 96–7
  distrust of migrants, 40–1
  increased ethnonationalism, 40–1, 43–4
  perceptions of ethnic diversity, 5
  on raids and semi-legal violence, 89
  on socialism and USSR, 63, 64–5
  on the West as the enemy, 66–7
  on Western model, 64
  xenophobia, 40
  see also NEORUSS surveys
Pussy Riot, 239, 291, 302, 313, 316–17, 351
Putin, Vladimir
  article on nationalism (*Nezavisimaia gazeta*), 5–6, 254, 256
  Crimea speech (2014), 18, 160, 206, 259–60, 331–2
  declining popular support (2011), 237
  early statist nationalism, 19, 251–2
  economic strategies, 337–8, 347–53
  ethnic understanding of identity, 18–19, 160–1, 255–6
  ethnonationalism, stance on, 38–9, 252–3, 254–6, 354
  leadership style, popular support for, 233–4, 238

Medvedev as successor to, 226, 235–6, 237, 254, 287
Millennium Manifesto, 251, 252, 258
national identity strategy, 255–7, 266–7
nationalism and annexation of Crimea, 6, 17, 18, 44, 160, 206, 222
nationalist issues and public support for, 6, 200–1, 228–9, 241
nation-building strategy, 251–2, 256
patriotic centrism, 282–4
as patronal president, 224
personal political networks, 224, 348
presidential elections (2000), 230–2, 233–4
public approval ratings, post-annexation of Crimea, 6, 72, 162, 198–9, *199*, 244–5, 247–8, 358
public support for, pre-Crimea, 234–7
response to terrorist attacks, 231–2, 233, 234
response to Western sanctions, 357–9
selection as Eltsin's successor, 230–1
succession of 2008, 226
2012 campaign strategy, 238–9
use of *rossiiane*, 260
use of *russkii/rossiiskie* terms, 18–19, 259, 275–6
use of term *russkie*, 160, 206, 259, 266, 271, 275–6
Valdai Club speech, 257–9, 294

radical nationalism
  Biriulevo-Zapadnoe riots, 86, 94–5, 240–1, 325–6
  coalition with national democratic nationalists, 79, 91–3
  Day of Russian Wrath, 94
  declining support for, 96–7

divisions in, post-annexation of Crimea, 82, 97–8
ethnic criminality activities, 84, 86, 94, 95
football hooliganism and, 85
future of, 99–100
grassroots activism, 88–9
internal organization, 77
Manezhnaia riots, 81, 85, 96
membership fighting in Ukraine, 98–9
non-political activities, 90–1
political activities, 78–9, 95–6
political marginalization of, 80–1
political strategies, 90
political structures, 90–7
political terror tactics, 84
racist violence, 77, 80, 83, 84, 87
raids (semi-legal violence), 87–9
relations with the authorities, 80–3
revolutionary violence, tactics for, 84–8
riot tactics (Kondopoga technique), 84–5, 86, 87, 96
Russian Spring, support for, 97–8
state support for, 2–3
suppression of by the Kremlin, 80–1, 253–4
2011 protest movement and, 3, 86, 92–3, 238
within the united opposition, 91, 92–4
violence, use of, 83–8
youth groups membership and support for, 80–1, 85, 90, 94–5, 96, 99
see also neo-Nazis
raids (semi-legal violence), 87–9
rally-round-the-leader effect
as rally-round-the-political-system effect, 200
support for Putin, post annexation of Crimea, 6, 72, 162, 198–9, 199, 244–5, 247–8
temporary nature of, 169, 193, 217–18
Rasputin, Valentin, 36

red-brown opposition, 20, 28–9, 53, 68–9
Regamey, Amandine, 134
Riabykh, Father (Abbot) Georgii, 110, 111
Rodina (party), 81, 92, 253, 285, 356
Rogozin, Dmitrii, 81, 253, 285
Romanov era, 33, 55, 61, 249
Rossiia, 301, 328–9
see also television, state-aligned; Vesti (Rossiia)
rossiiane
cultural core of, 270
ethnonationalist opposition to, 36
and the Russian language, 33
use by Eltsin, 3–4, 160, 252
use by Putin, 260
rossiiskaia natsiia, 38, 262, 264, 299
rossiiskii
and ethnic Russian nationalism, 229–30, 275–6
usage of term, state-aligned media, 309–10
rossiiskii model, 3, 6, 13, 33, 37, 39, 40, 42, 44, 202, 249, 309–10
rossiiskii narod, 18, 33, 38, 252, 256
Rowley, David, 21
Russia
entry to WTO, 353
as a European country, 276
federal structure of, 267–8, 300
party structure, 355
political isolation of, 72
Russia for Russians (Rossiia dlia russkikh), 40, 187, 202, 265
Russian All-National Union (Russkii obshchenatsional'nyi soiuz) (RONS), 75n, 76, 92, 97
Russian All-People's Union (Rossiiskii obshchenarodnyi soiuz) (ROS), 75n, 90, 92
Russian civic nation (rossiiskaia grazhdanskaia natsiia), 264, 299–300
Russian Image (Russkii obraz), 78, 79, 80, 83, 90, 91
Russian Imperial Movement (Russkoe imperskoe dvizhenie) (RID), 91, 92, 93, 97

Russian language
　for interethnic communication, 161
　as language of the state, 270
　and national identity, 13, 33
　during the Soviet Union, 43
Russian Liberation Front 'Pamiat' (*Russkii Front Osvobozheniia 'Pamiat'*), 92
Russian March, 2, 9, 54, 92, 95, 96, 118, 253
Russian National Union (RNS), 30–1
Russian National Unity (RNE), 31, 72, 89, 105–6
Russian (*Rossiiskaia*) Orthodox Autonomous Church (ROAC), 117
Russian (*Rossiiskaia*) Orthodox Church (RosOC), 116
Russian Orthodox Church
　concept of Russian world (*russkii mir*), 110–11, 262–3
　as key value, national patriots, 106
　moral values and, 291–2
　Orthodox nationalists in, 108, 113, 115, 118–20
　rejection of ethnic nationalism, 111–13
　relationship with the state, 108–10, 115, 262–3, 292, 316
　role in nation-building strategy, 258
　and Russian identity, 105
　television news coverage, *307–8*, 313–17, *314–15*, 329
　universality of Russian civilization, 111–12
　veneration of the tsar, 114
　work with migrants, 110
　see also Orthodox nationalism
Russian Orthodox Church Abroad (ROCA), 116, 117
Russian Public Movement (*Russkoe obshchestvennoe dvizhenie*) (ROD), 79
Russian Spring, 97–8
Russia's special path, 49, 50, 72, 343–5, 347
Russification, 24, 42, 266

russkie
　conceptual shift towards (post-2012), 160–1
　understanding of the term, 40, 205–6, 265–6
　use by Putin, 160, 206, 259, 271, 275–6
Russkie movement, 34, 76, 86, 88, 91–2, 94, 98, 100, 263
russkii
　cultural element of, 275–6
　ethnonationalist concept of, 36
　and multi-ethnic Russian nationalism, 229–30
　new boundaries of, 266
　public acceptance of russkii-centred identity, 266–71
　Putin's use of, 19, 259, 275–6
　in Russian for Russians slogan, 202, 265–6
　usage of term, state-aligned media, 309–10
russkii mir (Russian world)
　Russian Orthodox Church's concept of, 110–11, 262–3
　term, 72, 83, 250, 256, 271
russkii narod, 18, 38, 256, 262, 263, 264, 354
　see also ethnic Russians

secularism
　anti-immigrant stance, 127
　anti-Islamic orientation, 127–8
　as dynamic sector of ethnic nationalism, 128–9
　nationalists in, 124–6
　and personal religious practices, 127
　use of Orthodox rhetoric, 126
security forces (*siloviki*), 349
Sergeev, Sergei, 35, 36–7
Seton-Watson, Hugh, 25
Sevastianov, Aleksandr, 35, 37, 125, 127
Shafarevich, Igor, 28–9, 36
Shaimiev, Mintimer, 224
Sharafutdinova, Gulnaz, 291
Shenfield, Stephen, 29
Shevchenko, Maksim, 310

INDEX

Shevel, Oxana, 23, 33
Shevtsova, Lilia, 5
Shiropaev, Aleksei, 55, 56
Simonovich-Nikshich, Leonid, 118–19, 129
Simonsen, Sven Gunnar, 22
Slavic Community of St Petersburg, 124, 127
Slavic Force (*Slavianskaia sila*), 91–2
Slavic Union
   Crimean annexation as step towards, 188
   public support for, 176–8, *177*, 186, 213
Slavic Union (*Slavianskii soiuz*) (SS), 34–5, 83, 91
Slavophiles, 50–1, 62, 105, 340
social identity approach, 167–8, 182
Solovei, Valerii, 54, 126
Solov'ev, Vladimir, 47–8
Solzhenitsyn, Aleksandr, 20, 26, 31
sootechestvenniki (compatriots), 32
Sorokin, Vladimir, 68
sovereign democracy (*suverennaia demokratiia*), 285, 355
sovereignty, 47, 48, 59–60, 183, 197
Soviet Union (USSR)
   ethnic identity, 43, 55–6, 268–9
   nationalism, 25–6, 42
   nostalgia for, 55–6
   Russian language, 43
   state television, 329–30
   statist nationalism during perestroika, 28–30
   see also collapse of the Soviet Union
Sputnik i Pogrom, 54, 55, 128
Stalin, Iosif, 25, 65–6, 67, 162, 292
state, the
   relationship with the Church, 108–10, 115, 262–3, 292, 316
   role in neoliberal economies, 339
   Russian pride in, 204
   state identity, public preferences for, 182–5, *184*

strength of and statist nationalism, 1, 5, 19, 43, 353–4
   see also ideological state posture; Kremlin
stateless nations, 21
statists (*gosudarstvenniki*)
   as alternative to radical nationalism, 81
   during the Eltsin Administration, 20
   ethnic neutrality of, 29
   national democratic nationalism opposition to, 53–4
   national patriots as, 106–7
   opposition to ethnonationalism, 1
   Putin's early stance on, 19, 251–2
   shift to ethnocentrist nationalism, 19
   state strength, importance of, 1, 5, 19, 43, 353–4
   tension with liberals, 352
   USSR-focused statism, 28–30, 63–4
Steger, Manfred, 277
Stolypin, Petr, 24
Strategy 2020 reform programme, 350
Strelkov, Igor, 71
Strukova, Marina, 127
Struve, Petr, 24
supremacist nationalism, 23, 30–1, 43
Surkov, Vladislav, 238, 285–6, 350, 352, 355
Sviatenkov, Pavel, 37
Szporluk, Roman, 22–3

Tatarstan
   response to annexation of Crimea, 161–2, 163
television, state-aligned
   annexation of Crimea coverage, 330–3
   anti-immigration campaign, 81–2, 88, 94, 323
   'ethnic cohesion' use of term, *307–8*, 310–13
   ethnicity-related news, 303–4, 305–6, *307–9*
   inter-ethnic conflict, coverage of, 324–6

television, state-aligned (*cont.*)
  Kremlin's approaches to ethno-cultural diversity, 300–1
  migration, coverage of, *307–8*, 319–23, *321–2*
  migration in Europe coverage, 321–3, 324
  nation-building function, 299, 306–10, 328–9
  North-Caucasus-related stories, 303–4, 326–8
  Russian Orthodox Church coverage, *307–8*, 313–17, *314–15*, 329
  Ukraine coverage, 324
  the West, negative portrayal of, 312, 313, 318–19, 323, 324, 329, 331–2
  see also Channel 1; Rossiia
territorial expansion *see* expansionism
territory
  geography as destiny rhetoric, Eurasianists, 62
  preferences for territorial boundaries, NEORUSS survey, 171–2, *175*, 213, *214*, 241–2, 242
  territorial legitimacy of Ukraine, 196
  territorial state identity preference, ethnic minorities, 171–2, *175*, 175
  see also expansionism
terrorism
  Domodedovo International Airport, 302, 327–8, 329
  North-Caucasus-related stories and, 303–4, 326–7
  public opinion on Chechen terrorists, 232–3
  Putin's response to, 231–2, 233, 234
  radical nationalist attacks as, 77–8, 84
  Vladikavkaz bombing, 327, 329
31st day of the month rally, 245
Tishkov, Valerii, 32–3, 36–7, 38, 43, 263–4
Tolz, Vera, 22, 36

Tor, Vladimir, 37, 54
tozherossiianin (also-a-Russian-citizen), 104
Treisman, Daniel, 348
Tuminez, Astrid, 24
2011 protest movement
  Bolotnaia movement, 281, 287, 291
  consequences for nationalist strategies and, 243–4, 255–6
  Kremlin's response to, 238, 351
  nationalist opposition activity, 93–4
  political parties participating in, 3, 237–8, 243, 255
  radical nationalism and, 3, 86, 92–3, 238
  united opposition formation, 93–4

Ukraine
  current leadership, survey, 195–6, *195*
  as EU or Eurasian Union member, 196
  Kremlin narrative of Western-backed government, 67, 195–6, 201–2, 206, 211, 217, 245
  Novorossiia concept, 197, **198**
  Orange Revolution (2004), 284
  ousting of Yanukovych, 243, 260
  presidential elections (2014), 194–5
  radical nationalists fighting in, 98–9
  re-incorporation of, ethnonationalists, 23
  rejection of Ukrainians as marriage partners, 207–9, *208*, 212
  Russian ethnic identity of, 23
  in the Russian media, 196, 324
  Russian perceptions of Ukrainians, 206, 207–9
  territorial legitimacy and borders of, 196
  Ukraine question and anti-migrant views, 138n
  Ukrainian ethnic identity in Crimea, 188
  uniting/dividing factors between Russians and Ukrainians, 210–12, *211*
  see also Crimea, annexation of

INDEX

Union of Russian People (*Soiuz russkogo naroda*) (SRN), 51, 91, 92, 108
United Russia (party), 3, 235, 237, 240, 254, 284, 285, 286, 287
United States of America (USA)
  attitudes towards migrants, 139, 140, 141
  as the enemy of Russia, 66–7
Unity (party), 287
USSR (Union of Soviet Socialist Republics) *see* Soviet Union (USSR)
USSR 2.0, 188–9, 213
USSR-focused statism, 28–30
Uvarov, Sergei, 49–50, 60

Valuev, Petr, 49–50
Verkhovsky, Alexander, 34, 106, 111, 120, 134–5, 253n
Vesti (Rossiia)
  annexation of Crimea coverage, 312–13
  anti-immigration campaign, 81–2, 88, 94, 323
  'ethnic cohesion' use of term, *307–8*, 310–13
  ethnicity-related news, 305–9, *307–9, 311*
  as flagship news programme, 301–2
  inter-ethnic conflict coverage, 324–6
  Islam and radical Islam coverage, 317–19
  migration coverage, 320, *322*
  North-Caucasus-related stories, 306, 326–8
  other religions coverage, *307–8*, 317–19
  portrayal of Crimean Tartars, 332
  Rasul Mirzaev case coverage, 325
  Russian Orthodox Church coverage, *307–8*, 313–17, *314–15*, 329
  Vladikavkaz bombing coverage, 327

Vremia (Channel 1)
  annexation of Crimea coverage, 312–13
  anti-immigration campaign, 81–2, 88, 94, 323
  'ethnic cohesion' use of term, *307–8*, 310–13
  ethnicity-related news, 305–9, *307–9, 311*
  as flagship news programme, 301–2
  inter-ethnic conflict coverage, 324–6
  Islam and radical Islam coverage, 317–19
  migration coverage, 320, *321*
  North-Caucasus-related stories, 306, 326–8
  other religions coverage, *307–8*, 317–19
  Russian Orthodox Church coverage, *307–8*, 313–17, *314–15*, 329
  Vladikavkaz bombing coverage, 327

Waldinger, Roger, 137, 139
the West
  economic sanctions, Ukraine crisis, 357–9
  as the enemy of Russia, 66–7
  inter-ethnic relations, 329–30
  multiculturalism in, 254, 258, 299, 312, 318, 323, 329
  national democratic nationalism orientation towards, 55, 281
  negative portrayal of, Russian state-aligned television, 312, 313, 318–19, 323, 324, 329, 331–2
  preordained differences with Russian civilization, 50–1, 60–2, 340
  within Russian civilisational grammars, 278, 280–1, 293–4, 295
  Western-backed government, Ukraine, 67, 195–6, 201–2, 206, 211, 217, 245
  see also Europe

World Trade Organization (WTO), 352–3
Wortman, Richard, 61

xenophobia
 anti-migrant campaign (2013), 81–2, 87, 88, 94, 95, 323
 and extreme nationalism, 5–6
 global prevalence of, 137–8
 within historical imperial ideology, 5
 manifest xenophobia, 157
 in post-Soviet generation, 265
 public attitudes and, 40
 racist violence, 77, 80, 84, 87
 see also migrants, perceptions of

Yanov, Alexander, 28
Yanukovych, Viktor, 82, 192, 216, 243, 260, 344, 357, 359
youth groups
 pro-Kremlin youth groups, 2–3, 78, 80–1, 88, 253, 285
 radical nationalist membership of, 80–1, 86, 90, 94–5, 96, 99

Zelenskii, Roman, 119
Zevelev, Igor, 37
Zhirinovskii, Vladimir, 29, 198, 200, 235
Zhuchkovskii, Aleksandr, 118, 125–6
Ziuganov, Gennadii, 29, 63, 200, 232

EU representative:
Easy Access System Europe
Mustamäe tee 50, 10621 Tallinn, Estonia
Gpsr.requests@easproject.com

www.ingramcontent.com/pod-product-compliance
Lightning Source LLC
Chambersburg PA
CBHW070006010526
44117CB00011B/1445